Commercial Dispute Resolution in China:

An Annual Review and Preview (2016)

Beijing Arbitration Commission
Beijing International Arbitration Center

Published by Wolters Kluwer Hong Kong Limited

Wolters Kluwer Law & Business serves customers worldwide with CCH, Aspen Publishers, Loislaw and Kluwer Law International products.

Printed by Beijing Congreat Printing Co., Ltd

ISBN 978-988-13955-1-1

Preface

In the year of 2015, the Beijing Arbitration Commission (the "BAC") celebrated its twentieth anniversary. With the enforcement of the BAC Arbitration Rules 2015 and the concurrent use of its new name the "Beijing International Arbitration Center", the BAC quickened its pace of internationalization. During the past two decades, the BAC stuck to its core values of independence, fairness, professionalism and high efficiency, and proactively explored diversified dispute resolution methods that can meet the ever growing requirements of parties. Such endeavors include the revisions of the BAC Arbitration Rules for more flexible and efficient arbitral proceedings, the making of the BAC Construction Dispute Board Rules and the introduction of dispute board system into China, the establishment of the BAC Mediation Center along with the independent BAC Mediation Rules, the adoption of international commercial mediation theories and training experience and skills, by which to improve the professional competence of mediators and thus to strengthen the professionalism and effectiveness of commercial mediation, and to provide more client-friendly and cost-effective dispute resolution services.

Since the year of 2013, the BAC has planned and composed the annual report series entitled the Commercial Dispute Resolution in China: An Annual Review and Preview (the "Annual Report"). This well reflects that the BAC is not satisfied with its own practice of diversified dispute resolution, but devotes itself to promote diversified dispute resolution systems and to consolidate the international exchange and cooperation in this industry, which is the best evidence of the BAC's strong sense of social accountability and persistent spirit of responsibility. The planning and composition of the Annual Report are of unique values and significance. From the Annual Report, readers either domestic or abroad will have an overall, in-depth and continuous understanding of the developments and changes of commercial dispute resolution in China, and more importantly, they can observe the progress and growth of Chinese arbitration and arbitrators. It is reasonable to believe that the historical value of this work will further emerge as time goes on.

Economic and trade exchanges have become increasingly frequent in today's world, and countries have been closely connected in economy with each other and are interdependent and interrelated. China is now the second economy of the world, and so its changes in economy and law have naturally become the concerns of commercial and legal communities around the world. However, under the background of an era of informatization and digitization, incomplete, fragmentary and inaccurate information and data might lead to misunderstanding and misjudgment. It is therefore precious to have persistent observation, complete, systematic, authentic and refined data information as well as accurate and intensive professional analysis. And that is exactly the original intention of the Annual Report, which is aimed to conduct continuous record, analysis and reading of commercial dispute resolution in China, to reveal the business and legal environments of China objectively, and to promote the economic and legal communication and cooperation between China and other countries.

The Annual Report has been published for three consecutive years. The Commercial Dispute Resolution in China: An Annual Review and Preview (2016) (the "Annual Report 2016") is the fourth issue of the annual report series, with 11 chapters split into general reports and special reports. The general reports focus on Arbitration and Mediation, and the special reports cover dispute resolution in nine industries including Construction Project, Real Estate, Energy, Finance, Investment, International Trade, Intellectual Property, Film and Television and General Aviation. Each of these sub-reports provides a survey on dispute resolution of the past year within the specific field, interpretation of new laws and regulations, summary of hot topics, analysis of important cases, summary and prospect of developments. As for the BAC, it is a hard work and a huge devotion to organize the authorization and publication of such a high level report which is of hundreds of thousands of words and in both Chinese and English languages, as well as to host overseas conference year by year. As for authors of the Annual Report, they are renowned scholars, senior judges and lawyers, and it is also an endeavor beyond imagination to author the report and to make presentation in English and have interaction with conventioneers during the overseas conference in addition to their busy daily work. It is because of the deep devotion to commercial dispute resolution in China, the persistence of the common ideal and the spirit of dedication and team work that made the Annual Report and overseas conference increasingly perfected and well received. As the planner and the organizer, we not only enjoy the sweetness of success, but also confirm our confidence to carry on this valuable work.

We hereby extend our sincere thanks to all the authors, editors, translators, publishers and others who have contributed to the Annual Report, as well as those institutions and individuals, either domestic or abroad, for their assistance in and support to the overseas conference. The Annual Report 2016 is now about to be released. We expect to get more feedback and suggestions. Also, we look forward to more and more professionals of insight and experts with competence joining us, with whom we can further improve the Annual Report and the overseas summits, and further promote and develop commercial dispute resolution in China.

WANG Hongsong
Vice-Chairperson
Beijing Arbitration Commission/Beijing International Arbitration Center

Contents

About the Authors

Annual Review on Commercial Arbitration in China (*2016*):

SONG Lianbin holds a doctor degree in laws and he is a professor and Ph. D. advisor at China University of Political Science and Law and the Vice-Secretary General of China Society of Private International Law. He is on the Panel of Arbitrators for the Beijing Arbitration Commission, Guangzhou Arbitration Commission, Shanghai Arbitration Commission, Hainan Arbitration Commission, Nanjing Arbitration Commission, Xiangtan Arbitration Commission, Zhengzhou Arbitration Commission, Weinan Arbitration Commission, Zhuhai Arbitration Commission, Wuhan Arbitration Commission, Shenzhen Arbitration Commission, Dalian Arbitration Commission, Chongqing Arbitration Commission, Huizhou Arbitration Commission, China International Economic & Trade Arbitration Commission, South China International Economic & Trade Arbitration Commission, Shanghai International Economic & Trade Arbitration Commission, Singapore International Arbitration Center and Kuala Lumpur Regional Center for Arbitration. Mr. Song has served as a member of the editorial board of the "Chinese Yearbook of Private International and Comparative Law", "Arbitration in Beijing" for BAC, "Commercial Arbitration" for Wuhan Arbitration Commission and "Commercial Arbitration Review" for South China International Economic and Trade Arbitration Commission. Since 1991, Mr. Song has published many books as well as over 100 journals and translated works at home and abroad.

FU Panfeng is a doctor in law and a post-doctoral research member at the law school of Chinese Academy of Social Sciences. Her major research areas are private international law and international arbitration. She has published many works on study of arbitration since 2009. She was also the first-prize winner of the first "BAC Cup", a competition between student from Universities Nationwide on Commercial Arbitration and the third-prize winner for the second BAC Cup. Her representative works published in recent years include: "Discussions on the System Construction and its Practical Predicament in Multi-parties Arbitrations" (2014), "Discussions on the System of Emergency Arbitrators in ICC Arbitration Rules" (2015) and "Standards for res judicata in International Investment Arbitration— from formalism to substantialism" (2016).

Helena H. C. CHEN is a partner at Pinsent Masons LLP. She holds two doctorates in law: one from National Taiwan University and the other from Peking University. Helena is qualified to practice law in mainland China, Taiwan and New York State. She is a Fellow of the Chartered Institute of Arbitrators (FCIArb) and is listed on the panels of arbitrators of Arbitration institutions such as China International Economic & Trade Arbitration Commission, Singapore International Arbitration Center, Kuala Lumpur Regional Center for Arbitration, Korean Commercial Arbitration Board, Australian Centre for International Commercial Arbitration, Shenzhen Court of International Arbitration, Shanghai International Economic & Trade Arbitration Commission, Beijing Arbitration Commission, The Chinese Arbitration Association, Taipei and LCIA-MIAC Arbitration Centre. She is a member of the SIAC Users' Council and is listed as one of the Recommended Experts of the Construction Dispute Board (DB) of BAC. Helena is the Vice-Chairperson of the Mediation Center of CAA, Associate Mediator for the Singapore Mediation Center and is listed on the panel of mediators of China Council for the Promotion of International Trade/China Chamber of International Commerce (CCPIT/CCOIC) Mediation Center. Helena has received 'The International Who's Who of Construction Lawyers' every year since 2011. She composed "PPP Project Contract Guidelines (Trial Version)" for the PPP center of the Ministry of Finance and she is an international consultant for the Asian Development Bank (ADB). She is one of the founding supervisors of Taiwan Construction Law Society and served as a director thereof. She writes widely on arbitration, mediation and construction law topics and her articles were published on SSCI and TSSCI. She is frequently invited by international forums such as IBA and ABA to give speeches during international conferences.

Annual Review on Commercial Mediation in China (2016):

YANG Yan is the Deputy Chief of the case-filling court (Court of Register) of Beijing Higher People's Court and has participated in the construction of intermediation mechanism in Beijing courts. She wrote research articles such as "The Breakthrough of the 'Policy Bottleneck' in Mediation during Case-Filing —A Sample of Mediation Practice During Case-Filing in Beijing Courts".

ZHANG Hua is a judge at the case filling court (Court of Register) of Beijing Higher People's Court and has participated in the construction of intermediation mechanism in Beijing courts. He published articles such as "Tentative Construction of the System of Pre-litigation Mediation in People's Court: The Rationality and Feasibility of the ADR Mode of Pre-litigation Mediation".

Annual Review on Construction Project Dispute Resolution in China (2016):

TAN Jinghui is the Director of City Development Law Firm (Beijing). Prior to this, she worked in China State Construction Engineering Corporation for many years and served as General Counsel for CSCEC International. She holds a Master of Law and a Master in Structure Engineering. She is an arbitrator of Beijing Arbitration Commission, member of the Chartered Institute of Building, registered cost engineer in mainland China, level 1 project manager and senior economist. She also serves as legal adviser to the Ministry of Housing and Urban-Rural Development of the People Republic of China, executive director of China Real Estate Association and deputy secretary general of its Specialized Committee for legal Affairs, specialist of China Engineering Cost Association and China Tendering & Bidding Association, bidding evaluation specialist of Beijing Municipality. She is the Editor-in-Chief of the "Standard Form of Construction Contract, "Standard Form of Construction Subcontracting Contract 2015" and "Tender Exam Textbook", and participated in the legislation activities of several ministries.

She has published the monograph "Complicated Issues on Construction Engineering" and co-authored "Construction Law of UK". Journals or work published on a national level include "Value Realization of Mediation in Arbitration", "The Characteristics and Resolutions of International Engineering Legal Disputes", "Validity of Construction Contract", "New Explanation of Legal Issues concerning Tendering and Bidding" and "Status Quo of Construction Engineering Legal System, Development of Related Disputes", "7 Legal Conundrums in Government Purchase of PPP Projects", "Legal analysis of the investment decisions in PPP Projects" and "Legal Nature and Application of EPC Mode".

Annual Review on Real Estate Dispute Resolution in China (2016):

Dennis DENG is a senior partner at Dacheng Law Offices (China) and an arbitrator at the Beijing Arbitration Commission/Beijing International Arbitration Centre. Mr. Deng focuses on PE, M&A, Real Estate, and Litigation & Dispute Resolution. Furthermore, Mr. Deng has expertise in business negotiations and legal decisions making. Mr. Deng has considerable trial experience. He has a solid grasp of the habits of reasoning and overall disposition and temperament of judges and arbitrators alike, and is an experienced oral advocate in the courtroom or tribunal setting with excellent debating and reasoning techniques. Mr. Deng understands the importance of examining a client's case from the perspective of the judges and arbitrators. He emphasis that the lawyer's task is not merely to convey to the court or tribunal the views of lawyers and wishes of their client, but to subtly influence the decision maker to reach a judgment favourable to his client. Mr. Deng is skilled at presenting the underlying facts of a dispute in a client-favoured manner that is both credible and persuasive to arbitrators and judges, with the ultimate goal that the decision maker will trust and ultimately side with his client. At the same time, Mr. Deng is experienced at showing the ultimate decision maker how the underlying facts of the case fit within a legal theory or interpretation consistent with his client's desired outcome.

Annual Review on Energy Dispute Resolution in China (2016):

ZHANG Libin graduated from the University of International Business and Economics in 1987 with a B. A. in economics and graduated from the University of Texas at Austin School of Law with a J. D. degree in 1997. Mr. Zhang worked in many well-known American law firms both as an associate and a partner from 1997 to 2010. He worked in Siemens Ltd (China) as the head of Legal M&A in Asia & Australia from 2011 to March 2015, and joined Broad & Bright as a partner in April 2015.

Mr. Zhang focuses on foreign direct investment, M&A, overseas investment, energy, environment and arbitration. Being a member of the New York and Chinese Bar and having practiced law for over 18 years, Mr. Zhang has accumulated significant experience in representing numerous domestic and foreign enterprises in cross-border investment and M&A. Mr. Zhang participated in Siemens's many significant M&A projects in energy, industry, healthcare, infrastructure and urban transportation business when he worked there. Mr. Zhang is an arbitrator at the China International Economic and Trade Arbitration Commission (CIETAC) and Beijing Arbitration Commission (BAC), and he has served as the chief arbitrator or arbitrator in many arbitration cases (especially cases concerning energy). He also served as the Chinese Law consultant and expert witness in overseas arbitrations.

Mr. Zhang is a consultant and visiting professor in the UT Austin School of Law and Business School KBH Energy Canter; he is the Deputy Director of Peking University Energy Law and Policy Research Institute and a specially invited professor for the International LL. M. Program at Tsinghua University School of Law. He is also a visiting professor at the China University of Political Science and Law, the Law School of the University of International Business and Economics and the Law School of Beijing Foreign Language Studies University and taught courses on energy law, foreign investment law, etc. He is managing director of the Energy Law Academy of China Law Society, member of AIPN and consultant for Beijing Energy Club. In his spare time, he takes interests in academic studies, legal writing and translation and has published books and translations including the second edition of "US Energy Law (nutshell)", "American Contract Law: Case Law, Rules and Value", "Mergers and Acquisitions in the United States: A Practical Guide for Non-US Buyers" And "Latin Manuel for Legal Personnel". He also writes articles and gives lectures on PRC energy issues.

Annual Review on Investment Dispute Resolution in China (2016):

BAO Zhi is a partner at Fenxun Partners. Mr. Bao's practice focuses on foreign direct investment, mergers and acquisitions, private equity and competition law. Before joining in the Fenxun Law Firm, he spent several years in the ministry of commerce (Mofcom) in Beijing and subsequently at a leading Chinese law firm.

Mr. Bao has been one of the few lawyers who are able to transform the structure of complex overseas transactions into that of domestic investment. He participated in the design of models for transnational restructuring and structures for domestic transaction and obtained approvals from different regulation authorities.

Mr. Bao is an arbitrator of the Beijing Arbitration Commission. In addition, he serves as the legal advisor for China Association of Private Equity and an independent director of Zhongtai Trust Co. ,Ltd. Mr. Bao received his legal education from Anhui University (LL. B.), east China University of Politics and Law (LL. M.) and University of California, Berkeley (LL. M.). He is fluent in Chinese and English.

WANG Zekun is a lawyer at Fenxun Partners. His fields of practice include structure financing, insurance fund investment and dispute resolution. He participated in many kinds of securitisation, debt financing, insurance fund investment and relevant investment dispute projects.

Mr. Wang holds abachelor degree and a doctorate of law from Nanjing University. He is fluent in Chinese, English and Italian.

Annual Review on International Trade Dispute Resolution in China (2016):

WANG Xuehua is the founding Partner of Beijing Huanzhong & Partners. Dr. Wang graduated from UIBE with a Ph. D. in Law. He serves as the dean of WTO and International Business Commission of Chinese Bar Association, director of Beijing Bar Association, vice-director of Foreign Affairs Commission of Beijing director of Anti-Dumping and Anti-Monopoly Committee and director of WTO Law Research Society of China Law Society. Dr. Wang is also an adjunct law professor of University of International Business & Economics (UIBE), an arbitrator of China International Economic and Trade Arbitration Commission and Shenzhen Court of International Arbitration, and as a mediator of Shanghai International Arbitration Center.

Dr. Wang is the former Associate Dean of the Law School of the University of International Business & Economics. He acted as a member on the Drafting Committee of Anti-Dumping, Anti-Subsidy and Safeguard Regulations by Ministry of Foreign Trade and Economic Cooperation (predecessor of Ministry of Commerce), the director of the International Trade and Investment Committee of Beijing Bar Association, an adjunct professor of University of Law and Politics of China and a joint-tutor of Tsinghua University's LL. M. program.

LIU Jing is a partner of Beijing Huanzhong & Partners and adjunct professor at the University of International Business and Economics. Ms. Liu obtained her LL. M. degree from UIBE and has a LL. B. degree from China Youth College of Political Science (CYCPS) as one of the first graduates of CYCPS Law School. Ms. Liu had also visited and worked for six months in a distinguished law firm in USA in a lawyer exchange program.

The main practice areas of Ms. Liu are international trade law, corporation law, franchising and commercial arbitration. Ms. Liu, with her great experience in the field of international commercial dispute resolution, has represented clients in hundreds of arbitration cases under the arbitration rules of China International Economic and Trade Arbitration Commission, Beijing Arbitration Commission, Wuhan Arbitration Commission, Shanghai Arbitration Commission, International Court of Arbitration of the International Chamber of Commerce, the Arbitration Institute of the Stockholm Chamber of Commerce, Hong Kong International Arbitration Center, Singapore International Arbitration Center, Kuala Lumpur Regional Center for Arbitration and UNCITRAL.

Ms. Liu has also represented clients in the planning, negotiation, contracts drafting and reviewing of dozens of cases involving international trade, foreign investment, franchising, real estate, construction and finance projects.

Since 2011, Ms. Liu has been serving as an arbitratorat China International Economic and Trade Arbitration Commission, and has dealt with dozens of arbitration cases in the areas of international trade, foreign investment and financial leasing. In addition, Ms. Liu has joined International Arbitration Chamber of Paris as an arbitrator in 2015.

Besides her devotion to the above legal practices, Ms. Liu serves as a member of the Expert Lawyers Group of China Chambers of Commerce and secretary-general of the Arbitration Committee of the Eighth Session of Beijing Bar Association. Ms. Liu acted as the deputy director of the International Trade Committee of the Seventh Session of Beijing Bar Association. The working languages of Ms. Liu are Chinese and English.

Annual Review on Financial Dispute Resolution in China (2016):

TAO Xiuming is the founding partner and managing partner of Jun Ze Jun Law Offices. Mr. Tao has been practicing for over 20 years and has rich experience and excellent expertise in the area of international finance, securities, foreign investment and international business dispute resolution.

Mr. Tao currently acts as an arbitrator of the China International Economic and Trade Arbitration Commission (and member of Expert Advisory Committee), an arbitrator of Beijing Arbitration Commission, arbitrator of Hong Kong International Arbitration Center (HKIAC), a conciliator of Conciliation Center of China Council for Promotion of International Trade (CCPIT)/China Chamber of International Commerce (CCOIC), mediator of US-China Business Mediation Centre, and a member of Financial Derivative Committee, Legal Committee and Qualification Committee of National Association of Financial Market Institutional Investors ("NAFMII") of China, a member of Legal Experts of China Banking Association, a member of Expert Committee of China Insurance Assets Management Association, member of Finance and Security Committee of All China Lawyers Association, a part-time professor in the Law Institute of Chinese Academy of Social Sciences, a part time Master advisor in University of International Business and Economics and an executive member of Chinese Society of International Economic Law and etc.

Mr. Tao has served as the Director of the Financial Derivative Committee of Beijing Lawyer's Association and the Deputy Director of the Banking Law Committee of Beijing Lawyer's Association and etc. He was also a member of the Documentation, Collateral and Legal& Regulatory Committees of International Swap and Derivative Association (ISDA).

Mr. Tao got his bachelor degree of law in Ji Lin University in 1986, a master degree of international private law in Chinese Academy of Social Sciences in 1989, a postgraduate diploma in Institute of Social Studies (the Netherlands) 1995 and a Ph. D. in international law in University of International Business and Economics in 2007.

Annual Review on Intellectual Property Dispute Resolution in China (2016):

XIE Guanbin is the managing partner of Lifang Law Firm's Beijing Office. Mr. Xie's major practice areas include intellectual property, antitrust and competition law, legal counselling for hi-tech companies and venture capital, finance and insurance related issues. He has gained fame in these areas with his solid academic background, government experience and professional dedication. He has also been recognised as a well-known lawyer in IP law by many international legal magazines and government agencies.

Mr. Xie has an extensive client base in the technology industry providing long term legal services to many notable multi-national enterprises and institutions including IBM, Microsoft, Heinz, RHODIA, Trend Micro, EPSON, YAMAHA, SMUSUN, Panasonic Electric Works, UFIDA Software, Midea, China Unicom, PICC, China National Publications Import and Export (Group) Corporation, China Internet Network Information Centre (CNNIC) and the China Institute of Science and Technology Information.

Mr. Xie has successfully represented clients in a number of important IP litigations. In the trademark and domain name dispute field, he succeeded in having the courts recognize "Gome" as a well-known trademark; he helped the China's biggest property insurance company to retrieve its domain name "PICC"; and he represented Danone China to resolve trademark disputes on "Wahaha." In the area of patent, he represented a Taiwanese company in a MPU patent infringement dispute against Intel; he represented Heinz to enforce its package design patent; he represented a famous Chinese telecommunication manufacturer to defend a patent and copyright infringement assertion on over 100 patents raised by Huawei; he represented

Kangshifu (Taiwan) in a suit against UNI over infringement of design; he defended a vital patent of the French catalyst maker RHODIA against a hi-tech company in Tianjin. In the copyright field, his non-infringement argument for a Taiwanese financial software company was accepted by the Supreme Court; he represented Yahoo China to deal with MP3 copyright infringement problems, and he represented Microsoft China asserting copyrights and dealing with damages issues against some giant state-owned companies. In antitrust field, Mr. Xie defended China Netcom in China's first major judicial case for abuse of market dominance and participated in several collective antitrust declaration by influential business dealers. He represented many other clients including Qihoo in second instance against Tencent for abuse of market dominant position, the first antitrust action in China before the Supreme People's Court, the film "Lost in Thailand" in its unfair competition dispute, a public company suing a Shanghai company for misappropriation of trade secrets claiming RMB 100 million damages, a famous electronics company to deal with the company names and trademark disputes, China Network Information Canter against a domestic software company over infringement of reputation.

Mr Xie is also active in public service by acting as a legal consultant of Dongcheng District government in Beijing. He used to be a legal consultant in ministries such as the Ministry of Science and Technology to provide legal advice in industrial policies.

JIAO Shan is an attorney of Lifang & Partners. She got her J. D. degree from Columbia University School of Law and her LL. B. & B. A. degree in Economics from Peking University School of Law. Ms. Jiao joined Lifang in August 2013 and has been providing legal services for domestic and multinational clients. In the field of competition law, she participated in making notifications and obtaining clearance for several proposed M&As, as well as multiple anti-monopoly investigations representing informants or companies under probe. In the investigation against Qualcomm, she acted as a consultant to NDRC. She also assisted clients in anti-monopoly litigations, including the case filed by Qihoo against Tencent. In the field of IP law, Ms. Jiao has been advising software giants such as Microsoft in copyright suits. She also contributed to some legal research projects, including Investment Laws in Africa for Beijing Lawyers' Association and Railroad Law Amendment for Railroad Bureau.

CHE Luping is an associate of Lifang's Law Firm. She holds a bachelor degree in laws from East China University of Politics and Law and a master degree in laws from Queen Mary University of London. Ms. Che joined Lifang's Law Firm in October 2014. From then on, she provided legal services for domestic and multi-national corporations. In the field of intellectual property, she assisted several times to deal with copyright litigations for giant commercial software companies such as Microsoft. In the field of legal researches, she used to conduct a great deal of research works on the Research Project of Foreign Railway Legal System and Basic Framework in Relevant National Law directed by National Railway Administration.

Annual Review on Film and Television Dispute Resolution in China (2016):

XU Bo is a dean and a senior partner in of Beijing Tiantai Law Firm. He also serves as an arbitrator of Beijing Arbitration Commission. He is an adjunct professor at the China Foreign Affairs University, joint tutor of Tsinghua University Law School LL. M. programme and cooperative tutor of the Postgraduate Program at the China University of Political Science and Law. He is also the director of the Legal Department of Television Production Committee of China Federation of Radio, Film and TV Social Organizations. Mr. Xu has been practicing law related to copyright, film and television and publications for many years.

Annual Review on General Aviation Dispute Resolution in China (2016):

DONG Nianqing is a professor of law at Civil Aviation Management Institute of China and a dean at its center of aviation law. He is the president of the Research Committee on Aviation Law of Beijing and a distinguished technology leader of Civil Aviation Administration of China in 2013. He is an adjunct professor at East China University of Political and Law, a visiting professor at Civil Aviation University of China and the director of Chinese Society of International Law. He is an arbitrator of China International Economic and Trade Arbitration Commission (CIETAC), Beijing Arbitration Commission/Beijing International Arbitration Center, Shanghai Arbitration Commission, Shanghai International Arbitration Center, And South China International Economic and Trade Arbitration Commission (Shenzhen Court of International Arbitration). His research interests focus on international aviation law, air transportation policy and competition law.

ZHANG Qihuai is a leading lawyer with 24 years of experience specialising in aviation practice. His experiences in handling with numerous landmark cases further the development of his expertise and provided him with deep insight into the field of aviation law. Cases which he has worked on include: Malaysia Airlines MH370 air crash case, Pusan CA129 flight air crush case; Indonesia air crush case; Asiana Airlines Flight 214 air crush case; The Yichun air crash, the first case in China in which a pilot faced criminal charges as a result of an aviation disaster; China's first "aviation blacklist" case; China's first aircraft smuggling case; The damages to a third party's property due to the water pollution caused by the China Eastern "11.21" crash in Baotou, the first case in which an aviation disaster caused lake water pollution leading to property damage; The damages caused by aviation disasters in Nanjing, Panjin, Dunhuang; The damages caused to a client who climbed atop and fell from an aircraft body in Kunming; The first case in China in which the Montreal Convention was applied; The damages caused by an aviation disaster in Dunhuang; Aiding Tasly Holding Group returning corporate aircraft Bombardier Challenger 605 Aircraft; The case of an unmanned aerial vehicle endangering public safety, which is the first criminal case of unmanned aerial vehicle in China; The personal injury and property damage inflicted upon a client who was barred from boarding an aircraft while traveling to a hospital for surgery; Several hundred labour dispute cases for domestic airline captains, pilots and stewardesses, including a landmark case in which a resigning pilot successfully disputed the employer's claim for compensation as a result of the resignation; Mr. Gong suing Civil Aviation Administration of China and Civil Aviation Administration of East China for administrative omission.

Mr. Zhang is the founder and managing partner of Lanpeng Law Firm. He is also an arbitrator of Beijing Arbitration Commission, China International Economic and Trade Arbitration Commission, Shanghai International Economic and Trade Arbitration Commission, South China International Economic and Trade Arbitration Commission, Wuhan Arbitration Commission, Langfang Arbitration Commission and Tianjin Arbitration Commission. He is a scholar at the Air and Space Law Research Center of China University of Political Science and Law. Mr. Zhang is the executive vice-president and secretary-general of Beijing Aviation Law Society. He provides legal counsel on legislature for the Standing Committee of Beijing Municipal People's Congress. He is the chief consultant for China's Aviation Law Service Center.

Annual Review on Commercial Arbitration in China (2016) *

SONG Lianbin [1] *FU Panfeng* [2] *Helena H. C. CHEN* [3]

I. Overview

This article aims to provide an overview of the status and developments of China's arbitration practice in 2015. 2015 marks the 20th anniversary of the implementation of the *Arbitration Law of the People's Republic of China* (hereinafter referred to as the "Arbitration Law") as well as 20 years of successful operation of the China's first pilot group of the reorganized and established arbitration institutions. In 2015, 244 arbitration commissions nationwide administered a total number of 136,924 arbitration cases—an increase of 23,264 cases from 2014, with a growth rate of 20%. The cumulative value of these cases amounts to RMB 411.2 billion, which is an increase of RMB 145.6 billion, with a growth rate of 55%, as compared to 2014. [4] Although no legislation for arbitration was promulgated in 2015, the Supreme People's Court has issued three important judicial interpretations concerning arbitration. Meanwhile, there are still new arbitration institutions being established in 2015, such as the Arbitration Center across the Straits set up by the China Council for the Promotion of International Trade and China Chamber of International Commerce in the Fujian Pingtan Comprehensive Pilot Zone on 29 December. Foreign arbitration institutions are also setting up offices in Mainland China, such as the representative office of Hong Kong International Arbitration Centre set up in the China (Shanghai) Pilot Free Trade Zone on 19 November 2015. The major arbitration institutions in China, represented by the Beijing Arbitration Commission, the China International Economic and Trade Arbitration Commission ("CIETAC") and the China Maritime Arbitration

---

* Translated by Helena H. C. CHEN

1 SONG Lianbin, male, Ph. D., Professor and doctorial supervisor at the School of International Law of China University of Political Science and Law.

2 FU Panfeng, male, Ph. D., Post doctorate at the Institute of Law of Chinese Academy of Social Sciences.

3 Helena H. C. CHEN, female, Ph. D., Partner at Pinsent Masons LLP.

4 Please refer to http://www.ylzcwyh.com/ylac/zxdt/gnxw/641.html, accessed on 22 March 2016. The national average of cases per arbitral commissions is 561. In all, 62 arbitral commissions, constituting 25% of the number of arbitration commissions nationwide, that accepted above this national average, accepting cumulatively 108,710 cases in all, which correspondingly accounts for 79% of all cases. There were 182 arbitration commissions, constituting the remaining 75% of the number of arbitration commissions nationwide, that accepted less than this national average, accepting cumulatively 28,214 cases, which correspondingly accounts for 21% of all cases. There were 56,659 cases which were settled through mediation, accounting for 41% of all cases. There were 209 cases annulled by the people's courts, and 84 not enforced. There were 163 arbitration commissions that had no cases in relation to non-enforcement or annulment; 20 arbitration commissions that each had more than 5 cases that were annulled or not enforced by courts; 62 arbitration commissions that cumulatively had 2,085 cases with Hong Kong, Macau, Taiwan and/or other foreign elements, accounting for 1.5% of the total number of cases.

Commission have officially implemented new arbitration rules on their part and other arbitration institutions including the Guangzhou Arbitration Commission ("GZAC") also amended their respective arbitration rules. The GZAC has also formulated online arbitration rules and special online arbitration rules applicable to credit card disputes, small-sum online shopping disputes and online lending disputes, amongst others. As to case authorities, we have randomly selected 50 cases, out of the 1,000 cases collected for the purposes of this article from available official databases, as our target for observation to analyze the reasons in each case in relation to issues of recognition of the validity of an arbitration agreement; annulment of an arbitral award and recognition or enforcement or non-enforcement of an arbitral award while providing an in-depth review into the significant cases and the issues involved. This article does not represent the position of any organization and is only intended to provide relevant information to individuals and organizations for further insights into China's arbitration-related matters.

II. Commentary on New Arbitration Regulations and Arbitration Rules

The Supreme People's Court issued three important judicial interpretations concerning arbitration in 2015, namely, the *Interpretation of the Supreme People's Court on the Application of the Civil Procedure Law of the People's Republic of China* (Fa-Shi [2015] No. 5) effective as of 4 February 2015; the *Provisions of the Supreme People's Court on Recognition and Enforcement of Arbitral Awards Made in the Taiwan Region* (Fa-Shi [2015] No. 14) effective as of 1 July 2015 and the *Official Reply of the Supreme People's Court on the Requests of the Higher People's Court of Shanghai Municipality and Other Courts for Instructions on Cases Involving Judicial Review of the Arbitral Awards Issued by the China International Economic and Trade Arbitration Commission, Former Sub-Commissions Thereof and Other Arbitration Institutions* (Fa-Shi [2015] No. 15) effective as of 17 July 2015. These judicial interpretations have clarified certain difficult issues in China's arbitration practice and serve as direct guidelines for the arbitration industry and the courts.

A. Judicial Interpretation of the Civil Procedure Law

Based on the *Civil Procedure Law of the People's Republic of China* promulgated in 2012 (hereinafter referred to as the "*Civil Procedure Law*"), the Supreme People's Court issued the *Interpretation of the Supreme People's Court on the Application of the Civil Procedure Law of the People's Republic of China in* 2015. This new judicial interpretation is known as the longest judicial interpretation in the legal history of Mainland China, containing 552 articles in all. There are 17 articles in this judicial interpretation which are related to arbitration but most of them are a continuation of the already well-established *Civil Procedure Law* and related judicial interpretations. The new provisions and key points worth emphasizing are summarized as follows:

1. Courts having jurisdiction over a lawsuit claiming damages resulting from improper property preservation measures before the commencement of an arbitration: An action instituted by the respondent or an interested party for losses resulting from a party's failure to institute an action or apply for arbitration within the statutory period after applying for preservation before the institution of action shall be under the jurisdiction of the people's court taking the preservation measures. An action instituted by the respondent or an interested party for losses resulting

from the preservation measures shall be under the jurisdiction of the people's court which accepts that action or takes the preservation measures. This is a new provision targeting property preservation measures before the commencement of arbitration.

2. Degree of proof of the facts that have been affirmed in an effective award: A party need not provide evidence for facts confirmed by effective awards rendered by arbitration institutions, unless the other party has contrary evidence which suffices to overturn.

3. Anti-suit effect of an arbitration clause: Where the parties have concluded a valid arbitration agreement, they should not file a lawsuit to a court for the subject matter that is governed by the arbitration agreement. A court, having accepted an action that is provided for by a valid arbitration agreement, shall dismiss the action based on an objection raised by the other party concerned.

4. Arbitral awards and court retrial procedures: A court shall issue a ruling to permit retrial if a petition for retrial is made on the grounds that the award on which a judgment or ruling is made has been annulled or modified.

5. Partial non-enforcement of an arbitral award: Where a party requests the non-enforcement of an arbitral award, the party shall file the request with the enforcement court before the termination of enforcement. Where the matters being arbitrated by an arbitral institution partly fall under the circumstances as set forth in the *Civil Procedure Law*, the people's court shall render a ruling not to enforce the part of matters. Where, after the people's court issues a ruling not to enforce an arbitral award, a party raises an objection to or applies for reconsideration of the ruling, the people's court shall not accept it. The parties may either reach a new written arbitration agreement on the civil dispute and then apply for arbitration, or may institute an action in the people's court.

6. Enforcement procedures not affected by confirmation of a third party's right to or distribution of property through arbitration proceedings: Where, during enforcement, the person subject to enforcement confirms the right of a person that is not a party to the case to any property already seized, impounded or frozen by the people's court or divides and distributes such property to the person that is not a party to the case under the arbitration procedure, the proceeding of the enforcement procedure of the people's court shall not be affected. This is a new article added for the purpose of clarifying existing practice.

7. Exclusion by an arbitration agreement of a court's exclusive jurisdiction: the parties shall not select a foreign court for jurisdiction by an agreement; unless they agree in writing to settle the dispute through arbitration.

8. Application for provisional measures, review of such application and security: Where an international arbitral institution of the People's Republic of China submits a property preservation application filed by the party to a people's court for ruling, the people's court may examine the application and decide whether or not to take the preservation measure. The people's court that issues a ruling of preservation shall order the applicant to provide the security, and if the applicant fails to do so, the people's court shall render a ruling to dismiss the application.

9. Recognition and enforcement of foreign arbitral awards: A foreign arbitral award (including an ad hoc award) may be recognized and enforced in China pursuant to a valid convention that is binding on the People's Republic of China or pursuant to the principle of reciprocity. Recognition and enforcement are two separate proceedings and the court will make its determination specifically in relation to the precise application, whether it is one for recognition or enforcement or both, as made by the party concerned. During the period when one party ap-

plies for the recognition and enforcement of an effective judgment or ruling of a foreign court or a foreign arbitral award, the *Civil Procedure Law* shall apply. The period of application for enforcement shall be recalculated from the date when the ruling issued by the people's court on the recognition application comes into force.

10. Applying, mutatis mutandis, to cases involving Hong Kong, Macau and Taiwan: The people's courts may apply, mutatis mutandis, the special provisions on foreign-related civil procedures to civil actions that involve the Hong Kong Special Administrative Region, the Macao Special Administrative Region, or the Taiwan region.

B. Recognition and Enforcement of Arbitral Awards Made in Taiwan Region

Along with the continuous ease of cross-strait relations and deepening of cross-strait civil and commercial exchange since the 1980s, the *Provisions on the People's Court's Recognition of the Verdicts on Civil Cases Made by Courts of Taiwan* (Fa-Shi [1998] No. 11) promulgated on 22 May 1998 and the *Supplementary Provisions of the Supreme People's Court on the People's Courts' Recognition of Civil Judgments of the Relevant Courts of the Taiwan Region* (Fa-Shi [2009] No. 4) promulgated on 24 April 2009 by the Supreme People's Court are no longer fully adaptable to current practice. Therefore, the Supreme People's Court issued a new judicial interpretation in 2015 in respect of the recognition and enforcement of arbitral awards made in Taiwan, that is, the *Provisions of the Supreme People's Court on Recognition and Enforcement of Arbitral Awards Made in Taiwan Region*, which contains 22 articles in total. Amongst those articles, the most important article is undoubtedly Article 14, which specifies the circumstances under which an arbitral award made in Taiwan shall not be recognized and enforced. Article 14 provides that where, with respect to an arbitral award in question in an application for recognition or enforcement, the people's court shall not recognize the award if the people's court is satisfied that the respondent has provided sufficient evidence showing any of the following circumstances:

1. One party to the arbitration agreement lacked competency under the applicable law at the time the parties entered into the arbitration agreement, or the arbitration agreement is invalid in accordance with the governing law as agreed on by the parties, or the provisions of the Taiwan Region on arbitration, in the event that the parties did not agree on the applicable governing law, or the parties did not enter into a written arbitration agreement, unless an application for recognition of arbitration mediation of the Taiwan Region was filed;

2. The respondent did not receive proper notice on the selection and appointment of arbitrators or the arbitration procedure, or the respondent did not state its opinions due to any other reason not attributable to the respondent;

3. The dispute addressed in the arbitral award was not the dispute submitted for arbitration, or did not fall within the scope of the arbitration agreement. Where the arbitral award includes any decision exceeding the scope of items submitted by the parties for arbitration, but the decision in the arbitral award exceeding the scope of items submitted for arbitration may be separated from the decision on the items submitted for arbitration, the part of the decision in the arbitral award on the items submitted for arbitration may be recognized;

4. The formation of the arbitral award or the arbitration procedure violates the agreement between the parties, or, in the absence of the agreement between the parties, fails to comply with the provisions of the Taiwan Region on arbitration;

5. The arbitral award is not yet binding on the parties, or a court of the Taiwan Region has revoked the arbitral award or dismissed an enforcement application.

Where the item in dispute cannot be resolved through arbitration in accordance with the state law, or recognition of the arbitral award violates the One-China principle or any other fundamental principle of the laws of the state, or damages social and public interest, the people's court shall issue a ruling not to recognize it.

It is apparent that other than the special circumstances of the One-China principle, the conditions for recognition and enforcement of arbitral awards made in Taiwan by Mainland China basically mirror the provisions of the well-known Article V of the *Convention on the Recognition and Enforcement of Foreign Arbitral Awards* (i.e. the New York Convention).

C. Judicial Review of Arbitral Awards Made by the CIETAC and Its Former Sub-Commissions

The split between CIETAC and its former Shanghai Sub-Commission and South China Sub-Commission's in 2012 has resulted in a peculiar issue of conflict that concerns jurisdiction determination, i.e. which arbitration institution, after the spilt, has jurisdiction over a matter where, the parties, before the split, have entered into an arbitration agreement stipulating that disputes shall be submitted to the "China International Economic and Trade Arbitration Commission South China Sub-Commission" or the "China International Economic and Trade Arbitration Commission Shanghai Sub-Commission" for arbitration. This has not only caused disputes among arbitration institutions but has also confused the parties concerned. The courts were also placed in a difficult position when conducting judicial review over the relevant arbitral awards. As an attempt to provide a permanent cure for this problem, the Supreme People's Court issued the *Official Reply of the Supreme People's Court on the Requests of the Higher People's Court of Shanghai Municipality and Other Courts for Instructions on Cases Involving Judicial Review of the Arbitral Awards Issued by the China International Economic and Trade Arbitration Commission, Former Sub-Commissions thereof and Other Arbitration Institutions* (hereinafter referred to as "Official Reply") in 2015 as an official reply in the form of judicial interpretation to address this matter. Based on the principle of respecting parties' autonomy, this judicial interpretation aims to settle the controversy over jurisdiction between CIETAC and its two former Sub-Commissions by looking at the dates the two Sub-Commissions' split from the CIETAC (the South China Sub-Commission was renamed on 22 October 2012 and the Shanghai Sub-Commission was renamed on 17 April 2013). If the parties have reached an agreement before the abovementioned respective dates to submit the disputes to South China Sub-Commission or Shanghai Sub-Commission, the renamed South China International Economic and Trade Arbitration Commission ("SCIA") or the renamed Shanghai International Economic and Trade Arbitration Commission ("SHIAC") shall have jurisdiction over disputes between the parties. If the parties have reached an agreement on or after the above-mentioned dates to submit the disputes to South China Sub-Commission or Shanghai Sub-Commission, the CIETAC shall have jurisdiction over the disputes between the parties. In the interim between the above mentioned dates (respectively) and before this *Official Reply* came into force, for cases which were not accepted in accordance with this *Official Reply* and the respondent did not object to the jurisdiction or after an arbitral award was rendered, if a party applies for annulment or non-enforcement of the arbitral award on the grounds that the arbitration institution has no jurisdiction, the people's court shall not support such argument.

D. Online Arbitration Rules and Practice in China

In continuation of the trend in both international and Chinese domestic arbitration industries in updating arbitration rules in 2014, various Chinese arbitration institutions kept on improving their respective arbitration rules in 2015. In the 2014 Annual Review, the authors have made their observations on commercial arbitration rules and system which are most representative. The section below serves to introduce the development of China's online arbitration practice by using the online arbitration rules of the GZAC as an example.

After 20 years of development, the GZAC has accepted a total of 10,631 cases with claim amounts amounting to RMB 31.6 billion (figures below are similarly tagged with the RMB currency) in 2015, among which more than 1,000 cases involved foreign elements. The GZAC has been devoted to build up an online arbitration platform and promoting online case filing and online arbitration. In 2015, more than 2,000 cases were filed online and some of them were heard online throughout the process. In light of the special characteristics of online trading, the GZAC has formulated its online arbitration rules specifically so that they can be applicable to the online trading model and in doing so, providing basic principles for the conduct of arbitration online. The GZAC has also formulated specific online arbitration rules for small-sum online shopping to deal with online shopping disputes and specific online arbitration rules for online lending disputes to deal with P2P lending disputes. On 24 September 2015, the GZAC promoted the establishment of the China Internet Arbitration Association, whose members include more than 160 arbitration institutions, colleges and universities, industry associations, lawyers associations and other organizations nationwide. Through cooperation of the members on an equal footing, a unified internet arbitration platform will be set up and members will share their internet arbitration expertise and offline experience networks; recognize each other's panels of arbitrators and adopt unified internet arbitration procedural rules and laws applicable to internet disputes.

The GZAC Online Arbitration Rules consist of 31 articles in total and were brought into effect as of 1 October 2015. The main provisions of these arbitration rules include: (a) case filing and payment of fees online. The parties concerned shall submit requests for arbitration, upload evidence and pay fees online through the internet arbitration platform; (b) service of legal documents and hearing of cases online. The GZAC will receive the documents submitted by the parties online and arrange for service of arbitration-related documents to the parties via email, cell phone, fax or other electronic means of communication as confirmed by the parties who may also submit statement of defense, evidence or other relevant documents through the online arbitration platform. The arbitral tribunal will conduct the hearing mainly in written form but may also hear the case through online sessions via video conference, conference call or others as it deems necessary; (c) verification of the original form and validity of electronic evidence. Key evidence derived from e-commerce transactions is in the form of electronic data and the verification of the original form of the electronic evidence and determination of its degree of proof is therefore vital to ascertaining the facts of a case; (d) shortened time limit for submitting defense and hearing of case. Compared to the traditional arbitration model, the time limits under the online arbitration mechanisms are relatively shorter. For example, the timeframe for submitting a defense is shortened to 5 days and the timeframe for the tribunal to render an award is shortened to 30 days after the arbitral tribunal is constituted, resulting in an improvement in efficiency of the arbitration process; (e) conversion of proceedings—if the parties concerned reach an agreement or if the arbitral tribunal deems that the case involved is complicated, such case may be converted into one to be heard offline according to the Arbitration Rules of the GZAC. [5]

III. Statistical Analysis of Judicial Supervision Cases

A. Collection of Data and Overview

We have collected data in respect of 1,000 arbitration related cases and have classified them into four major categories. Out of these cases, 206 are claims for recognition of the validity of an arbitration agreement; 585 are claims for annulment of an arbitral award; 139 are claims for enforcement (including recognition, enforcement and non-enforcement) of arbitral awards and 70 are claims for provisional measures in arbitration. In order to ensure the correctness of the analysis, the cases mentioned above are sourced from the "Judicial Opinions of China", the official website created two years ago for law reports. By examining the data collected from various means, and having cross-referenced these data against those from pkulaw.cn and other law databases, the authors believe that the data reflects a rough picture of the respective percentages of the four major categories in judicial practice. Using these data as a starting point and having considered the influence of the cases, the authors have carefully selected 50 cases which they find to be most representative. Out of these cases, there are 10 cases for recognition of the validity of an arbitration agreement, 29 cases for annulment of the arbitral award, 7 cases for enforcement and 4 cases for provisional measures in arbitration. These cases are set out in the table below:

Table 1: Sample statistics of arbitration-related cases accepted by PRC courts

	Claim	Court and Case Number	Causes of Action	Court Judgment	Reasons
1	Recognition of the validity of an arbitration agreement (scope of jurisdiction)	The Supreme People's Court Civil Ruling (2015) Min-Si-Zhong-Zi No. 15	Appeal as to jurisdictional objection	People's Court has jurisdiction	Although the behavior in connection with the case has certain factual relevance to one party's termination of the contract, the behavior itself is neither governed by the rights or obligations under the contract involved in the case, nor arising from the excise of the rights or the performance of the obligations under such contract. Instead, such behavior is an independent civil conduct. The infringement of reputation caused by it has no concurrence relation with the liabilities for breach of the contract involved in the case. Therefore there is no issue of a repeated trial.

5 China Guangzhou Arbitration Commission Online Arbitration Rules Issued and Implemented, published on 25 June 2015 at the China arbitration website with link below: http://www.china-arbitration.com/news.php?id=3325, accessed on 2 February 2016.

	Claim	Court and Case Number	Causes of Action	Court Judgment	Reasons
2	Recognition of the validity of an arbitration agreement	Jiangxi Higher People's Court Civil Ruling (2015) Gan-Li-Zhong-Zi No. 13	Appeal as to jurisdictional objection	The Civil Ruling by Jiangxi Pingxiang Intermediate People's Court is overturned; case referred to Shanghai First Intermediate People's Court	The arbitration clause in connection with the case does not explicitly specify the name of the arbitration institution, and both parties did not provide sufficient evidence to prove the signing place of the contract, therefore the case shall be governed by the court at the domicile of the respondent, namely Shanghai First Intermediate people's Court.
3	Recognition of the validity of an arbitration agreement	Jiangxi Higher People's Court Civil Ruling (2015) Gan-Li-Zhong-Zi No. 52	Appeal as to jurisdictional objection	People's Court has jurisdiction	1. Unable to identify the arbitration institution based on the agreed wording that "application for arbitration shall be submitted to Shanghai Municipal Arbitration Commission"; 2. The arbitration agreement was signed in Ningdu County, Jiangxi, and the domicile of the respondent in the first trial is Shanghai. Therefore, both Jiangxi Ganzhou Intermediate People's Court and Shanghai First Intermediate People's Court have jurisdiction over the case; given that the former has accepted the case before the latter, there is nothing wrong to find that the case falls within the jurisdiction of the Jiangxi Ganzhou Intermediate People's Court.
4	Recognition of the validity of an arbitration agreement	Beijing Second Intermediate People's Court Civil Ruling (2015) Er-Zhong-Min-Te-Zi No. 00021	Declaration of the invalidity of an arbitration agreement	Withdrawal of application permitted	The applicant voluntarily applied for withdrawal ofthe application on the grounds that both parties have reached a settlement through negotiation.

	Claim	Court and Case Number	Causes of Action	Court Judgment	Reasons
5	Recognition of the validity of an arbitration agreement	Liaoning Shenyang Intermediate People's Court (2015) Shen – Zhong – Min – San – Te – Zi No. 00011	Declaration of the invalidity of an arbitration agreement	Application rejected	The registered addresses of both parties to the contract as well as the construction site in question are both located in Shenyang and there is only one arbitration commission in Shenyang. Therefore it was held that both parties to the contract in this case have selected an arbitration institution, which is the Shenyang Arbitration Commission.
6	Recognition of the validity of an arbitration agreement	Guangdong Shenzhen Intermediate People's Court (2015) Shen–Zhong–Fa–She – Wai – Zhong –Zi No. 158	Declaration of the invalidity of an arbitration agreement	Application rejected	Although the wording "Shenzhen City Arbitration Commission" is not accurate, it is only different from the official name "Shenzhen Arbitration Commission" by one word. It can therefore be held that the arbitration institution selected by both parties shall be the Shenzhen Arbitration Commission.
7	Recognition of the validity of an arbitration agreement	Shanghai First Intermediate People's Court (2015) Hu – Yi – Zhong – Min – Ren (Zhong–Xie) –Zi No. 9	Declaration of the invalidity of an arbitration agreement	Application rejected	Although there is an unnecessary word "Municipal" in the name "Shanghai Municipal Arbitration Commission Lingang International Arbitration Center", it shall be deemed that both parties have agreed to submit disputes tothe Lingang International Arbitration Center subordinated to and established by the Shanghai Arbitration Commission for arbitration.
8	Recognition of the validity of an arbitration agreement	Shanghai First Intermediate People's Court (2015) Hu – Yi – Zhong – Min – Ren (Zhong–Xie) –Zi No. 7	Declaration of the validity of an arbitration agreement	Arbitration agreement valid	The validity of the arbitration agreement itself is not in dispute between the parties. One party's disagreement with the other party's proposal (via an email) that the arbitral tribunal shall consist of three arbitrators has no impact on the recognition of the validity of the arbitration agreement concerned.

	Claim	Court and Case Number	Causes of Action	Court Judgment	Reasons
9	Recognition of the validity of an arbitration agreement	Beijing Second Intermediate People's Court Civil Ruling (2015) Er-Zhong-Min-Te-Zi No. 04731	Declaration of the invalidity of an arbitration agreement	Application rejected	1. No ambiguity in the wording "China International Economic and Trade Arbitration Commission Beijing Headquarter", which should refer to the CIETAC established in Beijing; 2. In this case, it is not a situation of a clause stipulating "either arbitration or trial" as alleged by one party.
10	Recognition of the validity of an arbitration agreement	Beijing Third Intermediate People's Court Civil Ruling (2015) San-Zhong-Min (Shang)-Te-Zi No. 03811	Declaration of the invalidity of an arbitration agreement	Application rejected	1. Lack of sufficient evidence to support the allegation that the concerned "Exploration Right Transfer Contract" explicitly excludes dispute settlement by arbitration; 2. Since the effectiveness of the arbitration clause and that of the exploration right transfer are not the same concept, it is baseless toapply for the concerned arbitration clause to be held invalid on the grounds that the exploration right transfer has not been approved by the Ministry of Land and Resources.
11	Recognition of the validity of an arbitral award	Beijing Second Intermediate People's Court Civil Ruling (2015) Er-Zhong-Min-Te-Zi No. 08817	Annulment of an arbitral award	Application rejected	1. The court did not admit the grounds, based upon Article 58 ofthe *Arbitration Law*, raised by the party; 2. Verification of facts and application of law both relate to the arbitral tribunal's handling of substantivematters of the case and they do not fall within the circumstances for annulment of an arbitral award set out in Article 58 of the *Arbitration Law*.
12	Recognition of the validity of an arbitral award	Beijing Third Intermediate People's Court Civil Ruling (2015) San-Zhong-Min (Shang)-Te-Zi No. 02092	Annulment of an arbitral award	Application rejected	1. The evidence raised by the applicant is not strong enough to prove that the evidence, which the award is based on, is forged; 2. The applicant has no strong evidence to support its claim that the arbitral tribunal has rendered the award by bending the law.

	Claim	Court and Case Number	Causes of Action	Court Judgment	Reasons
13	Recognition of the validity of an arbitral award	Beijing Third Intermediate People's Court Civil Ruling (2015) San-Zhong-Min (Shang)-Te-Zi No. 03812	Annulment of an arbitral award	Application rejected	1. Lack of factual basis in the applicant's claim that the arbitral tribunal has failed to comply with legal procedures; 2. Verification of the concerned contract, admission of the evidence and the examination as well as verification of the rights and obligations of both parties concerned based on contractual agreements and ascertained facts are within the scope of the arbitral tribunal's examination of the substantive matters of the case, rather than the circumstances for annulment of an arbitral award set out in Article 58 of the *Arbitration Law*.
14	Recognition of the validity of an arbitral award	Beijing Third Intermediate People's Court Civil Ruling (2015) San-Zhong-Min (Shang)-Te-Zi No. 04964	Annulment of an arbitral award	Application rejected	The arbitration agreement is valid. The Beijing Arbitration Commission has jurisdiction over the case.
15	Recognition of the validity of an arbitral award	Beijing Third Intermediate People's Court Civil Ruling (2015) San-Zhong-Min (Shang)-Te-Zi No. 01648	Annulment of an arbitral award	Application rejected	1. There are no such circumstances whereby the respondent has concealed evidence which would affect the impartiality of the award; 2. It is within the arbitral tribunal's scope to verify the evidence submitted by the parties concerned while examining the substantive matters of the case and when rendering an award. This is not within the scope of the court when examining a claim for annulment of an arbitral award. Therefore the applicant has no legal basis for making the application based on these reasons.

	Claim	Court and Case Number	Causes of Action	Court Judgment	Reasons
16	Recognition of the validity of an arbitral award	Shanghai First Intermediate People's Court Civil Ruling (2015) Hu-Yi-Zhong-Min-Si (Shang)-Che-Zi No. 12	Annulment of an arbitral award	Application rejected	1. The applicant claims that the respondent has concealed evidence which would affect the impartiality of the award but in fact, its supporting arguments actually dealt with the distribution of the burden of proof, which is not within the scope of the court's examination of annulment of an arbitral award; 2. According to the arbitration rules, the parties shall submit evidentiary materials within the period of adducing evidence specified by the arbitral tribunal. Should a party concerned fail to do so, it will be subject to the arbitral tribunal's decision on whether or not to accept and arrange the cross-examination. The fact that the arbitral tribunal did not accept further evidence submitted by the applicant after the second hearing should not lead to the conclusion that the arbitral tribunal violated the arbitration rules; 3. The applicant's allegation that the arbitral tribunal exercised favoritism and bent the law when rendering the award was not accepted by the court for the lack of evidence.
17	Recognition of the validity of an arbitral award	Shanxi Jincheng Intermediate People's Court Civil Ruling (2015) Jin-Shi-Fa-Min-Chu-Zi No. 53	Annulment of an arbitral award	Arbitration agreement invalid	1. There were no circumstances under which the legal procedures were violated; 2. The applicant failed to provide evidence proving that the other party concealed evidence which would affect the impartiality of the award; 3. Whether the award, rendered by the arbitral tribunal based on the evidence adduced by both parties concerned and the cross-examination of such evidence, is partial falls within the tribunal's scope of the substantive examination of the matter and these do not fall within any of the circumstances, set out in Article 58 of the *Arbitration Law*, for annulment of an arbitral award.

	Claim	Court and Case Number	Causes of Action	Court Judgment	Reasons
18	Recognition of the validity of an arbitral award	Tianjin Second Intermediate People's Court Civil Ruling (2015) Er-Zhong-Min-Er-Chu-Zi No. 491	Annulment of an arbitral award	Application rejected	There were no circumstances under which the respondent has concealed evidence which would affect the impartiality of the award.
19	Recognition of the validity of an arbitral award	Shandong Jinan Intermediate People's Court Civil Ruling (2015) Ji-Zhong-Li-Chu-Zi No. 66	Annulment of an arbitral award	Application rejected	1. The arbitration procedure did not violate legal procedures; 2. There were no circumstances under which the respondent has concealed evidence; 3. The applicant's dissatisfaction with the substantive result is not a subject of the court's examination of annulment of an arbitration award.
20	Recognition of the validity of an arbitral award	Henan Luoyang Intermediate People's Court Civil Ruling (2015) Luo-Min-San-Chu-Zi No. 82	Annulment of an arbitral award	Application rejected	1. The applicant failed to provide evidence to prove that the legal procedures have been violated; 2. The applicant failed to provide evidence to prove that the Luoyang Arbitration Commission had exercised favoritism for personal gains; 3. The applicant's allegation of inappropriateness in the arbitration commission's verification of evidence and rendering of award is included in the scope of the arbitration commission's examination of the substantive matters of the case, and the relevant allegations shall not be accepted for examination by the court.

	Claim	Court and Case Number	Causes of Action	Court Judgment	Reasons
21	Recognition of the validity of an arbitral award	Hubei Wuhan Intermediate People's Court Civil Ruling (2015) E - Wu - Han - Zhong - Zhong - Jian - Zi No. 00045	Annulment of an arbitral award	Application rejected	1. The applicant failed to prove that the respondent deliberately concealed the real address of the applicant for personal purpose and failed to serve the arbitration documents to the true and effective address; 2. The applicant failed to provide evidence proving that the appraisal opinion is false in any way; 3. The applicant's assertion that there is inconsistency in the relevant information in the award and that the contract involved in the award does not reflect the real intentions of both parties are issues to be considered by the arbitral tribunal in its examination of the substantive matters of the case and does not fall within the circumstances for annulment of an arbitration award.
22	Recognition of the validity of an arbitral award	Zhejiang Taizhou Intermediate People's Court Civil Ruling (2015) Zhe-Tai-Zhong-Che-Zi No. 31	Annulment of an arbitral award	Application rejected	1. Unable to verify the circumstance where the respondent was alleged to have concealed evidence which would affect the impartiality of the award; 2. Distribution of the burden of proof, admission of evidence and the evidential effect are substantive issues in the case to be considered by the tribunal, and not within the scope of the court's examination of annulment of an arbitration award.

	Claim	Court and Case Number	Causes of Action	Court Judgment	Reasons
23	Recognition of the validity of an arbitral award	Guangdong Shenzhen Intermediate People's Court Civil Ruling (2015) Shen–Zhong–Fa–She–Wai–Zhong–Zi No. 49	Annulment of an arbitral award	Application rejected	1. The CIETAC South China Sub–Commission is a duly established arbitration institution. It has been renamed as SCIA. Therefore, the SCIA is competent to accept the case and render the award; 2. The SCIA has served the arbitration documents to the applicant in accordance with the applicable arbitration rules, and there were no circumstances under which the legal procedures were violated; 3. The three arbitrators composing the arbitral tribunal for the case are on the panel of arbitrators maintained by the SCIA and are qualified to be arbitrators. The composition of the arbitral tribunal complies with the applicable arbitration rules.
24	Recognition of the validity of an arbitral award	Fujian Fuzhou Intermediate People's Court Civil Ruling (2015) Rong–Min–Ren–Zi No. 62	Annulment of an arbitral award	Application rejected	The evidence submitted by the applicant is not sufficient to prove that the respondent has concealed evidence which would affect the impartiality of the award.
25	Recognition of the validity of an arbitral award	Jiangxi Yichun Intermediate People's Court Civil Ruling (2015) Yi–Zhong–Min–Shang–Che–Zi No. 2	Annulment of an arbitral award	Application rejected	The arbitration clause in the contract is valid for two reasons: 1) the parties to the arbitration did not raise any objection to the validity of the arbitration agreement before the first hearing conducted by the tribunal; 2) the arbitration clause is concluded after the *Arbitration Law* became effective and before the Yichun Arbitration Commission was established. However, after the establishment of the Yichun Arbitration Commission, both parties had neither amended the subject arbitration clause nor entered into a new agreement. Therefore, it shall be regarded that both parties have agreed that such arbitration clause was to remain valid.

	Claim	Court and Case Number	Causes of Action	Court Judgment	Reasons
26	Recognition of the validity of an arbitral award	Hainan Haikou Intermediate People's Court Civil Ruling (2015) Hai-Zhong-Fa-Zhong-Zi No. 7	Annulment of an arbitral award	Application rejected	The arguments made by the applicant for annulment of the arbitration award are all related to substantive issues and do not constitute legal basis upon which an arbitral award shall be annulled.
27	Recognition of the validity of an arbitral award	Hebei Hengshui Intermediate People's Court Civil Ruling (2015) Heng-Zhong-Che-Zi No. 31	Annulment of an arbitral award	Application rejected	1. The arbitral tribunal merely conducted the hearings for 29 arbitration cases in one session but did not consolidate the 29 cases into one. Therefore, the allegation made by the applicant that the amount claimed under the arbitration has obviously exceeded the amount of claim allowed to be heard in summary procedures, asset forth in the arbitration rules, is not upheld by the court; 2. Although it is a fact that the arbitration award is made beyond the time limit provided by the arbitration rules, both parties have confirmed that the time spent for mediation during the arbitration proceedings is not to be included as part of the duration of the arbitration proceedings. In addition, this does not fall within the circumstances for annulling an arbitral award pursuant to Article 58 of the *Arbitration Law*.
28	Recognition of the validity of an arbitral award	Jilin Liaoyuan Intermediate People's Court Civil Ruling (2015) Liao-Min-Ta-Zi No. 3	Annulment of an arbitral award	Application rejected	The applicant failed to prove that the arbitral award satisfies any of the six circumstances stipulated in Article 58 of the *Arbitration Law* that justify a court to annul an arbitral award. In addition, there is no evidence to prove that this award has been made against social and public interest.

	Claim	Court and Case Number	Causes of Action	Court Judgment	Reasons
29	Recognition of the validity of an arbitral award	Hunan Changde Intermediate People's Court Civil Ruling (2015) Chang-Min-Yi-Che-Zi No. 7	Annulment of an arbitral award	Application rejected	The applicant failed to submit sufficient evidence to prove that the evidence upon which the award was based on has been forged.
30	Recognition of the validity of an arbitral award	Jiangsu Suzhou Intermediate People's Court Civil Ruling (2015) Su-Zhong-Min-Zhong-Shen-Zi No. 00005	Annulment of an arbitral award	Application rejected	1. No evidence of forged evidence or procedural irregularities in the arbitration proceedings; 2. Review of the arbitral award by the court is limited to the scope defined by Article 58 of the *Arbitration Law*. The substantive issues raised by the applicant concerning payment for construction work do not fall within the scope of review by the court.
31	Recognition of the validity of an arbitral award	Shanxi Xi'an Intermediate People's Court Civil Ruling (2015) Xi-Zhong-Min-Si-Zhong-Zi No. 00066	Annulment of an arbitral award	Application rejected	1. The issues arbitrated fall within the scope of the agreed arbitration agreement and the Xi'an Arbitration Commission has jurisdiction over the case; 2. The applicant's allegations that the arbitral tribunal has erred while verifying the facts and that the tribunal has violated public order and good moral does not comply with the requirements of Article 58 of the *Arbitration Law*, which provides the grounds for the court to annul an arbitral award. In addition, the applicant has failed to submit new evidence to support its allegation.

	Claim	Court and Case Number	Causes of Action	Court Judgment	Reasons
32	Recognition of the validity of an arbitral award	Anhui Hefei Intermediate People's Court Civil Ruling (2015) He-Min-Zhong-Zi No. 00124	Annulment of an arbitral award	Application rejected	1. The applicant insisted that the presiding arbitrator should be disqualified but failed to raise this issue in the course of the hearing. Such objection is merely based on the reason that the presiding arbitrator and the applicant's attorney are former colleagues before 2006, which does not constitute a statutory reason for disqualification. Therefore, the applicant's allegation that the arbitration procedure violated statutory procedural requirements based on such allegation is untenable. The applicant failed to submit an application for appraisal within 5 days before the expiration of the time period for producing evidence and therefore it is not in violation of any procedural requirements for the arbitral tribunal to reject such application; 2. The respondent is not found to have concealed evidence; 3. Verification of facts and application of law are duties of the arbitral tribunal in hearing cases and therefore do not constitute statutory reasons for applying for annulment of an arbitration award.

	Claim	Court and Case Number	Causes of Action	Court Judgment	Reasons
33	Recognition of the validity of an arbitral award	Hubei Wuhan Intermediate People's Court Civil Ruling (2015) E – Wu – Han – Zhong – Zhong – Jian – Zi No. 00134	Annulment of an arbitral award	Substantive issues referred back for re-arbitration and application for annulment suspended	1. The applicant's allegations in relation to the evidence upon which the arbitral award was rendered; the degree of proof; distribution of the burden of proof; practice in dealing business and logical reasoning etc., failed to satisfy the requirements set forth in Article 58 of the *Arbitration Law* under which an arbitral award should be annulled; 2. The applicant failed to submit sufficient evidence to prove that the respondent has concealed evidence that would affect the impartiality of the award; 3. The arbitral tribunal violated the basic principles of the rules of evidence stipulated in the *Civil Procedure Law* in its substantive award and therefore, according to Article 61 of the *Arbitration Law*, the court decided to refer the case back to the Wuhan Arbitration Commission for re-arbitration.
34	Recognition of the validity of an arbitral award	Shandong Jinan Intermediate People's Court Civil Ruling (2015) Ji-Zhong-Li-Chu-Zi No. 55	Annulment of an arbitral award	Application withdrawn	The applicant requested to withdraw the case on the grounds that both parties had reached a settlement agreement.
35	Recognition of the validity of an arbitral award	Beijing Second Intermediate People's Court Civil Ruling (2015) Er-Zhong-Min-Te-Zi No. 00515	Annulment of an arbitral award	Application withdrawn	The applicant has voluntarily withdrawn the application.

	Claim	Court and Case Number	Causes of Action	Court Judgment	Reasons
36	Recognition of the validity of an arbitral award	Hunan Shaoyang Intermediate People's Court Civil Ruling (2015) Shao-Zhong-Min-Er-Chu-Zi No. 103	Annulment of an arbitral award	Award annulled	The service procedures were illegal.
37	Recognition of the validity of an arbitral award	Yunnan Kunming Intermediate People's Court Civil Ruling (2015) Kun-Min-Yi-Chu-Zi No. 107	Annulment of an arbitral award	Award annulled	The respondent has concealed evidence that would have affected the impartiality of that award.
38	Recognition of the validity of an arbitral award	Guangdong Shenzhen Intermediate People's Court Civil Ruling (2015) Shen-Zhong-Fa-She-Wai-Zhong-Zi No. 61	Annulment of an arbitral award	Award annulled	Both parties did not conclude any arbitration agreement.
39	Recognition of the validity of an arbitral award	Zhejiang Zhoushan Intermediate People's Court Civil Ruling (2015) Zhe-Zhou-Zhong-Che-Zi No. 2	Annulment of an arbitral award	Award annulled	1. The arbitral tribunal deliberated and rendered an award without soliciting the applicant's opinions on cross-examination and without organizing a cross-examination on the opposing evidence; 2. The arbitral tribunal failed to fulfill its basic obligations of fulfilling the notification requirements when handling the applicant's request to conduct a financial audit and assent appraisal on the cooperation project.
40	Enforcement or non-enforcement of arbitral awards	Jiangsu Wuxi Intermediate People's Court Civil Ruling (2015) Xi-Shang-Zhong-Shen-Zi No. 00052	Enforcement of a CIETAC arbitral award	Award enforced	Enforcement conditions provided by law were fulfilled.

	Claim	Court and Case Number	Causes of Action	Court Judgment	Reasons
41	Enforcement or non-enforcement of arbitral awards	Jiangsu Wuxi Intermediate People's Court Civil Ruling (2015) Xi-Shang-Zhong-Shen-Zi No. 00073	Enforcement of a SHIAC arbitral award	Award enforced	Enforcement conditions provided by law were fulfilled.
42	Enforcement or non-enforcement of arbitral awards	Shanghai First Intermediate People's Court Enforcement Ruling (2015) Hu-Yi-Zhong-Zhi-Zi No. 275	Enforcement of a Shanghai Arbitration Commission arbitral award	Enforcement proceedings terminated	The other party applied for annulment of the arbitral award during the enforcement proceedings. The court terminated the enforcement proceedings in accordance with the law.
43	Enforcement or non-enforcement of arbitral awards	Jiangsu Yangzhou Intermediate People's Court Enforcement Ruling(2015) Yang-Zhi-Zi No. 00528	Enforcement of a Yangzhou Arbitration Commission arbitral award	Application rejected	This is a maritime dispute and should be under the jurisdiction of a maritime court at the place where the properties of the party subject to enforcement are located or where the party subject to enforcement is domiciled.
44	Enforcement or non-enforcement of arbitral awards	Shanghai Second Intermediate People's Court Enforcement Ruling (2015) Hu-Er-Zhong-Zhi-Yi-Zi No. 29	Non-enforcement of a Shanghai Arbitration Commission arbitral award	Application rejected	1. The party had initiated legal proceedings with the competent court for annulling the arbitral award on the grounds that the other party concealed evidence that would affect the impartiality of the award and such application had been rejected. The same party is now applying for non-enforcement of the award on the same grounds; 2. The parties did not raise any objection to the validity of the arbitration agreement or argue that the issues subject to decision did not fall into the scope of the arbitration agreement during the arbitration proceedings. Yet the parties, in these enforcement proceedings, now claimed that the arbitration clause contained in their contract does not govern their OEM relationship.

	Claim	Court and Case Number	Causes of Action	Court Judgment	Reasons
45	Enforcement or non – enforcement of arbitral awards	Inner Mongolia Chifeng Intermediate People's Court Civil Ruling (2015) Chi – Min – Zhong – Zi No. 21	Non – enforcement of a Chifeng Arbitration Commission arbitral award	Award not enforced	If the arbitral award were to be enforced, the applicant might end up paying twice the amount of the contract price for construction work, thereby damaging the national and social public interest.
46	Enforcement or non – enforcement of arbitral awards	Qinghai Xining Intermediate People's Court Enforcement Ruling (2015) Ning–Zhi – Yi – Zi No. 00033	Non – enforcement of a Shaoxing Arbitration Commission arbitral award	Award not enforced	The subject contract clearly provides that if both parties fail to reach an agreement through consultation, either party may submit the dispute to the arbitration commission located at the place where the contract is concluded for arbitration. The agreed place for conclusion of the contract is Xining City, Qinghai Province. Therefore the Shaoxing Arbitration Commission does not have jurisdiction over the subject case.
47	Provisional measures in arbitration	Guangdong Jiangmen Intermediate People's Court Civil Ruling (2015) Jiang–Zhong–Fa–Li–Bao–Zi No. 7	Application for a ruling of property preservation in arbitration proceedings.	Application rejected	The applicant did not provide property guarantee.
48	Provisional measures in arbitration	Hunan Liuyang Intermediate People's Court Civil Ruling (2015) Liu–Min–Bao–Zi No. 00031	Application for a ruling of property preservation in arbitration proceedings.	The bank accounts of the respondent were frozen, or other equivalent assets seized.	Fulfilled all the requirements for property preservation.

	Claim	Court and Case Number	Causes of Action	Court Judgment	Reasons
49	Provisional measures in arbitration	Fujian Yongchun County People's Court Civil Ruling (2015) Yong-Min-Te-Zi No. 4	Application for a ruling of property preservation in arbitration proceedings.	Injunction over the respondent's right to commercial forest	Fulfilled all the requirements for property preservation.
50	Provisional measures in arbitration	Guangdong Shenzhen Intermediate People's Court Civil Ruling (2015) Shen-Zhong-Fa-She-Wai-Zhong-Zi No. 36	Application for a ruling of property preservation in arbitration proceedings.	The real estate assets of the respondent were seized.	Fulfilled all the requirements for property preservation.

Table 2: Categories of case laws

Types of Cases	Total Cases	Percentage	Sample Size
Recognition of the validity of the arbitration agreement	206	20.6%	10
Annulment of an arbitral award	585	58.5%	29
Recognition, enforcement or non-enforcement of arbitral awards	139	13.9%	7
Provisional measures in arbitration	70	7%	4
Total	1000	100%	50

Table 3: Case laws on the recognition of the validity of an arbitration agreement

Type of cases	Judgment	Number	Percentage
Recognition of the validity of an arbitration agreement	Valid	136	66%
	Application withdrawn	40	19%
	Invalid	24	12%
	Others	6	3%
	Total	206	100%

Table 4: Case laws on annulment of arbitral awards

Type of cases	Judgment	Number	Percentage
Application for Annulment of an arbitral award	Application rejected	424	72.5%
	Application withdrawn	129	22%
	Award annulled	23	4%
	Referred back for re-arbitration	9	1.5%
	Total	585	100%

Table 5: Case laws on non-enforcement of arbitral awards

Type of cases	Judgment	Number	Percentage
Application for non-enforcement of arbitral awards	Application rejected	38	86%
	Non-enforcement	3	6%
	Application withdrawn	1	2%
	Others	3	6%
	Total	45	100%

Table 6: Case laws on enforcement of arbitral awards

Type of cases	Judgment	Number	Percentage
Application for enforcement of an arbitral award	Award enforced	79	84%
	Application rejected	6	6%
	Application withdrawn	2	2%
	Others	7	8%
	Total	94	100%

Table 7: Case laws on provisional measures in arbitration

Type of cases	Judgment	Number	Percentage
Provisional measures in arbitration	Application granted	56	80%
	Application rejected	7	10%
	Application withdrawn	2	3%
	Others	5	7%
	Total	70	100%

From the above statistics, it appears that more than half the vast number of arbitration-related cases heard by the Chinese Courts in 2015 seeks to annul the arbitral award. The remaining categories ranked by proportion percentages from high to low are: cases that seek recognition of the validity of arbitration agreements; applications for enforcement or non-enforcement of arbitral awards followed by applications for provisional measures in arbitration. Based on the judgments or rulings rendered by the courts, the majority of the applications concerning the validity of arbitral awards; the validity of the arbitration agreements; recognition and enforcement of arbitral awards and provisional measures in arbitration have all received support from the people's courts. This is in addition to the significant number of cases in which the parties had withdrawn their applications in accordance with the principle of party disposition. It can be said that in practice, there are very few instances where an arbitral award is annulled; an arbitration agreement is declared invalid; an arbitral award is not enforceable or an application for provisional measures being rejected.

B. Issues and Reflections on the Recognition of the Validity of Arbitration Agreements

The statutory provisions that relate to the validity of arbitral awards are mainly found in Chapter 3 of the *Arbitration Law* and the Interpretation of the *Supreme People's Court Concerning Some Issues on Application of the Arbitration Law of the People's Republic of China* (hereinafter referred to as the "Judicial Interpretation of Arbitration Law"). On one hand, the *Judicial Interpretation of Arbitration Law* has expanded the grounds upon which an arbitration agreement may be declared invalid [6] but on the other hand, it has also improved the predictability and feasibility of ascertaining the validity of arbitration agreements. In practice, the majority of arbitration agreements were held to be invalid by the Chinese Courts due to contravention of Article 16 of the *Arbitration Law* (and its related judicial interpretations). It is rare for arbitration agreements to be held invalid on the grounds prescribed by Article 17 of the *Arbitration Law*. In the cases collected by the authors for this Review, the major categories of reasoning handed down by the Chinese Courts in determining that an arbitration agreement is invalid can be said to be as follows:

1. Cases with issues in relation to the "intention to arbitrate": (a) it is not the true intention of one party to arbitrate; [7] (b) one party's evidence fails to prove that the other party has agreed to submit the dispute to arbitration; [8] (c) the absence of evidence to prove that one party has reached an agreement with the other party to arbitrate and the arbitration agreement therefore does not bind the other party; [9] (d) "there is no contractual relationship or agreement to submit disputes arising from the contract to arbitration and the parties did not reach a valid arbitration agreement" between the parties; [10] (e) "based on the evidence available, it is insuf-

---

6 See also page 14 of the Annual Review of Commercial Arbitration in China (2015) authored by Song Lianbin, Yang Ling and Helena H. C. Chen and published in Commercial Dispute Resolution in China: An Annual Review and Preview (2015), compiled by Beijing Arbitration Commission and published by LexisNexis (2015).

7 Jiangsu Taizhou Intermediate People's Court Civil Ruling (2015) Tai-Zhong-Shang-Zhong-Shen-Xiao-Zi No. 00003; Zhejiang Taizhou Intermediate People's Court Civil Ruling (2015) Zhe-Tai-Zhong-Que-Zi No. 5; Hunan Changsha Intermediate People's Court Civil Ruling (2015) Chang-Zhong-Min-Wu-Zhong-Zi No. 0363.

8 Beijing Third Intermediate People's Court Civil Ruling (2015) San-Zhong-Min-(Shang)-Te-Zi No. 08771.

9 Beijing Second Intermediate People's Court Civil Ruling (2015) Er-Zhong-Min-Te-Zi No. 07460; Hunan Changsha Intermediate People's Court Civil Ruling (2015) Chang-Zhong-Min-Wu-Zhong-Zi No. 00548.

10 Hunan Yueyang Intermediate People's Court Civil Ruling (2015) Yue-Zhong-Min-Er-Zhong-(Que)-Zi No. 4.

ficient to prove that the arbitration agreement in the relevant contract was agreed by both parties";[11] (f) the agreement between the parties was only that when negotiations fail, any party can notify the other party (or parties) of his intention to submit the dispute to arbitration and there was no clear and common intention between both parties to submit the dispute to arbitration.[12]

2. Cases with issues in relation to the "agreed arbitration commission": (a) the agreement stipulates that "the dispute will be submitted to the local arbitration commission at the location where the contract was signed, in accordance with that commission's institutional rules" which also means that parties have not agreed to a specific arbitration commission;[13] (b) the contract stipulates that "where the parties have failed to reach a settlement in relation to a dispute, the parties agree that the dispute would be resolved by Method (1) below—(1) Submit to (□Suzhou, □__) Arbitration Commission to arbitrate".[14] As such, the arbitration clause does not indicate a clear and equivocal agreement between parties as to the choice of the arbitration commission; (c) "submit the dispute to the arbitration commission that has jurisdiction at the location of the Project"[15]—such an agreement does not specify the arbitration commission; (d) an agreement which provides for the dispute to be referred to the arbitration commission in X City, where there is more than one arbitration commission in the specified city;[16] (e) an agreement which provides for the dispute to be referred to the arbitration commission located in the city where the contract was signed, where there is more than one arbitration commission in that city;[17] (f) the agreement provides that the method of dispute resolution was for arbitration to be applied for at the local people's court where party A is based at. However, this agreement is unclear since the people's court is not an arbitration commission;[18] (g) an agreement between parties which stipulates "for the dispute to be submitted to the Hainin City Arbitration Commission". However, there is no such arbitration commission as the Hainin City Arbitration Commission;[19] (h) an agreement between parties for the dispute to be referred to the arbitration institution at Siming District of Xiamen City but this specific arbitration institution does not exist.[20]

3. Cases with issues in relation to clauses that provide for "litigation or arbitration": (a) an agreement between parties for mediation, arbitration and litigation to be the three methods of dispute resolution and a right of selection amongst these methods. In other words, the contracting parties can choose to submit the dispute to either arbitration or litigation;[21] (b) a right granted upon parties, by one clause, to either submit the dispute to arbitration or

---

11 Zhejiang Hangzhou Intermediate People's Court Civil Ruling (2015) Zhe-Hang-Zhong-Que-Zi No. 1.

12 Guangdong Guangzhou Intermediate People's Court Civil Ruling (2015) Sui-Zhong-Fa-Zhong-Yi-Zi No. 24.

13 Shanghai Second Intermediate People's Court Civil Ruling (2015) Hu-Er-Zhong-Min-Ren-(Zhong-Xie)-Zi No. 10.

14 Jiangsu Suzhou Intermediate People's Court Civil Ruling (2014) Su-Zhong-Min-Zhong-Shen-Zi No. 00102.

15 Tianjin Second Intermediate People's Court Civil Ruling (2015) Er-Zhong-Min-Er-Chu-Zi No. 209.

16 Beijing Second Intermediate People's Court Civil Ruling (2015) Er-Zhong-Min-Te-Zi No. 07608.

17 Beijing Second Intermediate People's Court Civil Ruling (2015) Er-Zhong-Min-Te-Zi No. 10009.

18 Fujian Xiamen Intermediate People's Court Civil Ruling (2015) Xia-Min-Ren-Zi No. 21.

19 Zhejiang Jiaxing Intermediate People's Court Civil Ruling (2015) Zhe-Jia-Zhong-Que-Zi No. 1.

20 Fujian Xiamen Intermediate People's Court Civil Ruling (2015) Xia-Min-Ren-Zi No. 4.

21 Jiangsu Yangzhou Intermediate People's Court Civil Ruling (2015) Yang-Shang-Zhong-Shen-Zi No. 00050.

to litigation when negotiations fail;[22] (c) different clauses in one contract which provide, respectively, that when negotiations fail, the parties can submit the dispute to arbitration or litigation;[23] (d) separate contracts, which form the entire agreement between parties and lacking any provision of hierarchy between them, allowing, respectively, the dispute to be submitted to arbitration as well as for the dispute to be litigated;[24] (e) the contract stipulating that "where the parties have failed to reach a settlement in the event of a dispute, they can submit the dispute to the arbitration commission located in the city of the Project or resolve the dispute in accordance with the relevant legal procedures." The Court held that while parties have expressed an intention to arbitrate, the clause meant that the dispute resolution mechanisms included both arbitration by an arbitration commission and litigation before the courts because the agreement provides for resolving disputes in accordance with "the relevant legal procedures". Accordingly, since arbitration is not the only means of resolving a dispute, the arbitration agreement is invalid.[25]

4. Cases related to invalid arbitration agreements: (a) the arbitration clause in Contract A was substituted by the litigation clause in Contract B (which was signed later on), therefore invalidating the prior arbitration agreement;[26] (b) Contract A includes litigation clause, Contract B includes arbitration clause and it was agreed between parties that where there are inconsistencies between the two contracts, Contract A shall prevail. The arbitration agreement is therefore invalid.[27]

5. Cases relating to other categories: (a) one of the parties to the contract was coerced into signing the contract, therefore leading to the conclusion that the arbitration clause in the contract was correspondingly entered into by coercion as well, and the arbitration agreement is therefore deemed to be invalid;[28] (b) on one hand, the court rejected the application seeking to invalidate the arbitration agreement and confirmed that the arbitration agreement binds the respondent. On the other hand, the court held that the valid arbitration agreement does not have legal binding force upon the applicant since the applicant has not signed the contract.[29]

The notable points from our analysis of the above cases are as follows:

Firstly, the most common reasons why an arbitration agreement is held to be invalid in judicial practice are that there is a lack of intention to refer the dispute to arbitration; a lack of a clearly agreed arbitration commission as well as a provision for "litigation or arbitration". There are some instances where the validity of an arbitration agreement has expired and therefore held to be invalid, but these instances are rare. Usually, the validity of arbitration agree-

---

22 Fujian Xiamen Intermediate People's Court Civil Ruling (2015) Xia-Min-Ren-Zi No. 100.

23 Guangdong Guangzhou Intermediate People's Court Civil Ruling (2015) Sui-Zhong-Fa-Zhong-Yi-Zi No. 62.

24 Guangdong Shenzhen Intermediate People's Court Civil Ruling (2015) Shen-Zhong-Fa-She-Wai-Zhong-Zi No. 150.

25 Guangdong Foshan Intermediate People's Court Civil Ruling (2015) Fo-Zhong-Fa-Min-Yi-Zhong-Zi No. 4.

26 Fujian Xiamen Intermediate People's Court Civil Ruling (2014) Xia-Min-Ren-Zi No. 113.

27 Guangdong Guangzhou Intermediate People's Court Civil Ruling (2015) Sui-Zhong-Fa-Zhong-Yi-Zi No. 44; Tianjin Second Intermediate People's Court Civil Ruling (2015) Er-Zhong-Min-Er-Chu-Zi No. 223.

28 Jiangsu Yangzhou Intermediate People's Court Civil Ruling (2015) Yang-Shang-Zhong-Shen-Zi No. 00042.

29 Guangdong Foshan Intermediate People's Court Civil Ruling (2015) Fo-Zhong-Fa-Min-Yi-Zhong-Zi No. 1; Guangdong Foshan Intermediate People's Court Civil Ruling (2014) Fo-Zhong-Fa-Min-Yi-Zhong-Zi No. 14.

ments expires due to two reasons: one is that the contract containing the arbitration clause has been substituted by a contract without an arbitration clause; the other reason is that different contracts are in conflict with each other and the contract without the arbitration clause prevails. We have yet to see a case where the arbitration agreement was held to be invalid on the grounds that the dispute was outside the scope of arbitration as prescribed by law, or the arbitration agreement was made by persons without legal capacity or limited legal capacity. There was only one case where the arbitration agreement was held to be invalid due to the fact that one party coerced the other party to enter into an arbitration agreement. It is evident, therefore, that the courts have rarely held an arbitration agreement to be invalid pursuant to Article 17 of the *Arbitration Law*.

Secondly, with respect to the lack of intention to arbitrate, two common outcomes were found in the courts' rulings: one, the arbitration agreement was held to be invalid; second, the arbitration agreement itself is valid, but does not bind the applicants. The latter can almost be viewed the same as the invalidation of the arbitration agreement. Although it is less common than the former, it is also commonly encountered. In addition, another issue worth noting is that an expression of intention to arbitration is not the same as the parties' intention to submit a dispute to arbitration. If the parties only agree that in the event of a dispute, one party shall notify the other party of its intention to submit the dispute to arbitration, even if there was a clear agreement on the arbitration commission, it still cannot be regarded as a common and clear intention by the parties to actually submit disputes to arbitration.

Thirdly, in relation to instances where there is no clear agreement of a specific arbitration commission, it may appear that there are already clear prescriptive criteriaset out in the *Judicial Interpretation of Arbitration Law* and the court therefore has little room of discretion. However, this is not true. Take for example the more commonly encountered example of submitting the dispute to "arbitration commission in X City", courts in many provinces or cities, especially the courts in the more commercially active provinces or cities, such as Beijing or Shanghai, view these as clear agreements and not contentious. [30] However, there are still courts, and High People's Courts, that view these agreements as being unclear. [31] Without judging the correctness of the latter instance, it at least shows that there is still a degree of judicial discretion in relation to whether the parties had reached a clear agreement on an arbitration commission which correspondingly determines whether the arbitration agreement is valid. The authors are of the view that if the courts could adopt a more transparent stance in supporting arbitrations, it would mean that instances where an arbitration agreement is held invalid due to an unclear a-

---

30 For example: Beijing Third Intermediate People's Court Civil Ruling (2015) San-Zhong-Min-(Shang)-Te-Zi No. 10183. In this case, the court deems that "…the arbitration institution agreed in the arbitration clause is 'Beijing Municipality Arbitration Commission', which is just one word difference (an extra word 'Municipality') from 'Beijing Arbitration Commission'. This should be considered an improper expression of the arbitration institution by the parties and does not prejudice the true intent of the parties to submit the dispute to Beijing Arbitration Commission for arbitration and therefore the parties should be deemed to have reached a specific agreement on the selected arbitration institution…"

31 Jiangxi Higher People's Court Civil Ruling (2015) Gan-Li-Zhong-Zi No. 52. In this case, the court deems that "…as to the agreement of the parties to 'submit a dispute to Shanghai Arbitration Commission for arbitration', due to the fact that there does not exist such an institute called Shanghai Arbitration Commission within the jurisdiction of Shanghai, the court is unable to determine the specific arbitration institution agreed in the said arbitration agreement during the appellate review period of this case concerning an objection to jurisdiction."

greement on arbitration commissions would decrease drastically.

Lastly, in relation to the issue of "arbitration or litigation", even though the relevant judicial reasoning are usually controversial,[32] the authors are of the view that these instances where the arbitration agreements are held to be invalid arose mostly due to the oversight of the parties or their insufficient understanding of the *Arbitration Law*. When the parties agree to submit their disputes to arbitration, an agreement in the same contract to submit the disputes to litigation appears to be nothing but superfluous. In cases where there are agreements, in separate contracts, to submit the dispute to arbitration as well as litigation, this may have been caused by the oversight of the parties on one hand but, on the other hand, the court should handle it based on the specific circumstances of each case rather than to hold in a uniform fashion that all such arbitration agreements are invalid. The circumstances that the court would take into account include whether a rank hierarchy applies to the different contracts or not.

C. Issues and Reflections on Judicial Cases Regarding the Annulment and Non-enforcement of Arbitral Awards

Two methods of exercising judicial supervision on arbitral awards by the Chinese courts are by annulment and non-enforcement of arbitral awards. Although the amendments to *Civil Procedure Law* in 2012 have standardized the grounds for non-enforcement with the grounds for annulment in *Arbitration Law*, there are still differences in practice, between the courts' reasoning with respect to annulment and non-enforcement. Hence, it is worthwhile to do a comparison exercise at this juncture. The authors have grouped the cases relating to annulment and non-enforcement into two categories.

In cases where the arbitral award was annulled, the reasons handed down by the Chinese courts can generally be categorized as follows:

1. Cases relating to "no arbitration agreement": (a) the arbitration agreement signed by the applicant was reached in relation to X arbitration, rather than this particular arbitration. Therefore there is no arbitration agreement between the parties in this case;[33] (b) the parties have never signed an arbitration agreement;[34] (c) the respondent's entering into the "Release and Return of Equity Agreement" with the applicant and the implementation of the equity transaction without the approval at the shareholders meeting, shareholders' general meeting or board meeting is in violation of the prohibited practices under the *Company Law of the People's Republic of China* because the respondent is the applicant's shareholder, executive board mem-

---

32 Annual Review of Commercial Arbitration in China (2015) made note to a case (Beijing Third Intermediate People's Court Civil Ruling (2014) San-Zhong-Min-Te-Zi No. 06308). In this case, the arbitration clause in question provides that "either party may submit an arbitration application to Beijing Arbitration Commission; either party disagreeing with the arbitration award may initiate legal proceedings to a people's court at the domicile of Party B." This arbitration clause is later on determined by the court as invalid. However, this clause is different from a typical "arbitrate or litigate" clause in that it can be inferred from the clause that the parties clearly agree to submit to arbitration but only that they have no idea of the legal requirements of "arbitral award being final and binding" and deem that an arbitral award may be appealed. The authors take the view that a reasonable judgment shall be to determine that the later part of the clause is invalid due to a violation of the mandatory legal requirements but the rest of the clause shall be valid and the parties may apply to Beijing Arbitration Commission for arbitration.

33 Sichuan Guangyuan Intermediate People's Court Civil Ruling (2015) Guang-Min-Te-Zi No. 24.

34 Guangdong Shenzhen Intermediate People's Court Civil Ruling (2015) Shen-Zhong-Fa-She-Wai-Zhong-Zi No. 61.

ber and/or legal representative. Therefore, such agreement (including the arbitration clause) cannot be deemed as the applicant's true expression of intention and does not legally bind the applicant. In other words, there is no legal and valid arbitration agreement between the parties;[35] (d) the contract provided for three possible options to resolve a dispute. At the time when the applicant signed the contract, all the options were not ticked. The respondent could not prove that the parties had intended to select arbitration in the course of supplementing terms to the contract;[36] (e) the dispute between the applicant and the respondent regarding whether there was a change of the legal representative of X company did not fall in the scope of the contract executed between them, therefore the arbitration clause in the contract cannot be held to be an agreement to arbitrate this particular dispute;[37] (f) the contract in question provides two means of dispute resolution: arbitration or litigation. The respondent has elected arbitration but the applicant did not make any choice. Therefore, it is insufficient to demonstrate that both parties have agreed to submit to arbitration as a means of resolving disputes.[38]

2. Cases relating to "the issues to be arbitrated is outside the scope of the arbitration agreement or the arbitration commission does not have jurisdiction": (a) even though the contract provides that in the event of a dispute, it will be referred to X arbitration commission for arbitration, a subsequent amendment to the contract clearly provides that in the event of a failed negotiation, either party can commence an action at the court with proper jurisdiction. This therefore nullifies the jurisdiction of the arbitration commission;[39] (b) partial annulment: item X of the arbitral award exceeds the scope of the request for arbitration and can be separated from other parts of the arbitral award;[40] (c) partial annulment: where item X of the arbitral award exceeds the scope of the request for arbitration and item Y of the arbitral award cannot be separated from item X, the parts of the award dealing with both parts are therefore annulled together.[41]

3. Cases relating to "procedural irregularity": (a) the arbitral tribunal deliberated and rendered an award without soliciting the applicant's opinions on cross-examination and without organizing a cross-examination of the opposing evidence; in addition, the arbitral tribunal failed to fulfill the basic obligation of providing notifications for the applicant's request to conduct a financial audit and assent appraisal on the cooperation project;[42] (b) the tribunal has not made any investigation as to the whereabouts of the applicant, nor has it used various means of service, such as direct delivery; leaving a notice at an appropriate location; mail delivery etc. Instead, the tribunal directly resorted to public notices to serve the Request for Arbitration, the Notice of Hearing and the arbitral award and other important legal documents, thereby violating the legal requirements;[43] (c) while the last hearing date was 7 January 2015; the Notice of

---

35 Guangdong Shenzhen Intermediate People's Court Civil Ruling (2015) Shen-Zhong-Fa-She-Wai-Zhong-Zi No. 149.

36 Shandong Binzhou Intermediate People's Court Civil Ruling (2015) Bin-Zhong-Min-Si-Yi-Zi No. 1.

37 Liaoning Benxi Intermediate People's Court Civil Ruling (2015) Ben-Min-Er-Te-Zi No. 00006.

38 Hebei Shijiazhuang Intermediate People's Court Civil Ruling (2015) Shi-Min-Si-Cai-Zi No. 00035.

39 Sichuan Guangyuan Intermediate People's Court Civil Ruling (2015) Guang-Min-Te-Zi No. 18.

40 Hunan Yiyang Intermediate People's Court Civil Ruling (2015) Yi-Fa-Min-Er-Zhong-Che-Zi No. 2.

41 Jiangsu Yangzhou Intermediate People's Court Civil Ruling (2015) Yang-Shang-Zhong-Shen-Che-Zi No. 00001.

42 Zhejiang Zhoushan Intermediate People's Court Civil Ruling (2015) Zhe-Zhou-Zhong-Che-Zi No. 2.

43 Hunan Shaoyang Intermediate People's Court Civil Ruling (2015) Shao-Zhong-Min-Er-Chu-Zi No. 103.

Hearing was delivered on 4 January 2015. The arbitration commission failed to inform the parties of the hearing date five days prior to the hearing;[44] (d) inconsistency between the timing of the applicant's request for an amendment to its Request for Arbitration with the timing stipulated in the arbitration rules, hence infringing the other party's rights;[45] (e) the tribunal arbitrarily amended the applicant's Request for Arbitration;[46] (f) the arbitration commission failed to organize cross-examination of evidence in relation to whether the applicant breached the contract or whether the contractual relationship between the parties should be terminated, which if admitted and evaluated, would affect the impartiality of the award;[47] (g) the tribunal failed to adhere to the period set forth in the arbitration rules to notify the applicant of the hearing date and proceeded to a hearing;[48] (h) the agreed expert institution declined its engagement on the basis of a lack of materials for appraisal or a lack of clarity of the matters to be appraised. In those instances, an alternative expert institution should have been engaged but the tribunal rejected the Request for Arbitration even before taking such steps;[49] (i) the tribunal failed to take into account an objection made by the application during the hearing and did not provide its assessment of the objection in the arbitral award;[50] (j) the fourth applicant in the arbitral award passed away before the issuance of the arbitral award and should not have been listed as an applicant but was nevertheless included in the arbitral award.[51]

4. Cases relating to "concealing evidence that would affect the impartiality of an award": (a) two loan receipts contained important information on the parties' rights and obligations under the contract but was concealed by the respondent in the arbitration. The concealment would affect the impartiality of the award;[52] (b) a construction contract signed by a third party and the respondent may affect the force or performance of another construction contract between the parties but was concealed by the respondent. The concealment would affect the impartiality of the award;[53] (c) the respondent concealed the product compliance certificate and evidence which would prove that the serial numbers on the product compliance certificate and those of the hardware and software are consistent. The concealment would affect the impartiality of the award;[54] (d) the respondent only presented evidence to the arbitration commission that X amount has been paid towards the housing price but concealed evidence that he has received deed tax and administrative fees on behalf of the applicant. The concealment of such evidence would affect the impartiality of the award;[55] (e) the respondent refused without any val-

---

44 Zhejiang Huzhou Intermediate People's Court Civil Ruling (2015) Zhe-Hu-Zhong-Che-Zi No. 13 - the last hearing date being 7 January 2015 but the Notice of Hearing was delivered on 4 January 2015.

45 Guangdong Shaoguan Intermediate People's Court Civil Ruling (2015) Shao-Zhong-Fa-Min-San-Zhong-Zi No. 4.

46 Heilongjiang Mudanjiang Intermediate People's Court Civil Ruling (2015) Mu-Min-Ta-Zi No. 7.

47 Guangxi Guigang Intermediate People's Court Civil Ruling (2015) Gui-Min-Er-Chu-Zi No. 11.

48 Zhejiang Taizhou Intermediate People's Court Civil Ruling (2015) Zhe-Tai-Zhong-Che-Zi No. 8.

49 Heilongjiang Mudanjiang Intermediate People's Court Civil Ruling (2015) Mu-Min-Ta-Zi No. 6.

50 Sichuan Mianyang Intermediate People's Court Civil Ruling (2015) Mian-Min-Zhong-Zi No. 17.

51 Shanghai First Intermediate People's Court Civil Ruling (2015) Hu-Yi-Zhong-Min-Si-(Shang)-Che-Zi No. 33.

52 Zhejiang Jiaxing Intermediate People's Court Civil Ruling (2015) Zhe-Jia-Zhong-Che-Zi No. 11.

53 Hunan Changsha Intermediate People's Court Civil Ruling (2015) Chang-Zhong-Min-Wu-Zhong-Zi No. 00707.

54 Hunan Zhangjiajie Intermediate People's Court Civil Ruling (2015) Zhang-Zhong-Li-Min-Te-Zi No. 1.

55 Hunan Loudi Intermediate People's Court Civil Ruling (2015) Lou-Zhong-Li-Ta-Zi No. 13.

id reason to present evidence explaining his legal relationship with X, which is directly relevant to the issues contended in the arbitration and directly affected the tribunal's ability to correctly determine the factual circumstances of the case.[56]

5. Cases relating to "forged evidence that the award relies upon": the three "Confirmed Tables of Construction Project's Certified Final Account(s)" produced by the applicant to the respondent were proved by investigation records to be forged.[57]

In cases where the courts rendered rulings of non-enforcement of arbitral awards, the reasons cited by the Chinese courts can be generally categorized as follows:

(1) Cases relating to "the parties did not include an arbitration agreement in the contract" or "did not subsequently reach a written agreement to arbitrate": the arbitration commission issued an arbitral award in the absence of a written arbitration agreement.

(2) Cases relating to "the arbitration institution lacks jurisdiction": The contract clearly stipulates that if both parties fail to reach an agreement through consultation, either party may submit the dispute to the arbitration commission at the place where the contract is concluded for arbitration. The agreed place for conclusion of the contract is Xining City, Qinghai Province. Therefore the Shaoxing Arbitration Commission does not have jurisdiction over the subject case.[58]

(3) Cases relating to "the arbitration procedure violates the procedural requirements provided by law": (a) the arbitration commission did not serve relevant legal documents to the respondent and rendered a default award. Such proceedings violated the law;[59] (b) the arbitration commission failed to serve the arbitration-related documents pursuant to the arbitration rules and rendered a default award. The respondent was therefore not given any opportunity to participate in the arbitration proceedings and was not able to exercise his legal rights granted by the *Arbitration Law*;[60] (c) the arbitration commission, knowing that the applicant is not a local resident, nevertheless issued public notices in the local area or local media during the arbitration proceedings and after rendering an award. Therefore the service of process was illegal.[61]

(4) Cases relating to "concealing evidence that would affect the impartiality of an award": (a) A third party's criminal record has substantial influence in determining whether the respondent had actually purchased the real estate in dispute, which would affect the impartiality of the award but the respondent has failed to disclose these relevant details to the tribunal;[62] (b) the respondent submitted to the arbitration commission the Loan Guarantee Contract No. 005451 in support of his claims, but did not disclose Loan Guarantee Contracts No. 005741, No. 005724 and No. 005701; thereby concealing the evidence that would affect the

---

56 Zhejiang Wenzhou Intermediate People's Court Civil Ruling (2015) Zhe-Wen-Min-Zhong-Che-Zi No. 38.

57 Sichuan Guangyuan Intermediate People's Court Civil Ruling (2015) Guang-Min-Te-Zi No. 5.

58 Qinghai Xining Intermediate People's Court Enforcement Ruling (2015) Ning-Zhi-Yi-Zi No. 00033.

59 Henan Pingdingshan Intermediate People's Court Enforcement Ruling (2015) Ping-Zhi-Zi No. 161.

60 Guangdong Zhongshan Intermediate People's Court Civil Ruling (2015) Zhong-Zhong-Fa-Min-Si-Zhi-Zhong-Zi No. 1.

61 Hunan Loudi Intermediate People's Court Enforcement Ruling (2015) Lou-Zhong-Zhi-Yi-Zi No. 56.

62 Guangdong Shenzhen Intermediate People's Court Civil Ruling (2015) Shen-Zhong-Fa-She-Wai-Zhong-Zi No. 54; Guangdong Shenzhen Intermediate People's Court Civil Ruling (2015) Shen-Zhong-Fa-She-Wai-Zhong-Zi No. 55; Guangdong Shenzhen Intermediate People's Court Civil Ruling (2015) Shen-Zhong-Fa-She-Wai-Zhong-Zi No. 56.

impartiality of the award;[63] (c) whether the applicant was entitled to unilaterally terminate the flat lease contract depends on whether the respondent's sub-leasing of the flat met the requirements set out in law and in the contract. This directly affects a determination of which party is responsible for the breach of contract and directly influences the outcome of the arbitration. Therefore, during the arbitration, the applicant's concealment of the fact that he sub-let the flat in question would affect the impracticality of the award.[64]

(5) Cases relating to "an award violating social and public interest": A portion of the ancillary construction work was sub-contracted to a third party, Mr. Mao, for construction. The applicant has already paid more than RMB 400,000 of construction payment and that portion of construction work was included in the Final Construction Plain annexed to the audit report. If the award was to be enforced, the applicant might end up paying twice the contract price for construction work, thereby damaging national as well as social and public interest.[65]

The following points of interest can be discerned from an analysis of the above and with reference to both tables 4 and 5:

Firstly, although both annulment and non-enforcement of an award are means of judicial supervision, cases of the former obviously outnumbered those of the latter as seen from the data collected by the authors. Be that as it may, in the few numbers of applications for non-enforcement, there are still some cases where the courts have decided on non-enforcement. It is well known that the mode of double judicial supervision in *Chinese Arbitration Law* has been criticized by many experts. Currently, the grounds for annulment and non-enforcement have been amended to be consistent with each other. However, in practice, there are still several instances where an applicant, after his failed attempt to seek annulment of the award, subsequently seeks non-enforcement of the award.[66] Article 26 of the *Judicial Interpretation of Arbitration Law* stipulates that: "where, after the application filed by a party concerned to the people's court for annulment of the arbitral award is rejected, the said party raises objection for non-enforcement of the award in the enforcement proceedings on the same grounds, such an objection shall not be supported by the people's court". However, in practice, a party can take separate legal actions on the grounds that are consistent under the current law, in two different legal proceedings in order to delay the enforcement of the arbitral award.

Secondly, in relation to cases where the arbitral award has been annulled, as in previous years, violation of arbitration procedural requirements is the most common reason relied upon. Judicial supervision of arbitration proceedings is common practice in many countries' judicial supervision systems. However, when the courts are determining whether there is a violation of the legal procedural requirements, the courts not only need to investigate whether a violation has occurred but also need to consider the nature of the violation. The courts shall not easily

---

63 Henan Shangqiu Intermediate People's Court Enforcement Ruling (2015) Shang-Zhi-Zi No. 155.

64 Guangdong Shenzhen Intermediate People's Court Civil Ruling (2015) Shen-Zhong-Fa-She-Wai-Zhong-Zi No. 198.

65 Inner Mongolia Chifeng Intermediate People's Court Civil Ruling (2015) Chi-Min-Zhong-Zi No. 21.

66 Jiangsu Nanjing Intermediate People's Court Enforcement Ruling (2015) Ning-Zhi-Hui-Zi No. 32. In this case, Nanjing Intermediate People's Court has previously rejected an arbitral award annulment application submitted by Mr./Ms. Bian. During the enforcement proceedings, the court ordered that the enforced party, Mr./Ms. Bian, to continue performing the relevant obligations imposed by valid legal documents. Mr./Ms. Bian applied to the court for not enforcing the arbitral award. The case is now being heard but as it takes relatively longer to render a judgment on a claim for non-enforcement of the arbitral award. The applicant for enforcement, XX Company, has applied to the court for terminating the said enforcement proceedings. The court has finally ruled to terminate the enforcement proceedings.

determine that there is a violation of legal procedural requirements and annul an award just because of some minor flaws in the arbitration proceedings or a few reasonable deviations from the legal procedural requirements. After all, the beauty and advantage of arbitration is that the tribunal, subject to the respect for parties' autonomy, may decide the procedures based on the specific circumstances of each case. To sum things up, in relation to the grounds of violation of legal procedural requirements, the courts should focus on one basic point: which is whether the parties are given a fair and adequate opportunity to present their case. Due to difference in complexity of the relevant evidence, witnesses and other elements, there is no one rule which fits all when evaluating fairness and adequacy. With respect to other circumstances that relate to procedure, the courts should treat them with even more caution. To summarize the cases above, the circumstances where the courts have annulled the arbitral award on the grounds of violation of legal procedural requirements include: no cross examination of evidence; no performance of the basic duty to notify; illegal service of process; amendment to the Request for Arbitration at a time not allowed under arbitration rules; unilateral amendment to the Request for Arbitration; assessment of certain objections which were not heard during the arbitration proceedings in the award and listing a deceased person as one of the parties to the arbitration. It is evident from the list that there are various circumstances which constitute a violation of legal procedural requirements. In relation to non-enforcement cases, violation of legal procedural requirements is also a ground often relied upon. More frequently, however, as opposed to annulment cases, the courts seem to hold that an award shall not be enforced due to illegal service of process. Therefore, arbitration institutions should handle service of process carefully in order to avoid the unfortunate situation where an award could not be enforced due to illegal service of process.

Thirdly, from certain perspective, there is one issue which warrants even more attention than procedural irregularity: annulment or non-enforcement of an award owing to issues relating to evidence. There is a degree of doubt over the authority granted by the *Arbitration Law* to the Chinese courts to review domestic awards in substantive reasoning regarding evidence. On one hand, such authority has, to a certain extent, suppressed the development of domestic arbitration but on the other hand, it can potentially encourage the users of domestic arbitration to deliberately involve foreign elements in order to avoid this overly stringent supervisory mechanism. It cannot be overlooked that this has resulted in the repeated discussion of the core issue "whether there exist foreign elements" in recent cases. Having said that, the courts do not appear to have restrained themselves from handing down annulment or non-enforcement rulings based on evidence-related statutory grounds. From the cases categorized above, whether it is annulment of arbitral awards or non-enforcement of arbitral awards, a frequent reason cited by the Chinese courts is that the opposite party has concealed evidence that would affect the impartiality of an award. The current situation has to be attributed primarily to the work of the legislation. Aside from how the issue of "affecting the impartiality of an award" requires an investigation into the substantive matters of an award, it is also an obvious problem when it comes to an examination of the issue of "concealment of evidence" which involves the distribution of the burden of proof. In China, the rules of evidence in commercial arbitration generally stem from civil proceedings. Namely, the claimant is normally charged with the burden of proof, unless in special circumstances which require the reverse. Therefore, the notion of "concealment of evidence" acts in contrary to the usual principles of civil proceedings. In the absence of amendment to related legislation, the authors are of the opinion that the judiciary should adopt a more stringent approach to review and determine whether there exists any concealment of evidence that would affect the impartiality of an award. Specifically, as reference, the author suggests that first, concealment of evidence must be discovered after, rather than before, the issuance of the award and the concealed evidence must be directly relevant to the legal arguments and claims in the arbitration. Second, the impact on the impartiality of an award must be obvious. In other words, the courts only need to undertake a preliminary investigation to be able to see the serious consequences of such conduct. In addition to concealment of evidence, the forgery of evidence is also often referred to by a party to apply for annulment or non-enforcement of an award. In terms of the statutory provisions, the issues that can arise from this particular ground can be said to be as many as, if not more than, those that can arise from concealment of evidence. Fortunately, from the cases selected this time, there was only one case relating to forged evidence amongst cases of annulment and non-enforcement. It is hoped that the Chinese courts can follow the international trend to implement more advanced arbitration principles and to eliminate the possibility of awards being annulled or not enforced owing to evidence-related issues through judicial means.

D. Sample Review and Commentary on Foreign-related Arbitration Cases

Foreign-related arbitrations reviewed by the Chinese courts are mainly foreign-related arbitrations administered by Chinese arbitration commissions; recognition and enforcement of awards made in Hong Kong, Macau or Taiwan and recognition and enforcement of foreign arbitral awards. These types of cases, especially cases in the latter two categories, receive a high degree of publicity and are few in numbers compared to domestic arbitration cases. As a result, undertaking individual review of these cases appears to be the more sensible approach. Out of the 50 foreign-related arbitration cases collected by the authors this time, we have selected 10 individual cases as analyzed below:

Table 8: Sampling statistics of foreign-related arbitration cases heard by PRC courts

	Claim	Court and Case Number	Causes of Action	Court Judgment	Basis of Judgment
1	Recognition of the validity of an arbitration agreement	Jiangsu Changzhou Intermediate People's Court Civil Ruling (2015) Chang-Shang-Xia-Zhong-Zi No. 146	Appeal as to jurisdictional objection	People's court has jurisdiction	In a commercial or civil dispute without any foreign elements, if the parties agree to submit the dispute to a foreign arbitration institution or to have the dispute arbitrated abroad, such arbitration agreement is null and void. Judicial review over an arbitral award made in Hong Kong, Macao or Taiwan shall be dealt with in the same manner as that of a foreign arbitral award.

	Claim	Court and Case Number	Causes of Action	Court Judgment	Basis of Judgment
2	Recognition of the validity of an arbitral award	Beijing Second Intermediate People's Court Civil Ruling (2015) Er-Zhong-Min-Te-Zi No. 00618	Annulment of an arbitral award	Application rejected	1. The arbitration commission received the applicant's Request for Arbitration on 11 April, 2012 and commenced the arbitration proceedings. Once the arbitration proceedings are initiated, the arbitration commission shall determine the applicable arbitration rules. At that time the Arbitration Rules (2005) are the arbitration rules in force and therefore the arbitration commission did not make any mistake in determining to apply the Arbitration Rules (2005) to the case; 2. Whether or not to approve the applicant's application for postponing the hearing or remote testifying shall be decided by the arbitral tribunal, at its sole discretion, based on the specific circumstance of the case. The tribunal's decision to disapprove the applicant's application for postponing the hearing and remote testifying does not violate the Arbitration Rules (2005).
3	Enforcement of an arbitral award	Jiangsu Wuxi Intermediate People's Court Civil Ruling (2015) Xi-Shang-Wai-Zhong-Shen-Zi No. 3	Enforcement of a CIETAC arbitral award	Enforcement of the award granted	The statutory conditions for enforcement were satisfied and none of the statutory conditions, as stipulated in Articles 274 of the *Civil Procedure Law*, exists such that enforcement should be denied.
4	Enforcement of an arbitral award	Jiangsu Yangzhou Intermediate People's Court Civil Ruling (2015) Yang-Shang-Zhong-Shen-Zhi-Zi No. 00143	Enforcement of a Yangzhou Arbitration Commission arbitral award	Application rejected	The applicant is Japanese. Both the enforcement application and a power of attorney submitted by the applicant have not been notarized nor authenticated or otherwise certified, nor been signed before the court staff. The documents submitted by the applicant are not in the required form as stipulated by the Chinese law and the relevant procedures were not made up within a reasonable period of time.

	Claim	Court and Case Number	Causes of Action	Court Judgment	Basis of Judgment
5	Recognition, enforcement or non - enforcement of arbitral awards	Tianjin Maritime Court Civil Ruling (2015) Jin - Hai - Fa-Que-Zi No. 2 -1	Jurisdictional objection in enforcement proceedings	Tianjin Maritime Court has jurisdiction	The claim is for recognition and enforcement of a Hong Kong International Arbitration Center maritime arbitral award in respect of a charter party for XX Ship. According to Article 11 of the *Special Maritime Procedure Law of the People's Republic of China*, the Tianjin Maritime Court being the maritime court at the defendant's domicile enjoy exclusive maritime jurisdiction over the case.
6	Recognition, enforcement or non - enforcement of arbitral awards	Beijing First Intermediate People's Court Civil Ruling (2014) Yi-Zhong -Min-Te-Zi No. 878	Recognition of an International Centre for Dispute Resolution/American Arbitration Association (ICDR/AAA) arbitral award	Recognition of the award granted	1. The application is submitted within the statutory time limit. 2. Objection to the determination of substantive issues in the case does not constitute any of the circumstances provided in Article V of the *New York Convention*, under which recognition or enforcement of a foreign arbitral award may be refused.
7	Recognition, enforcement or non - enforcement of arbitral awards	Jiangsu Suzhou Intermediate People's Court Civil Ruling (2014) Su - Zhong - Shang - Wai-Chu-Zi No. 00031	Recognition and enforcement of an ICC International Court of Arbitration arbitral award made in Hong Kong	Recognition of the award granted	The respondent acted in violation of law in that it did not raise any objection to the validity of the arbitration clause during the arbitration proceedings but later on applied for non - recognition of the arbitral award after it has been rendered based on an argument that the arbitration clause is invalid.
8	Recognition, enforcement or non - enforcement of arbitral awards	Shanghai Second Intermediate People's Court Civil Ruling (2014) Hu -Er-Zhong-Min-Ren - (Wai - Zhong)-Zi No. 1	Recognition and enforcement of a Japanese Commercial Arbitration Association (JCAA) arbitral award	Recognition and enforcement of the award granted	There were no circumstances, according to the *New York Convention*, which warranted a refusal of recognition or enforcement of a foreign arbitral award.

	Claim	Court and Case Number	Causes of Action	Court Judgment	Basis of Judgment
9	Recognition, enforcement or non-enforcement of arbitral awards	Shandong Dezhou Intermediate People's Court Civil Ruling (2015) De-Zhong-Min-Chu-Zi No. 3	Recognition and enforcement of an International Cotton Association arbitral award	Recognition and enforcement of the award granted	There were no circumstances, according to the *New York Convention*, which warranted a refusal of recognition or enforcement of a foreign arbitral award.
10	Recognition, enforcement or non-enforcement of arbitral awards	Jiangsu Wuxi Intermediate People's Court Civil Ruling (2013) Xi-Shang-Wai-Zhong-Shen-Zi No. 0009	Recognition and enforcement of an International Cotton Association arbitral award	Recognition and enforcement of the award refused	No arbitration clause found in the case. The requirement provided in Article II of the *New York Convention* was not satisfied.

In general, it is rare for foreign-related arbitration agreements to be held invalid, or foreign-related arbitral awards to be annulled or not enforced or foreign arbitral awards to be annulled or not enforced. On the one hand, this is closely related to the fact that the number of foreign-related arbitration cases is few and the quality of such cases is generally better. On the other hand, it is also attributable to the exceptional support that China affords to foreign-related arbitrations. There are many aspects that differ in terms of the treatments afforded to domestic arbitrations and foreign-related arbitrations under the *Arbitration Law*. It is the so-called "dual-track regime". Specifically, foreign-related arbitration differs in at least three aspects for domestic arbitration: Firstly, in relation to judicial supervision, other than those that relate to the public policy, the Chinese courts cannot investigate any substantive matters in foreign-related arbitration. Secondly, in relation to foreign-related arbitration, there is a "Reporting System" in China, under which all lower courts' proposed adverse rulings in relation to foreign-related arbitration agreements or arbitral awards have to be reported to a court at a higher level. Lastly, in relation to jurisdictional hierarchy, despite the fact that the enforcement of both domestic and foreign-related awards are under the jurisdiction of local court located at where the party subject to enforcement has his domicile or where the assets are located, the enforcement of a foreign-related arbitration award has to be done at an intermediate people's court.

Although the "dual track regime" has supported foreign-related arbitration, it has also created a series of issues. Currently, a particular topic of interest is, whether a dispute without any foreign element can be submitted to a foreign arbitration institution for arbitration. The Supreme People's Court has clearly ruled in the negative in a recent series of high publicity cases.[67] At

67 These cases include the Liupanshui Heng Ding in 2011, the Jiangsu Hang Tian Wan Yuan in 2012 and the Chao Lai Xin Sheng in 2014. See also pages 22-24 of the Annual Review of Commercial Arbitration in China (2015) authored by Song Lianbin, Yang Ling and Helena H C Chen and published in Commercial Dispute Resolution in China: An Annual Review and Preview (2015), compiled by Beijing Arbitration Commission and published by LexisNexis (2015).

the same time, the attitudes of the local courts are also worth noting. The Jiangsu Changzhou Intermediate People's Court ruled that,[68] in a dispute on jurisdiction, due to the fact the dispute in question did not involve any foreign elements, the agreement to submit the dispute to the Hong Kong International Arbitration Center (the "HKIAC")[69] is invalid. The same issue was encountered in a ruling rendered by the Hebei Higher People's Court[70]. In that case, the court held that due to the fact the parties to the contract are both legal entities set up within China; the relevant products were produced and transported in China and the contract was performed in China, the contract therefore does not contain any foreign elements and the arbitration agreement in the contract[71] was invalid. However, a recent high profile civil ruling rendered by the Shanghai First Intermediate People's Court concerning recognition and enforcement of an SIAC arbitral award is regarded as a breakthrough in what can be considered as a foreign element. This case will be discussed in details in the next section.

Since her accession to the *New York Convention* in 1987, China has gained more and more experiences in recognition and enforcement of foreign arbitral awards. In terms of the source of the foreign awards that have been recognized and enforced by the Chinese courts, they came from locations across the world as can be seen by the above table. From the treatment of cases, the courts in China have strictly followed Article V of the *New York Convention*[72] to review foreign arbitral awards, especially in applying the public policy strictly. The majority of the foreign arbitral awards have received recognition and enforcement by the Chinese courts. With re-

68 Jiangsu Changzhou Intermediate People's Court Civil Ruling (2015) Chang-Shang-Xia-Zhong-Zi No. 146.

69 The arbitration clause in question provides that "any dispute, claim or controversy arising out of or in relation to this Agreement shall be exclusively and finally resolved through arbitration. Such arbitration shall be conducted in Hong Kong in English by Hong Kong International Arbitration Center in accordance with the Hong Kong International Arbitration Center Administered Arbitration Rules then in force."

70 Hebei Higher People's Court Civil Ruling (2015) Ji-Li-Min-Zhong-Zi No. 70.

71 The arbitration clause in question provides that "both parties shall strive to settle any controversy, dispute or claim arising out of this Agreement through friendly consultation. If such controversy, dispute or claim cannot be resolved through consultation within sixty (60) days after the same has been submitted by either party to the other, the dispute shall be resolved through arbitration in the Hong Kong Special Administrative Region in accordance with the ICC Rules of Arbitration ("Rules") in effect at the time of the arbitration."

72 Article V of the New York Convention provides that "1. Recognition and enforcement of the award may be refused, at the request of the party against whom it is invoked, only if that party furnishes to the competent authority where the recognition and enforcement is sought, proof that: (a) the parties to the agreement referred to in Article II were, under the law applicable to them, under some incapacity, or the said agreement is not valid under the law to which the parties have subjected it or, failing any indication thereon, under the law of the country where the award was made; or (b) the party against whom the award is invoked was not given proper notice of the appointment of the arbitrator or of the arbitration proceedings or was otherwise unable to present his case; or (c) the award deals with a difference not contemplated by or not falling within the terms of the submission to arbitration, or it contains decisions on matters beyond the scope of the submission to arbitration, provided that, if the decisions on matters submitted to arbitration can be separated from those not so submitted, that part of the award which contains decisions on matters submitted to arbitration may be recognized and enforced; or (d) the composition of the arbitral authority or the arbitral procedure was not in accordance with the agreement of the parties, or, failing such agreement, was not in accordance with the law of the country where the arbitration took place; or (e) the award has not yet become binding on the parties, or has been set aside or suspended by a competent authority of the country in which, or under the law of which, that award was made. 2. Recognition and enforcement of an arbitral award may also be refused if the competent authority in the country where recognition and enforcement is sought finds that: (a) the subject matter of the difference is not capable of settlement by arbitration under the law of that country; or (b) the recognition or enforcement of the award would be contrary to the public policy of that country."

spect to arbitral awards made in the Hong Kong Special Administrative Region, including awards from Hong Kong-based arbitration institutions, such as the HKIAC, and awards made in Hong Kong by foreign arbitration institutions, such as the ICC, the courts in Mainland China has reviewed these awards in accordance with the *Arrangements of the Supreme People's Court on the Mutual Enforcement of Arbitral Awards between the Mainland and the Hong Kong Special Administrative Region* (hereinafter referred to as the "Arrangements") that came into force in 2000.[73] Similarly, the majority of the awards made in Hong Kong have received recognition and enforcement by Mainland China courts, with few exceptions.

From the cases listed in Table 8, there are two issues worth paying attention. One concerns the notarization and authentication of documents. In one application for enforcement of foreign-related arbitral award, the Intermediate People's Court in Yangzhou, Jiangsu[74] rejected the award that the application was based on. One key factor was that the Japanese applicant did not supply the application to enforce or the Power of Attorney in a notarized, legalized or otherwise authenticated manner. Therefore, applicants should be extra careful in the compliance of procedures related to document-notarization in seeking to enforce foreign-related arbitral awards, and avoid an outcome that the award ends up unenforceable due to non-compliance with these requirements. The second question relate to the jurisdiction for the enforcement of maritime arbitrations. Many applications for the recognition and enforcement of foreign arbitral awards relate to maritime arbitrations and the jurisdiction of enforcing maritime arbitral awards. Article 11 of the *Special Maritime Procedure Law of the People's Republic of China* stipulates that: "When the parties apply for enforcement of maritime arbitral award, apply for recognition and enforcement of a judgment or written order of a foreign court and foreign maritime arbitral award, an application shall be filed with the maritime court of the place where the property subjected to execution or of the place where the person subjected to execution has its domicile. In case of no maritime court in the place where the property subjected to execution or

---

73 Article 7 of the Arrangements of the Supreme People's Court on the Mutual Enforcement of Arbitral Awards between the Mainland and the Hong Kong Special Administrative Region provides that "The party against whom an application is filed may, after receiving notice of an arbitral award, whether made in the Mainland or in the HKSAR, adduce evidence to show any of the situations set out below. Upon such evidence being examined and any of the said situations being found proved, the relevant court may refuse to enforce the arbitral award: (1) A party to the arbitration agreement was, under the law applicable to him, under some incapacity, or the arbitration agreement was not valid under the law to which the parties subjected it, or, failing any indication thereon, under the law of the place in which the arbitral award was made; (2) The party against whom the application is filed was not given proper notice of the appointment of the arbitrator or was otherwise unable to present his case; (3) The award deals with a difference not contemplated by or not falling within the terms of the submission to arbitration, or the award contains decisions on matters beyond the scope of the submission to arbitration. However, if the award contains decisions on matters submitted to arbitration that can be separated from those not so submitted, that part of the award which contains decisions on matters submitted to arbitration shall be enforced; (4) The composition of the arbitral authority or the arbitral procedure was not in accordance with agreement of the parties or, failing such agreement, with the law of the place where the arbitration took place (5) The award has not yet become binding on the parties, or has been set aside or suspended by the court or in accordance with the law of the place where the arbitration took place. If the relevant court finds that under the law of the place of enforcement, the dispute is incapable of being settled by arbitration, then the court may refuse to enforce the award. The enforcement of the award may be refused if the court of the Mainland holds that the enforcement of the arbitral award in the Mainland would be contrary to the public interest of the Mainland, or if the court of the HKSAR decides that the enforcement of the arbitral award in Hong Kong would be contrary to the public policy of the HKSAR."

74 Jiangsu Yangzhou Intermediate People's Court Civil Ruling (2015) Yang-Shang-Zhong-Shen-Zhi-Zi No. 00143.

in the place where the person subjected to execution has its domicile, an application shall be filed with the intermediate people's court of the place where the property subjected to execution or of the place where the person subjected to execution has its domicile." In an application for enforcement involving a Hong Kong element, the maritime court in Tianjin rejected the application for challenging jurisdiction pursuant to this provision.[75] In addition, it is worth noting that where it comes to the jurisdiction to determine the force of arbitration agreements, Article 12 of the *Judicial Interpretation of Arbitration Law* states: "[a] case on the effectiveness of an agreement for arbitration of a maritime dispute shall be under the jurisdiction of the maritime court at the locality of the arbitration institution agreed upon in the agreement for arbitration, at the locality of conclusion of the agreement for arbitration, or at the claimant's or respondent's domicile; if there is no maritime court at the above-mentioned places, it shall be under the jurisdiction of the nearest maritime court." From the above we can refer that maritime court has the exclusive jurisdiction over cases on the effectiveness of an agreement for arbitration of a maritime dispute.

IV. Review of Notable Arbitration Case Authorities

A. Developments of Law Concerning the Determination of the Existence of "Foreign Elements"

In recent years, whether an arbitration case involves foreign elements has been a focal point in case authority studies. In 2011 and 2012, the Supreme People's Court held in the cases of *Liupanshui Heng Ding*[76] and *Jiangsu Hang Tian Wan Yuan*[77], respectively, that Chinese parties cannot submit disputes without foreign elements to overseas arbitration institutions including the HKIAC. In 2014, the Supreme People's Court reiterated its views in the case of *Chao Lai Xin Sheng*[78] and further held that the arbitral awards thereof will not be enforced by Chinese courts. The views of the Supreme People's Court in these series of cases have caused heated debate in the legal fraternity.[79]

Even while the debate is still ongoing, a new judgment has been issued. This new judgment, however, marked somewhat of a shift for the current situation. In November 2015, the Shanghai First Intermediate People's Court issued its civil ruling concerning an application made by Siemens International Trading (Shanghai) Co., Ltd (hereinafter referred to as "Siemens") for the recognition and enforcement of an arbitral award issued by the SIAC (the "*Siemens*" case). Its decision has been deemed a remarkable breakthrough for the determination of

75 Tianjin Maritime Court Civil Ruling (2015) Jin-Hai-Fa-Que-Zi No. 2-1.

76 See pages 94-98 of the Guidance on Case Filing, Su Zelin and Jing Hanchao (ed) (2011 vol. 1) (vol. 28) published by People's Court Press (2011).

77 Reply of the Supreme People's Court to the Request for Instructions Regarding Validity of the Arbitration Agreement between Jiangsu Hang Tian Wan Yuan Wind Power Equipment Manufacturing Co., Ltd and LM Wind Power Blades Product (Tianjin) Co., Ltd ([2012] Min-Si-Ta-Zi No. 2).

78 Beijing Second Intermediate People's Court Civil Ruling (2013) Er-Zhong-Min-Te-Zi No. 10670.

79 See also pages 22-24 of Annual Review of Commercial Arbitration in China (2015) authored by Song Lianbin, Yang Ling and Helena H. C. Chen, published in the Commercial Dispute Resolution in China: An Annual Review and Preview (2015), compiled by Beijing Arbitration Commission and published by LexisNexis (2015).

what constitutes "foreign element", [80] and much attention is paid to this decision by both the media and legal professionals. [81] The facts of the case are as follows: in September 2005, Shanghai Golden Landmark Co., Ltd (hereinafter referred to as "SGL") signed a supply contract with Siemens. It was agreed that any disputes arising from the contract shall be submitted for arbitration. During the performance of the contract, a dispute arose and SGL submitted the dispute to the SIAC for arbitration in September 2007. SGL alleged that Siemen's conducts constituted a fundamental breach of contract and sought to recover damages from Siemens. Siemens challenged the SIAC's jurisdiction on the basis that the dispute does not involve any foreign element and the SIAC therefore does not have jurisdiction over this matter. The tribunal issued a decision on this in March 2009 and rejected Siemens' jurisdictional challenge. During the arbitration proceedings, Siemens made a counterclaim that they did not breach the contract and sought damages against SGL. The tribunal ultimately held that Siemens' acts did not constitute a fundamental breach and awarded Siemens damages from SGL. However, unlike the proactive attitude taken in the arbitration, SGL adopted a passive stance after receiving the arbitral award and failed to pay the damages to Siemens. In order to recover the debts, Siemens applied to the Shanghai First Intermediate People's Court for recognition and enforcement of the SIAC award.

In this case, the core issue for determination is whether the case involved any foreign element. In making this determination, the court focused on two aspects: one, even though both SGL and Siemens are Chinese legal entities, they are both incorporated in the China (Shanghai) Pilot Free Trade Zone. In addition, in terms of the nature of both entities, they are both wholly-foreign-owned enterprises. Compared with domestic-funded enterprises, their source of capital, ultimate beneficiaries and management policies are closely related to their foreign investors and thus can be deemed to have more obvious foreign elements. The Court held that considering that the Pilot Free Trade Zone was intended to facilitate business and trade, it is necessary to attach importance to the aforesaid foreign element. On the other hand, even though the delivery of the subject matter in question (i.e. the equipment) pursuant to the contract was concluded inside China, having examined the process of contract-signing and performance, the equipment was first shipped from overseas to the Pilot Free Trade Zone under bond and then, in accordance with the implementation of the contract, cleared customs within a reasonable timeframe and delivered out of the Pilot Free Trade Zone. It is only after then can the import obligations be said to be completed. Therefore the arrangement for the supply of the equipment as prescribed in the contract has, to some extent, the characteristics of international trade. Accordingly, the court held that the contract in dispute has a foreign element.

People associated the still-debated *Chao Lai Xin Sheng* case with the above case as soon as its judgment was released to the public. Though the facts of the two cases were similar, totally different outcomes were reached since the courts adopted different views on the concept of foreign element.

---

80 Shanghai First Intermediate People's Court Civil Ruling (2013) Hu-Yi-Zhong-Min-Ren (Wai-Zhong) Zi No. 2.

81 See also "Judgment Made for the First Case in the Shanghai Pilot Free Trade Zone on Recognition and Enforcement of Foreign Arbitral Award", published on page 3 of the People's Court Daily on 1 January 2016.

In *Chao Lai Xin Sheng*, the Beijing Second Intermediate People's Court took the view that Beijing Chao Lai Xin Sheng Sports and Leisure Co., Ltd (the applicant, hereinafter referred to as "Chao Lai Xin Sheng") and Beijing Suowangzhixin Investment Consulting Co., Ltd (the respondent, hereinafter referred to as "Suowangzhixin") are both Chinese legal entities. The legal facts for establishment, alteration or termination of a civil legal relationship between the parties concerned took place in China. The subject matter of the action is also located in China. According to Article 304 of the *Interpretation of the Supreme People's Court on the Application of the Civil Procedure Law of the People's Republic of China*,[82] this case is not foreign-related. Pursuant to Article 271 of the *Civil Procedure Law*[83] and Article 128(2) of the *Contract Law of the People's Republic of China*[84], only parties to a foreign-related dispute can submit the dispute to a foreign-related arbitration institution in China or other arbitration institutions. Therefore, the arbitration clause involved is invalid for stipulating the dispute to be submitted to The Korean Commercial Arbitration Board.

What has led to such a dramatic difference in identifying foreign elements despite the similarities in the facts of the two cases? This question can be answered after examining the social background and legal basis of these two cases. In terms of the social background, even though both cases involve foreign investors and foreign arbitral awards, the *Siemens* case was in a more special context, namely that both parties are registered in the Shanghai Pilot Free Trade Zone. The contractual obligations and their performance are closely related to the Shanghai Pilot Free Trade Zone. As such, one must consider the context of China's plans to widely implement Pilot Free Trade Zones strategically across China. It can therefore be said that the court's breakthrough for the *Siemens* case reflects the spirit of "to explore and to try" intended for the Pilot Free Trade Zones. In terms of legal basis, the Shanghai First Intermediate People's Court citied Article 1 of the *Interpretations of the Supreme People's Court on Several Issues Concerning Application of the Law of the People's Republic of China on Choice of Law for Foreign-Related Civil Relationships (I)*[85] which came into effect as of 7 January 2013. Different from the previous relevant law, Article 1 introduces a catch-all provision, giving the court discretion to determine whether the civil relationship involved constitutes foreign civil re-

82 Article 304 provides that "Civil cases in which one party or both parties are foreigners, stateless persons, foreign enterprises or organizations or the legal facts for establishment, alteration or termination of a civil legal relationship between the parties concerned take place at abroad, or the subject matter of an action is located at abroad shall be the civil cases involving foreign elements."

83 Article 271 of the Civil Procedure Law provides that "where disputes arising from economic, trade, transport or maritime activities involve foreign parties, if the parties have included an arbitration clause in their contract or subsequently reach a written arbitration agreement that provides that such disputes shall be submitted for arbitration to an arbitration institution of the People's Republic of China for foreign-related disputes or to another arbitration institution, no party may institute an action in a people's court."

84 Article 128 (2) of the Contract Law of the People's Republic of China provides that "Parties to a foreign-related contract may apply to a Chinese arbitration institution or another arbitration institution for arbitration."

85 Article 1 provides that "Where a civil relationship falls under any of the following circumstances, the people's court may determine it as foreign-related civil relationship: (1) where either party or both parties are foreign citizens, foreign legal persons or other organizations or stateless persons; (2) where the habitual residence of either party or both parties locate outside the territory of the People's Republic of China; (3) where the subject matter is outside the territory of the People's Republic of China; (4) where the legal fact that leads to establishment, change or termination of the civil relation happens outside the territory of the People's Republic of China; or (5) other circumstances under which the civil relationship may be determined as foreign-related civil relationship."

lationship based on the facts of the case. [86] This discretion granted by this statute was fully utilized by the Shanghai First Intermediate People's Court.

In the commentary on the *Chao Lai Xin Sheng* case in the "Annual Review of Commercial Arbitration in China (2015)", the authors predicted that "*it cannot rule out the possibility of future expansion of cases concerning foreign elements*", [87] a statement which has now been affirmed by the *Siemens* case. At least two positive significances can be derived from the *Siemens* case: firstly, it demonstrates a willingness to support arbitration, which is consistent with the notion of respecting parties' autonomy in arbitration; secondly, it shows the spirit of keeping up with the times, reflecting the open attitude of the Intermediate Courts located within the Shanghai Pilot Free Trade Zone in the context of the internationalization of Chinese commercial arbitration. From the preliminary commentary in the industry, it is expected that that this case will have a significant demonstrative effect on similar cases in the future.

B. Intellectual Property Court and Judicial Supervision on Arbitral Awards

On 31 August 2014, the tenth meeting of the Twelfth Session of the National People's Congress Standing Committee voted and approved the Standing Committee of the National People's Congress' Decision on Setting up Intellectual Property Courts in Beijing, Shanghai and Guangzhou, thereby marking a new development stage of the judicial protection of intellectual property in China. In terms of the trial class system in China, the Intellectual Property Court is essentially at the same level as the Intermediate People's Court. On the other hand, under the Chinese arbitration system, the judicial supervision of arbitral awards is conducted by the Intermediate People's Courts. Therefore, a question may be raised as to whether, in regions where Intellectual Property Courts have been set up, the Intellectual Property Courts shall have jurisdiction over cases regarding judicial review of arbitration. In this regard, the Provisions of the Supreme People's Court on the Jurisdiction of the Intellectual Property Courts of Beijing, Shanghai and Guangzhou over Cases has failed to provide a direct answer. Thus relevant cases from judicial practices are especially worth attention. The recent case involving *Hainan Honz Pharmaceutical Co., Ltd* (hereinafter referred to as "Honz Pharmaceutical"), in relation to the application for annulment of an arbitral award, is one such case. The facts of the case are as follows:

Due to disputes over the patent licensing contract, Xiangbei Welman Pharmaceutical Co., Ltd (hereinafter referred to as "Welman") applied for arbitration to Qingyuan Commission Arbitration in accordance with the arbitration agreement. In December 2014, Honz Pharmaceutical applied to the Guangzhou Intellectual Property Court for annulment of the arbitral award. In March 2015, the Guangzhou Intellectual Property Court decided not to accept the application. [88] Honz Pharmaceutical appealed to the Guangdong Higher People's Court. The Guangdong Higher People's Court constituted a collegial bench according to law, heard the case and is-

---

[86] Article 522 of the Interpretation of the Supreme People's Court on the Application of the Civil Procedure Law of the People's Republic of China implemented as of 4 February, 2015 contains exactly the same provisions as that in Article 1 of the Interpretations of the Supreme People's Court on Several Issues Concerning Application of the Law of the People's Republic of China on Choice of Law for Foreign-Related Civil Relationships (I).

[87] See page 25 of Annual Review of Commercial Arbitration in China (2015) authored by Song Lianbin, Yang Ling and Helena H. C. Chen and published in Commercial Dispute Resolution in China: An Annual Review and Preview (2015), compiled by Beijing Arbitration Commission and published by LexisNexis (2015).

[88] Guangzhou Intellectual Property Court Civil Ruling (2015) Yue-Zhi-Fa-Li-Min-Chu-Zi No. 11.

sued its ruling.

The ruling is as follows: According to Article 2 of the *Decision of the Standing Committee of the National People's Congress on Establishing Intellectual Property Right Courts in Beijing, Shanghai and Guangzhou*[89], Articles 1[90], 2[91] and 3[92] of the *Provisions of the Supreme People's Court on the Jurisdiction of the Intellectual Property Courts of Beijing, Shanghai and Guangzhou over Cases*, as well as the *Official Reply of the Supreme People's Court on the Approval of the Jurisdiction of the Two-Tier Courts of Shenzhen, Guangdong to Hear Patent and other Intellectual Property Related Cases*, the *Guangzhou Intellectual Property Court has cross-region jurisdiction over civil and administrative cases in relation to patent, new plant variety, integrated circuit layout designs, technical secrets computer software and civil cases relating to the recognition of famous trademarks which fall beyond the jurisdiction of Shenzhen's two-tier courts.* In the present case, Honz Pharmaceutical's application to the Guangzhou Intellectual Property Court for annulment of the Qingyuan Arbitration Commission's arbitral award is with regard to a dispute on patent licensing contract. The Qingyuan Arbitration Commission is located in Guangdong which is outside the jurisdiction of Shenzhen's two-tier courts. According to Article 58 of the *Arbitration Law of the People's Republic of China*, Honz Pharmaceutical can make an application to the Guangzhou Intellectual Property Court for annulment of the arbitral award. The court of first instance's view that Honz Pharmaceutical should apply to the Qingyuan Intermediate People's Court is an inappropriate application of law. Honz Pharmaceutical's application to revoke the original ruling accorded with Article 58 of the *Arbitration Law* shall be supported. The Guangdong Higher People's Court decided that (1) the ruling of the Guangzhou Intellectual Property Court be revoked; and (2) the Guangzhou Intellectual Property Court be designated to hear the case.

It can be seen from the ruling of the Guangdong Higher People's Court on designation of jurisdiction that the Guangzhou Intellectual Property Court has exclusive jurisdiction over cases

---

89 Article 2 provides that "an intellectual property right court as the court of first instance shall have jurisdiction over a civil or administrative intellectual property case involving a patent, a new variety of plant, an integrated circuit layout design, or technical know-how, among others, which is highly technical. An administrative case involving the granting or confirmation of any intellectual property right filed against a ruling or decision of an administrative department of the State Council shall be under the jurisdiction of the Intellectual Property Right Court of Beijing as the court of first instance. An intellectual property right court shall exercise interregional jurisdiction over cases specified in the first paragraph hereof. Interregional jurisdiction in the province (or municipality directly under the Central Government) where an intellectual property right court is located may be first implemented within three years of establishment of the intellectual property right court."

90 Article 1 provides that "an intellectual property court as the court of first instance shall have jurisdiction over the following cases within its municipal jurisdiction: (1) a civil or administrative case involving a patent, a new variety of plant, an integrated circuit layout design, technical know-how or computer software; (2) an administrative case concerning an administrative act of a department of the State Council or a local people's government at or above the county level regarding copyright, trademark or unfair competition; and (3) a civil case involving the determination of a well-known trademark."

91 Article 2 provides that "the Intellectual Property Court of Guangzhou shall exercise interregional jurisdiction over cases specified in the Items (1) and (3) of Article 1 herein within Guangdong Province."

92 Article 3 provides that "all intermediate people's courts of Beijing Municipality and Shanghai Municipality as well as Guangzhou Intermediate People's Court shall no longer accept any civil or administrative intellectual property case. Other intermediate people's courts of Guangdong Province shall no longer accept any case specified in the Items (1) and (3) of Article 1 herein. All basic people's courts of Beijing Municipality, Shanghai Municipality and Guangdong Province shall no longer accept any case specified in the Items (1) and (3) of Article 1 herein."

regarding the application for annulment of arbitral awards in Guangdong in relation to intellectual property (except Shenzhen). In other words, the Intermediate People's Courts in which the arbitration institutions are located are no longer responsible for the judicial supervision over arbitral awards relating to intellectual property. It will undoubtedly help to unify the extent of judicial supervision over arbitral awards and reduce the risk of courts' arbitrary annulment of arbitral awards. This is particularly helpful in the case of Guangdong Province where there are disparities in regional development and the degree of the legalization of the region is inconsistent across different parts of the region. On the other hand, with regard to arbitral awards in relation to intellectual property rendered by the arbitration institutions located in cities far away from Guangzhou (e. g. Zhanjiang and Shantou), commencing a legal proceeding to annul an arbitral award in the provincial capital will be troublesome as much as it will increase the costs involved. Therefore, this may potentially dissuade parties from applying for annulment of arbitral awards.

The Intellectual Property Courts set up in Beijing, Shanghai and Guangzhou are still at the pilot stage. With further developments, the establishment of intellectual property courts may be generalized in other places in China. It is expected that the relationship between the Intellectual Property Courts and the judicial supervision over arbitral awards will become clearer and more institutionalized.

C. Definition of the Term "China" as Used in the Clause "Commencing Arbitration in China in Accordance with the ICC Rules of Arbitration"

In the past decade, the recognition of the validity of an arbitration agreement providing "commencing arbitration in China in accordance with the ICC Rules of Arbitration" is a question Chinese courts have been facing over and over again. From the *Zublin International GmbH* case in 2003,[93] the *Ningbo Arts & Crafts I/E Co., Ltd* case in 2006,[94] the *Anhui Long Li De* case in 2013,[95] to the *Ningbo Beilun Licheng* case in 2014,[96] Chinese courts have increasingly been adopting a more open attitude towards such agreements. At present, the validity of such agreements is not controversial. However, it still involves questions in other aspects, including how to ascertain the place of arbitration under such an agreement. It will certainly not be an issue for the courts in Mainland China. But what if this issue is brought up in Hong Kong? The case of *Z* v *A*[97] heard by the Hong Kong Court of First Instance in 2015 is one such notable case. The core issue in this case is whether "China" stated in "commencing arbitration in China in accordance with the ICC Rules of Arbitration" refers to the Mainland China or does it include Hong Kong. The facts of the case are as follows:

---

93 See also the Reply of the Supreme People's Court to the Request for Instructions on the Case Concerning the Application of Züblin International GmbH and Wuxi Woke General Engineering Rubber Co., Ltd for Determining the Validity of the Arbitration Agreement ([2003] Min-Si-Ta-Zi No. 23).

94 Zhejiang Ningbo Intermediate People's Court Civil Ruling (2008) Yong-Zhong-Jian-Zi No. 4.

95 Reply of the Supreme People's Court to the Request for Instructions on the Case Concerning the Validity of the Arbitration Agreement between Anhui LD Package Printing Co. Ltd (Claimant) and BP Agnati S. R. L (Respondent) ([2013] Min-Si-Ta-Zi No. 13).

96 Reply of the Supreme People's Court to the Request for Instructions on the Case Concerning the Validity of the Arbitration Clause Contained in the Sale and Purchase Contract between Ningbo Beilun Licheng Lubricating Oil Co. Ltd and Famo Wanchi Company ([2013] Min-Si-Ta-Zi No. 74).

97 Z v. A and others (HCCT 8/2013).

Z and A have signed the "CKD Agreement" and "TC Agreement" respectively in 2007. Both agreements incorporated arbitration clauses, among which the CKD Agreement provided that "[I]n case of breach of any of the Articles of this agreement by either of the parties, both Parties agree to put best efforts to remedy by negotiations. Otherwise, those Parties agree to arbitration as per the International Chamber of Commerce and held in CHINA?"[98] The TC Agreement states that "any dispute, controversy or difference which may arise between the parties out of or in relation to this Agreement or for the breach thereof shall be settled amicably by the parties, but in case of failure, it shall be finally settled in CHINA by arbitration pursuant to the Rules of the International Chamber of Commerce whose award shall bind the parties hereto."[99] Disputes arose between the parties afterwards. A and its subsidiaries submitted an application for arbitration to the ICC International Court of Arbitration in October 2011, requesting an award that Z violated the aforementioned agreements and thus should compensate A.

The parties held different opinions on the place of arbitration during the arbitration proceeding. Party A considered Hong Kong to be the place of arbitration while Z held the view that Mainland China should be the place of arbitration. In the end, the arbitral tribunal (sole arbitrator) decided that Hong Kong is the place of arbitration and that the Hong Kong Arbitration Law should be the procedural law of arbitration. After the arbitral tribunal rendered a partial award, Z objected to this award and commenced a legal proceeding before the Hong Kong Court of First Instance, requesting the Court to revoke the partial award. The Presiding Judge was Justice Mimmie Chan. In the ruling, Justice Chan supported the arbitrator's determination of the place of arbitration for two reasons: first, there was an inherent ambiguity on whether the word "China" refers to Mainland China or does it also include Hong Kong and the ICC International Court of Arbitration is therefore entitled to determine Hong Kong as the place of arbitration according to Article 14(1)[100] of ICC Rules of Arbitration; second, it is an established principle of contractual interpretation that the parties are presumed to be aware of the relevant legal background surrounding the formation of their contract and that they intend their contract to be legally enforceable. Consequently, the Parties must have been aware that the PRC had resumed sovereignty over Hong Kong when they signed the two Agreements and it would have been artificial for them to refer to "China" as meaning "China excluding Hong Kong" or "China including Hong Kong". It was therefore open for the ICC Court to fix Hong Kong as the place of arbitration. In addition, the Parties would also have been aware that there was uncertainty over whether a mainland Chinese court would enforce an ICC arbitral award that was seated in Mainland China. This is because arbitral awards in Mainland China must be administered by a registered arbitral commission pursuant to the *PRC Civil Procedure Law* and the ICC is not such a commission. Both parties' Mainland Chinese law experts provided conflicting evidence on this issue, which was largely due to conflicting mainland Chinese case law on the en-

98 CKD Agreement provides that: "In case of breach of any of the Articles of this agreement by either of the parties, both Parties agree to put best efforts to remedy by negotiations. Otherwise, those Parties agree to arbitration as per the International Chamber of Commerce and held in CHINA?"

99 TC Agreement provides that: "Any dispute, controversy or difference which may arise between the parties out of or in relation to this Agreement or for the breach thereof shall be settled amicably by the parties, but in case of failure, it shall be finally settled in CHINA by arbitration pursuant to the Rules of the International Chamber of Commerce whose award shall bind the parties hereto."

100 Article 14 (1) of the ICC Rules of Arbitration, applicable to the case, provides that "the place of the arbitration shall be fixed by the Court, unless agreed upon by the parties."

forceability of ICC arbitral awards in Mainland China. By contrast, an ICC arbitral award rendered in Hong Kong would face no enforcement difficulties, either in Mainland China or Hong Kong. Accordingly, Justice Chan held that "realizing that the purpose of an arbitration agreement is to make the dispute to be resolved through a procedure which could produce a final, binding and executable award, I agree with the arbitrator's opinion that the arbitration involving both parties shall be commenced in Hong Kong."

The arbitral tribunal's decision on the place of arbitration and Justice Chan's support on this decision have caused some debates in the industry. The tribunal's decision to take "China" as "Hong Kong" is not sufficiently justified. Unless specified, it is commonly understood that the word "China" refers to Mainland China, with the exclusion of Hong Kong, unless otherwise specified. Notwithstanding so, it also cannot be said that Justice Chan's legal reasoning is impeccable. Given that the case took place in the Hong Kong Special Administrative Region, the term "China" might be interpreted in a way different to how it is interpreted usually. To this issue, the authors' understanding is that as long as China is not interpreted as other countries such as the UK or France, it is unnecessary to over criticize the tribunal's decision to determine Hong Kong, China as the place of arbitration.

In international commercial arbitration, the place of arbitration plays a very important role. Once the place of arbitration has been decided, the applicable law to recognize the validity of an arbitration agreement (i. e. the procedural law of arbitration place) is usually decided accordingly. The body to exercise the supervision power over arbitration (i. e. the courts at the place of arbitration) is decided as well. Some inspirations from the case of Z v A for Chinese business people are, when signing an arbitration clause such as "commencing arbitration in China in accordance with the ICC Rules of Arbitration", if the parties intended to exclude Hong Kong from the scope of the word "China", express explanation should be made to avoid any troubles encountered in the case of Z v A.

D. The Application of the Case of Noble Resources for the Recognition and Enforcement of an HKIAC Arbitral Award

In March 2015, after having reported to the Supreme People's Court, the Shenzhen Intermediate People's Court issued acivil ruling, rejecting a company's application for the recognition and enforcement of an arbitral award rendered by the HKIAC[101]. This was the first case that the Mainland China people's court rejected the recognition and enforcement of an arbitral award made in Hong Kong since the implementation of the *Arrangement of the Supreme People's Court on the Mutual Enforcement of Arbitral Awards between the Mainland and the Hong Kong Special Administrative Region* (hereinafter referred to as the "Arrangement") in February 2000. This case has attracted the attention of the industry. Noble Resources Pte., Ltd (hereinafter referred to as "Noble Resources") is a renowned international enterprise based in Hong Kong and is listed on the Singapore Exchange. It engages in the import and export of agricultural products. Shenzhen Cereals Group Co., Ltd (hereinafter referred to as "SZCG") is a state-owned holding company registered in China. Noble Resources has filed an application for arbitration to HKIAC and received a favorable award on a dispute over the sale and pur-

---

101 Guangdong Shenzhen Intermediate People's Court Civil Ruling (2011) Shen-Zhong-Fa-Min-Si-Chu-Zi No. 270.

chase contract for the sales of soybeans (hereinafter referred to as the "Soybeans Contract") concluded between the parties. Noble Resources subsequently applied to the Shenzhen Intermediate People's Court for recognition and enforcement of this arbitral award rendered in Hong Kong. SZCG thought that Noble Resources' recognition and enforcement application should be rejected on the grounds that: firstly, given that the CFR term applies in this case, the subject matter in the award should be covered in the loss of the chartered freight under the Voyage Charter. It should not be governed by the arbitration clause under the Soybeans Contract[102]; secondly, the subject of the HKIAC award dealt with the dispute in relation to soybeans with a seed coating agent, which was agreed explicitly or implicitly in the Supplementary Contract. It should be governed by the Chinese court according to Chinese laws as explicitly agreed in the Supplementary Contract; thirdly, recognition and enforcement of this arbitral award may violate social and public interest in Mainland China. All factors considered this case involves two main legal issues: firstly, whether the HKIAC arbitral tribunal has jurisdiction over the case, i. e. whether the concerned award falls in the circumstance prescribed in Article 7. 1 (3) of the *Arrangement*[103]; secondly, whether the enforcement of the award will violate any social and public interest in the Mainland.

The Shenzhen Intermediate People's Court held the view that the Supplementary Contract between Noble Resources and SZCG provides for "costs of delay" which includes, but is not limited to, "demurrage", while the "demurrage" under the Supplementary Contract alters the agreements on the "demurrage" under the Soybeans Contract. According to the Supplementary Contract, disputes arising from the "demurrage" shall be governed by the Chinese court. Thus the HKIAC arbitral tribunal has no jurisdiction over the dispute concerned. As for the argument on social and public interest, the Court believes that the enforcement of the arbitral award will not violate the social and public interest of the Mainland.

Since the Civil Ruling of this case has not been officially published yet, the authors can only make the following two comments based on the information from media reports: firstly, though the outcome is that the recognition and enforcement of the arbitral award rendered in Hong Kong has been rejected by the Mainland China people's court when the applicant for the enforcement is a foreign company and the respondent is a Chinese company, it cannot be concluded that the Mainland China people's court is conservative and unenlightened in dealing with recognition and enforcement applications where the arbitral award was rendered in Hong Kong. In this case, the court examined the arbitral award in strict accordance with Article 7 of the *Arrangement*. The court made intensive analysis of the reason on why it ruled that the arbitral tribunal had no jurisdiction over the case. This should be viewed in a positive light. Secondly, although the party concerned asserted that the award violates social and public interest, the court adopted quite a strict approach and rejected the applicant's assertion upfront and explicitly. This in fact represents the consistent attitude of the Mainland China people's courts

---

102 It is agreed in the arbitration clauses under the Soybeans Contract that: "Disputes arising from the performance of the contract shall be submitted to arbitration by either side. If the purchaser is the defendant, the dispute shall be submitted to the Hong Kong International Arbitration Center; if the vender is the defendant, the dispute shall be submitted to the Grain and Feed Trade Association in London for arbitration. Disputes arising out of the contract shall be resolved in accordance with English law."

103 For details of Article 7 of the Arrangement, please refer to the relevant footnotes under the preceding section "sample review and commentary on foreign-related arbitration cases".

when dealing with these types of issues.

E. Re-arbitration due to the Absence of a Member of the Tribunal

Notification of re-arbitration occurs from time to time in the course of judicial supervision. Article 61 of the *Arbitration Law* provides that "if, after accepting an application for annulment of an arbitral award, the people's court considers that the case may be re-arbitrated by the arbitral tribunal, it shall notify the tribunal that it shall re-arbitrate the case within a certain time limit and shall rule to suspend the annulment procedure. If the arbitral tribunal refuses to re-arbitrate the case, the people's court shall rule to resume the annulment procedure". This provision offers a general principle but lacks operational details. In practice, there are different understandings and applications of this provision amongst the people's courts. [104] Article 21 of the *Interpretation of the Supreme People's Court concerning Some Issues on Application of the Arbitration Law of the People's Republic of China* sets forth two circumstances where People's Courts may order for the case to be re-arbitrated: (1) the evidence on which the arbitral award is based is forged; or (2) the other party concealed any evidence, which is enough to impact the impartiality of an award. These circumstances appear to relate to issues of evidence alone. In the case of an application for annulment of an arbitral award, Hubei Yichang Intermediate People's Court ruled to suspend the annulment procedure and re-arbitrate the case on the ground that the arbitrator was absent from the hearing, a ruling which is quite refreshing. [105]

On 9 January 2015, Yichang Arbitration Commission accepted a request for arbitration in relation to a private lending dispute between Zhang XX and Tang XX. Within the specified period, Zhang XX appointed Ge XX as the arbitrator, while Tang XX failed to appoint an arbitrator. Both parties failed to agree on the presiding arbitrator. The Yichang Arbitration Commission then appointed Ke XX as the presiding arbitrator and Yan XX as another arbitrator. Thereafter the arbitral tribunal held two hearings. During the first hearing, all three arbitrators were present. However during the second hearing, arbitrator Yan XX was absent. The reason for his absence and whether this was approved by both parties was not stated in the record of the hearing. Yan XX did not affix his signature to the hearing record either.

After the award was rendered, Tang XX applied for the annulment of the arbitral award and stated three reasons, one of which was that the award was rendered in violation of due process as the arbitrator Yan XX was not present at the hearing and neither did he affix his signature to the record of the hearing. Upon examination, Yichang Intermediate People's Court affirmed that the arbitrator Yan XX neither attended the second hearing nor affixed his signature to the record of the hearing. This hearing was held under the circumstances whereby the party concerned had applied for the postponement of the exchange of evidence and an amendment to the arbitration claim. Several basic arbitration proceedings shall be conducted and completed in this hearing, including, the exchange of evidence and cross-examination, the arbitrator's inquiry of the concerned parties, mutual inquiries between the concerned parties, debate between the concerned parties, etc. Arbitrator Yan XX's absence from this hearing violated the princi-

---

104 Please refer to page 49-64 of the Thesis on Basis of Sending Back for Re-arbitration in China - Take Practice of Domestic Courts as Example by Yang Ling, which was published on the 61th edition of Beijing Arbitration by China Legal Publishing House (2007).

105 Hubei Yichang Intermediate People's Court (2015) E-Yi-Chang-Zhong-Min-Zhong-Zi No. 00010.

ples of direct hearing and the principle of a verbal trial, according to which the arbitrators are obliged to attend the hearing and listen to the opinions of the concerned parties in ordinary arbitration procedures. It is prescribed in Articles 31 and 32 of the *Interim Arbitration Rules of Yichang Arbitration Commission* that in the event that an arbitrator is prevented from fulfilling his/her functions for whatever reason therefore affects the examination of the case, the arbitrator can be replaced or Chairman of the Arbitration Commission may appoint a new arbitrator. Hence, there was a material defect in the arbitration procedure of this case, which may have affected the impartiality of the award. According to Article 61 of the *Arbitration Law*, Yichang Intermediate People's Court ruled as follows: (1) suspend the annulment procedure; (2) the case of the private lending dispute between the applicant Tang XX and the respondent Zhang XX shall be re-arbitrated by Yichang Arbitration Commission within 30 days from the receipt of the notice of this court (under Article 61 of the *Arbitration Law*, the court shall notify the arbitral tribunal to re-arbitrate within a certain time limit).

It is widely believed that, under the framework of judicial supervision over arbitral awards, a notification to re-arbitrate is a choice that reflects a mentality to "support arbitration proceedings", a choice that contrasts with a simple ruling to annul an arbitral award. Providing arbitral tribunal with an opportunity to correct mistakes may expedite the dispute settlement process, saving judicial resources and reduce the burden on parties concerned.

In this case, Yichang Intermediate People's Court did not simply rule to annul the arbitral award on the grounds that the arbitrator was absent from the hearing which led to a material defect in the arbitration procedure and may have sufficiently affected the rendering of a fair award (a violation of Article 58 of the *Arbitration Law*). Instead, it found another way out by giving the arbitral tribunal an opportunity to re-arbitrate in accordance with Article 61 of *the Arbitration Law*, an approach that can be said to be open-minded. Having said that, it can also be said that such an open-minded approach appears to contravene the relevant provisions of the *Arbitration Law*. It is expressed in Article 58 of the *Arbitration Law* that the people's court shall "rule to annul an arbitration award" if a collegial panel formed by the people's court verifies, upon examination, that the award involves one of the six circumstances set forth in the preceding paragraph. In this case, Yichang Intermediate People's Court held that a material defect existed in the arbitration procedure which would have sufficiently affected the rendering of a fair award. This clearly meets the criteria that "the arbitration procedure was not in conformity with the statutory procedure". As a matter of fact, this highlights the tension between rationality in judicial practice and the present situation of the arbitration legislation. In revision of the *Arbitration Law*, attention should be paid to further streamline re-arbitration from the legislative perspective, clarify different approaches to various issues in practice as well as encourage people's courts to try to exercise the option of re-arbitration rather than annulment of arbitral awards.

In addition, this case involves an issue of arbitrators' professional ethics and is worth reflecting on. Arbitration is only as good as its arbitrators. In this case, the Arbitrator Yan XX did not attend the hearing for reasons unknown. However, an arbitrator, once having received and accepted an appointment, should diligently and responsibly devote him/herself to the appointment, especiallyin terms of the duties such as attending hearings and deliberations on time. An arbitrator should notify other tribunal members if he/she is unable to attend the scheduled hearing for certain reason. Such notification should be made as early as possible to allow others to make appropriate arrangements. This does not only relate to the reputation of an individual arbitrator, but also a fair and efficient resolution of the case. This may also have a direct impact on the social reputation of the arbitration system. Nowadays, arbitration undertakings in China are developing vigorously and have been attracting tremendous attention. The quality of arbitrators, however, still varies. In this context, it is an urgent need to improve the panel of available arbitrators. Arbitration institutions obviously play an indispensable and important role. Externally, they should strengthen trainings for newly-recruited arbitrators and provide arbitration professionals a platform for communication and mutual promotion etc. Internally, they should formulate and improve regulations on the arbitrators' code of conducts. It is also necessary to improve the quality of case management to ensure that arbitrators handle each case appropriately. All of these suggestions must be implemented thoroughly.

V. Summary and Prospects

2015 has been a meaningful year for arbitrations in China. The *Arbitration Law* has been in force for 20 years and the earliest seven arbitration commissions that were set up based on the *Arbitration Law* (Beijing, Shanghai, Tianjin, Guangzhou, Xian, Hohhot and Shenzhen) have also been running successfully for these 20 years. During this time, 200 odd arbitration commissions have been set up around the country, creating an increasing competition between Chinese arbitration commissions. On the other hand, the new free trade zones that have been set up as well as the "One Belt One Road" Initiative will translate to new opportunities for Chinese arbitration to become more international. The representative office set up by the HKIAC in the China (Shanghai) Pilot Free Trade Zone on 19 November 2015, being one of the first foreign arbitration institutions to set foot within Mainland China. On 29 December of the same year, the China Council for the Promotion of International Trade and the China Chamber of International Commerce set up the Arbitration Center Across the Straits in the Pingtan Comprehensive Pilot Zone in Fujian, which is dedicated to afford more convenient arbitration services to parties on both sides of the Taiwan Strait. At the beginning of 2016, the SIAC and the ICC International Court of Arbitration announced, respectively, that they would be setting up representative offices in the China (Shanghai) Pilot Free Trade Zone. This announcement coupled with the existing Nansha International Arbitration Centre, the Zhuhai Court of International Arbitration and the Shenzhen Qianhai Court of International Arbitration, show how arbitrations in China have, together with the development of the Chinese economy, become more international and the services offered have also become more internationalized to a point where they can boldly compete with fellow arbitration institutions on the international stage. There is no doubt that internationalization will not merely be a hot topic of the year, but will become a more and more distinctive feature of contemporary arbitration in China.

Annual Review on Commercial Mediation in China (2016) *

YANG Yan [1], *ZHANG Hua* [2]

I. Summary

As the market economy grows, commercial mediation has been developing in China to meet diverse needs of commercial parties for dispute resolution in this new era. It could be said that parties in commercial disputes are more rational, comparing to parties in civil disputes, as they would like to solve their problems, keep their benefits and satisfy their needs while they repair business relationships with the other parties, maintain or even raise their reputation, ultimately they would like to achieve a "harmonious", "mutual-beneficial" and "win-win" outcome for all parties. Nowadays, mediation organisations in various fields are more or less established and they have realised the importance of developing jointly with each other. For instance, the mediation alliance of the Capital area, the Guangdong, Hong Kong and Macau Mediation Alliance have been established throughout recent years. Till 2015, the horizontal alliance between mediation organisations is getting more and more connected and frequent. At the same time, commercial mediation as a widely applicable alternative dispute resolution mechanism is developing towards the trend of professionalism, specialization and standardization. It is becoming more well-recognized and influential in the society.

II. The New Development of Commercial Mediation

A. State Policies and Judicial Policies in Support of the Development of Commercial Mediation

1. Supporting policy from central committee of the communist party of China ("CCCPC")

On 6 December 2015, the General Office of the CCCPC and General Office of the State Council jointly issued the *Opinion on Improving the Multidimensional Dispute Resolution Mechanism* (Zhong Ban Fa (2015) No. 60) (hereinafter referred to as "Opinion 60") and for the first time set out overall arrangements for the establishment of the multidimensional dispute resolution mechanism on a CCCPC level by issuing a separate opinion. The *Opinion* spec-

* Translated by Smyth & Co in association with RPC.

1 YANG Yan, Deputy of the Case Registration of Beijing People's High Court.

2 ZHANG Hua, Judge of the Case Registration of Beijing People's High Court.

ifies that "the improvement of a multidimensional dispute resolution mechanism is a necessity for protecting legitimate rights of citizens and promoting fairness and justice, it is a crucial part of improving and updating the management of the society and deepening the construction of a "peaceful" China. Despite the fact that the Opinion 60 was only issued at the end of 2015, high attention had already been paid to the establishment of multidimensional dispute resolution mechanism, including commercial mediation, at the Eighteenth National Congress of the Communist Party of China, the 3rd and 4th Session of Eighteenth Central Committee of Communist Party of China, in which the establishment of multidimensional dispute resolution mechanism had also been included into the system of social governance. It is without doubt that the policy support from CCCPC plays a vital role in the promotion of multidimensional dispute resolution mechanism. Over a very long period of time, it is very difficult for the exploration from bottom to top in specific areas to break the predicament brought by lack of related applicable laws and suitable regimes. Mediation organisations would have been struggling had there not been the great support from the Party committees and governments at all levels. Opinion 60 promotes the establishment of multidimensional dispute resolution mechanism from top to bottom. It has a profound impact across the country on the recognition and unification of concept, the unification of the structuring as well as the reconfiguration of resources and thereafter boost the development of multidimensional dispute resolution mechanism in a way that is scientific, rational and more sustainable.

Commercial mediation, as an important part of the multidimensional dispute resolution mechanism, has a prominent role in the establishment of rule-of-law society and market economy and has raised high attention of the CCCPC. The CCCPC has pointed out in various meetings and documents that the judicial and administrative authorities shall foster the establishment of industry-focused and specialised people's mediation organisation; the people's court shall strengthen its cooperation with commercial mediation organisations and improve the interface system of lawsuits and mediation mechanism; industrial associations and other social organisations are encouraged to establish mediation organisations to handle civil and commercial disputes between members of the association and between members of the association and other parties; to categorize as government purchase of services those conflicts in the public service area which can be handled by social organisations and have relevant social organisations take on such conflicts after a competitive selection. Opinion 60 further points out that those relevant departments of CCCPC shall guide and support the establishment of industrial mediation organisations, support those chambers of commerce, industrial associations, private non-enterprise entities, commercial arbitration organisations who have the capability set up commercial mediation organisations and encourage those commercial mediation organisations who are independent legal entities to provide mediation services in the area of investment, finance, securities and futures, insurance, real-estate, project contracting, technology transfer, intellectual property and international trade to make full use of the expertise and professionalism of commercial mediation organisations. CCCPC has promoted a series of policies and measures to provide larger space and better external support for the development of commercial mediation. Such support from CCCPC shall fasten establishment of commercial mediation organisations and the capability of providing an efficient mediation service platform to its members shall become a vital indicator of the function of an industrial association.

2. Policy support from the Supreme People's Court

The "One Belt One Road" (the "Silk Road Economic Belt" and the "21st-Century Maritime Silk Road") is a state strategy, some even call it the third "reform and opening up" of China. The core of "One Belt One Road" is to strengthen and promote the economic cooperation and the joint development with countries along the "One Belt One Road" by establishing a fair and just legal system is essential for promoting economic and trade cooperation. The Supreme People's Court issued *Several Opinions of the Supreme People's Court on Judicial Services and Safeguards for Building the "One Belt and One Road" Initiatives* (Fa Fa (2015) No. 9) in an attempt to better facilitate the establishment of the "One Belt One Road" in which people's court at all levels are required to establish and improve the establishment of multidimensional dispute resolution mechanism and further promote the linkage between commercial mediation, conciliation in arbitration and other mediation mechanisms. This would allow them to play to their strengths to resolve disputes in relation to the construction of the "One Belt One Road" and satisfy the need for dispute resolution of both domestic and international parties.

B. Changes in the Construction of Mediation Organisations

In 2015, with the strong support from CCCPC and the Supreme People's Court, the increasing demand in society, based on the foundation lay down by prior development, the commercial mediation in China is booming: more emphasis has been placed on the use of integrated mediation resources in the establishment of organisation, more emphasis has been placed on the linkage and mutual complementation between mediation and arbitration, litigation, neutral evaluation organisations in the establishment of mechanisms , there are more frequent training and communication activities, the formation of mediators are also becoming more professional and standardized.

In 2015, the development of commercial mediation organisations can be categorized by the division of various commercial and industrial areas. The longitudinal development is rapid and there are two distinct characteristics: the horizontal cooperation have been strengthening, and the external cooperation have been strengthening.

1. Beijing: The establishment of industrial associations for industrial and specialized mediation organisations

Disputes in Beijing area are more specialized and more categorized to certain types. Also, such disputes occur frequently and in large volumes, industrial and specialized mediation organisations who focus on commercial mediations have been developing rapidly in the area to deal with these disputes. Statistics show that up to the end of 2015, there are about 30 industrial mediation organisations in various commercial fields including the internet, securities, futures, insurance, the pawn and logistics. These industrial and specialised mediation organisations were scattered in different industries and were basically "on their own", there was no unified specifications and the development was uneven. There was no effective communication channel between such organisation and the Party Committee, the government and judicial authorities. It was, in general, very difficult for such organisations to improve the overall effectiveness or to raise social awareness. On 23 December 2015, Beijing Multidimensional Mediation Development Association, China's very first provincial industrial self-discipline association which consists of industrial and specialized mediation organisations and aims to provide service support to them, was established in Beijing. The newly established Beijing Multidimensional Mediation Development Association shall commit itself to the establishment of external promotion platforms as well as communication and exchange platforms among the industrial and specialized mediation organizations. In the meantime it will strengthen the standardized construction of those organizations and formulate industrial mediation procedure standards, charging standards, performance appraisal standards and mediator qualification criterion, in order to standardize the codes of practice, promote the self-regulation of the industry and foster the establishment of new mediation organisations. Besides, the association will strengthen the communication with the Party committee and governments to seek for their support and improve the interface system of lawsuits and mediation mechanism to create a healthy external environment for the development of industrial and specialized mediation. It will fully play its role as the linking bridge and service support to facilitate the establishment of a mediation network where industrial and specialized mediation, people's mediation and administrative mediation work together in a cooperative and comprehensive way, so as to improve the multidimensional mediation mechanism at the capital. As one important change made to the multidimensional mediation framework, the establishment of Beijing Multidimensional Mediation Development Association indicates that the industrial and specialized mediation organizations in Beijing have ushered in a new phase where the industry has realized self-regulation and self-management, and has been integrating the mediation resources and seeking for common development.

2. Hong Kong: The establishment of the Mainland-Hong Kong Cross-border Mediation Centre

Almost at the same time when Beijing Multidimensional Mediation Development Associationis established, on 9 December 2015, "China Mainland-Hong Kong Joint Mediation Centre" was set up in Hong Kong. In the opening ceremony, China Council for the Promotion of International Trade/ China International Chamber of Commerce Mediation Centre signed the cooperation contract with Hong Kong Mediation Centre. The set-up of this cross-border organization is prospective. At the present juncture, the "Belt and Road" construction of the country and such regional cooperative development strategies such as Asian investment banks and regional comprehensive economic partnership agreement have stepped up. As more cross-border economic trade and cooperation in other fields between commercial subjects have been promoted, there come more expected commercial disputes and more needs from commercial subjects for legal and dispute resolution service. The centre is set up to provide a platform to solve cross-border commercial disputes for the mainland and Hong Kong, and to provide cross-border dispute resolution service. Cross-border mediation will help solve the problems encountered when resolving the disputes between different legal systems and those involving more than one judicial jurisdiction, which consist of procedure and substantive issues. Such mediation contributes to the package solution of all the disputes between concerned parties in an environment of equal consultation, and also indicates the new direction of multidimensional mediation development in the overall picture of frequent international intercourse. [3]

3. International: The establishment of China-Arab Commercial Mediation Centre

China-Arab Commercial Mediation Centre was initiated and jointly founded by China Council for the Promotion of International Trade, Lebanon Mediation Centre, Jordan Amman Chamber of Commerce and Cairo International Arbitration Centre. The centre is set up to help resolve the increasingly critical economic and trade conflicts as the trade and investment volume between China and Arab states expands. With more application of joint mediation, it will help protect China's and Arab states' enterprises from business risks in trade, resolve commercial disputes and promote trade investment cooperation. [4]

4. The establishment and development of Commercial Mediation Organisations in Free Trade Areas such as Fujian, Tianjin, Guangdong, etc.

Driven by the country's "Belt and Road" strategy, all regions have attached great emphasis to the construction and development of free trade areas. It has been put on the agenda to build a multidimensional dispute resolution platform and to create a healthy legal environment for commercial parties, which necessitates the formulation of commercial mediation mechanisms. In 2013, Shanghai Cultural and Creative Industries Legal Service Platform and Intellectual Property Mediation Centre/ Shanghai Economic and Trade Centre for the Mediation of Intellectual Property Rights Specialized Committee were established in China (Shanghai) free trade experimental area. Right after that on 6 June 2015, Xiamen International Commercial Arbitration Court and Xiamen International Commercial Mediation Centre were officially founded in Xiamen District of China (Fujian) free trade experimental area. It attracted a group of arbitrators and mediators, and professional steering committee members from Taiwan, which shows advantage in free trade area commercial dispute resolution when Taiwan is involved. [5] In November 2015, Tianjin International Trade Promotion Committee and China Tianjin International Economic and Financial Arbitration Centre delegated professional mediators to Tianjin Binhai New Area People's court to help solve commercial disputes in a flexible and effective way by playing to their strengths of specialization and internationalization. [6] At the same time free trade areas in Guangdong and other provinces have also accelerated their construction of international commercial mediation mechanisms.

---

3 Xinhuanet: "Yuan Guoqiang: Hong Kong's Provision of Cross-border Dispute Resolution Service by the Advantage of 'One Country, Two Systems'", http://news.xinhuanet.com/gangao/2015-12/09/c_1117411682.htm, accessed on 25 January 2016.

4 Xinhuanet Ningxia Channel: "The Establishment of China-Arab Commercial Mediation Centre in Ningxia", http://news.xinhuanet.com/local/2015-09/10/c_1116527206.htm, accessed on 29 January 2016.

5 People's Daily Online: "The Opening Ceremony of Xiamen International Commercial Arbitration Court and Xiamen International Commercial Mediation Center in Xiamen District, Fujian", http://fj.people.com.cn/n/2015/0607/c337006-25148682.html, accessed on 5 March 2016.

6 Enorth: "The Start-up of the Litigation and Mediation Platform in Free Trade Area", http://news.enorth.com.cn/system/2015/11/06/030614177.shtml, accessed on 5 March 2016.

C. Changes in the Construction of Mechanisms

In the construction of mechanisms, all kinds of dispute resolutions tend to work in an increasingly obvious way of advantages complementation and interface, with the mediation becoming especially closely related to litigation and arbitration. This satisfies the need of the concerned party to enforce the mediation results, making mediation more appealing to the society while raising its credibility. Neutral evaluation mechanism, as a new kind of multidimensional dispute resolution mechanism, has also attracted the attention of legal professionals in resolving disputes.

1. The establishment of a perfect interface system of lawsuits and mediation mechanism to support the mechanism construction

The implement of the reform of lawsuit registration system has lowered the threshold of lawsuit filing and further motivated the concerned party's protective consciousness of the right to sue. In the real situation where the multidimensional dispute resolution mechanism is not perfected yet, the recognition in public is low, and multidimensional mediation's advantages is not as obvious as litigation, there is a significant increase of lawsuits at people's courts at all levels. Take Beijing as an example, there was 601747 cases filed in the city courts in 2015, with a year-on-year growth of 136648 cases and a growth rate of 29.4%, reaching a record high in both the increment and the increase. Courts at all levels, especially in medium and large cities including Beijing and Shanghai, have encountered critical conflicts between more cases and few personnel, too much pressure have been placed on judges, which inevitably results in the impact on trial quality and efficiency. To cope with the overloaded trial task, internal potentials exploration and trial management mechanism improvement can only solve part of the problem. Increasing the court staffing also could not meet the needs in the long run. Looking forward from the whole picture, the key to solving the problem fundamentally lies in the development of multidimensional dispute resolution mechanism, which will muster social strengths to solve disputes jointly while diverse and defuse disputes outside of litigation. On the eve of the day to implement the registration system reform, Supreme People's Court called a meeting of national courts multidimensional dispute resolution mechanism promotion in Meishan, Sichuan. The meeting called on people's courts to play the leading, pushing and protective role in the construction of multidimensional dispute resolution mechanism, in order to build an interface system of lawsuits and mediation platform with powerful functions, adequate resources and in-place services, and to establish an interface system of lawsuits and mediation mechanism with various forms and standardized operations. It also addressed the necessity to give full play to the professional and technical advantages of the experts in the building of the special mediator team, to enhance the guidance to industrial mediation organisations in relevant fields, to strengthen judicial safeguard while enlarging mediator team and establishing fund guarantee system. The meeting consolidated the role and responsibilities of court in promoting multidimensional mediation mechanism and pointed out the emphasis attached to the building of industrial mediation organisations and teams of professional mediators, playing a significant guiding role in the promotion of commercial mediation.

Based on the lawsuit registration system, courts have shown an urgent need for multidimensional mediation and vigorously promoted it, along with an increasing need to deal with commercial disputes in the economic downturn. In 2015, commercial mediation organisations and courts cooperated in an active way by jointly seeking to improve the interface system of lawsuits and mediation mechanism, and establishing various forms of interface system of lawsuits and mediation in fields such as insurance disputes, disputes over protection of consumer rights and interests, intellectual property disputes, financial disputes, securities and futures disputes, etc. Among all the fields, the establishment of insurance disputes interface system of lawsuits and mediation mechanism draws the most attention. On 29 September 2015, the Supreme People's Court and China Insurance Regulatory Commission (CIRC) jointly called the "National Insurance Disputes Litigation and Mediation Interface Mechanism Construction Promotion Meeting". The meeting summarized the experience learned from the pilot experience of insurance litigation and mediation interface starting from 2013 and further promoted the experience. It also established 12 courts and 12 regional offices of CIRC as demonstration units.[7] Besides, China Council for the Promotion of International Trade and its branches in Beijing, Tianjin, Suzhou, etc. have been actively communicating with local courts and have set up several commercial disputes interface system of lawsuits and mediation platforms. In this way, the role of courts in leading, promoting and protecting the construction of multidimensional disputes resolution mechanism has become increasingly significant.

2. The prominent advantage of the interface system of arbitration and mediation in the commercial disputes resolution mechanism

At present, the mediation agreement presided over by people's mediation organisations or industrial and specialized mediation organisations is only endowed with contract validity by law. To expand civil mediation's effect in dispute resolution, *Provisions of the Judicial Recognition Procedure on the People's Mediation Agreement* (Fa Shi [2011] No. 5) was issued by the Supreme People's Court on 21 March 2015. The provision has placed clear obligations on the judicial recognition procedure and its effect on the people's mediation agreement. It solved the problem that people's mediation agreement does not have the enforcement effect through the interface system of litigation and mediation. After 2012 when such system was established in the form of the basic law by *Civil Procedure Law of the People's Republic of China*, in 2015, *Interpretation of the Supreme People's Court on the Application of the Civil Procedure Law of the People's Republic of China* further expanded the judicial recognition case scope from people's mediation agreement to the agreements reached and presided over by administrative organs, commercial mediation organisations, industrial mediation organisations and other mediation organisations with mediation function.[8]

Inspired by the judicial recognition system of mediation agreement, arbitration institutions started to notice the benefits of the interface of arbitration and mediation in the process of independent commercial mediation. South China International Economic and Trade Arbitration Commission (also known as Shenzhen Court of International Arbitration) has already made a

---

7 CIRC's website: "The National Insurance Disputes Litigation and Mediation Interface Mechanism Construction Promotion Meeting called by the Supreme People's Court and China Insurance Regulatory Commission", http://www.circ.gov.cn/web/site0/tab5207/info3975656.htm, accessed on 25 January 2016.

8 Shen Deyong ed., The Understanding and Adaptation of the Judicial Interpretation of the Supreme People's Court in the Civil Procedure Law (Part 2), The People's Court press: 2015, 3, 1st edition, pp. 923.

beneficial attempt in this regards. If the mediation is successful, the person concerned could apply to arbitration institution for accelerated approval procedure, which will refer to the mediation agreement and make the arbitration award in accordance with the law, thus endowing the agreement with enforcement effect. The advantage of the combination of mediation and arbitration becomes clearer in the resolution of commercial disputes concerning foreign affairs. Early in 1987, China has joined the *Convention on the Recognition and Enforcement of Foreign Arbitral Awards* (also known as *New York Convention*), which placed emphasis on the recognition and execution problems in dealing with foreign arbitral awards and pointed out that the arbitral awards by any member state will be recognized and executed in other member states. [9] Till now, 156 states have joined the convention, which is very attractive to the clients of commercial disputes concerning foreign affairs. The interface system of mediation and arbitration positively combines the advantages of the two fields, making up for mediation's deficiencies in effect while improving the attractiveness and credibility of mediation, thus expanding the path of disputes resolution.

3. The application of neutral evaluation mechanism in multidimensional mediation at the early period of civil and commercial disputes

Local courts actively seek to build a neutral evaluation mechanism as they promote multidimensional mediation. People's court of Yuexiu District, Guangzhou, with the cooperation with Guangdong University of Technology, has hired professional teachers of the specialty of law to assume the position of neutral assessor, who, by playing their respective professional advantages, will help clients evaluate the litigation risk, make the legal relations clear for the clients, sort out the dispute resolution, and find a more effective relief, which provides a new option for the effective resolution of civil and commercial disputes. [10] Besides, Dongguan Second People's Court, Fujian Hanjiang District People's Court, Xiamen Haicang District People's Court, Anhui Hanshan County People's Court, and Meishan City People's Court of Sichuan have established a counterpart of specialized evaluation system to deal with the difficulties in medical disputes, traffic accident liability disputes, disputes involving real estate, product quality disputes, etc. by offering professional suggestions from professionals and helping the clients in getting a better understanding of the case, the litigation risk and cost. On the basis of neutral evaluation, the client can then decide on the way of dispute resolution with reasons. China's neutral evaluation system is still at the initial exploration stage where it has not been recognized widely and not being paid enough attention to yet. With a narrow application range, the system has not been attached enough importance to as it has effect in promoting judicial justice. Besides, the evaluation subjects not only come from a broad range and are inexperienced in law, but also intervene unexpectedly during the process and there is a lack of procedure standardization. Therefore, the concepts need transformation and the operation proce-

---

9 Sina Court Channel: "The Cross-border Mediation from Hong Kong", http://finance.sina.com.cn/sf/news/2015-12-19/151814072.html, accessed on 26 January 2016.

10 Shang Chao website: "The Pilot Work of Neutral Evaluation Mechanism in Civil and Commercial Disputes by Yuexiu Court", http://www.999ws.com/dzsw/201601/20/5192.htm, accessed on 6 March 2016.

dure still has a large room to improve. [11]

D. Professional and Standardized Development of the Mediator Team Building with Frequent Communication and Training Activities

1. The active and promoting role of Guangdong, Hong Kong and Macao Commercial Mediation alliance in the commercial mediation cooperation, communication and mediator training between the Mainland and Hong Kong and Macao

At the end of June 2015, the first Guangdong, Hong Kong and Macao Commercial Mediation Forum was held. The forum, themed "Cross-border Commercial Mediation and Free Trade Area Legal Environment", was attended by responsible persons, legal experts and businessman in charge of 14 member units from the mainland, Hong Kong and Macao. The participants exchanged their mediation experience and mediation system, and have reached a consensus that Guangdong, Hong Kong and Macao Commercial Mediation Alliance could give a full play to its platform strength of "mediation plus arbitration", providing service to the "Belt and Road" strategy. [12] On 22 November 2015, with the duration of 44 hours and only 20 trainees, the Guangdong, Hong Kong and Macao Commercial Mediation Alliance's Cross-border Qualification Recognition Commercial Mediation Training was held at South China International Economic and Trade Arbitration Commission (also known as the Shenzhen Court of International Arbitration). However, the small-sized training has raised great response. Featuring the mediator-training model introduced from Hong Kong, the training combines the mediation content of the mainland and Hong Kong, carrying out a mediator joint training and qualification recognition among Guangdong, Hong Kong and Macao. With more than twenty years of development, Hong Kong's mediation training and assessment model is rather advanced in Asia and around the world. The trainees consist mostly of lawyers and responsible persons of chamber of commerce in Guangdong. A brand new mediation concept and a more practical training model will infuse fresh energy to the mainland commercial mediation. [13]

Furthermore, Zhuhai Arbitration Commission, Hengqin New Area Management Committee and Hong Kong Joint Mediation Line Office jointly held the "Diversified Dispute Settlement Mechanism of Free Trade Area and the Practice of Commercial Mediation in the Zhuhai, Macao and Hong Kong" seminar. Combining the commercial activities in Zhuhai, Macao and Hong Kong, the seminar addressed the legal constructionin free trade areas and the small-to-medium enterprises commercial disputes resolution practice.

2. The responsibilities of developed areas' governments in cultivating commercial mediators

From the end of 2014 to the end of 2015, Shanghai Municipal Commission of Commerce

---

11 Jiang Heping, and Huang Qi, "The Development of Neutral Employment Mechanism of Civil and Commercial Disputes in China", Law Application, 2015, Vol. 7, pp. 22-27.

12 China Economy website: "The Discussion of Cross-border Commercial Mediation in Free Trade Area", http://district.ce.cn/newarea/roll/201507/01/t20150701_5813360.shtml, accessed on 26 January 2016.

13 Sina Court Channel: "The Cross-border Mediation from Hong Kong", http://finance.sina.com.cn/sf/news/2015-12-19/151814072.html, accessed on 26 January 2016.

carried out the "100 Talents Cultivation Plan for the Mediation of Commercial Disputes". By holding the "Seminar on Commercial Dispute Mediation" and a series of "International Trade and Business Mediator Senior Seminar", the plan cultivated a group of high-quality professional commercial dispute mediation talents who are equipped with mediation theory and mediation procedure knowledge and practice skills for the business field and key industries.[14] The fact that governments have taken the initiative to assume the responsibility of cultivating commercial mediator indicates that governments have transformed their concepts of social governance and fully used social strengths to assist social governance and resolve conflicts. It is a beneficial attempt to realize the central social governance capability and system modernization.

3. Shanghai Kai Sheng Commercial Professional Mediation Qualification Training Centre's active exploration of the commercial mediation personnel training and qualification certification system

To develop more professional talents for commercial mediation, approved by Shanghai Municipal Education Commission at the end of 2013, Shanghai Kai Sheng Commercial Professional Mediation Qualification Training Centre was established by Shanghai Economic and Trade Mediation Centre and Shanghai Jiao Tong University. It became China's first marketing operative non-governmental institution of mediator skill training. Initiated by the Division of the Supreme People's Court and compiled by professor Ji Weidong, Professor Mike Palmer and Vice Dean Zou Bihua, etc., the nation's first mediator skill training textbook that not only meets the international standards, but also includes our own Chinese characteristics was released. So far the training centre has successfully held four mediation skill trainings with more than 100 trainees from across the country attending the training. The trainees include court judges at all levels who work in the interface system of lawsuits and mediation, lawyers, corporate legal officers and working personnel engaged in import and export trade. Upon successful completion of the course, the training centre will award every trainee the "Chinese Commercial Mediator Certificate".[15]

III. Typical Cases of Commercial Mediation

In 2015, all commercial mediation organisations applied their professions and advantages to actively expand the channel in receiving cases. By employing their professional advantage and further playing the role of absorbing and resolving disputes, such organisations have successfully solved a series of cases.

The Mediation Centre of Beijing Arbitration Commission still went on in the mode of market-oriented operation in 2015, with certain proportion of mediation fees charged. In the situation where all kinds of commercial mediation organisations are emerging and the competition of mediation market has intensified, the centre insists on its professional mediation service to attract commercial subjects, and promoting the sustainable development of independent media-

---

14 Shanghai Municipal Commission of Commerce: "100 Talents Cultivation Plan for the Mediation of Commercial Disputes Fulfilled", http://www.scofcom.gov.cn/swdt/239376.htm, accessed on 29 January 2016.

15 Wtoutiao: "[Reform Forefront] Shanghai Economic and Trade Mediation Centre: The Establishment of Commercial Dispute Resolution Mediation", http://www.wtoutiao.com/p/s10CjC.html, accessed on 6 March 2016.

tion, resulting in a great increase of the cases in its types and volume. In a mediation case of the dispute over naming right, the mediator fully showed his professionalism substantively and procedurally. Substantively, the mediator accurately grasped the real requirements of the two parties behind their stands. By presenting a third people's understanding of the facts and the law, the mediator helped clients to understand the situation correctly without misreading the facts, so as to find overlaps in the two parties' mediation plans and to further promote reconciliation. Procedurally, the mediator held the pace of the mediation accurately. By reaching the agreement of the parties to the arrangement of the procedure, the mediator eased the opposition of the clients and resolved to ensure an agreement about substance problems. The professional value of mediation was fully recognized by clients. Although there were mediation fees incurred, the number was far lower than that of arbitration fees. Clients greatly welcomed the low cost. In another complex and controversial case of construction contract dispute, the mediation centre first arranged professional mediators of the construction industry to help the dispute resolution and made adequate and detailed preparation to win the clients' trust with its professional inquiry. Secondly, the mediators helped the two parties sort the central issues and clarified the facts, industry rules and laws respectively. Thirdly, the acceptable mediation scope for two parties around the dispute focus was settled by a multidimensional mediation way. Although the case was not successfully mediated at the end and entered into arbitration proceedings, issues of the dispute were made clear and the content and scope of the dispute were narrowed through mediation, which greatly saved the costs of the follow-up dispute resolution and won the recognition of the clients for specialized mediation service.

In 2015, China Internet Association Mediation Centre ("Internet Mediation Centre") successfully mediated more than 500 cases of concerning online intellectual property disputes, online transaction disputes, unfair competition disputes, etc., including one case which concerns an intense contradiction about protection of group consumer rights that involved almost 50 persons. As it involved the problem of food safety, the case drew a wide range of social attention and exerted great influence on the society. Internet Mediation Centre was entrusted by court to mediate. In the mediation process, the mediation centre worked closely with the court's full-time mediation judge to communicate again and again with both parties. On one hand, by informing the clients the litigation risk and cost, they offered both parties the guidance to actively agree on the mediation. On the other hand, they patiently guided the e-commerce business person to think from other people's perspective and to focus on the long-term benefit and business reputation protection. The largest highlight of this successfully mediated case was that the judge fully participated in the mediation and offered detailed guidance. The judge made full use of his rich experience accumulated as a judicial officer and the advantage of being familiar with legal rules. The mediation has achieved good social effects. It is a helpful and practical attempt of the interface system of lawsuits and mediation practice. Another entrusted case by court was about copyright infringement of audio and video works. Since the antagonism between the two parties was serious, mediator firstly communicated unilaterally with the client to understand the real requirement and previous related disputes behind the presented proposition. Secondly, by communicating patiently and in detail, the mediator tied to filter out the emotional elements and help the two parties return to the track of mediation. Thirdly, focusing on the substantial dispute of the two parties, the mediator presented a resolution plan acceptable to both sides, and contacted the entrusting court to reassure the clients. Finally they reached a mediation agreement presided over by judge, and the dispute was successfully resolved by nolle prosequi.

In this case of mediation, the mediator followed the case step by step by grasping the real interest requirements of the concerned parties in time. He actively managed to remove the mediation obstacles brought by the distrust between the two sides. This fully displayed mediation's advantage of large negotiation space and the capability to resolve the dispute thoroughly.

By "seeking common ground while reserving differences", China Council for the Promotion of International Trade Xiamen Mediation Centre successfully mediated a case of disputes over the international sale of goods in just 5 hours. The applicant, an importer of canned food in Africa, signed the sales contract of goods which was labelled as some canned seafood, with the respondent, a domestic enterprise. When confirming the food sample, the applicant pointed out that the sample flavour was different compared to before, so he proposed to terminate the contract with a refund of the advance payment for more than 10,000 dollars. The two parties could not reach an agreement and were caught up in disputes. In the process of mediation, the mediator firstly tried to persuade the two parties to maintain the trade contract relation by suggesting that the applicant offer another opportunity to the respondent to provide the sample again, so as to ensure the contract relations intact, but this suggestion turned out be to infeasible due to time constraints. On the transformation of idea, the mediator suggested to terminate the contract on the basis that the applicant shall compensate the respondent for its costs incurred in carrying out the contract. But the amount of compensation was not recognized and accepted by the applicant, who thought it in the lack of evidence. To resolve the dispute, the mediator further presented another plan that the respondent shall return the rest of the advance payment after the deduction of its incurred costs in carrying out the contract, and the applicant was suggested to file a civil action separately on the decision of the amount of the incurred costs which the respondent claimed in carrying out the contract. A multidimensional mediation resolution acceptable for both sides was thus formed and was a successful close to this international trade dispute that was rendered impossible to solve at first. Such mediation of "shelving disputes while seeking common ground and solving the problem by multidimensional resolution" shows the excellent skills of the mediator, and indicates again that the professionalism of mediators is the key to the success of mediation and the vitality of commercial mediation.[16]

Though such cases were collected from different mediation organisations and were of different case types, they have shown that more and more significance has been placed on the professionalism of China's commercial mediation. Moreover, there has been some qualified mediators with good legal cultivation and mediation skills coming into the picture, who have set examples in practice. In the meantime, mediation organisations have fully employed the interface system of lawsuits and mediation while mediators have been working cooperatively with judges in mediation. Such practice has enhanced the authority of mediation and achieved good results in reality.

---

16 China Council for the Promotion of International Trade: "The Success of International Trade Dispute Mediation", ed. by Guo Tao of Commercial Law Service Center of CCPIT, http://www.ccpit.org/Contents/Channel_3388/2015/0910/487533/content_487533.htm, accessed on 30 January 2016.

IV. Hot Issues

A. The Promotion of the Legislation on Setting Mediation as a Procedural Prerequisite

In the Opinion 60 of CCCPC, it is addressed in "III. The Promotion of the Healthy Development of Various Types of Non-Litigation Dispute Resolution, 8) The Standardization and Enhancement of Mediation" that "courts at all level shall actively explore the previous mediation case types and promote the pilot implementation of setting mediation as procedural prerequisite at grass-roots courts with conditions when dealing with the cases suited for mediation, including family disputes, disputes over the adjacent relations, petty debts disputes, labour disputes, consumer rights disputes, traffic accident disputes, etc." It demonstrates a fundamental change of CCCPC in its core concept of mediation, which has a very important guiding significance. It marks as an opening in the policy of the setting the mediation as procedural prerequisite at grass-roots court levels, and indicates that the legislation of the procedural prerequisite of mediation has been put on the agenda.

At present, China has not established a compulsory mediation system. In this situation, the institutional advantages of non-litigation mediation have been greatly weakened by China's low litigation fee system, the unique time limit system, the developed judge mediation in litigation, and the certainty and authority of judicial judgment. Most parties who have sued to the court are unwilling to resort to multidimensional mediation. There are "litigation explosions" in large and medium cities, making the courts unable to handle the overloaded cases; mediation organisations of every industry have actively established more than one lawsuit and mediation interface platforms with the courts, and have set up mediation procedure rules. But due to the lack of case resources, those platforms are impossible to be put into practice. Since the reform of registration system started, all kinds of cases have flooded into courts without limitation, which further enhances the litigation consciousness of the clients to protect their rights, and weakens the attractiveness of non-litigation mediation, including commercial mediation. It also explains the decrease of cases in some industrial specialized commercial mediation organisations.

The reason why legislation is so serious about compulsory mediation is that pre litigation compulsory mediation violates the voluntary principle of mediation, and contradicts the mediation procedure's nature of equal consultation and participation according to previous mainstream academic viewpoints. So, to establish mediation as the prerequisite of litigation will impose limitation on the right of judgment of the parties.[17] However, this is not the case. On one hand, litigation system cannot deal with all the cases, nor can it solve all of them effectively, especially certain types of disputes. Therefore, simple emphasis on the protection of the right of judgment of the parties will fall far from the original intention of the judicial pursuit of justice and count against the effective achievement of the judicial function. On the other hand, compulsory mediation is established only to regulate the mediation procedures, while the par-

---

17 Li De'en: "On the Legal Theory and Practice of Compulsory Mediations", Journal of JiangxiI University of Finance and Economics, 2009, Vol. 4, pp. 109.

ties are entitled to decide whether they want to reach conciliation and what the detailed mediation contract should include. Compulsory mediation is not established to deprive the parties' rights of judgment, but merely to make certain procedure restrictions to specific types of disputes, which will purify the judicial function of the court, realize the reasonable allocation of social public resources and fully exemplify the effectiveness and value of the other social dispute resolution resources. Therefore, it is just and reasonable to place mediation as the necessary procedure before certain specific types of disputes enter the proceedings of litigation.

But at the same time, the author also noticed that it is still possible for compulsory mediation before litigation to delay the parties' obtainment of judicial relief. So it is necessary to conduct further study and research, and make an in-depth theoretical study of its nature, organisation form, applicable dispute types, legal effects and its link with litigation procedure, etc., so as to provide a sufficient reference basis for legislation.

Combined with the practice of court to mediate before litigation and drawing lessons from the rule of law developed countries' judicial ADR experience, an attempt of the mechanism design can be applied. Firstly, compulsory mediation before litigation should be defined as quasi-judicial mediation in nature and should be carried out under strict supervision and guidance of the court, in order to guarantee that the mediation will proceed according to the law and the procedures. And this would prevent the violation of the parties' right to seek judicial relief in a timely manner due to the arbitrary nature of the mediation procedure. Secondly, compulsory mediation before litigation should be conducted by institutions including the multidimensional mediation team established by the courts of justice, organisations that have established joint mediation mechanisms with courts, and institutions of quasi-judicial power like labour dispute arbitration institution, traffic accident processing institution, or other institutions with adjudication power. Thirdly, regarding the case type, some suitable disputes through mediation including disputes over marriage and family inheritance, adjacent relations, property heating, labour, road traffic accident damage compensation, etc., are suggested to be included in the scope of compulsory mediation before litigation. Fourthly, regarding the mediation agreement reached by compulsory mediation before litigation, such agreement will be recognized by the judiciary and the effectiveness of compulsory execution will be enforced accordingly after it is confirmed to be in conformity with the provisions of law by the court. In the meanwhile, as a supporting mechanism for compulsory mediation before litigation, the punishment mechanism for refusing to mediate is also necessary for the promotion of multidimensional mediation and requires research and promotion as well. [18]

B. The Construction of Mediator Training, Test and Qualification System

To meet the realistic needs for professional and socially developed mediators, theorists have also begun to pay attention to the mediator team training, evaluation, as well as the mediator qualification certification issues. The official account of multidimensional dispute resolution mechanism on Wechat ("SIFAADR") has released one article written by Lv Zheying—

---

18 Zhai Jingmin and yang Yan: "The Breakthrough of Entrusted Mediation System in Filing Stage—The Sample Case of Beijing Court's Entrusted Mediation System in Filing Stage", China's mediation system and the best mediation case, 2015, 11, 1st edition.

"The Revival of Hong Kong Mediator Accreditation System", which presented a detailed introduction of the mediation training standard and evaluation mechanism of the Hong Kong mediator accreditation system. Hong Kong Mediation Accreditation Association Limited ("HKMAAL") is currently the only mediator qualifications assessment agency in Hong Kong. Concerning mediation training specification, the successions and changes of HKMAAL are as follows: 1) the prerequisite for admission. Whether there should be conditions for admission, including the requirements for a bachelor degree or the lawyer qualification, or certain professional background. The mainstream holds the opinion that the applicant does not need any professional degree for admission because there is no proof that a person who holds a certain college degree will be more competent to be a mediator. Such core skills of being a mediator as listening carefully, speaking fairly and creating benefit of both parties, and possessing the ability to deal with the complex sequence of events, have little relations with a college degree. One of the principles of HKMAAL in qualification evaluation is to encourage more people who are interested in mediation to participate in the industry in order to prevent the formation of a small circle from opening only to the industry practitioners. However, at the last stage of mediator qualification application where the training courses are completed and tests have been passed, the applicant needs to submit a proof of education or equivalent working experience. Therefore, the assessment of the qualifications of the mediator will not completely abandon the element of degree or equivalent work experience, thus making the threshold of mediator qualification equal to that of other profession qualifications in Hong Kong. 2) Training courses. There are a lot of factors that can affect the mediator's quality, including training, experience, personality and style. A qualified mediator is expected to think in-depth of the mediation theories and endeavour to improve him/her psychologically, mentally and in knowledge. After the establishment of HKMAA, few changes have been made to the mediation course content and the 40-hour standard courses still remain. It is an attempt to unify the evaluation criteria. Only by being practical and feasible, and also widely accepted by the public, can mediation get support from all the fields.

With respect to the assessment mechanism. In Hong Kong, before the establishment of the HKMAA, different institutions used their own score forms respectively to evaluate the performance of the candidates in role-play. The score form was in the form of a list, splitting the mediation into several stages according to the enhancement mediation mode. Listed on the form were the ability coefficients which a mediator is supposed to display, including survey, empathy, creativity, problem-solving skills, persuasion, speech ability, the ability to decentralize attention, the ability to control the interaction between the two sides, actual knowledge, etc. There was a rating score with 1 standing for excellent, 5 for unqualified. After the establishment of HKMAA, the previous score form was replaced by form 1. The difference of form 1 was to change the original 1-5 level rating to 4 clear pointers: level 1 stood for qualified, level 2 stood for in need of progress, level 3 was lower than the average, and level 4 was unqualified. The new evaluation criteria indicated the core competencies, objectives, and the small skills of each phase of the mediation. Besides, by using role-play as field assessment, the examiner can make an accurate assessment of the mediator's performance, and the case used for assessment and the arrangement of the roles in the case were also worth studying.[19]

The reason why the author made such a detailed introduction about this article of Hong Kong mediator training and assessment system written by Lv Zheying lies in the fact that Hong Kong's training and evaluation system is rather advanced in the world. This effective and practical training and evaluation system of the mediator has contributed to the fast development of Hong Kong's multidimensional mediation. It is a growth not only outstanding in local social governance, but also influential along the China coast, with the establishment of Guangdong, Hong Kong and Macao Mediation Alliance and its performance in 2015 fully illustrates this point. The training and evaluation of mediators in China are in the initial stage, with a lack of unified training and evaluation system even in large cities like Beijing and Shanghai. All industrial mediation organisations hold the training and evaluation on their own. Also, their training courses are mainly focused on class teaching which lack of interaction and practical operation. What is more, the evaluation criteria are loose. More attention is paid to previous work experience. It has been clearly pointed out in Opinion 60 that we need to "promote the establishment of a professional and socialized mediator team, establish the occupational level evaluation system of the mediator team, improve the training management mechanism of the mediator team, strengthen social work knowledge training and the construction of professional ethics, regulate the behaviour of mediation, improve the level of mediation, and encourage the development of specialized and professional mediation training institutions". Therefore, to achieve this goal as soon as possible, it is very important to learn from the more developed mediators training and evaluation mechanism of places like Hong Kong and the United States, which will help to train a group of professional mediators and meet the demands of the community in a relatively short period of time, so as to avoid detours and to facilitate the development of mediation in China.

C. The Funding Guarantee for Commercial Mediation Organisations

Considering the circumstances in Beijing, insufficient fund can be regarded as one of the major difficulties that almost all the commercial mediation organisations have encountered in their development in common. According to different funding resources, there are two different modes of operation of commercial mediation organisations: government supporting mode and marketing operation mode. The mediation organisations supported by the Government are included in the scope of the people's mediation, like People's Mediation Committee of China Internet Association, which offers free mediation service to people by relying on government funds to support the maintenance of its operation. On the other hand, due to the fact that non-litigation mediation charges is still unacceptable for the community and the lack of standardization and authority, most industrial specialized mediation organisations in the marketing operation mode have limited case resources and are struggling to exist by relying on mediation service. Some industry associations or running corporation state clearly that at present, the concerns of mediation service focus more on serving the association members and the community, and expanding the service scope, instead of achieving any profit from it.

---

19 Lv Zheying: "The Revival of Hong Kong Mediator Accreditation System", source: wechat official account SIFAADR, firstly published by the journal of Negotiation, accessed on 31 January 2016.

The author believed that in the early stage of the development of multidimensional mediation, the support to the pattern of government buying services is necessary for the development of all the multidimensional mediation organisations. But looking in the long run, the disputes should be categorized into different groups: for those disputes concerning people's livelihood including marriage and family disputes, neighbourhood disputes, residential land disputes, medical disputes, etc. , the resolution should resort to the government support to provide low cost mediation service; for commercial disputes over purchasing, selling, lending, insurance, securities and futures, etc. , the resolution should resort to the marketing operation. To tackle the issue that non-litigation mediation charging is not recognized and accepted by commercial subjects, court, as an important force behind the multidimensional mediation development. We could coordinate actively with the government to come up with a solution, such as to transfer part of the litigation fees to the industrial specialized organisations. For instance, China (Shanghai) Free Trade Area Court has already made some attempts in this regard. It only charged 40% of the litigation fees for the cases entrusted to commercial mediation organisations and transferred 20% of the charged fees to the mediation organisation. This conduct not only encouraged the parties to resort to non-litigation mediation, but also, to some degree, solved the commercial mediation organisation's lack of funds. Some local government departments have also established docking mechanism with mediation organisations and granted the organisation certain amount of mediation fees from the special fund set up by the government for those successfully mediated cases through the way of "taking the case to make up".

D. The Development of Online Dispute Resolution System

In today's world where the internet exerts great influence on people's life and work, the traditional "face to face" dispute resolution could not meet people's need for a convenient, efficient, low-cost dispute resolution any more. Since the online dispute resolution system overcomes the obstacles of time and space, and realizes an indoor dispute resolution. It has drawn attention and importance from every party, and has shown a strong momentum of development and vitality. Under the guidance of the country's strategy of "Internet plus", many domestic e-commerce platforms have established online dispute resolution system and have resolved a massive amount of disputes between consumers and e-commerce retailers. Some courts also started to make attempts on setting up online filing and mediation system, which provided convenience to the parties and was expected to guide more clients to resolve disputes by non-litigation mediation. So it would help to ease the prominent contradiction that there were "more cases and few personnel" in the court. Based on the realistic demand of an improved interface system of lawsuits and mediation, Beijing courts developed an entrust mediation network system, in order to realize the informatization of the entrusted mediation data transmission and recording between the court and people's mediation organisations or industrial mediation organisations. It would improve the timeliness of communication and the standardized management of the court's litigation and mediation interface work. But looking from the current situation, information network technology remains rather limited in its application in the work of litigation and mediation interface. The communication, contact, case export and import between court and other social organisations in the litigation and mediation interface system are still in the manual form, which is disadvantageous to the standardized management of the work of litigation and mediation interface, which decreases the efficiency of the interface, thus impacting on the attractiveness of the system to the parties.

Judge Long Fei, from the Reform Office of the Supreme Court, introduced in "Six Development Trends of Internet plus Dispute Resolution Mechanism" about the development of ODR (Online Dispute Resolution) in China and abroad, and pointed out the six development trends of ODR in the future. She maintained that besides e-commercial disputes, more disputes types should be included in ODR; and that the power of the internet should be exerted effectively on the dispute resolution and the combination of multiple fields; and that the construction of ODR should pay great attention to the reasonable resources allocation and sharing between the legal and the non-legal, the official and the non-official, the domestic and the international; and that the system should be able to offer more effective dispute resolution service, being effective not only in the approaches, but also in facts identification, evidence collection, contact and interface with the judicial office for the parties; and that e-commerce enterprises should be encouraged to form a sound corporate trust mark and reliable plan, in order to promote the self-regulation of the e-commerce industry, while in setting up a ODR website, there should be established ODR regulations and standards to define the subject qualification, practitioner's qualification, training and selection of employees, the establishment of social evaluation system, reward and punishment and withdrawal mechanism, etc., and to define the charging standards and the legal liabilities of website fraud, breach of contract and tort, etc. to keep the neutral, impartial and efficient procedure rules of ODR intact; and that in order to enhance people's trust of ODR, a set of more common, authoritative and neutral dispute resolution rules should be established, including the rules of procedure, ODR mediator or judge neutrality guarantee mechanism, evaluation system and evaluation mechanism, training mechanism, implementation procedures of ODR results, etc.; and that the country should ensure the legal authority of ODR and its service by laws and regulations, and make specific operation rules to support ODR system take effect. Combining the current problems that the online dispute resolution system have encountered, Judge Long Fei accurately analysed its future development trend, which played a very enlightening and guiding role in the development of various dispute resolution institutions including government, court and e-commerce enterprises.[20]

V. Conclusion and Future Development

In 2015, the commercial mediation has showed a development trend of "vertical and horizontal combination": vertically, some industrial mediation organisations went deep inside the industry, playing an increasingly important role in the resolution of disputes between organisation members, member and other social members; horizontally, there not only emerged mediation organisations' own self- disciplined industry association like the Multidimensional Mediation Development Association of Beijing, the substantive cooperation between domestic and overseas mediation organisations was also enhanced. Commercial mediation organisation has attached more and more emphasis to the specialized mediation strength that will provide professional legal service to the community. And as a mediation approach closely connected with the

---

20 Long Fei: "Six Development Trends of Internet plus Dispute Resolution Mechanism", source: wechat official account SIFAADR, accessed on 31 January 2016.

economic society, such organisation has gradually displayed its attractiveness and vitality. But undeniably, commercial mediation still faces difficulties including the unbalance of regional development, less specialized mediator team, limited case resources, charging difficulty, and the inability to support the marketing operation. For those difficulties and problems, the reasons are also multiple, including the lack of legislative support, unreasonableness of the design of the judicial system that has affected the multidimensional mediation mechanism to play its comparative advantage, and the lack of professionalism and social recognition of the commercial mediation itself.

Looking into the future, under the guidance of the multidimensional dispute resolution construction policy promoted vigorously by CCCPC, the external environment of commercial mediation is believed to be further optimized. It is known that some courts have already been working actively to promote the procedural prerequisite of mediation under the guidance of Opinion 60. Initially the procedural prerequisite of mediation will be carried out in the cases of disputes suited for mediation including marriage and family and inheritance disputes, road traffic accident liability compensation disputes, property heating contract disputes, small business loan disputes, etc. Procedural prerequisite of mediation breaks through the voluntary principle of mediation in the application phase, and enlarges the space of use for judicial ADR. In this way, it is expected that a significant amount of disputes will be split into multidimensional mediation organisations, and will allow more adequate case resources for commercial mediation organisations. Besides, multidimensional dispute resolution mechanism is included in the system of social governance, where the government's transformations of its governance concept and approach have also provided a good opportunity for the development of the commercial mediation organisations. In the future, the government will provide more funding and policy support for multidimensional mediation, and will resolve disputes in more fields by the way of government purchasing service. Regarding the internal construction of commercial mediation organisations, the path of the professional development of the mediator team has been very clear, while it becomes vital to achieve a unified, standardized and orderly development. The developed commercial mediation organisations should learn from other region's advanced system and practice, and establish a set of a complete, rigorous training and accreditation mechanism and seek to popularize it. Furthermore, the online dispute resolution mechanism has a broad prospect of development in the times of Internet plus and is worth the participation of commercial mediation organisations with creative thinking. Looking back, commercial mediation is a dispute resolution field with a long history. But given in consideration to its era and its operation mechanism, it is rather a brand new field with great developing space that awaits those talents and organisations interested in business mediation to join in and make an effort.

Annual Review on Construction Project Dispute Resolution in China (2016)*

TAN Jinghui [1]

I. Overview

According to data published by the National Bureau of Statistics of China, growth of the national economy further slowed in 2015, and the year-on-year growth rate of annual GDP was estimated at 6.9%. Investment in fixed assets (excluding rural households) maintained a moderate growth, and the national investment in fixed assets was RMB 55,159 billion, an increase of 10% over the previous year. The actual growth rate was 12% after deducting the price factors, which indicates slowed growth. Of total investment, investment in real estate development was RMB 7,0535 billion in the first three quarters with a year-on-year nominal increase of 2.6%. The actual growth was 4.2% after deducting price factors, and the growth rate had a decreased 2.0% in the first half year; investment in infrastructure (excluding electricity power) was RMB 10,127.1 billion , up by 17.2% from the previous year.

In addition, by mid December 2015, the National Development and Reform Commission ("NDRC") introduced 2,529 public-private partnership ("PPP") model projects, where the total investment was around RMB 4,244.3 billion; the Ministry of Finance ("MOF") launched 233 PPP demonstration projects, the total investment of which was around RMB 817 billion. Contracted projects for around 755 have been concluded and the aggregated contract sum is around RMB 1,800 billion. PPP projects are becoming the mainstream construction model for infrastructure and public utilities projects in China.

From 1 January 2015 to 31 December 2015, the Supreme People's Court closed 231 cases concerning construction disputes, 36 of which were second instance cases accepted by the Supreme People's Court, and 195 of which were retrials. In terms of the subject matter, 50 cases (21.65%) involved carrying out construction works using other contractors' qualifications, sub-contracting of entire construction projects to other contractors and the illegal sub-contracting of works to disqualified sub-contractors, 23 cases (9.96%) involved tendering and bidding disputes, 29 cases (12.55%) involved project costs authentication, 42 cases (18.18%) involved construction quality issues, 41 cases (17.75%) involved delay in completion, 7 ca-

---

* Translated by Mayer Brown JSM.

1 TAN Jinghui, LL. M. and Master in Structural Engineering, member of the Chartered Institute of Building, Director of City Development Law Firm (Beijing), arbitrator of Beijing Arbitration Commission / Beijing International Arbitration Centre, former Deputy General Manager of the Legal Department of China State Construction Engineering Corporation and General Counsel of China State Construction International Co., Ltd.

ses (3.03%) involved performance security, and 9 cases (3.9%) involved priority of compensation for project costs [2] (see the following chart).

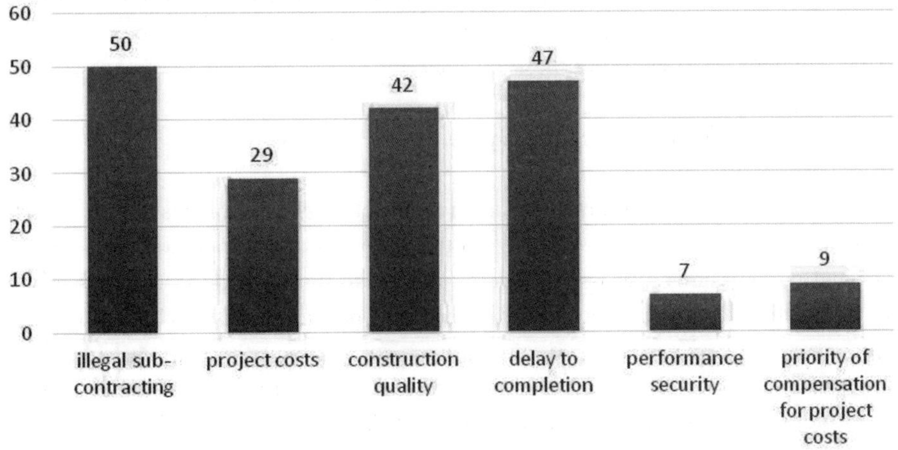

Generally, in 2015, real estate and construction investment in China witnessed a downturn. Benefiting from the promotion of the PPP model and the "One Belt One Road" Strategy, infrastructure investment maintained a relatively fast growth, its industrial structures were continually optimized, and its structural recession and structural prosperity coexisted. Its industry differentiation and regional disparity became more prominent. Taking the construction industry as an example, the laws and policies issued by the State in 2015 focused on the PPP model, new urbanization, the "One Belt One Road" Strategy, and the structure of a uniformly developed construction market. In respect to construction disputes, due to the impact of the decline of national economic growth, industrial structure adjustment, and the downturn of real estate investment, construction disputes in 2015 became more frequent: the number and disputed amount of construction cases increased significantly. Construction disputes mainly arose out of the discharge of creditor's rights, delay in completion, quality defects and other relating contractual disputes.

II. Major Changes in Law

2014 was the first year when the Chinese Government advocated the PPP model. Stepping into 2015, China's economy entered into a phase of further adjustment, in which the growth of the real estate and construction sector decelerated. From the perspective of realizing modernized management and pursuant to the policy of "pooling people's ideas and talents through a synergy of business start-ups and innovation", the Government further promoted the PPP model with integrated private investment as the focus of China's economic development. On the basis of last year, this year, the Government actively provided support from a variety of aspects, such as project financing, industry promotion and encouraged private investment in new urbani-

2 The source of the above data is the Judicial Opinions of China (http://www.court.gov.cn/zgcpwsw/). Relevant data have been included in the statistics according to the judgment documents published on the website containing reasons, without regard to those containing unreasoned judgments.

zation, sponge city construction, underground utility tunnels, and etc. From the market situation promotion of the PPP model 2015, it can be seen that the PPP model may change the development of China's construction sector in the future, and will have a great impact on the causes, nature and dispute resolution approach of construction related disputes, as well as increasing the complexity of handling these disputes.

A. Establishment of PPP Legal System

In 2015, the Chinese Government issued a series of laws and policies for the infrastructure and public utilities sector, with specific regard to the standardized operation of the PPP model. Ministries and commissions also issued several policies to promote the PPP model in municipal utilities, urban utility tunnels, water pollution control, pension industry, hydraulic engineering and public rental housing, and issued supporting regulations on the appraisal of PPP projects and its financial support. Meanwhile, the issuance of the *Draft Public-Private Partnership Law for Consultation* at the national legislation level with the MOF taking the lead on its promulgation demonstrated that the Government had placed significant emphasis on the PPP model as well as its objective feasibility.

1. With the release of the *Draft PPP Law for Consultation* and continuous issuance of documents by the State Council, top-level design of the PPP legal system improves

On 7 January 2016, the MOF issued the *Draft PPP Law for Consultation*, which provides a basic definition, scope of its application, regulatory authority, generation of project, cooperation agreement, implementation and dispute resolution, and specifies that PPP projects to include infrastructure and public service projects, and that private investors can submit their own proposals for project implementation. In this draft, disputes arising out of PPP projects are expressly classified as civil disputes, which is helpful for the resolution of legal disputes derivative of the operation and the implementation of PPP projects in practice and further facilitating the realization of the spirit of contract equality.

On 19 May 2015, the General Office of the State Council forwarded the *Guiding Opinions of the MOF, the NDRC and the People's Bank of China on Promoting the PPP Model in the Public Service Sector* (Guo Ban Fa No. 42 of 2015), which warranted the PPP model as a major innovation in the public service supply mechanism, and required the MOF in conjunction with relevant departments to improve the PPP institutional mechanism. For instance, financing platform companies are prohibited from participating in PPP projects by means of undertakings of minimum returns to conduct financing in a disguised form. Central finance institutions will establish a PPP financing support fund to participate in the projects as private investment so as to enhance the availability of project financing. In addition, project companies are encouraged to issue project yield bonds, project yield notes and asset-backed notes. Also, social security funds and insurance funds are encouraged to use a variety of innovative ways such as debt investment plans, equity investment plans and project asset-backed plans to participate in the projects. Moreover, the reliance on the exchange market of various types of property rights and equities, diversified, standardized and market-oriented exit channels are provided for private investment. This document identifies, on a macro view, the basic framework under which insurance funds can enter into the PPP projects.

2. Value for Money ("VfM") assessment of PPP projects was regulated and the VfM assessment system was specified

On 18 December 2015, the MOF issued the *PPP Value for Money Assessment Guidelines (For Trial Implementation)* (Cai Jin No. 167 of 2015), which defines the VfM assessment and provides that the MOF (or the PPP Centre), together with the industry-specific competent authority, shall conduct the VfM assessment of PPP projects. Also, at this stage, the qualitative assessment shall be its focus and it is encouraged to conduct the quantitative assessment. The conclusion of the VfM assessment shall be drawn on the basis of combination of the conclusions of qualitative and quantitative assessments. The Guidelines also set out the to-be-followed principles, preparation of the VfM assessment, the specific indices and calculation methods of the qualitative and quantitative assessments, and the basic content and information disclosure of the assessment report.

3. PPP demonstration and integrated information platform were launched to promote the open, transparent and orderly implementation of PPP projects

On 18 December 2015, the MOF issued the *Circular on Regulating the Operation of the Integrated PPP Information Platform* (Cai Jin No. 166 of 2015), which specifies that the MOF PPP Centre shall be responsible for management and maintenance of the database, collection, entry and management of the relevant PPP policies and regulations, dynamics, guidebooks, training materials, classic cases and other PPP information. After the issuance of the Circular, the national and provincial model projects and those listed on the local annual and mid-term PPP plans are all required to be selected and identified from the database of the integrated information platform. For those projects that are not incorporated in this database shall not be listed in the relevant local PPP project catalogue and, in principle, shall also not be allocated for any expenditure from the financial budget.

The building of the integrated PPP information platform helps to promote an open, transparent and orderly competition of the implementation of the projects and enhances the level and efficiency of the government services for and the supervision of PPP.

4. Adjustment of capital ratios and other financing and investment measures attract more capital to PPP projects

On 9 September 2015, the State Council issued the *Circular on Adjusting and Improving the Capital System for Fixed Asset Investment Projects* (Guo Fa No. 51 of 2015), under which the minimum capital ratio of urban rail transportation projects shall be adjusted from 25% to 20%; ports, coastal and inland water transportation, and airport projects from 30% to 25%; railway and highway projects from 25% to 20%; low-income housing and ordinary commercial housing projects remained at 20%; and the other projects from 30% to 25%. In addition, approved by the State Council, the minimum capital ratios may be appropriately reduced for the individual national key construction projects in special cases.

On 12 November 2015, the MOF issued the *Interim Measures for Management of Government Investment Funds* (Cai Yu No. 210 of 2015), which provides that the departments of finance at all levels shall establish government investment funds in the sectors that support infrastructure and public services, innovation and entrepreneurship, and etc., in different organization forms such as companies, limited partnership and contract; And in that the departments of finance should not participate in the daily management of the funds; and that the government investment funds shall be prohibited from offering guarantees other than financing guarantees, mortgage and entrusted loans during the operation.

The issuance of the above-mentioned policy documents should assist in the control of financial risks, promote the adjustment of industrial structures, improve the benefits from the use of financial capital, enhance credit in the project financing sector, and specifically regulate the establishment, operation and risk control of government investment funds.

5. Sector-specific regulations on, among other things, public utilities and urban utility tunnels accelerate the implementation of the PPP model.

(1) The compensation system for use of urban utility tunnels promotes the application of the PPP model

The urban utility tunnels are one of the sectors where PPP projects are promoted and operated. In 2015, the compensation system for use of urban underground utility tunnels was specified for the first time and a number of policy documents were formulated to ensure the benefits of private investment in the utility tunnel PPP projects.

On 3 August 2015, the General Office of the State Council issued the *Guiding Opinions on Promoting the Building of Urban Underground Utility Tunnels* (Guo Ban Fa No. 61 of 2015), which introduces the PPP model formally to the underground utility tunnels sector. Specifically, as from 2015, underground utility tunnels are required to be built simultaneously with newly built roads in new areas, parks, and development tracts in the cities on the basis of functional requirements; in the old urban areas, the underground utility tunnels should be built, as necessary and in accordance with the overall urban plan, by integrating with the renewal of such areas, transformation of roads, river regulation and development of underground space. The compensation system for use of urban underground utility tunnels shall be implemented and pipeline owners are required to pay the fees for networking with such utility tunnels and for daily maintenance to the operators of the undergraduate utility tunnels. The establishment of such a system will help guide private investors to participate in PPP projects of underground utility tunnels, as well as improve the issue of repeated excavation of roads, and optimize the urban landscapes.

On 26 November 2015, the NDRC and the Ministry of Housing and Urban-Rural Development ("MOHURD") issued the *Guiding Opinions on Implementing the Compensation System for Use of Urban Underground Utility Tunnels* (Fa Gai Jia Ge No. 2754 of 2015). The *Guiding Opinions* specify that utility tunnel builders and operators shall be responsible for the building, operation and management of urban underground utility tunnels and their ancillary facilities; and that pipeline owners shall be responsible for the maintenance and daily management of the pipelines networked with the utility tunnels. The *Guiding Opinions* also provide that the compensation rates for use of urban underground utility tunnels shall, in principle, be determined by the utility tunnel construction and operation entities and the pipeline owners through consultation; government-fixed or government-guided prices may be adopted for use of the underground utility tunnels in cities where there is no way of determining such rates by consultation or by supply and demand.

The implementation of the compensation system for the use of underground utility tunnels helps to develop a reasonable fee mechanism of underground utility tunnels construction projects, to motivate private investors to make investment, and to promote the scientific development of urban constructions.

(2) Special provisions on PPP in the water pollution control sector

On 9 April 2015, the MOF and the Ministry of Environmental Protection issued the *Implementation Opinions on Promoting Public-Private Partnership in Water Pollution Control Sector* (Cai Jian No. 90 of 2015). The *Implementation Opinions* encourage the promotion of PPP in the water pollution control sector and require integrity of land development, water supply, under-forest economy, ecological agriculture, ecological fishery, ecological tourism and other water pollution control-related ancillary project resources that have a stronger capacity to generate revenue so as to achieve integration of water drainage and supply in villages and towns, integration of production and distribution as well as combined development of the industry. The *Implementation Opinions* also provide guiding opinions on promoting PPP in the water pollution control sector from the aspects such as the design of systems and specifications, management model, basic principles, overall objectives, organizational and implementation structure, market, fund, financing initiatives and ancillary support. Those provisions help guide private investors to participate actively in PPP projects of water pollution control and standardize the operational procedures of PPP projects in the water pollution control sector.

(3) Special provisions on PPP projects of public rental housing

On 21 April 2015, the MOF, the Ministry of Land and Resources, MOHURD, the People's Bank of China, the State Administration of Taxation and the China Banking Regulatory Commission jointly issued the *Circular on Applying Public-Private Partnership Model to Promote Public Rental Housing Investment, Development, Operation and Management* (Cai Zong No. 15 of 2015). The *Circular* encourages application of the PPP model on the establishment of the public rental housing investment, development, operation and management model of "construction by enterprises, rental by residents, subsidies from government and management by the public". The Government shall formulate a development plan and annual plan for public rental housing and organize the adoption of the PPP model in any appropriate public rental housing projects on a trial basis.

[Summary] In 2015, in order to implement three major reforms in the administrative system, financial system and investment and financing systems in the course of economic development, the Chinese Government basically completed the system design in respect of the whole process that operation and administrative regulations of PPP projects by reference to experiences and practices abroad, which included vigorously promoting the systematic implementation of steps such as project feasibility study, project financing, land use, tax incentives and support in key areas. The Government expressly emphasized that PPP model is not simply a financing mode, but an important reform initiative to transform governmental function, absorb private capital, implement the transformation in investment approaches and foster new sources of economic growth, with the view to upgrade the quality of infrastructure and public utilities services and achieving positive social effects.

With the improvements in the PPP model, 2016 will welcome an increase in the implementation of PPP projects, which may give rise to construction disputes in relation to those projects. Such disputes require the promulgation of the *PPP Law* and other regulations at all levels of the legal process to regulate and to guide the implementation of PPP projects in China.

B. Changes in the Legal Environment for Construction Works

In view of new circumstances and new needs of social and economic development, the State vigorously promoted the establishment of a sound, unified and open construction market system with orderly competition. It further regulated the construction agent system and general contracting system, as well as actively improving the electronic tendering system and continued focusing on the quality and safety of the construction works. The amendment and improvement in laws and regulations with respect to the domestic construction industry will further promote standardized operations in the construction industry, reduce regional barriers and administrative intervention, so as to achieve market-orientation and full competition, which will have positive impacts on reducing construction disputes and the resolution thereof.

1. The establishment of the unified and open construction market

On 21 September, 2015, MOHURD issued the *Circular on Issuing the Several Provisions on Promoting the Unity and Openness of Construction Market* (Jian Shi No. 140 of 2015), which is applicable to the inter-provincial processing of housing building projects and municipal infrastructure projects by the construction enterprises in China. The *Circular* requires that competent authorities of housing and urban and rural development at provincial level shall uniformly announce the information in respect of the project team members of the bid-winning enterprises (including the contractors determined by way of direct contracting) in the supervision information platform for local construction market and integrate the bid-winning information with onsite law enforcement inspections. The competent authority of housing and urban and rural development at the provincial level at location of registration shall assist other provinces and cities in verifying the information such as the qualifications of the local construction enterprises and qualifications of relevant personnel. It will also cooperate in handling any illegal acts by construction enterprises in the inter-provincial processing of construction works, so as to achieve joint supervision. Such regulations will have an important impact on the establishment of a sound construction market with orderly competition as well as creating a positive market environment for construction enterprises.

2. The development of a general contracting system

On 26 June 2015, the Ministry of Transport ("MOT") issued the *Measures for the Management of General Contracting in Road Engineering Design and Construction* (Order No. 10 of 2015 of the MOT), which stipulates that the competent departments of transport at all levels shall supervise general contracting in accordance with their responsibilities. The *Measures* provide that the developer of the project may, based on actual circumstances, determine, at its sole discretion, the implementation method, such as general contracting of the entire project, general contracting of certain sections or professional general contracting of single projects. The *Measures* also provide that the general contracting costs or bidding quotation shall include costs such as survey and design costs for construction drawings, construction and installation costs, equipment purchase costs, maintenance fees for defects liability period and insurance expenses with respect to relevant projects. General contracting shall adopt the lump sum contract, and the total contract price thereof is usually not subject to adjustment except the risk costs borne by the developer of the project; the developer of the project shall set bidding limits within the scope of the budget approved in the preliminary design. This provision will help promote the integration of road engineering design with construction works, enhance the integrated effect of road engineering design and construction, and improve the realization, overall, of construction projects by way of work division and risk allocation between the investor and the contractor.

On 21 January 2015, the Department of Construction Market Supervision of MOHURD, based on the original document, issued a *Letter Soliciting Opinions on the Several Opinions on Further Promoting the Development of General Contracting for Construction Projects* (*Draft for Comment*) (Jian Shi She Han No. 10 of 2015), which stipulates that the developer may, based on the actual needs of the project, determine at its discretion the contracting method, which includes for example: Engineering, Procurement and Construction/Turnkey, Design-Build, Design-Procurement, and Procurement-Build. It also requires the improvement of the management system of general contracting and pushes forward the organization and implementation of the general contracting. Such provisions will help deepen the reform on the method of organization and implementation of construction projects, improve the management level of construction works, and to some extent, prevent corruption arising from contracting activities.

3. Incorporation of the construction industry into the pilot program of replacement of business tax with value-added tax

At the National Financial Work Conference on 28 December 2015, Lou Jiwei, the Minister of the MOF pointed out that in 2016, the Government will comprehensively promote the reform on the replacement of business tax with value-added tax to include the construction industry, real estate industry, finance industry and domestic service industry into the pilot program. The promotion of "Replacement of Business Tax with Value-added Tax" in the construction industry will eliminate multi-level and duplicated taxation in the construction industry under the current taxation system where value-added tax and business tax coexist, which will help the integration of the construction industry with its upstream and downstream industries, drive the structure of the entire industry to become more reasonable, which will have positive meaning for improving management, technological advancement, innovation and market competitiveness of construction enterprises, and will influence the development strategy of the construction enterprises in the future. In the meantime, the "Replacement of Business Tax with Value-added Tax" in the construction industry will increase the costs of carrying out construction works using other contractors' qualifications, and therefore will help with the governance of critical issues such as illegal sub-contracting of entire construction projects to other contractors and carrying out construction works using other contractors' qualifications, as well as the regulation on business activities of the construction enterprises, so as to facilitate the orderly and healthy development of the construction industry.

4. The development of the construction industry is constantly becoming more information-based, modernized, and standardized

On 16 June 2015, MOHURD issued the *Guiding Opinions on Promoting the Application of the Building Information Modeling*, which stipulates the development goals of the promotion of BIM (Building Information Modeling) application. For instance, by the end of 2020, a survey and design institute with construction industry class A certificate and house building construction enterprises with special grade and first grade should acquire the BIM and implement the integrated application of the BIM with corporate management systems and other information technology. The *Guiding Opinions* would vigorously promote the application of BIM in China's construction industry, provide technological support for the cooperation through industry chains, industrialized construction and prosperous development of architectural design, and provides basis for the optimization of the whole process of construction project and scientific decision-making. In the meantime, the *Guiding Opinions* would also greatly facilitate the technological upgrade of the construction industry and the reform of production methods.

In order to achieve modernization in supporting industries, in June 2015, MOHURD issued the *National Construction Standardized Design System for the Modernization of the Construction Industry*. Such Standardized Design System will further strengthen standardized constructions and provide technological support for the industrialization of the construction industry.

5. Developments in the Form of Construction Contracts

(1) MOHURD and the State Administration for Industry and Commerce ("SAIC") issued the Standard Form of Design Contract for Construction Projects

On 4 March 2015, MOHURD and SAIC issued the *Standard Form of Design Contract for Construction Projects (Building Works)* (GF-2015-0209) and the Standard Form of Design Contract for Construction Projects (Specialist Works) (GF-2015-0210), which came into effect on 1 July 2015. The 2015 standard form is more specific on consortium design, requirements for engineering design, professional liability and project insurance, ownership and use of intellectual property rights, liability for damages and dispute review in project design compared with previous drafts.

(2) MOHURD and SAIC issued the Standard Form of Cost Consultancy Agreement for Construction Projects

On 24 August 2015, MOHURD and SAIC issued the *Circular on Issuing the Standard Form of Cost Consultancy Agreement for Construction Projects* [Jian Biao No. 124 of 2015], which came into effect on 1 October 2015. The 2015 standard form is different from the 2012 standard form in the following aspects: scope of services, work content, and consultants' deliverables are provided for in its appendix; in terms of a client's obligations, the 2015 Standard form adds that a client shall assume negative consequences for failure to respond; in terms of the project consultancy team and personnel, the client may request the consultant to include in the special terms the qualification and number of major members of the consultation team, and name of project leader; in relation to liabilities for breach of contract, the 2015 Standard form cancels the ceiling of compensation in favour of the consultant set out in the 2012 Standard form. In addition, the 2015 Standard form enumerates the conditions for contract cancellation for the first time, and also includes clauses of intellectual property rights for the first time.

[Summary] In 2015, China's issuance of policies and standard forms in the field of construction projects, aiming at regulating competitions in the industry is conducive to promoting the standardized development of the domestic construction market. Prior to the replacement of old regulations with new regulations, disputes relating to time for completion and quality may arise out of modification to such regulations. The promotion and application of new technologies in the field of construction projects will help the construction industry to move towards being more information-based, modernized and standardized, and would compel enterprises to pay attention to the application of innovative technologies and strengthen the management of intellectual property rights, which may give rise to more disputes relating to intellectual property rights in the construction industry in the future.

C. Developments in the Polices and Laws on Urbanization

1. The issuance of the National Comprehensive Pilot Scheme for New Urbanization constitutes a favorable policy to the construction industry

On 4 February 2015, the NDRC and other authorities jointly issued the *National Comprehensive Pilot Scheme for New Urbanization*, listing two provinces, Jiangsu and Anhui, and 62 cities (townships) including Ningbo as the national comprehensive pilot areas for new urbanization. According to the Scheme, supporting policies to this pilot are required to: strengthen policy synergies between authorities, promote release of relevant policies and reform measures on new urbanization in the pilot areas first; improve transfer payment measures and establish the mechanism where fiscal transfer payment is linked with granting urban residency to people with rural household registration; use provincial government lending in favor of pilot areas, and etc.

The issuance of the Scheme will give rise to moderate preferential policies for the construction of low-income housing units and improvement of municipal infrastructure in pilot areas; meanwhile, acceleration of urbanization in pilot areas will lead to a population explosion and a drastic increasing demand for residential, commercial and office space, that will provide huge and ongoing increments in the market for the construction industry.

2. With accelerated transformation of shanty towns, trouble with financing may be solved

On 25 June 2015, the State Council further issued the *Opinions on Further Conducting Urban Shanty Town and Urban and Rural Dilapidated House Transformation and Supporting Infrastructure Construction Well* (Guo Fa No. 37 of 2015). The *Opinions* require the intensification of the transformation construction, and put forward specific measures for accelerating the transformation of urban shanty towns, improving the supporting infrastructure and promoting the transformation of rural dilapidated houses. The *Opinions* specify four paths to innovate institutional mechanisms for finance, namely promoting purchases by the Government of the transformation services of urban shanty towns, promoting the PPP model, constructing diversified implementers of transformation of urban shanty towns, and exerting the support role of development finance. The issuance of the *Opinions* means more private investment will participate in the transformation of urban shanty towns in the future, which will help to solve the implementer's trouble with financing. In addition, judging from successful cases of transformation of urban shanty towns, numerous contractors will participate in the financing and investment construction and project contracting in the future.

3. The MOF issues specific matching measures for urbanization

On 26 August 2015, the MOF issued the *Circular on Better Implementing the Transforma-*

tion of Urban Shanty Towns (Cai Zong No. 57 of 2015), specifying that the targets and tasks in respect of the national transformation of urban shanty towns in 2015 shall have 5.4 million units, and central and provincial finance shall be required to give proper aid on the basis of fiscal difficulties and the accomplishment of the transformation of urban shanty towns in different regions. The land used for construction of resettlement houses during the transformation of urban shanty towns shall be supplied by allotment, and shall be free of land transfer fees other than land compensation fee and compensation for demolition in accordance with relevant laws; various administrative fees such as fees for relocation of air defense basement construction, charges for urban infrastructure and educational surcharges, and government-managed funds shall be exempted in accordance with the regulations of the MOF[3]; meanwhile, various administrative fees imposed at the provincial level shall be exempted in accordance with relevant provisions. Preferential treatment shall be given in accordance with relevant provisions in urban land use tax, stamp tax, land value-added tax, deed tax and individual income tax involved in the transformation projects of urban shanty towns. The issuance of such policy plays an active role in accomplishing the target of constructing urban low-income housing projects and promotes the transformation of urban shanty towns.

[Summary] New urbanization is a major strategy to realize social transformation and sustainable economic development in China that will help to promote a balanced infrastructure and basic public services. Since urbanization has a huge demand for funds, especially for the transformation of old towns and urban shanty towns where there are numerous participants and complicated legal relationships are faced with insufficient supporting funds and mechanisms, and uncertainty in selection of contractors in practice, China needs to constantly improve institutions supporting construction. Meanwhile, given the specificity of new urbanization projects, more disputes in this area may become more prominent in the future.

D. Developments in Laws on Construction Dispute Resolution

1. Case filing and registration system was implemented and construction lawsuits increased

On 15 April 2015, the Supreme People's Court promulgated the *Provisions of the Supreme People's Court on Several Issues concerning the Registration and Case Filing by People's Courts* (Judicial Interpretation No. 8 of 2015). According to these provisions, the people's courts should implement case filing and registration system with respect to civil prosecutions at first instance, administrative prosecutions and criminal private prosecutions. Also, the people's courts should accept pleadings for both public and private prosecutions, and complete case registration and filing on the spot for such public and private prosecutions that are in compliance with legal requirements. In cases of rejecting pleadings, if there is any of the fol-

3 The Circular on Better Implementing the Transformation of Urban Shanty Towns: 5. Tax preferential policies involved in implementing the transformation of urban shanty towns (1) implementing preferential policy of exemption of various fees and funds. For transformation projects of urban shanty towns, fees for relocated air defence basement construction, charges for termite prevention, charges for urban infrastructure, special fund for bulk cement, special fund for new wall materials, educational surcharge, local educational surcharges, and urban public utility surcharges shall be exempted in accordance with MOF regulations. Various administrative fees imposed at the provincial level shall be exempted in accordance with relevant provisions.

lowing: failing to issue written confirmation after accepting pleadings, failing to notify parties involved to make additions or corrections to pleadings, and other legal or discipline violations including rejecting to file a case, delays in filing a case, interference with case filings as well as failing to file a case and make a ruling or decision, the parties involved may complain to the people's court that accepted the pleading or the people's court at a higher level. In the short term, the case filing and registration system may lead to an increase of lawsuits arising from construction disputes, but it can help to resolve construction disputes effectively and promptly in the long term.

2. 44 departments jointly signed the *Cooperation Memorandum on the Joint Discipline and Penalty against Dishonest Persons subjected to Legal Execution*

On 20 January 2016, 44 departments including the NDRC and the Supreme People's Court jointly signed the *Cooperation Memorandum on the Joint Discipline and Penalty against Dishonest Persons subjected to Execution* (the "Memorandum"). The main contents of the Memorandum include: the party against whom joint discipline and penalty is implemented (i. e. dishonest persons subjected to legal execution ordered by the Supreme People's Court), the method of information sharing and joint discipline and penalty, disciplinary measures, shared contents and implementation organizations. The introduction of the Memorandum creates a joint power to punish dishonest or guilty persons, which will force such persons subject to a court order or legal execution to actively comply with such rulings.

[Summary] In the long term, the setting up and implementation of the case filing and registration system by the people's courts will help to solve more disputes within the judicial framework by opening up a channel for construction dispute resolution. In regard to the implementation of a joint discipline and penalty system against dishonest persons who are the subject of a court order or form of legal execution, it will contribute to the acceleration of the resolution to a wide range of construction disputes that are "hard to execute".

E. The "One Belt One Road" Brings More International Project Opportunities to Construction Enterprises

In order to create a new situation of collaborative economic construction and development between China and neighbouring countries, and basing on the needs of adjustment of industrial structure and solving overcapacity in China, the Chinese Government has issued policy documents focusing on the "One Belt One Road" Strategy.

As for the top-level system design, the NDRC, the Ministry of Foreign Affairs and MOFCOM jointly published the *Vision and Actions on Jointly Building Silk Road Economic Belt and 21st-Century Maritime Silk Road* on 28 March 2015, which defines five major international channels for China's foreign economic development, i. e., three silk road economic belts. The "One Belt One Road" creates great opportunities for construction enterprises to solve overcapacity and realize internationalization.

As for the implementation of transportation strategies, the MOT held a meeting in May 2015 where it reviewed and approved the *Planning and Implementation Scheme of the Ministry of Transport on the Implementation of the "One Belt One Road" Strategy (Draft for Examination)*. According to public reports, the focus of "One Belt One Road" transportation projects is to advance the transportation infrastructure construction for interconnection of China-Laos-Thailand, China-Mongolia, China-Russia, China-Pakistan, China-Kirghizstan-Uzbekistan, China-Kazakhstan, China-Tajikistan-Afghanistan-Iran, China-India and China-Vietnam. The socio-political environment and policy and legal environment in these regions will attract close attention from construction enterprises.

As for services and safeguards provided by state judicial authorities, the Supreme People's Court issued the *Several Opinions on Providing Judicial Services and Safeguard for the Construction of the "One Belt One Road" by People's Courts* on 16 June 2015. According to these opinions, people's courts should actively respond to the judicial concerns and needs of Chinese and foreign market players in the construction of the "One Belt One Road", make great efforts to strengthen judicial review in foreign criminal, foreign civil and commercial, maritime and maritime commercial, and international commercial and maritime arbitration cases as well as trials in cases concerning free trade areas, and create a positive legal environment for the construction of the "One Belt One Road". It is also emphasized that international commercial and maritime arbitrations should play an important role in the construction of the "One Belt One Road", and reciprocal recognition. Enforcement of arbitration awards between China and countries along the "One Belt One Road" that have not entered into the *New York Convention* should also be promoted.

[Summary] The "One Belt One Road" creates great opportunities for the implementation of the internationalization strategy of construction enterprises in China, but it should be noted that given the complexity of political, economic and social situations in some countries along the "One Belt One Road", construction enterprises need to pay high attention to the political and security environment of countries at which projects are located and the integrity of project owners and governments, and make a full evaluation on regional protection, technical barriers and other issues to prevent and reduce cross-border construction disputes.

III. Significant Cases in respect of Construction Disputes

[Case 1] The validity of intermediary behaviour in construction projects and the determination of intermediary fee standard

[Basic Facts]

On 14 May 2004, Mr. Hu and a construction company's Shanghai branch entered into an Intermediary Contract under which it was agreed that Mr. Hu shall provide intermediary services by recommending the company for construction projects in Anhui Province. The intermediary payment was agreed at equal to 5% of the total amount of the construction contract concluded. In November 2006, Mr. Hu told Mr. Mo of the construction company's Shanghai branch that the project of Wuhu Liansheng International Commercial Plaza was inviting bids. Through Mr. Hu's efforts, Wuhu Liansheng Real Estate Development Co., Ltd contracted out construction works with a total value of RMB 85,808,881 to the construction company. The construction company did not pay Mr. Hu any intermediary fee after it won the bid, therefore, Mr. Hu filed a lawsuit with a court on 11 January 2010, demanding payment of the intermediary fee. In this case, the court of first instance decided that the Intermediary Contract was legitimate and valid, while the intermediary fee agreed by both parties shall, based on the principles of equitableness and reasonableness, be reduced to 1% of the total amount of the construction contract. Mr. Hu and the construction company did not accept the first-instance judgment and lodged an appeal to the Higher People's Court of Anhui Province. The court of second instance upheld the first-instance judgement. Mr. Hu believed that the first- and second-instance judgments arbitrarily reduced the intermediary fee agreed by both parties from 5% to 1%, which was against the principle of autonomy of will in contracts and damaged the legitimate rights and interests of the intermediary. Therefore, Mr. Hu applied for a retrial with the Supreme People's Court. The case has already been concluded. [4]

[**Case Summary**]

The focus of dispute in this case includes two issues: one, the validity of intermediary behaviour in construction projects, the other, whether it is appropriate for the courts to reduce the proportion of intermediary payment by exercising their discretion.

[**Court's Opinions**]

Opinion of the Higher People's Court of Anhui Province:

1. In respect to the validity of the construction intermediary behavior, the construction company claimed that Mr. Hu's intermediary behavior breached the provisions of laws and regulations, but the evidence provided by it was not within the scope of laws and administrative regulations. The relevant provisions of intermediary contract provided by the *Contract Law* shall be applied to this case, and the law applied by the court of first instance is proper.

2. The court adjusted the standard of intermediary payment. Whether there is factual and legal basis for the court of first instance to adjust the charging rate of intermediary payment from 5% to 1%. According to the relevant provisions on intermediary contract provided by the *Contract Law*, the client shall make the payment as agreed if the intermediary facilitated the formation of the contract. The parties in this case agreed to charge 5% of the total amount of construction contract as the intermediary payment. Although the laws make no clear regulations of the standard of intermediary payment, the payment to intermediary shall be determined on the principle of fairness and equity. In view of the fact that the standard agreed by the parties represented an excessively high ratio of the target profit of the construction contract involved, the court of first instance made a proper reduction of the intermediary payment to 1% of the total amount of construction contract. Combined with the facts of this case and taking into account the work and risks undertaken by the intermediary Mr. Hu, it is in line with the principle of fairness and there is no obvious inappropriateness that the court of first instance reduced the intermediary payment from 5% to 1% of the total amount of construction contract.

Opinions of the Supreme People's Court:

1. The validity of the intermediary behavior in construction. The Intermediary Contract signed by Mr. Hu and the construction company on 14 May 2004 as evidence that there was an intermediary civil legal relationship between the parties and Article 2 of the Intermediary Contract expressly agreed the intermediary payment to be 5% of the total amount of construction contract. This Intermediary Contract is in line with the relevant provisions on intermediary contract provided by Article 424 of the *Contract Law*. As to the construction project which must follow the procedure of tendering and bidding pursuant to laws, the tendering information re-

---

4 Case No.: Min Ti Zi No. 74 of 2014. Source: Judicial Opinions of China, the Supreme People's Court at http://www.court.gov.cn/cpwsw/zgrmfy/ms/201412/t20141226_5596824.html, accessed on 6 January 2016.

leased by the project owner may not be well-known due to constraints of time, place and manner, therefore, reporting the tendering information to the enterprises and individuals who conduct construction work and bringing the project owner and the construction party together to sign the Construction Contract through negotiation is an objective phenomenon in reality and is not prohibited by law. Accordingly, it is correct for the courts of first instance and second instance to determine the Intermediary Contract involved as valid.

2. The court adjusted the standard of intermediary payment. It is proper for the courts of first instance and second instance to, at their discretion, adjust the intermediary payment agreed by the parties from 5% to 1% of the total construction price on the premise that the Intermediary Contract involved is determined as valid. First, according to the provisions of the *Tendering and Bidding Law*, the project of Wuhu Liansheng International Commercial Plaza was within the scope of mandatory tendering and bidding, and the contracting right thereof was also obtained by winning in the procedure of tendering and bidding. As the tendering and bidding of the project involved, it must comply with the provisions of Article 43 of the *Tendering and Bidding Law*, i. e. "*Before the winning bidder is determined, the tenderee may not negotiate with any bidder on such substantial contents as bid price or bidding plan.*" Therefore, the intermediary role of Mr. Hu in the bid winning by the construction company in the project of Wuhu Liansheng International Commercial Plaza is merely limited to reporting the tendering information and bringing the relevant responsible persons of the tendering and the bidding parties together to know each other, and the intermediary payment obtained by him shall be consistent with his work in the intermediary activities. If Mr. Hu believes that he has other intermediary activities in addition to the above mentioned in the bid winning of the project involved, then he must provide evidence of his work and that his intermediary activities do not breach the provisions of Article 43 of the *Tendering and Bidding Law*. However, the evidence adduced by Mr. Hu during the trials of first instance and second instance did not show that he had other lawful intermediary activities and work. Second, in recent years, the construction industry in our country has made meager profits. The excessively high fee agreed by the parties in respect of intermediary payment in the intermediary contract has the possibility of interest imbalance. The practice of the courts of first instance and second instance that, at their discretion, adjusting the intermediary payment agreed by the parties in the intermediary contract from 5% to 1% of the total amount of the construction conforms to the basic situation that construction industry conforms to the basic practice of an industry of meager profits and is also consistent with the work that Mr. Hu had done in the intermediary activities, which better balances the interests of the parties, and thus such adjustment is not an abuse of their discretion.

[**Observations**]

In accordance with the provisions of the *Contract Law*, an intermediary contract refers to a contract by which the intermediary informs the client of an opportunity to enter into a contract or provides intermediary service for entering into a contract, for which the client shall make a payment. If the establishment of a contract is facilitated by the intermediary, the client shall make a payment as agreed. The intermediary behavior in the field of construction projects refers to the behavior where one party provides to the other party who engages in construction with services such as informing tendering information, assisting with the participation in bidding and facilitating the execution of construction contracts, and charges intermediary payment as agreed. However, the legitimacy of the intermediary behaviour in the field of construction projects has always been controversial and will become a bigger challenge after the issuance of the *Tendering and Bidding Law*:

One opinion is that in accordance with the provisions of the *Tendering and Bidding Law*, in order to win the tender for construction projects, bidders shall actively respond to the bidding requirements and fairly participate in the competition of bidding. While the intermediary behavior in the field of construction projects often demonstrates where the intermediary brings the client and the tenderer together to conduct substantial negotiations and helps the client win the bidding by way of collusive and conspired bidding. It is obvious that such behavior violates the relevant provisions of the *Tendering and Bidding Law*. It not only disturbs the fair competition in the tendering and bidding procedures, but also damages the competitive environment of the construction market. Therefore, the kind of construction intermediary contract that conceals illegal intentions with a lawful form shall therefore be identified as invalid.

Another opinion is that the legal provisions regarding intermediary contract are established by the *Contract Law*, the intermediary behavior of construction contract is not prohibited by the law of the PRC. Although the bidding announcement is open to the public, it does not necessarily mean that everyone knows that. Thus, there are circumstances where the matters subject to open bidding need to be informed to others and may give rise to an opportunity to enter into a contract, so bidders may entrust the bidding matters to others for their representation or help. Therefore, it is not that the basic principles of the *Tendering and Bidding Law* are violated so long as there is intermediary behavior in tendering and bidding activities, so construction intermediary behavior shall be identified as legal and valid.

In the author's opinion, the validity of construction intermediary contracts cannot be generalized. The validity of such kinds of contracts should be determined according to the specific content of the intermediary services provided by the intermediary. If the content of the intermediary service, such as agreeing to ensure the winning of the bidding, helping the client to obtain the subject matter or to conduct collusive bidding, obtaining the list of bid evaluation experts, etc., violating the prohibitive provisions provided by the *Tendering and Bidding Law* and other relevant laws, such intermediary contracts shall be identified as invalid. However, if the content of the intermediary service only includes providing bidding information, bringing the client and the tenderer together and helping preparing bidding documents, which does not violate the prohibitive provisions provided by the *Tendering and Bidding Law* and other relevant laws, such intermediary contracts shall be identified as legal and valid.

In respect of the determination of the intermediary payment standard, in the author's opinion, the agreement of the parties on the intermediary payment standard shall be respected in principle. However, in consideration of the provisions of the *Contract Law*, the exercise of the right to claim for intermediary payment shall be conditional on the establishment of a contract facilitated by the intermediary. Therefore, if a party claims that the intermediary payment is excessively high and shall be adjusted, the court shall determine whether the intermediary payment is reasonable so as to determine whether the intermediary payment standard shall be adjusted when trialing cases. In the author's opinion, when judging if the intermediary payment is reasonable, an especially prudent approach should be taken and many factors, such as the actual input of the intermediary into providing intermediary service, the effect of the intermediary service on facilitating the entry into of the construction contract and the actual returns brought about to the client by the projects so facilitated, should be taken into consideration. Otherwise, it is unfair to obtain a large of intermediary payment merely by the way of bringing the parties to the contract together.

[Case 2] Validity of an arbitration clause in an action filed by a contractor against the employer

[Basic Facts]

Jian'an (the "contractor") and Senke (the "employer") entered into a construction contract under which Jian'an would undertake construction works on Senke's site. Jian'an and a Mr. Xiong subsequently entered into an Agreement under which Mr. Xiong (the "actual contractor") would be responsible for organizing personnel, machinery, equipment and construction materials to carry out the construction works on Senke's site. Mr. Xiong completed the construction works as agreed but Jian'an failed to make payment to him as agreed. As such, Mr. Xiong filed an action in the court, requesting Jian'an (the "contractor") to make the outstanding payment and for an order that Senke (the "employer") be held jointly and severally liable for the outstanding payment. After Qinghai Higher People's Court accepted the case, Senke challenged the jurisdiction of the court on the basis of an arbitration clause contained in the construction contract between Senke and Jian'an and further requested a ruling that Mr. Xiong should apply for arbitration at the Xining Arbitration Commission. The court of first instance denied Senke's challenge to its jurisdiction. Senke disagreed, and considered that the Agreement between Mr. Xiong and Jian'an could not be grounds to determine the jurisdiction over this case. The two construction contracts between Senke and Jian'an both specified that any dispute should be submitted for arbitration. Senke appealed to the Supreme People's Court and requested dismissal of the judgment at first instance. [5]

[Case Issue]

In this case, the dispute focused on whether the actual contractor's claim against the employer for payment was subject to the arbitration clause between the employer and the contractor under circumstances where an arbitration agreement existed between the employer and the contractor.

[Court's Opinions]

With respect to the issue of the dispute mentioned above, the Qinghai Higher People's Court and the Supreme People's Court held different opinions:

The Qinghai Higher People's Court held that this case involved a dispute over the claim for the payment made by the actual contractor Mr. Xiong against Jian'an and Senke and that a direct contractual relationship existed between Mr. Xiong and Jian'an and also between Jian'an and Senke. The Agreement between Mr. Xiong and Jian'an provided that "The Parties shall, on the basis of the principles of fairness and amicability, resolve any disputes arising from their cooperation through negotiation. If such negotiation fails, either Party may refer the dispute to the people's court of the place where the project is located." In accordance with these provisions, Mr. Xiong and Jian'an expressly agreed on how to resolve any disputes arising, i.e. To file an action with the people's court. Mr. Xiong filed the action in accordance with the provisions of the Agreement as well as the relevant regulations on jurisdiction, and in compliance

---

5 Case No.: Min Yi Zhong Zi No. 170 of 2015. Source: Judicial Opinions of China, the Supreme People's Court at http://www.court.gov.cn/cpwsw/zgrmfy/ms/201510/t20151019_11816592.html, accessed on 14 January 2016.

with all applicable laws and regulations. Although the Contracts between Jian' an and Senke contained an arbitration clause, Mr. Xiong was not a party to those Contracts and the dispute resolution clause of these Contracts should not be naturally applicable to the party, namely Mr. Xiong. Therefore, it was appropriate for Mr. Xiong to file the action with the Qinghai Higher People's Court in accordance with the provisions of the Agreement and the law. The court of first instance had jurisdiction over this case and thus in accordance with the law, it dismissed the challenge raised by Senke in relation to its jurisdiction in this matter.

The Supreme People's Court held that the subject matter of this case is a dispute over the Contracts. Mr. Xiong as the actual contractor, has the right to claim the payment from the employer, Senke, and the contractor, Jian' an, involved the settlement of the payment between Mr. Xiong and Jian' an and also between Jian' an and Senke. However, because the Contracts between Jian' an and Senke expressly provided for arbitration, any disputes between the parties over settlement of payment should be referred to the arbitration commission agreed on by the parties and should not be subject to the jurisdiction of the people's court. It was inappropriate for the court of first instance to have accepted the action filed by Mr. Xiong against Senke and the action should have been dismissed. The Agreement between Mr. Xiong and Jian' an provided that "The Parties shall, on the basis of the principles of fairness and amicability, resolve any disputes arising from their cooperation through negotiation. If such negotiation fails, either Party may refer the dispute to the people's court of the place where the project is located." Since the project was located in Qinghai Province, the Qinghai Higher People's Court may, in accordance with the above-mentioned provisions of the Agreement and the applicable rule on jurisdiction, continue to hear the dispute over the construction contracts between Mr. Xiong and Jian' an. In conclusion, the grounds on which Senke filed the appeal were partially tenable and the first instance judgment was improperly rendered and should be corrected. Therefore, the Supreme People's Court reversed the ruling of first instance rendered by the Qinghai Higher People's Court and rejected the action filed by Mr. Xiong against Senke.

[**Observations**]

In accordance with Article 26[6] of the *Interpretations of the Supreme People's Court on the Application of Law in the Trial of Disputes over Construction Contracts* (the "Judicial Interpretations on Construction Contracts"), if the actual contractor makes a claim for any outstanding payment, it may file an action against the employer with whom it has no contractual relationship. However, if the employer and the contractor have agreed to arbitrate, there are no express provisions of law specifying whether an action filed by the actual contractor against the employer is subject to such arbitration clause. In this regard, different courts hold different opinions and the differences of the opinions can also be seen in the judgment rendered by the courts of the two levels that heard this case.

One opinion is that Article 26 of the *Judicial Interpretations on Construction Contracts* not

6 Article 26 of the Judicial Interpretations on Construction Contracts provides: If a contractor files an action with the person who illegally sub-contracts the entire construction project to other contractors or who illegally sub-contracts the works to disqualified sub-contractors as defendant(s), the people's court shall accept it in accordance with the law. If the actual contractor makes any claim with the employer as defendant, the people's court may list the person who illegally sub-contracts the entire construction project to other contractors or who illegally sub-contracts the works to disqualified sub-contractors as an additional party in the action. The employer shall bear the payment obligation to the actual contractor only within the scope of its outstanding project price.

only grants the actual contractor for the right of action which can be used to against the employer and the person who illegally sub-contracts the entire construction project to other contractors or who illegally sub-contracts the works to disqualified sub-contractors, but also limits the right of the actual contractor, namely the employer shall only bear liability to the actual contractor to the extent of the outstanding construction payment. On the basis of the above, whether and to what extent the claim made by the actual contractor for the construction payment shall be conditioned by the ascertainment of the facts such as the amount of the outstanding construction payment to be paid by the employer and the contractor. The arbitration institution shall ascertain such facts on the precondition that the contract between the employer and the contractor contains an arbitration clause. If the action directly filed by the actual contractor against the employer is not subject to an arbitration clause, the arbitration agreement between the employer and the contractor will become irrelevant. These understanding increases the rights of the actual contractor and is not conducive to safeguard the rights of the employer, particularly its right to choose how to resolve disputes. Therefore, the actual contractor should also be subject to the arbitration clause agreed on by the employer and the contractor if it directly requests the employer to bear liability.

Another opinion is that the existence of a legal and valid arbitration agreement between the parties is a precondition and grounds for the jurisdiction of the relevant arbitration institution over the case. The judicial interpretations provide that the actual contractor may only make its claim against the employer for the outstanding construction payment to be paid by the employer. It is therefore inevitable in such cases to ascertain the amount of the outstanding construction payment that the employer and the contractor have agreed to be subject to arbitration. However, no arbitration agreement exists between the actual contractor and the employer. Moreover, the subject matter of a dispute over a claim made by the actual contractor against the employer for the construction payment does not limit the matters that the employer and the contractor have agreed to be subject to arbitration and also involves matters not subject to arbitration, such as whether the actual contractor is entitled to make a claim and whether or not such claim has been time barred. Article 4 of the *Arbitration Law* provides that "An arbitration commission shall not accept an application for arbitration submitted by one of the parties in the absence of an arbitration agreement." It is therefore contrary to this provision if a claim is brought by the actual contractor against the employer for the construction payment is subject to the arbitration agreement between the employer and the contractor.

In the author's opinion, whether the actual contractor is subject to the arbitration clause between the employer and the contractor is highly controversial in current judicial practice. As such, it is useful to refer to the opinion of the Supreme People's Court in this case for the resolution of these lands disputes. In accordance with the relevant provisions of the *Arbitration Law*, however, an arbitration agreement is the precondition of an arbitration jurisdiction and also a significant ground for the arbitration institution to determine whether or not to accept the application for arbitration and the scope of any arbitration. If, in the absence of an arbitration agreement between the actual contractor and the employer, the arbitration institution exercises its jurisdiction over an application for arbitration filed by the actual contractor against the employer only pursuant to an arbitration agreement between the employer and the contractor, there is a risk that an award made by the arbitration institution may be be dismissed on the grounds that "(i) there is no arbitration agreement between the parties; or (ii) the matters of the award are outside the scope of the arbitration agreement or not subject to the jurisdiction of the arbitration commission."Therefore, in the author's opinion, whether an action filed directly by the actual contractor against the employer is subject to an arbitration clause between the employer and the contractor remains unresolved.

[Case 3] Relationship between the settlement and administrative audit of payment

[Basic Facts]

On 11 October 2010, Harbin No. 5 Hospital (the "Hospital") invited bids in respect of the construction of a complex for its orthopedics and burns ward (the "Project"). A company named Sihaiyuan won the bid. On 28 October 2010, the Hospital and Sihaiyuan entered into a contract under which Sihaiyuan was responsible for construction of the Project. The construction agreement provided that the provisional contract price would be RMB 149,539,066.49 (subject to the settlement of the final audit). The special conditions of contract provided that the contractor would file applications for interim payments to the construction supervision company for its review on a monthly basis. Upon completion of the review, the interim payment application would be submitted to a cost consultancy company appointed by the employer which will forward the same to the employer after completion of the review. Upon audit by the audit department, 95% of the construction payment would be made within 15 working days.

On 25 August 2010, the Hospital and Gongying entered into an audit contract under which the Hospital engaged Gongying to audit the final account of the Project. Gongying audited the cost of the Project in accordance with the terms of appointment agreed with the Hospital and issued the Audit Report (Ha Gong Ying Zi Shen Zi No. 2 of 2013), confirming that the audited amount of final account was RMB 329,825,640.37. The Hospital, Sihaiyuan and Gongying affixed their company chops to the Audit Report.

After completion of the Project, given that the Hospital failed to make payments as agreed, Sihaiyuan referred such disputes to the Higher People's Court of Heilongjiang Province, requesting that the Hospital be ordered to pay the overdue payments with interest accrued on the basis of the Audit Report. The Hospital alleged that on 3 July 2013, Harbin Audit Bureau, at the request of relevant administrative authority, included the Project in the audit plan of 2013, and served the audit notice on the Hospital. During the trial of the case, the Bureau issued a Draft Audit Report for Consultation to the Hospital, which stated the audited final account of the Project was RMB 252,693,277.43. Therefore, the final account of the Project shall be RMB 252,693,277.43 as determined in the Draft Audit Report for Consultation issued by Harbin Audit Bureau. The court of first instance ruled on the basis of the Audit Report issued by Gongying and ordered that the Hospital made payment to Sihaiyuan. The Hospital challenged the judgment rendered by the court of first instance and filed an appeal to the Supreme People's Court where this case was concluded. [7]

---

7 Case No.: Min Yi Zhong Zi No. 94 of 2015, Source: Judicial Opinions of China, the Supreme People's Court at http://www.court.gov.cn/cpwsw/zgrmfy/ms/201511/t20151119_12659117.html, accessed on 14 January 2016.

[**Case Issue**]

The dispute focused on whetherthe final account of the Project should be determined in accordance with the conclusion of administrative audit.

[**Court's Opinions**]

Opinions of the Higher People's Court of Heilongjiang Province:

An audit institution's audit of a project owner is in substance an administrative supervising act. There should be a specific agreement if the result of the administrative audit supervision is to be taken as the basis for determining project costs in civil legal relationships. After examination, Sihaiyuan had sufficient evidence to support its assertion that the costs of the Project should be subject to the audit by Gongying:

Firstly, review of the construction contract. The construction contract expressly provided that "the provisional contract price shall be subject to the settlement of the final audit", and "the construction supervision company shall review it within 3 days and then submit to the cost consultancy company appointed by the employer, and the cost consultancy company shall review it within 5 days and then submit it to the employer". It shows that the payment should be determined on the basis of the audit and that cost consultancy company has a role in reviewing the costs of the Project.

Secondly, review of the audit contract. The Hospital entered into the audit contract with Gongying before entering the construction contract with Sihaiyuan. The audit contract explicitly provided that the Gongying had an obligation to audit the final account of the Project.

Thirdly, review of actual implementation. After the completion of the Project, Gongying issued the Audit Report in accordance with the audit contract, which was signed and sealed by Gongying, the Hospital and Sihaiyuan.

Fourthly, review of facts in relation to administrative audit. The Project was not included in the audit plan of the Audit Bureau at the time of execution of the construction contract. The investigation of the Harbin Audit Bureau reveals that the bureau did not list this include the Project in its annual audit plan until 3 July 2013, and the bureau served the official audit notice on the Hospital in November of that year. The audit institution also testified that it had not issued an official and definite audit result of the Project yet. Therefore, the assertion of the Hospital that the competent institution requested an audit of the project when the Project was entered into contradicted the above facts ascertained on investigation. Therefore, one could not conclude that the audit agreed in the construction contract was an administrative audit.

Fifthly, the Hospital and Sihaiyuan have already confirmed the settlement of project costs by affixing their signatures and seals. Even if it is possible to determine the settlement by two audits, both parties have eventually selected the audit through actual performance. Therefore, the final account amount of RMB 329,825,640.37 audited by Gongying shall serve as the basis for settling the costs of the Project. There is no sufficient evidence to support the Hospital's allegation that RMB 252,693,277.43 as determined in the Draft Audit Report for Consultation issued by Harbin Audit Bureau are the costs of the Project.

Opinion of the Supreme People's Court:

The administrative audit between the audit institution and the audited entity falls into the category of an adjustment of administrative legal relations, whether the audited entity agrees or not, once it is included in an audit plan, it should unconditionally accept the audit to be conducted by the audit institution. Whilst the legal relationship under the contract between the employer and the contractor is a civil legal relationship between equal parties, the entrusting party and the entrusted party must also reach a consensus on audit. Under the construction contract, the reason for the parties concerned to introduce a third party for settling the final account audit is to take advantage of professional knowledge of third party to fill of gaps in expertise in project costs of the employer, and to control the cost of the project within a reasonable range. Explicit consent must be secured from the parties concerned if the audit institution steps into the civil legal relationship between the parties concerned, particularly when the conclusion of administrative audit will be taken into account for settling project costs.

Firstly, the parties concerned did not specify in the contract that the audit institution would be the Harbin Audit Bureau. As the audit institution conducts auditing in accordance with the law, and is not bound by the consent of the civil entities, if the construction contract provides that the result of administrative audit shall serve as the ground for settling project costs, then the precondition shall be satisfied that the audit institution has included the relevant project within the scope of audit. The Hospital asserted that the Project certainly fell into the scope of an administrative audit, but failed to produce the relevant evidence. On the contrary, from the investigation and verification by the court of first instance of the Harbin Audit Bureau, the Project was not included in the audit plan of the Bureau at the time of execution of the contract, and it was not until 3 July 2013 after the Project was in operation that the Bureau included it in the audit plan as instructed by the administrative chief. It was impossible for the parties concerned to foresee that the said instruction would have definitely occurred at the time of execution of the contract.

Secondly, prior to the execution of the construction contract, the Hospital and Gongying entered into an audit contract providing for the scope and fees for auditing the final account of the Project to be undertaken by Gongying. Considering the Contract, other terms of the audit contract and the actual performance, the audit agreed by the Hospital and Sihaiyuan should have been the audit conducted by Gongying rather than the administrative audit conducted by Harbin Audit Bureau. The Hospital's assertion that the audit institution agreed in the contract was referred to Harbin Audit Bureau, and the agreed final account audit was the administrative audit of such Bureau was not well grounded, and its reasoning untenable.

[**Observations**]

In recent years, many places such as Jiangxi, Beijing, Shanghai, Hainan, Anhui, Hebei and Chongqing have issued local regulations on audit, stipulating that "for construction projects involving government investment or funded mainly by government investment, the project owner or the agent shall specify in the bidding documents and the contract entered into with the contractor that an audit shall serve as the basis for the settlement of the final account upon completion of the project". The legality of such local legislation has given rise to numerous disputes amongst different parties. In resolving disputes arising from construction contracts, whether the conclusion of an administrative audit may serve as the basis for determining the final account or not has become a disputed judicial issue.

The reason of the Higher Court of Heilongjiang and the Supreme People's Court defined two types of legal relationships, i. e., (1) the administrative legal relationship between the audit institution and the audited entity; and (2) the equal civil legal relationship between the employer and the contractor. The reasoning of the two courts both reflect the fact that the conclusion of an administrative audit may not serve as the ground for determining the project costs unless the parties agree so.

In fact, the judicial rules on the issue of this dispute are reflected in the "*Telephone Replies of the Supreme People's Court on the Application of Laws on the Inconsistency between the Final Account Confirmed by the Parties and the Final Account Audited by an Audit Institution in Construction Contract Cases*" (Min Yi Ta Zi No. 2 of 2001), which states that "After research, it is held that an audit is a type of administrative supervision by the State of the project owner, which does not affect the validity of the contract between the project owner and the contractor." In a construction contract case, the agreement between the parties shall be taken as the basis for the court to render judgment. The conclusion of an audit may serve as grounds for judgment only when the contract specifically agrees to take the audit as grounds for the final account settlement or when the relevant provision is not specific or valid.

In the author's opinion, when handling disputes involving whether an audit shall serve as the ground for determining project price, "the application of an administrative audit shall be subject to agreement between the parties" stated by the Supreme People's Court in the said Replies should still be followed. However, "audits may be admitted as the grounds for judgment when the relevant provision is not specific or valid" as stated in the Replies, shall not be adopted for the following reasons: Article 2 of the *Judicial Interpretation on Construction Contracts* issued by the Supreme People's Court in 2005 specifically provides that "if the construction contract is invalid but the project is accepted after completion, the contractor's request to make payment under the contract shall be upheld." So even if the provision is invalid, the contract price shall be settled according to this provision. As long as the contract does not specify that the conclusion of the administrative audit as judicial grounds, and the price of the disputed project may not be determined on the basis of the administrative audit. If the contract does not specify the basis for settlement, the calculation method or calculation standards released by the Government should be consulted to calculate the payments in accordance with the *Judicial Interpretation on Construction Contracts*, thus, in such circumstances the settlement price should not be determined according to the conclusions of administrative audit.

Furthermore, in the author's opinion, the legal status of, and legal role played by audit, in project settlement should strictly follow the *Audit Law*, the *Budget Law* and the *Construction Law*, which shall be post-supervision in substance. If there is a need to adjust the audit which further affects the settlement of payment between equal parties, it should be specified in laws and regulations, otherwise creditor's contractual rights cannot be safeguarded.

[Case 4] Issues arising from initiating arbitration by a consortium

[Basic Facts]

In 2010, Company A (the "main contractor") and a consortium comprising of Company B and Company C (the "sub-contractors") entered into a sub-contract for the manufacture of Steel Decks and Installation Works relating to a stadium project (the "Sub-Contract"). Schedule 6 to the "Consortium Agreement" provided that Company B shall be the leader of the consortium and the division of responsibilities between Company B and Company C shall be as follows: Company B shall be responsible for the detailed design, material preparation, processing, transportation and technical services in relation to steel decks; Company C shall be responsible for construction works of the steel decks and related accessories and other relevant matters, appointing full-time managers stationed on site, and carrying out relevant work required on site under the Sub-Contract, including handling of payments and relevant material.

In addition, Company B and Company C jointly issued a Financial Statement to Company A setting out that both Company B and Company C agreed that all amounts under this Sub-Contract shall be paid by Company A (the "main contractor") to Company B, then Company B shall pay Company C the commensurate amounts within seven business days after receipt of the same.

In 2013, Company B submitted an arbitration notice to initiate an arbitration on the dispute over the Sub-Contract requesting Company A to compensate Company B for the outstanding payment, accrued interest and all losses suffered from non-payment.

Company A (the "main contractor") alleged that it was the consortium that entered into the Sub-Contract with Company A, therefore no arbitration agreement existed between Company A and Company B. Moreover, Company B was neither a legal representative of the consortium nor authorized by the consortium to initiate an arbitration on behalf of it, so Company B could not apply to the arbitration commission for arbitration in accordance with the arbitration clause set out in the Sub-Contract. Furthermore, Company A (the "main contractor") asserted that there was a connection between the project and the time that the consortium was in existence. As the project was not completed for acceptance and settlement, the application for arbitration solely made by Company B as a member of the consortium would make the distribution of rights and obligations within the consortium impossible, as a result, the interests of Company C would be seriously damaged. Therefore, Company A applied to the arbitral tribunal for an interim award on jurisdiction of the arbitral tribunal over this case.

This case closed with a settlement agreement reached between Company A and Company B.

[**Case Issue**]

The focus of dispute in this case includes two issues: first, whether the arbitration commission has jurisdiction over this case when Company B, as a member of the consortium, independently initiated an arbitration; second, whether Company B, without authorization from Company C, can independently issue an arbitration notice requesting Company A (the "main contractor") to settle the final account and make payment.

[**Arbitral Tribunal's Opinions**]

The arbitral tribunal rendered an interim award on the jurisdiction issue arising from the application for arbitration independently submitted by Company B. The arbitral tribunal held that Chinese laws and regulations in force did not provide that a bidding consortium can act as a legal entity to exercise its rights and obligation. According to Article 2 of *Arbitration Law* [8], Article 48 of the *Civil Procedure Law* [9] and Article 40 of the *Opinions of the Supreme People's Court on Some Issues Concerning the Application of the Civil Procedure Law of the People's*

---

8 Article 2 of the Arbitration Law: "Disputes over contracts and disputes over property rights and interests between citizens, legal persons and other organizations as equal subjects of law may be submitted to arbitration."

9 Article 48 of the Civil Procedure Law: "Any citizen, legal person or any other organization may become a party to a civil lawsuit. Legal persons shall be represented by their legal representatives in litigation. Other organizations shall be represented by their principal leading personnel in litigation."

Republic of China[10], bidding consortiums are not legal entities defined by these laws and regulations. In practice, no bidding consortium has ever initiated legal proceedings such as an arbitration or a civil lawsuit in its own name. The right of action can only be exercised by parties that enter into contracts after winning bids.

According to Article 31 of the *Tendering and Bidding Law*, "*Two or more legal persons or other organizations may form a consortium and jointly submit their bids as one bidder…Parties to a consortium shall enter into an agreement on joint submission of bid to define the work and responsibility to be assumed by each of them, and shall deliver the said agreement to the tenderer together with the bid documents. If a consortium wins the bid, the parties thereto shall jointly enter into a contract with the tenderer and assume joint and several liability over the winning project to the tenderer.*" In this case, the agreement made between the applicant Company B and Company C on matters concerning the bidding consortium is clear and definite. The division of work and responsibilities between members of the consortium is mainly based on the agreement on joint submission of bid. After winning the bid, all members of the consortium concurrently become the parties to the Sub-Contract, enjoying corresponding contractual rights and assuming joint and several liabilities to the employer.

[**Observations**]

In this case, the two parties to the Sub-Contract include Company A as the employer and the consortium as the sub-contractor comprising of Company B and Company C through the Consortium Agreement. In accordance with Article 31 of the *Tendering and Bidding Law*, "*the parties thereto shall jointly enter into a contract with the tenderer and assume joint and several liabilities over the winning project to the tenderer*", Company B and Company C shall jointly sign and affix their company chops to the Sub-Contract. As Company B and Company C were both members of one party to the Sub-Contract, and they affirmed the arbitration agreement in the Sub-Contract as independent entities respectively, and arbitration agreements did exist between company B and Company A as well as between Company C and Company A, therefore, Company B was entitled to apply for arbitration by itself. The interim award rendered by the arbitral tribunal held that it had jurisdiction over this case and also confirmed that Company B was entitled to apply for arbitration independently.

As to the question whether Company B as a member of the consortium could apply for arbitration individually over settlement with respect to the Sub-Contract, in accordance with the

---

10 Article 40 of theOpinions of the Supreme People's Court on Some Issues Concerning the Application of the Civil Procedure Law of the People's Republic of China: "The 'other organizations' as prescribed by Article 49 of the Civil Procedure Law refers to the organizations that are lawfully established, have certain organizational bodies and properties but do not have the status of legal person, and include: (1) sole proprietorships and partnerships that have been registered and obtained a business license according to law; (2) partnership associations that have been registered and have obtained business licenses according to law; (3) Chinese-foreign contractual joint ventures and foreign-funded enterprises that have been registered and have obtained business licenses in China according to law; (4) social organizations that have been approved and registered by the civil affairs administrative department and have obtained registration certificates of social organization; (5) branches that are established by legal persons and have obtained business licenses; (6) branches of the People's Bank of China or various professional banks that are established all over the country; (7) branches of the People's Insurance Company of China that are established all over the country; (8) enterprises run by towns, sub-districts or villages that have been registered upon approval and have obtained business licenses according to law; and (9) other organizations meeting the requirements set down in this Article." The Opinions of the Supreme People's Court on Some Issues Concerning the Application of the Civil Procedure Law of the People's Republic of China have been abolished.

Sub-Contract, the parties to the settlement were the sub-contractor and the employer, therefore, the settlement should be between the consortium (the "sub-contractor") and company A (the "employer"). Company B may not individually represent the sub-contractor to settle final accounts with Company A without authorization from Company C. If it was agreed under the Sub-Contract that the settlement shall be made by the leader of the consortium on behalf of the consortium or by a member of the consortium jointly commissioned by other parties to the consortium, such member's sole application for arbitration on settlement would be justifiable, and would not damage legitimate rights of contractual settlement or arbitration enjoyed by other members of the consortium. In addition, it would also prevent the arbitral tribunal from overlooking any issue that should have been heard or ruled on, or determining issues beyond its jurisdiction.

IV. Academic Focus

1. Legal validity of using "short list" in government procurement

With regard to government procurement activities of all local governments, they usually first include potential suppliers in their "procurement suppliers list" (hereinafter referred to as the "Short List") and then select suppliers from the "Short List". The relationship between such practices and the legal principle of government procurement and whether it violates full competition are subject to academic debate.

According to the provisions of the *Government Procurement Law* and the *Tendering and Bidding Law* tendering and procurement should follow the principle of openness, fairness, impartiality and good faith. Moreover, according to the provisions of the *Government Procurement Law*, open tendering, selective tendering, competitive negotiation, single source procurement, inquiry or other procurement methods identified by the procurement supervision and administration department of the State Council may be applied and that open tendering should be the main procurement method. In addition, according to the provisions of the regulations on the implementation of the *Government Procurement Law* and the rules of the relevant departments procurement methods in government procurement activities such as open tendering, selective tendering and competitive negotiation are subject to open prequalification and the selection of appropriate potential suppliers to conduct procurement activities.

It can be inferred that the legislative intention of the *Government Procurement Law* is that of openness, fairness, impartiality and good faith, which should be taken as basic principles. Yet, the Short List may possibly restrict open competition and impede fair trade. The main views on this topic are as follows:

Firstly, the Short List includes suppliers before implementation of procurement which may not be timely and effective at the time of implementing procurement. For instance, its original qualifications may not fully cover the requirements at the time of formally conducting a new procurement, or the original qualified suppliers may not still satisfy the relevant conditions at a new point in time;

Secondly, the short list directly violates the provisions of Article 25 of the *Government Procurement Law*, because the stipulated procurement method is usually open tendering, and selection of appropriate suppliers from the short list cannot ensure compliance with the provisions thereof, not to mention that selective tendering or competitive negotiation also requires the conduct of open prequalification;

Thirdly, the Government is under the suspicion of setting up an administrative license if it makes use of the Short List, which could be interpreted as only the short listed entities can qualify for participation, therefore, such short list constitutes a threshold; according to the provisions of Article 15 of the *Administrative License Law of PRC*, an administrative license established by a local regulation or government rule of the provinces, autonomous region and municipalities directly under the Central Government "*shall not hinder individuals or enterprises of other regions from manufacturing, doing business or providing services in the local region, and shall not restrict the commodities of other regions from entering the local market*". Therefore, such practice breaches the law and should be revoked. For example, in regard to current PPP projects, the governments of all levels are keen on setting up short lists for PPP projects and only select suppliers from the lists. Such practice will violate the *Administrative License Law* and also restrict legitimate competition.

2. Final account of incomplete works in lump sum contracts

Article 22 of the *Judicial Interpretations on Construction Contracts* stipulates that "*if the parties have agreed to settle the final account of the construction payment on a lump sum basis, and one party requests authentication of the project cost, it should not be upheld*". This regulation applies only to the settlement method of the final account of completed works in lump sum contracts but does not apply to the settlement of the final account of uncompleted works in lump sum contracts. In practice, the final account of a lump sum construction contract, which is terminated without completion due to the reasons of one or both parties, is an urgent issue which requires negotiation.

According to the guiding opinions of all regions' higher courts, there areusually three methods for settling the final account of imcomplete works in lump sum contracts:

The first is "quota calculation method". For instance, Article 15 of the *Guiding Opinions of Chongqing Higher People's Court on Several Legal Issues concerning Current Civil Trials* provides that, the construction price calculated by way of using quotas should be decreased by a certain ratio as compared with the lump sum price.

The second is "conversion of the quantity of completed works". For instance, Article 1 of the *Opinions of Guangdong Higher People's Court on Several Issues concerning the Trial of Disputes over Construction Contracts* provides that the payment should be calculated on the basis of a lump sum agreed in the contract as well as the completion percentage of the works set out under the contract.

The third is "the same proportion as a third party's standard". For instance, Article 13 of the *Reply of Beijing Higher People's Court on Several Difficult Issues concerning the Trial of Disputes over Construction Contracts* provides that, the method of "conversion in proportion" should be adopted, i. e., the authentication institute should separately calculate the price of the completed works and the total price of the entire project agreed in the contract set at the same charging standard, comparing and contrasting the two results and calculating the corresponding coefficient, and multiplying the lump sum agreed in the contract by the coefficient to determine the payment to be paid by the employer.

The opinion of the Supreme People's Court on these issues is reflected in the adjudication of "Disputes over Construction Contract between Qinghai Fangsheng Construction Engineering

LLC and Qinghai Longhao Properties Co. , Ltd" in 2015 bulletin cases[11]. The opinion of the Supreme People's Court on this case states that, for a construction contract with an agreed lump sum, if the parties failed to perform the contract as agreed resulting in a termination thereof, when deciding the payment due under the disputed contract, payment cannot be calculated simply by using the quotas published by the Government. It is also improper to directly take the ratio of the total price agreed in the contract to the total budget price of the entire project as the ratio to decrease and multiply such ratio by the budget price of the completed works to calculate the construction payment, which should, instead, be determined by taking into account the actual performance of the case with a special focus on such factors as the degree of the parties' fault and the value given by judicial decision.

In the above opinion, the Supreme People's Court does not clarify which settlement method should be adopted in case of early termination of a lump sum construction contract. But, it emphasizes that it is necessary to take into account of the actual performance of the contract and the degree of the parties' fault and determine the settlement method under the principle of fairness and by balancing the parties' interests. However, in the author's opinion, generally speaking, it is relatively reasonable to resolve such disputes by "the same proportion as the third party's standard" in accordance with the guiding opinion of Beijing Higher People's Court.

3. Confiscation of illegal income in the disputes of sub-contracting disputes of entire construction projects to other contractors and illegal sub-contracting of works to disqualified sub-contractors

Article 4 of the *Judicial Interpretations on Construction Contracts* provides that, "*the illegal sub-contracting of the entire construction project to other contractors or the illegal sub-contracting of works to disqualified sub-contractors by the contractors, or the execution of construction contracts between the actual disqualified contractors in the name of qualified construction enterprises and others shall be deemed to be invalid. The people's court may, in accordance with Article* 134 *of the General Principles of the Civil Law, confiscate illegal income which has been obtained by the parties.*" The scope of the definition of illegal income in this article is controversial in judicial practice. After taking into account the relevant interpretations of the Supreme People's Court and the opinions reflected in the adjudications, the issues are clarified as follows:

At present, the mainstream opinion is that the main function of the courts in trials of civil and commercial cases is to make impartial judgments. The sanction of confiscating illegal income as stipulated by the *Judicial Interpretations on Construction Contracts* should be used with caution. It is generally believed that the people's court should exercise such power of confiscation as stipulated by the above judicial interpretations. Therefore, the arbitration institutions should not take confiscation when dealing with such disputes.

As to the scope of "illegal income" to be confiscated, the prevailing opinion is that a restrictive interpretation should also be applied. Specifically, first, the *Judicial Interpretations on*

---

11 Case No. : Min Yi Zhong Zi No. 69 of 2014, Source: Judicial Opinions of China, the Supreme People's Court at http://www.court.gov.cn/wenshu/xiangqing-8389.html, accessed on 26 January 2016.

Construction Contracts expressly provide that the illegal income to be confiscated should be that which "has been obtained"; therefore, the management fee agreed by the parties but has not been obtained should not be confiscated pursuant to this article. Second, if the state administrative agency has imposed administrative punishments, it is inappropriate for the people's court to impose civil sanctions again.

It should be mentioned that there is a different opinion, on whether the illegal income which is agreed, but has not been obtained should be confiscated. This opinion holds that, if the court does not confiscate illegal income which is agreed but has not been obtained, it will cause the payer to make a profit due to the invalidity of contract, which does not comply with the basic principle that no one shall benefit from illegal actions. Therefore, the agreed illegal income should also be confiscated. It seems that this opinion is, on balance, reasonable, but it is generally believed that for the management fee which is agreed by the parties but has not actually occurred, the payee does not obtain profit according to an invalid contract. The payer simply does not impair its existing property due to the invalidity of contract and it does not make any additional profits according to the invalid contract. Therefore, those fees are not the illegal income to be obtained by any party based on the invalid contract and should not be subject to confiscation.

A specific explanation is required where the qualification-lending party or the person who illegally sub-contracts the entire construction project to other contractors who can prove its actual provision of management service to the qualification-borrowing party or sub-contractor, should comprehensively consider factors such as performance of contract, contracting fault, construction quality, and etc, based on the principle of fairness, to support the management fee matched with the actual management pay which is claimed by the qualification-lending party or the person who illegally sub-contracts the entire construction project to other contractors. If the qualification-lending party and the person who illegally sub-contracts the entire construction project to other contractors cannot prove actual provision of management services, its claim of management fee should not be supported.

4. Legal nature of waiving the priority of compensation for construction payments

For the purpose of protecting the lawful rights and interests of the contractor, Article 286 of the *Contract Law* grants a priority of compensation for construction payments to the contractor. However, in practice, the employer, who is in a dominant position and in order to meet its mortgage financing needs, always requires the contractor to issue a written document for waiving the priority of compensation for construction payments. However, as to whether the priority of compensation for construction payments may be waived in advance, the *Contract Law* and the relevant judicial interpretations of the Supreme People's Court make no clear regulations and there are different opinions in judicial practice:

One opinion is that it is a civil right of the contractor to have the priority of compensation for construction payments. therefore, on the basis of the principle of the autonomy of will provided by the *Civil Law*, the parties may either exercise or waive such right, which shall not be prohibited by law so long as it is the genuine intention of the rights owner. Therefore, if it is the contractor's genuine intention to waive the priority of compensation for the discounted or auctioned price of the projects when the construction payment is not paid off on schedule, the contractor's intention shall be identified as legal and valid and the contractor shall bear the legal consequences of being deprived of the priority of compensation. In a case concerning the dispute over construction contracts, i. e. *China Guangfa Bank Co. ,Ltd Changsha Branch vs. Hunan Landscape Architecture Co. ,Ltd and Hunan Hongjin Real Estate Co. , Ltd*, the Hunan Higher People's Court held a similar view. According to the judgment, the contractor has the legal right of priority for compensation from the project involved, which takes precedence over other rights. As this right is still a property right of the contractor that could be disposed freely, and the contractor, as the rights owner, who expressly waives such right under specific circumstances does not violate any prohibitive provisions under any laws and administrative regulations and therefore shall be a lawful and valid juristic act.

Another opinion is that the priority of compensation cannot be waived in advance. There are two main reasons. One is that the purpose of the priority of compensation for payment created by law is to protect the interests of the contractor so as to prevent the employer from deliberately owing payment through taking advantage of its dominant position. If it is possible to waive such right through agreement of the parties, then the purpose of the priority of compensation for payment provided by law cannot be achieved and the relevant law will only exist in name. The other is that being in a weak position in the legal relationship of construction projects, the contractor always has to accept the conditions imposed by the employer so as to get the construction projects. So, in practice it is hard to ensure that the contractor's intention to waive the priority of compensation is genuine. Therefore, the priority of compensation granted by law to the contractor should not be waived in advance through agreement or any unilateral undertaking.

In the author's opinion, the nature of the priority of compensation granted to the contractor of construction projects by Article 286 of the *Contract Law* is a kind of priority right stipulated by law. The purpose of such legislation is to solve the problem of owing payments which then to ensure the resolution of the problems such as workers' wages and payments of material supply. If the contractor is allowed to waive the priority of compensation for payment, the purpose of the legislation will be frustrated. Thus, the priority of compensation for payments should not be waived in principle. However, without prejudice to the rights and interests of the workers, when the employer has provided practically reliable guarantees or a tri-partite agreement has been entered into by a bank, the employer and the contractor by which the employer mortgages the uncompleted construction works to the bank and the bank directly pays the loan to the contractor, if the contractor elects to waive the priority of compensation for construction payments, it should be uphold.

Finally, in the author's opinion, the premise of being a kind of priorityright stipulated by law depends on the nature of the right and the legal interests it protects. If it shall not be waived absolutely, it shall be expressly provided by law. However, such right relates to a civil creditor's rights. A right direction of legislation should be the legitimate approach as to, in a fairly and reasonably way, consider the interests of the parties to the transaction, the basis of the consideration, and the essential elements that cannot be waived, because in any event, the purpose is to protect the rights and interests generated in the civil transactions.

V. Conclusion and Prospects

With the gradual improvement of the legal and policy system concerning the PPP model in 2015, the PPP model will be implemented and put into practice intensively in 2016, and the construction for infrastructure and public utilities projects will become very broad in space for development. As the PPP model involves multiple parties, complex legal relationships, long cycles of cooperation in projects and increased uncertainties during the performance of the construction projects, there may be a significant change in the number and type of disputes relating to PPP projects and construction projects in the future. In addition, with the expediting of new urbanization and the implementation of "One Belt One Road" Strategy, domestic and overseas construction markets will further develop and mix and the enterprises in relevant fields will enter into a new period of development with opportunities and challenges coexisting, in which the enterprises will have to improve their risk management capacities and comprehensive capacities so as to adapt to the new environment and situations and the regulatory authorities will impose stricter requirements.

Since 2015, with the adjustment of the industrial structure and China's financing policies, the slowdown of investment and the development of the construction industry encountering hardship, the number of disputes over construction contracts arising from the settlement of construction payments have constantly increased. In response to contractors' demands for payment, employers always advance a counter-claim for compensation for delay to completion, defective workmanship, and illegal sub-contracting of the entire construction project to other contractors and illegal sub-contracting of works to disqualified sub-contractors. Therefore, the disputes over construction contracts usually focus on the combination of many issues, such as the settlement of construction payments, determination of delay liability, analysis of the liability for defective works, breach of contract and determination of responsibilities, in addition to few disputes over a single issue arising from construction contracts. As there are many disputes arising under construction contracts, most of which involve professional issues and need to be determined through authentication, so, the resolution of the disputes of construction contracts requires a longer period of time, sustains lower efficiency and costs the parties a lot of money. Therefore, the mentioned above issues have been criticised by the parties who are anxious to recover the construction payments and have became the issues that need to be addressed in the resolution of the disputes over construction contracts.

Looking ahead into 2016, the situation in the field of construction projectsis still not optimistic. Disputes over construction contracts arising from the settlement of payment will remain as an increasing trend. Thus, by seeking a scheme resolving disputes over construction contracts efficiently that increases the efficiency of judgment is a key direction for research of dispute resolution institutes.

Annual Review on Real Estate Dispute Resolution in China (2016) *

Dennis DENG [1]

I. Overview

The dual impact of economic and policy factors has brought about a volatile housing market in China in 2015. Meanwhile, the government has stepped up its efforts to boost market demand and digest housing inventory by launching a series of relaxed housing policies, including multiple rounds of cuts to the reserve requirement ratio (RRR) and interest rates, the lowering of down payment requirements for housing purchases, increases in public housing fund loan ceiling, transaction tax exemptions and reductions and so forth. In the wake of such policies, however, the housing market has only become more polarized, resulting in a relatively tense supply and demand imbalance, with demand for housing thriving in top tier cities, while certain third and fourth tier cities continue to experience excess housing inventory and severe stagnation. By turning to various measures ranging from restructuring existing resources, modifying business models, forming alliances with other industry giants [2] to expanding financing channels—such as setting up real estate investment trust funds (REIT) [3], testing the waters of real estate crowd funding [4]—large real estate enterprises are getting increasingly stronger. Small and medium-sized enterprises, on the other hand, are being squeezed into a condensed living space, leaving them no choice but to sell off their real estate businesses and forge a different path. The real estate industry is seeing more and more mergers and restructurings (be it by way

---

* Translated by Hogan Lovells International LLP.

1 Dennis DENG, senior partner of Dentons (China), Beijing Arbitration Commission/Beijing International Arbitration Centre arbitrator.

2 e. g. on 14 May 2015, residential housing giant, China Vanke Co Ltd, entered into a strategic collaboration framework agreement with commercial property giant, Dalin Wanda Group Co Ltd, in Beijing. http://news.xinhuanet.com/house/suzhou/2015-05-14/c_1115289739.htm, accessed on 10 January 2016.

3 e. g. on 26 June 2015, Vanke partnered with Penghua Fund Management to launch the first public REITs in China ("Qianhai REITs"). http://news.ifeng.com/a/20150626/44045329_0.shtml, accessed on 10 January 2016; "Insane" 100 Billion Domestic Debt of RE Enterprises, http://info.3g.qq.com/g/index5/ttnews/chinamobile.jsp?id=house_20151014022769&g_f=23748&g_ut=3, accessed on 11 January 2016.

4 e. g. Beijing North Star announced its Coco Moma ICBC Credit Suisse Phase I Crowdfunding Project via 51wofang.com, Wanda's "Wen Zhuan Yi Hao" project, the Shanghai Jiading District "Country Garden-Pingan-Crowdfunded Housing Project" launched by Pinganfang and Country Garden, Greenland Group's "Wuhan Greenland Centre" and other like projects are all explorations into real estate crowdfunding.

of equity or projects)[5], which not only facilitate the integration of the industry's resources, but also continuously stage a chess game between industry and capital[6]. Products on the real estate market are gradually being diversified, with more and more businesses moving from residential housing towards senior housing, cultural and tourism real estate, logistics real estate and other areas.

As a result of fluctuations on the real estate market and frequent changes in real estate policies, there has been a marked uptick in real estate disputes. According to two sets of data obtained through public channels, in 2015, the courts in the entire Sichuan province adjudicated 23,489 cases concerning, among other things, use rights to land designated for construction purposes, real estate development and operations, and disputes arising from housing purchases and sales, involving an aggregate amount of RMB 30.897 billion, representing an increase of 41.19% and 89.1%[7] respectively over the previous year. In Zhejiang, the courts throughout the province adjudicated 32,000 real estate disputes (a 19.8% increase over the previous year), involving an aggregate amount of RMB 31.9 billion[8].

II. Review of New Laws

A. Real Estate Macro-control Policies

At the end of 2015, there were 718.53 million square metres[9] of commercial housing available on the market throughout China, a figure which is high and rising. Therefore, the central theme of the real estate industry in 2015 was "destocking". At both the central and local levels, the government has stepped up its efforts to boost market demand and digest housing inventory by launching a series of relaxed housing policies, including multiple rounds of cuts to the reserve requirement ratio (RRR) and interest rates, the lowering of down payment requirements for housing purchases, increases in public housing fund loan ceiling, transaction tax exemptions and reductions and so forth. In particular, the central government included destocking as one of the top five economic undertakings of the State in 2016 during the Central Economic Work Conference held from 18 to 22 December 2015[10].

B. Laws and Regulations on Land Administration

In the wake of the continued shift in rural labour force and growing demand for the circulation and trading of collectively owned rural land, the Standing Committee of the National

5 According to Wind Info, as of 28 September, there had been 176 M&As in the real estate industry in 2015, involving RMB 160 billion, which is close to the value of all real estate M&A deals in 2014. See "Large Companies are Busy Merging in 2015": http://www.yicai.com/news/2015/10/4698687.html, accessed on 13 January 2016.

6 The most classic example of real estate M&A in 2015 is Baoneng's acquisition of Vanke.

7 Sichuan Higher People's Court Working Report (Abstract): http://www.sc.gov.cn/10462/10464/10797/2016/2/6/10367891.shtml, accessed on 1 March 2016.

8 Zhejiang Higher People's Court Working Report: http://zjnews.zjol.com.cn/system/2016/02/02/021011445.shtml, accessed on1 March 2016.

9 State Statistics Bureau: "2015 Nationwide Real Estate Development, Investment and Sales", http://www.stats.gov.cn/tjsj/zxfb/201601/t20160119_1306094.html, accessed on 22 January 2016.

10 People.com.cn: "Central Economic Work Conference Held in Beijing", http://politics.people.com.cn/n1/2015/1222/c1024-27958128.html, accessed on 22 January 2016.

People's Congress promulgated the *Decision on Authorising the State Council to Temporarily Adjust the Implementation of Relevant Laws in the Administrative Regions of Thirty-Three Pilot Counties (or Municipalities or Districts) including Daxing District in Beijing* (the "Decision") on 27 February 2015, authorising the State Council to temporarily adjust the implementation of the relevant provisions of the *People's Republic of China Land Administration Law and the People's Republic of China Urban Real Estate Administration Law* with respect to the expropriation of rural land, the entry of collectively owned commercial construction land ("Co-owned Construction Land") into the market, and the administration system for rural homestead in the administrative regions of thirty-three pilot counties (or municipalities or districts) including Daxing district in Beijing[11]. On 24 August that year, the State Council subsequently promulgated its *Mortgage Loans on Contracted Rural Land Operating Rights and Rural Resident Housing Property Rights Pilot Programmes Launching Guidelines* (State Council Doc. No. 45 of 2015), launching pilot programmes for mortgaging, transferring and providing security for the property rights in the housing of residents in rural areas, as well as pilot programmes for mortgage loans on the operating rights to contracted land (i. e. arable land) in rural areas and property rights in rural resident housing[12].

The entry of Co-owned Construction Land into the market will certainly lead to a scenario where urban State-owned Construction land and Co-owned Construction Land enjoy the same status, which will inevitably impact the real estate and land market to a certain extent. However, since Co-owned Construction Land is in extremely short supply at the pilot stage, and the planning for and use of such land are strictly controlled, the scope of Co-owned Construction Land to be put and circulated on the market, as well as the mechanism for determining the transaction price of the land, the method for allocating gains from the land, and the means for regulating entry into the market and related transactions have yet to be determined. Therefore, the impact that Co-owned Construction Land's entry into and circulation on the market will have on the real estate market is currently unknown and will remain to be seen.

C. Real Estate Registration System

The *Real Estate Registration Interim Regulations* (State Council Decree No. 656) officially came into force on 1 March 2015, and were first implemented in cities including Harbin, Nanjing and Xiamen on a trial basis. According to the Registration System Office of the Real Estate Registration Center under the Ministry of Land and Resources, China has basically completed the top-level framework for its uniform real estate registration system, and following the implementation of the *Real Estate Registration Interim Regulations*, supporting policies such as the *Real Estate Registration Interim Regulations Implementing Rules* and *Real Estate Registration Technical Procedures* will be subsequently rolled out. [13]Among the aforesaid policies, the *Real Estate Registration Interim Regulations Implementing Rules* came into force on 1 January

11 See NPC's website: http://www.npc.gov.cn/npc/xinwen/2015-02/28/content_1906228.html, accessed on 12 January 2016.

12 See the Chinese Government's website: http://www.gov.cn/zhengce/content/2015-08/24/content_10121.html, accessed on 12 January 2016.

13 "Real Estate Registration Interim Regulations Implementing Rules to Be Released": http://www.legaldaily.com.cn/index_article/content/2015-06/26/content_6143041.htm?node=5955, accessed on 10 January 2016.

2016 as per Decree No. 63 of the Ministry of Land and Resources dated 1 January 2016.

The creation of a sound and uniform real estate registration system will be beneficial to clarifying property rights, improving transparency in real estate transactions, and lowering transaction costs. Moreover, the eventual development of a system for sharing real estate registration information nationwide will lay an important foundation for introducing real estate tax reform and other related policies and regulations.

D. Policies Allowing Entry of Foreign Capital into Real Estate Market

In order to facilitate the steady and healthy growth of the real estate market, MOHURD, NDRC, PBOC, SAIC and SAFE made changes to certain policies on foreign invested real estate enterprises, overseas institutions and housing purchases by individuals under the *Opinions on Regulating the Entry and Administration of Foreign Investment on the Real Estate Market* (MOHURD No. 171 of 2006), and promulgated the *Entry and Administration of Foreign Investment on Real Estate Market Policy Change Circular* (MOHURD No. 122 of 2015)[14], providing a more relaxed environment for foreign investment on China's real estate market.

Restrictions on foreign investment and housing purchases are both measures designed to prevent housing prices from rising too quickly on an overheated real estate market. However, given the current downturn of the real estate market and the overall sluggish increase in housing prices, the loosening of restrictions on foreign investment is inevitable, and will contribute to the steady growth of the real estate market.

E. Real Estate Advertising Standards

On 24 December 2015, the State Administration of Industry and Commerce promulgated the *Real Estate Advertising Provisions* (SAIC Decree No. 80)[15], which require that real estate advertisements be truthful, lawful, scientific and accurate, and free from contents which would deceive or mislead consumers. As of 1 February 2016, the use of wording in real estate advertisements claiming to "help residents with their household registration ("*hukou*"), school placement", as well as those promising "appreciation or returns on investment" or other promises such as "purchases entitle places at prestigious schools" and "guaranteed high returns on investment" will be deemed unlawful.

Previously, real estate advertising was fraught with exaggerations; deceptive advertising was fairly commonplace. The arrival of the *Real Estate Advertising Provisions*, however, will reduce the risk of home buyers being misled by false advertising; real estate developers, on the other hand, will be forced to abandon the old methods of advertising and marketing, and find new ways to attract buyers.

---

14 See MOHURD's website: http://www.mohurd.gov.cn/wjfb/201508/t20150828_224060.html, accessed on 11 January 2016.

15 See SAIC's website: http://www.saic.gov.cn/zwgk/zyfb/zjl/xxzx/201512/t20151231_165562.html, accessed on 10 January 2016.

F. Improvement of Residential Housing Rental System

On 6 January 2015, the Ministry of Housing and Urban-Rural Development promulgated its *Accelerating the Cultivation and Development of the Residential Housing Rental Market Guidelines* (MOHURD No. 4 of 2015)[16], which position the residential housing rental market as an integral part of China's housing supply system. The *Guidelines* also indicate that the market would play a decisive role in resource allocation, and the government would take on a better role, in order to actively advance the construction of a platform for rental services, vigorously develop rental agencies for residential housing, improve public housing rental systems, expand financing channels, push forward the transformation and upgrading of real estate developers, and, in 3 years' time, essentially create a diverse, balanced and reasonably structured residential housing rental market with standard services and a sound system.

At the Central Economic Work Conference held from 18 to 22 December 2015, the central government also specifically call for the next phase of development of China's housing system to move towards resolving the housing needs of new urban residents by creating a housing system which equally promotes housing rentals and purchases.[17]

III. Case Studies

A. Arbitration of China-Ghana Collaborative Real Estate Development Dispute[18]

1. Case background

The claimant is a private Chinese enterprise engaging in real estate development; the first respondent is a Ghanaian company engaging in real estate construction, and is wholly-owned by another Ghanaian company, XX (Ghana) Group Corporation[19] ("XX (Ghana) Corp"); the second respondent is a large Chinese State-owned enterprise which owns 100% of the equity in XX (Ghana) Corp.

On 6 April 2013, the claimant entered into a Strategic Collaboration Agreement (the "SCA") with the first respondent at the office of the second respondent located at a certain provincial capital in China, stipulating that the parties would establish a joint venture company (the "JV Co") in Ghana for the purpose of jointly developing real estate in Ghana. Under the SCA, the claimant was to hold 60% of the equity in the JV Co, while the first respondent was

---

16 See MOHURD's website: http://www.mohurd.gov.cn/zcfg/jsbwj_0/jsbwjfdcy/201501/t20150114_220094.html, accessed on 1 March 2016.

17 People.com.cn: "Central Economic Work Conference Held in Beijing", http://politics.people.com.cn/n1/2015/1222/c1024-27958128.html, accessed on 1 March 2016.

18 This was not a Beijing Arbitration Commission/Beijing International Arbitration Centre case. The author's reason for choosing this case as an example was not to probe into specific issues, but rather to illustrate two relatively macroscopic issues: first, the significant role that compatibility between business model and legal framework plays in risk control and dispute resolution; second, the arbitration tribunal in this case may very well be unique in its approach, and it is hoped that such approach will reflect the understandable yet indescribable flow of the adjudicator's thought process.

19 Said subsidiary was also set up by the second respondent in Ghana.

to hold 40%[20].

However, the shareholders and shareholding structure of the JV Co actually set up were as follows: Individual A held 50% of the equity in the JV Co, Individual B held 40% and Individual C held 10%. Individual A (a Chinese national) was the chairman of the claimant; Individual B (a Chinese national) was both the chairman of the first respondent and the chairman of its shareholder, XX (Ghana) Corp; Individual C is a natural person in Ghana (a Ghanaian national). According the claimant's statement, Individual A held equity in the JV Co on behalf of the claimant, while Individual B and Individual C held equity in the JV Co on behalf of the first respondent. While the first respondent neither confirmed nor denied this, the parties did not enter into any written instrument to address this issue specifically[21]. In particular, there was no written confirmation from Individual C in this regard. The board of directors of the JV Co was comprised of two directors, namely, Individual A and Individual B, with Individual A acting as the chairman.

During the course of the collaboration, a dispute arose between the parties. Following consultations, the claimant agreed to withdraw from the project, but the parties failed to reach a consensus on the claimant's investment losses. In particular, the respondents took the view that since the project had yet to be completed and expected returns were undetermined, a profit scenario and loss scenario were both still possible, and the claimant therefore should not claim compensation for losses on its investment. Ultimately, the parties executed meeting minutes, which stipulated, "[t]he parties agree to first submit the matters on which no agreement has been reached to arbitration, and the parties shall proactively cooperate with the arbitration institution with a view to rendering an award as soon as practicable; if no arbitral award were rendered within two months of the date on which these minutes are executed, then the claimant shall maintain that the second respondent shall first pay the amount of the principal actually invested and confirmed; while the first respondent shall maintain that all confirmed amounts shall be paid together by the second respondent and first respondent after a consensus is reached, or an arbitral award is rendered, with respect to other disputed matters". "The parties agree to submit the matters on which no agreement has been reached to arbitration, and all obligations under the arbitral award shall be performed within two weeks. The parties shall share the arbitration costs on a 50/50 basis".

In September 2014, the claimant filed for arbitration, demanding that the first respondent be held liable for default for terminating the collaboration between the parties in breach of the relevant agreements. The claimant's primary arbitration claims included: (1) the first respondent and second respondent jointly pay the collaborative development costs incurred by the claimant in the amount of RMB XXXX[22]; (2) the first respondent and second respondent jointly pay the claimant the expected profits from the JV Co's development of the DXS Plaza Project in the amount of RMB XXXX (tentative) due to the claimant. During the proceedings, the claimant requested that the appraiser appointed by the arbitration tribunal conduct an appraisal of the profits expected from the DXS Plaza Project.

---

20 According to the claimant's statement, the respective shareholding ratio of both parties was 50% each, with the claimant holding 10% on behalf of the first respondent. However, no written agreement was entered into between the parties.

21 The claimant submitted to the arbitration tribunal a nominee shareholding confirmation letter issued by its chairman, Individual A, confirming that Individual A was holding shares in the JV Co on behalf of the claimant.

22 Equivalent to the amount on which the parties failed to reach an agreement.

2. Opinion of the arbitral tribunal

The arbitral tribunal was of the opinion that the arbitration matter specified under the arbitration agreement was not a dispute over the termination of the contract by law, nor was it a dispute over the termination of the contract by agreement; rather, it equated to the creation of a contract for the parties by the arbitration tribunal. The contractual dispute at issue was not a dispute over the performance of the SCA, rather, it was a dispute which arose while the parties negotiated termination by mutual consent. Naturally, the arbitration tribunal must respect the true intent of the parties to attempt termination by mutual consent—as opposed to termination by law—and must not go against the parties' intent by determining termination by law. Yet, the parties failed to reach an agreement through consultations, and thus submitted the differences between their offers to be resolved by the arbitration tribunal. This essentially meant that the arbitration tribunal would be creating a contract for the parties, an act that would certainly exceed the scope of the tribunal's duties.

For this reason, the arbitration tribunal took the view that the arbitration application submitted by the claimant and respondents should be rejected. If the parties truly could not reach an agreement on mutual consent, then they could consider resolving their dispute through other remedial measures, such as directly initiating an action in a court in accordance with the relevant legal provisions governing termination by law.

3. Review of dispute

From a legal standpoint, most of the issues in the present case pertain to corporate law. However, the primary factor affecting the resolution of the dispute was the incompatibility between the business model and legal framework involved; and yet such incompatibility is extremely common in the real estate development industry. This case is therefore of great value. In addition, the outcome of this case is extremely uncommon, and is therefore worth a read.

In terms of the case itself, the parties had a clear development goal before establishing the JV Co, i. e. ,the DXS Plaza Project. The purpose of the parties' collaboration was not for the long-term engagement in real estate development activities, and the JV Co itself was a project company specifically set up to develop the DXS Plaza Project. From the claimant's point of view, the parties should have stated this point when entering into the SCA[23], while a compatible legal framework would have been one whereby the parties to the SCA (i. e. the claimant and first respondent) established the JV Co as shareholders. Yet in actuality, the parties arranged for Individual A, Individual B and Individual C to hold equity on their behalf when establishing the JV Co. Based on the evidence in the case, the arbitration tribunal would not have been able to determine that Individual C held equity in the JV Co on behalf of the first respondent; but rather, legally, the tribunal could only treat Individual C as an independent third party. Individual C's independent legal status played a major role in guiding the verdict of the arbitration tribunal in the case. If Individual C did not have an independent legal status, the case would purely be a dispute between the claimant and the first respondent, and the arbitration tribunal would not need to worry whether its decision would affect the JV Co or Individual C.

---

23 This would help the arbitration tribunal to determine that the JV Co was a means of performing the SCA.

Moreover, the parties' establishment of the JV Co could essentially be construed as a means of performing the SCA, while the business failure of the JV Co could directly lead to a conclusion of a breach by the claimant or the first respondent under the SCA, and the non-breaching party could directly pursue the breaching party for liability in accordance with the SCA. Conversely, the arbitration tribunal was now compelled to focus its attention on whether or not upholding the claimant's claims would affect the JV Co or Individual C (neither of whom was a party to the case), because an affirmative would greatly erode the tribunal's confidence in upholding the claimant's claims. From the claimant's perspective, the parties should have separately agreed on or confirmed in writing such nominee shareholding structure, so as to avoid the occurrence of such circumstances.

Due to the incompatibility between the business model and legal framework involved, the parties' collaborative relationship (based on the SCA) and shareholder relationship (based on the JV Co) were severed, and the rights and obligations at either end could not be matched. Add to this the mishandling of the dispute, and it would be substantively difficult to uphold the arbitration claims of the claimant. However, the arbitration tribunal did not turn down the claimant's claims in substance; rather, by interpreting the contract on its own initiative, the tribunal concluded the case in a fashion unexpected to the parties. As the parties did not differ in their understanding of the arbitration provisions and the related agreement, there was in fact no need for interpretation in the first place. Nevertheless, the arbitration tribunal took it upon itself to interpret the contract, and its methodology for interpretation was not based on any conventional approach, such as a literal, systematic or historical interpretation, or an interpretation in line with the purpose of the contract, or that which conforms to customs or practices; rather, the arbitration tribunal adopted the method of elimination[24]. When ruling out an interpretation based on termination by law, the arbitration tribunal also rejected said conventional means of interpretation. The author is of the opinion that an adjudicator should strictly respect the autonomy of the will of the parties. In civil proceedings, the public authority of the court is merely an instrument to resolve disputes between equal civil entities in the sphere of private rights. This does not mean that the parties, as equal civil entities in a dispute arising within the sphere of private rights, are at the mercy of the public authority. In commercial arbitration, the arbitration tribunal in particular needs to respect the autonomy of will of the parties. The reason for this is that the very nature of arbitration is for the arbitration institution engaged by the parties to make a decision on a dispute between such parties, and then to render such decision enforceable on the strength of the authority granted to the institution by the State. Specifically, in terms of contract interpretation, if the parties do not interpret the contract differently, then the adjudicator cannot interpret the contract on its own initiative, much less present its own understanding. If the parties do interpret the contract differently, then what the adjudicator can do is to determine the true intent of the parties by way of interpreting the contract, which is different from using its own interpretation to supersede the will of the parties. When interpreting a contract, the adjudicator must examine the true intent of the parties from the parties' perspective, rather than from its own.

---

24 That is, the means by which a contract is terminated include termination by agreement, termination by law and termination by mutual consent. However, the present case did not involve termination by agreement, while the parties ruled out termination by law, and termination by mutual consent could not be achieved. Therefore, the arbitration matter agreed upon by the parties was, in actuality, the creation of a contract for the parties by the arbitration tribunal.

B. Arbitration of a Dispute Over Late Delivery Under a Commercial Housing Purchase and Sale Contract

1. Case background

The claimant, a natural person, and the respondent, a real estate development company, entered into a series of documents, stipulating that the claimant would purchase certain commercial housing developed by the respondent. The claimant, taking the view that the respondent had delayed in delivering the property, filed for arbitration, requesting that the respondent compensate the claimant for loss of interest on the down payment, loss of the deposit and loss of rent.

The parties entered into a Subscription Agreement on 22 April 2014, whereby the claimant agreed to purchase the property at issue. It was further stipulated that prior to 22 April 2014 (i. e. prior to entering into the Subscription Agreement), the claimant was required to make a 50.1% down payment (with a_____% mortgage loan) to the respondent, and then enter into a Commercial Housing Purchase and Sale Contract, as well as a Supplemental Contract thereto (i. e. the parties were to enter into the Commercial Housing Purchase and Sale Contract and Supplemental Contract prior to entering into the Subscription Agreement), and carry out mortgage loan procedures. However, the parties neither agreed on a specific delivery date for the property, nor provided for a specific percentage for the mortgage loan. As agreed under the Subscription Agreement, the claimant paid the 50.1% down payment.

In actuality, the parties did not enter into the Commercial Housing Purchase and Sale Contract and Supplemental Contract until 4 December 2014, under which it was agreed that the respondent would deliver the property by 15 November 2014, and the claimant would pay the remainder of the purchase price by way of a mortgage loan, for which the respondent would carry out the relevant procedures on behalf of the claimant. However, the parties failed to specify a date by which the purchase price was to be paid in full; rather, it was only mentioned in the Supplemental Contract that if the respondent was to be responsible for taking out a mortgage loan on behalf of the claimant, then the claimant was to provide the respondent with the relevant materials within ten days of entry into the Commercial Housing Purchase and Sale Contract. The claimant completed the mortgage loan procedures on 4 June 2015, and paid off the remainder of the purchase price by way of the mortgage loan on 5 June. On the following day (i. e. 6 June 2015), the respondent delivered the property to the claimant.

The claimant was of the opinion that the Commercial Housing Purchase and Sale Contract expressly stipulated that the respondent was to deliver the property by 15 November 2014. Although such date was earlier than the execution date of the Commercial Housing Purchase and Sale Contract, it actually originated from the Subscription Agreement previously executed by the parties. This, coupled with the respondent committing orally to deliver the property on 1 May 2014, led to the backdating of delivery date under the Commercial Housing Purchase and Sale Contract, which in turn was confirmation of the remedial measures taken by the respondent in regard to its oral commitment. Therefore, the respondent should have delivered the property by 15 November 2014 and should assume liability for breach of contract due to the delayed delivery of the property.

The respondent was of the opinion that the respondent could not have been able to deliver the property to the claimant until the parties signed online ("Wang Qian") the executed Commercial Housing Purchase and Sale Contract; thus, clearly, delivery by 15 November 2014 could not have been possible. Moreover, the respondent was entitled to refuse delivery until the claimant completed the mortgage loan procedures and paid the purchase price in full. The claimant paid off the purchase price by way of the mortgage loan on 5 June 2015, and the respondent delivered the property on the following day; such conduct did not constitute a breach of contract on the part of the respondent.

2. Opinion of the arbitration tribunal

The arbitration tribunal was of the opinion that the point of contention in the case was whether or not the respondent committed a breach of contract by delivering the property only after the claimant had made full payment. The parties' failure to expressly provide for a number of matters (including the date on which the claimant was to pay the purchase price in full and conditions precedent to delivery) was the root cause of the dispute. While the arbitration tribunal should make its decision based on the contract provisions or usage of trade, the parties differed in their understanding of the contract terms; thus, it was necessary for the arbitration tribunal to interpret the contract. Ultimately, the arbitration tribunal comprehensively weighed the various factors at play, and found both parties to be equally liable. The tribunal ruled that the respondent compensate the claimant for a portion of the loss of interest on the down payment, and rejected all other arbitration claims.

3. Review of dispute

The dispute in this case is the result of the parties not clearly providing for a number of matters in the contract and the discrepancy between their understandings of the contract terms. The agreement between the parties contained many illogical absurdities[25] which evaded all rational thinking, making it an extremely trying test of the arbitration tribunal's skills to determine matters that were not clearly provided for and to conduct contract interpretation. The way the tribunal handled this case epitomises the ruling and reasoning process that arbitration tribunals adopt in handling similar cases.

First, the execution date of the Commercial Housing Purchase and Sale Contract agreed upon by the parties under the Subscription Agreement was earlier than the execution date of the Subscription Agreement itself. This is absurd in that: (1) a Commercial Housing Purchase and Sale Contract is generally entered into after a Subscription Agreement; (2) logically speaking, we can only confirm today what has transpired yesterday, but cannot stipulate what must have transpired yesterday. Therefore, the parties' agreement concerning the execution of the Commercial Housing Purchase and Sale Contract is unenforceable.

Second, the date for carrying out mortgage procedures as agreed upon under the Subscription Agreement fell earlier than the execution date of the Subscription Agreement; moreover, the Commercial Housing Purchase and Sale Contract had yet to be executed. This is absurd in that: (1) the execution of a legitimate and valid purchase and sale contract for the property at

---

25 This is not a clerical error. Ordinarily, an absurdity is already something illogical which evades rational thinking. However, the irrationality in this case is far from ordinary that it is almost illogical to the extreme, hence the author's use of "illogical absurdities".

issue was a necessary condition for carrying out mortgage procedures; thus the parties could not have carried out such procedures by 22 April 2014; (2) logically speaking, we can only confirm today what has transpired yesterday, but we cannot stipulate what must have transpired yesterday. Therefore, the parties' agreement concerning mortgage loan procedures is unenforceable. However, the respondent had reason to believe that the true intent of the parties as embodied in such agreement was for the claimant to complete the mortgage loan procedures - and even pay off the purchase price in full by way of such mortgage loan—prior to the delivery of the property.

Third, the parties failed to expressly stipulate under the Commercial Housing Purchase and Sale Contract the date on which the housing price was to be paid in full; likewise, they also failed to stipulate the timeline for the completion of mortgage loan procedures. Although the Supplemental Contract did stipulate that the claimant was to provide the respondent with the relevant materials within ten days of execution of the Commercial Housing Purchase and Sale Contract, this merely provided for the means by which the mortgage loan was to be taken out, and cannot lead one to presume that the respondent was supposed to have delivered the property to the claimant prior to the completion of the mortgage loan procedures (i. e. full payment of the purchase price). Therefore, the unenforceability of the provisions of the Subscription Agreement concerning mortgage loan procedures does not automatically mean that the true intent of the parties with respect to such procedures as embodied in the Subscription Agreement was bound to change as a result of the execution of the Commercial Housing Purchase and Sale Contract. In other words, the respondent still had reason to believe that the true intent of the parties at the time of execution of the Commercial Housing Purchase and Sale Contract was that mortgage loan procedures were to be completed prior to delivery of the property.

Fourth, the delivery date agreed upon under the Commercial Housing Purchase and Sale Contract was earlier than the execution date of the contract itself, and the respondent had not yet delivered the property to the claimant at that time. If there were no other conditions precedent, the respondent would have been deemed to have delayed delivery upon entering into the Commercial Housing Purchase and Sale Contract. This clearly evades all reasons, and the arbitration tribunal should not presume that the respondent's purpose for entering into the Commercial Housing Purchase and Sale Contract was to be in breach of the same. Therefore, the arbitration tribunal can presume that there were other conditions precedent agreed upon by the parties.

Based on the details of the case, one possibility is that the respondent would not carry out mortgage loan procedures for the claimant until the respondent itself satisfied the conditions for delivery. Another possibility is that the respondent had satisfied the conditions for delivery, but the claimant had not satisfied the conditions for taking out the mortgage loan, and the respondent could only wait until the mortgage loan procedures had been completed and it received the loan to deliver the property. Neither parties produced any evidence shedding light on the specific reason, nor did they raise any objections or claims during the performance of the contract. In short, neither of the parties' claims are completely tenable, while it is also difficult to quantify the proportion of their respective liability. Therefore, the arbitration tribunal's finding that both parties share equal liability is rather reasonable, and it was appropriate for the tribunal to rule that the respondent compensated the claimant for a portion of the loss of interest on the down payment.

C. Mediation of a Dispute Over a Property Purchase and Sale Contract between a Service Centre and a Limited Liability Company

1. Case background

The commercial-residential building in question (the "Property at Issue") is a real estate project developed and built by a certain limited liability company (the "Developer"). On 29 June 2010, a certain service centre (the "Service Centre", as the buyer) entered into a property purchase agreement (the "Agreement") with the Developer (as the seller), whereby the Service Centre purchased the commercial space on the ground floor of the Property at Issue, as well as the underground parking garage, in their existing condition; the total floor area of the purchased space and garage was approximately 28,800 square metres; the total price for the purchase was RMB 396 million (inclusive of the land premium).

Pursuant to the Agreement, the Service Centre was to pay 50% of the transfer price in the first instalment (i. e. RMB 198 million). The Service Centre paid the aforementioned amount in full in August 2010. Pursuant to the Agreement, the Developer was to carry out ownership registration procedures for the Service Centre within thirty business days after payment of said amount. However, the Developer failed to obtain the property ownership certificate for the Service Centre as agreed because, among other things, the land grant price had yet to be settled.

In June 2015, the Service Centre engaged counsel to send to the Developer a lawyer's letter concerning the Developer's assistance in registering the transfer of ownership of the property, yet there was no substantial progress. As a result, the Service Centre (acting as the plaintiff) filed a civil action in a certain people's court (the "Court").

2. Dispute resolution process

On 24 June 2015, the plaintiff filed an action in the people's court, requesting the court to order the defendant to assist the plaintiff in registering the transfer of ownership of the Property at Issue. Upon receiving the relevant materials, the Court concluded that despite the rather high amount involved, the basic facts of the case were clear and the parties' dispute could be resolved by the combined processes of litigation and mediation. As advised by the Court, the parties agreed to turn the case over to the mediation centre under the China Real Estate Association ("CREA")[26] for mediation.

On 28 July 2015, the Court issued a Letter of Referral to Pre-litigation Mediation, referring the case to CREA for pre-litigation mediation. On 4 August 2015, CREA's mediation centre arranged for mediation between the parties, during which the parties, with CREA acting as the mediator and through the joint efforts of the plaintiff and defendant, came to an agreement which was detailed in a written mediation opinion. CREA then issued a Mediation Agreement (CREA Mediation No. 1 of 2015).

---

[26] CREA's mediation centre was established by the China Real Estate Association, and is an industry mediation organisation designed to resolve disputes relating to real estate, construction, real estate finance, component and part procurement and other related fields. Its website has already gone online at CREA's official website: www.fangchan.com.

On 4 August 2015, the plaintiff and defendant jointly submitted an application to the Court, petitioning the Court for judicial confirmation of the Mediation Agreement issued by CREA (CREA Mediation No. 1 of 2015). During the course of judicial confirmation, employees of CREA's mediation centre were also on hand to supervise the plaintiff and defendant in their performance of the executed Mediation Agreement. Following several rounds of consultations, the plaintiff and defendant confirmed, one by one, the details of the issues arisen during the performance of the Mediation Agreement. Through the joint efforts of both parties, the plaintiff eventually fulfilled the aim of its action (i. e. obtaining the Property Ownership Certificate), while the defendant received the payment of the agreed upon purchase price. The dispute was thus resolved in a satisfactory manner.

3. Review of dispute

Although the case itself is not very complex, it is of special significance that it used a "combined litigation and mediation" approach, which gave full play to the overall advantages of the trade organisation in the industry. As a result, the dispute between the plaintiff and defendant, which had been unresolved for over five years, was quickly resolved in just a few months' time. This, in turn, conserved judicial resources, made dispute resolution more efficient, lowered the costs of the parties in the dispute resolution process, and fully exemplified the scientific and rational nature of a diverse dispute resolution mechanism.

Mediation exists in both litigation and arbitration. However, there is widespread worry among disputing parties that should they reject a judge or arbitrator's mediation decision, such judge or arbitrator may retaliate against them when rendering a decision. Therefore, judges and arbitrators must do their utmost to keep disputing parties from feeling threatened by their judicial authority during mediation, as this will help better assure the parties that the ruling is impartial. One way of doing this is for judges and arbitrators to conduct a pre-mediation assessment of the odds that mediation will be successful. If the odds are low, then they should not waste their efforts on mediation, as it is much more likely for the parties to have doubts as to the impartiality of the ruling if mediation is unsuccessful. Comparatively speaking, there is no threat of judicial authority in the case of industry mediators (such as CREA's mediation centre), thus the parties need not worry about whether the success or failure of mediation will affect the outcome of the ruling. One could therefore say that this is true mediation.

Mediation is not simply conciliation, nor is it purely a means of reasoning. Mediators[27] need to assist the parties in settling their overall differences (particularly those of an economic nature) concerning a variety of opportunity costs (including those related to commercial matters, legal matters, litigation and arbitration) and variables, and then formulate a solution for the parties on such basis. It is even necessary for mediators to use their own expertise to conduct in-depth analyses of their cases, so as to make the parties fully aware of how a judge or arbitrator would rule were they to resolve their dispute through litigation or arbitration. This would further encourage the parties to resolve their disputes through mediation.

Regardless of whether mediation is carried out during litigation or arbitration proceedings,

---

27 Meaning judges, arbitrators and mediators, similarly hereinafter.

oras an independent process, the success of mediation depends on multiple factors[28]—factors which interact with one another. Mediators must mobilise and balance such factors, so as to ease the antagonism between the parties, lower their expectations for winning the lawsuit and strengthen their resolve to settle their dispute through mediation.

D. Collaborative Real Estate Development Dispute between Factory A and Company B (Litigation)[29]

1. Case background

Factory A and Company B entered into an Agreement, the main terms of which were that Factory A was to provide allotted land, and Company B to make a capital contribution, such that the parties would jointly incorporate a new real estate project company for the collaborative development of real estate. (1) Company B was fully responsible for advancing on behalf of Factory A all upfront costs and expenses in connection with the relevant preliminary procedures, including those for audits, assessments, land conversion, obtaining the land certificate and so forth; (2) Factory A was responsible for providing all relevant materials required for submission when carrying out the aforementioned procedures; (3) Factory A was willing to put up the use rights to the commercial-residential land for collaborative real estate development as security for the advance payment made by Company B; the land covered an area of more than 70 mu (subject to the actual planned area for the expropriated land); (4) if, for one reason or another, Company B was unable to become a shareholder of the newly established company after having advanced the relevant expenses and completed the relevant procedures, Factory A must repay Company B in one lump sum all upfront expenses advanced by Company B to carry out the relevant preliminary procedures, plus interest at four times the bank lending rate for the period corresponding to the advance payment. If Company B became a shareholder of the new company, then the amount advanced by Company B would be converted into share capital in the new company, while the use rights to the 70-plus mu of land would be used by Factory A as in-kind contribution to the new company.

After signing the contract, Company B spent over RMB 15 million on the various preliminary procedures (including land grant costs, obtaining approvals and so forth), in addition to paying off Factory A's existing debts. However, once the allotted land being used by Factory A was converted into State-owned land with the use rights granted, the parties failed to incorporate the new company. Factory A invited bids for the land use rights at issue and actively assisted Company B in taking part in the bidding process, but, due to its own reasons, Company B could not participate in the bidding activities, and the collaboration between Factory A and Company B broke down.

---

28 e.g. whether the parties disagree on the basic facts of the case, and whether there is objective evidence supporting such facts; whether the criteria for the application of laws are clear; whether the business model and legal framework pertaining to the case are incompatible, and whether the resolution of the dispute would require a breaking through of the limitations of the legal relationship concerned.

29 From: How to Distinguish a Cleanup Clause in a Collaborative Real Estate Development Contract from a "Loan Contract in the Guise of a Collaboration Contract", by No. 1 Civil Tribunal of the Supreme People's Court; authors: FENG Xiaoguang, XIE Aimei; published in: Guide and Reference to Civil Trials, pp. 154-147, chief editor: DU Wanhua, compiled by: No. 1 Civil Tribunal of the Supreme People's Court, published in December 2015 by People's Court Press.

Company B subsequently filed an action requesting the court to order Factory A to refund the RMB 15 million contributed by Company B, and pay interest at four times the contemporary bank lending rate. Factory A argued that the actual nature of the relationship between the parties was that of a lender and a borrower, and the payment of interest at four times the contemporary bank lending rate as agreed was far higher than the actual losses of Company B. Factory A agreed to terminate the contract, refunded the principal and paid interest at the contemporary bank lending rate.

2. Key points of the judge's ruling

(1) Determining the nature of the contract at issue

According to the Agreement, the objective thereof was for Factory A to provide land, and Company B to make a capital contribution for the joint incorporation of a new company, with a view to jointly developing real estate. Company B was fully responsible for advancing on behalf of Factory A all upfront costs and expenses in connection with the relevant preliminary procedures. The Agreement also stipulated that Company B was to become a shareholder of the new company, whereupon the costs advanced by Company B would be converted into share capital in the newly established company, while Factory A would make its in-kind contribution by providing the 70-plus mu of land. Based on the foregoing, Company B invested capital for the purpose of participating in collaborative real estate development. The return on Company B's investment would be in the form of returns it would generate as the shareholder of the new company, which would be floating, and would not fall within the definition of "fixed profits" under Article 26 of the *Supreme People's Court Interpretation on Issues concerning the Application of Laws during the Adjudication of Contract Disputes Involving State-Owned Land Use Rights*. Thus, the nature of the agreement at issue is a contract for the collaborative development of real estate, rather than a loan agreement.

(2) On the issue of Factory A's liability: whether there is a legal basis for the parties to agree on the payment of interest at four times the bank lending rate.

Based on Articles 97 and 98 of the *Contract Law*[30], the nature of the provisions in question is that of a cleanup clause following the termination of the contract's performance, and is not a loan contract in the guise of a collaboration contract as set out under Article 26 of the *Supreme People's Court Interpretation on Issues concerning the Application of Laws during the Adjudication of Contract Disputes Involving State-Owned Land Use Rights*[31]. Thus, Factory A must refund the capital invested by Company B, and compensate Company B for its loss of profit, which should be calculated at four times the bank lending rate.

---

30 People's Republic of China Contract Law: Article 97 of People's Republic of China Contract Law, after a contract has been terminated, any obligations that have not been performed shall be discharged; where the obligations have already been performed, a party may request restitution or other remedial measures, based on the extent of performance and the nature of the contract; in addition, such party shall be entitled to claim damages. Article 98 of People's Republic of China Contract Law, the discharge of contractual rights and obligations shall not affect the validity of the contractual terms concerning settlement and cleanup.

31 Supreme People's Court Interpretation on Issues concerning the Application of Laws during the Adjudication of Contract Disputes Involving State-Owned Land Use Rights: Article 26 of People's Republic of China Contract Law, any collaborative real estate development contract which stipulates that the party providing funding shall only receive a fixed monetary amount without assuming operating risks shall be deemed a loan contract.

3. Review of dispute

In the real estate development industry, it is very common for parties to enter into relatively complex business arrangements for a variety of purposes and reasons; this case is a classic example of just that. China has adopted a special operating permit system in the financial sector, whereby credit is concentrated in banks, and non-financial institutions are not permitted to engage in credit activities, while lending between businesses is even expressly prohibited. In practice, when it is necessary for real estate businesses that are loath to be bothered with the cumbersome bank lending process to circulate funds, they often hasten to lend from other businesses or individuals under the guise of collaborative development. Article 26 of the *Supreme People's Court Interpretation on Issues concerning the Application of Laws during the Adjudication of Contract Disputes Involving State-Owned Land Use Rights* is designed to curb this type of legal circumvention. Once a dispute arises, the adjudicator is faced with the issue of how to determine the nature of the agreement made in the contract at issue, as this will play a vital role in the outcome of the case. The value of this case lies in its revelation about how the judge determined the nature of the agreement at issue by exploring the true intent of the parties.

In the present case, the Agreement executed by the collaborating parties provided for two scenarios: in the first scenario, Factory A and Company B establish the new company and engage in real estate development; the parties share profits and assume risks according to their respective investment ratios. In the second, the company is not established, in which case Factory A must refund Company B's investment plus interest. These provisions are misleading, and may easily cause one to believe that the relationship between the contracting parties would become a loan relationship should the second scenario occur. Pursuant to the *People's Republic of China Contract Law*, it would be more appropriate to interpret such provisions as cleanup provisions upon termination of the parties' rights and obligations, as the true intent of Company B was to invest funds for the purpose of engaging in collaborative real estate development, and it had actually performed its obligations. If the relationship between the parties was found to be a lending relationship, then the interests of Company B would be seriously prejudiced.

E. China Baoan Group Co., Ltd, Shenzhen Hengan Real Estate Development Co., Ltd et al v Inner Mongolia Jiatai Investment Group Co., Ltd in Equity Transfer Dispute (Litigation)[32]

1. Case background

On 19 April 2011, four parties (as transferors), including China Baoan Group Co Ltd ("Baoan Group") and Shenzhen Hengan Real Estate Development Co., Ltd ("Hengan Real Estate"), entered into an Equity Transfer Agreement with Inner Mongolia Jiatai Investment Group Co., Ltd ("Jiatai Group"), agreeing to transfer the equity interests held by Baoan Group et al in three Shanghai-based target companies (two of which were Sino-foreign joint ventures) to Jiatai Group and its subsidiary.

Under the Agreement, Jiatai Group was to pay the first instalment of the transfer price in

32 See Judicial Opinions of China: www.wenshu.court.gov.cn, http://wenshu.court.gov.cn/content/content?DocID=81ec79ef-a5d6-4da1-ab82-e8171f64fd1d, accessed on 1 March 2016.

the amount of RMB 100 million within 5 business days of execution of the agreement; once the Agreement became effective, Jiatai Group was to pay the remaining amount by 31 August 2011. The Agreement further stipulated that upon receiving Jiatai Group's payment of the first instalment of the transfer price, Baoan Group, Hengan Real Estate et al were to make arrangements for the execution of the relevant documents involved in the Equity Transfer Agreement pertaining to the three companies, as well as the approval documents from the relevant authorities. In addition, the first paragraph of Clause 8 (Miscellaneous) of the agreement stipulated as follows: this Agreement shall only become effective upon satisfaction all of the following conditions: "1. the legal representatives or authorised representatives of the parties sign the agreement and affix the parties' company seals hereto; 2. the transferors receive the first instalment of the transfer price in the amount of RMB 100 million; 3. Baoan Group's general shareholders' meeting approves the sale of the equity interests in the three companies, and the transfer is approved by the regulatory authority." The second paragraph stipulated: "The transferors and transferee agree in principle that Heng Feng International shall transfer the foreign equity held thereby in Baoqi Group and the hotel company to the transferee's Hong Kong company."

On 25 April 2011, Jiatai Group paid the first instalment of the transfer price in the amount of RMB 100 million to Baoan Group as agreed. On 16 May 2011, Baoan Group convened an interim shareholders' meeting and approved the Equity Transfer Agreement. On 26 October 2011, the four parties, including Baoan Group and Hengan Real Estate, jointly issued to Jiatai Group the *Letter concerning the Termination of the Equity Transfer Agreement*, informing Jiatai Group that the agreement would terminate with immediate effect on the grounds that Jiatai Group failed to pay the remainder of the transfer price by 31 August 2011, and that Jiatai Group would be charged RMB 20 million in liquidated damages.

Jiatai Group subsequently filed an action, requesting that: 1. the Equity Transfer Agreement be deemed formed but yet to become effective; 2. the *Letter concerning the Termination of the Equity Transfer Agreement* sent unilaterally by the four parties including Baoan Group and Hengan Real Estate to Jiatai Group on 26 October 2011 be deemed invalid; 3. the Equity Transfer Agreement be terminated, and the four parties including Baoan Group and Hengan Real Estate be ordered to refund the RMB 20 million charged to Jiatai Group, and pay relevant interest on the initial instalment of the transfer price (i. e. RMB 100 million).

2. Key points of the judge's ruling[33]

This case was adjudicated by the Shenzhen Intermediate People's Court at first instance (which ruled in favour of the defendant), the Guangdong Higher People's Court at second instance (which ruled in favour of the plaintiff), and was eventually retried by the Supreme People's Court (which ruled in favour of the defendant). The point of contention was the third condition precedent to the effectiveness of the Equity Transfer Agreement: whether or not the condition that "Baoan Group's general shareholders' meeting approves the sale of the equity interests in the three companies, and the transfer is approved by the regulatory authority" had been satisfied, and whether or not the Equity Transfer Agreement had become effective.

According to the Equity Transfer Agreement, there were a total of three target companies

33 Due to length limitation, this review only includes excerpts from the key points of the rulings of the court of first instance and court of retrial.

(two of which were Sino-foreign joint ventures, and the other a Chinese owned enterprise) involved in the equity transfer; the transferors were Baoan Group, Hengan Real Estate and two other parties, and the transferees were Jiatai Group and its Hong Kong company. The terms of the agreement indicate that, first, the agreement between the parties to the case was a blanket agreement for the transfer of equity, involving changes in the equity interests in three target companies. Second, it was unclear as to who the transferee (s) under the agreement was (were), and Jiatai Group would need to set up a separate company in Hong Kong to be the transferee of the equity interests held by the foreign party to the joint venture. Third, the parties should have been aware of the necessity to enter into specific equity transfer agreements separately, as the agreement at issue also contained such terms, and the Shanghai Commission of Commerce (i. e. the approval authority for the Sino-foreign joint ventures at issue) also gave an unequivocal response on this issue when being consulted by the parties to the agreement. In other words, the agreement at issue was a framework agreement between the parties with respect to the transfer of equity interests in the three target companies, and the specific transfer of equity interests in the various enterprises must be carried out by each of the parties in accordance with the framework agreement, including Jiatai Group's setting up of a company in Hong Kong to be the transferee of the foreign equity in the target companies, as well as the execution of the specific transfer contracts and so forth. The agreement at issue was essentially a preliminary agreement between the various parties regarding the transfer of the relevant equity interests, and it is not necessary to submit preliminary agreements such as this to the authority for foreign invested enterprises for approval.

The first paragraph of Clause 8 of the agreement at issue set out three conditions precedent for the agreement to take effect. There was no contention between the parties as to whether the first two conditions had been satisfied, while a dispute did arise as to whether or not the regulatory authority had approved the transfer as specified in the third condition (i. e. "Baoan Group's general shareholders' meeting approves the sale of the equity interests in the three companies, and the transfer is approved by the regulatory authority"). Jiatai Group was of the opinion that said regulatory authority ought to be the approval authority for foreign invested enterprises, whereas the four transferors believed it to be the regulatory authority for the equity transfer (i. e. the Shenzhen Stock Exchange). Judging from the context of the contract, it seemed more reasonable to determine that the Shenzhen Stock Exchange—rather than the approval authority for foreign invested enterprises—was the regulatory authority in question. By law, the transfer of equity interest in a foreign invested enterprise is automatically subject to review and approval, a requirement that does not need to be set out by the parties. Moreover, the equity transfer under the agreement at issue involved three enterprises, one of which was a Chinese invested enterprise whose equity transfer did not require approval by the approval authority. Since the resolution adopted by Baoan Group's shareholders' meeting concerning the equity transfer at issue had been reviewed by the Shenzhen Stock Exchange and then publicly announced, one can conclude that the regulatory authority had already approved the equity transfer in the present case.

For the above reasons, the agreement at issue did not require approval by the approval authority for foreign invested enterprises, the agreed upon conditions precedent to the effectiveness of the agreement have been satisfied, and Jiatai Group breached the agreement by failing to pay the remainder of the transfer prices as agreed. The deduction of RMB 20 million by the four transferors under the agreement complies with the provisions of the agreement.

3. Review of dispute

Due to the fact that real estate development is often carried out by way of a project company, the transfer of project is also often achieved by transferring the equity interest in the project company. This way, deed tax can be avoided and the parties will not be subject to conditions for the transfer of the project. Furthermore, the Chinese real estate industry is currently gearing up for integration due to the impact of the market downturn and other factors. Thus, it is of great practical significance to select this case as a classic example.

This case is a typical dispute over the interpretation of contract terms. The value of this case lies in that plaintiff Jiatai Group had two options, yet it chose the one the least favourable, thereby losing its control over the case and the ace up its sleeve, and ultimately losing the lawsuit as a result.

In objective terms, Jiatai Group was presented with two lines of thoughts from which it could choose. One would be to assert that the "regulatory authority" mentioned in the third condition (i. e. the "Baoan Group's general shareholders' meeting approves the sale of the equity interests in the three companies, and the transfer is approved by the regulatory authority") under the Equity Transfer Agreement at issue included the competent authority in charge of commercial affairs (in this case, the Shanghai Commission of Commerce), that the Equity Transfer Agreement at issue did not come into effect because no approval was granted by the Commission. The other line of thoughts would be that the aforementioned "regulatory authority" was either not specified or was meant to refer to the Shenzhen Stock Exchange, yet the parties failed to reach an agreement over the operative provisions that were to be submitted for approval, thereby rendering the Equity Transfer Agreement unperformable, in which case neither party should be held liable. Comparatively speaking, the first line of thoughts would result in complete reliance on the judge's interpretation of the contract, meaning that whatever the judge says goes; moreover, the judge would have little flexibility in interpreting the contract, which would be unfavourable to Jiatai Group. By contrast, the greatest advantage of the second line of thoughts is that Jiatai Group would have a great deal of room to seize the initiative as well as an ace up its sleeve, and would have a variety of objective reasons[34] at its disposal to explain why the parties failed to execute an operative equity transfer agreement for submission for approval, and why the parties ultimately were unable to actually perform the Equity Transfer Agreement at issue, and should therefore both be exempt from liability. These two paths are poles apart, and once a path is chosen, there is no turning back. If Jiatai Group had chosen the second option, it would need to have taken preventive measures by preparing to act both genuinely and insincerely during the performance of the Equity Transfer Agreement at issue.

In short, going to court is much like going to battle: one needs to do its utmost to seize the initiative, and must never err in putting one's fate in the hands of an adjudicator.

---

34 As the payment method agreed upon by the parties under the Equity Assignment Agreement at issue did not comply with foreign exchange control regulations, new arrangements would have been needed when executing an operative equity assignment agreement for submission for approval. Since this plan would have been very complex and would have subjected the parties to rigid compliance requirements, the parties would most likely fail to reach an agreement.

IV. Hot Topics in the Industry and Academia

A. Real Estate Crowd Funding

Given the downward trend of the real estate industry, certain third and fourth tier cities will continue to have high inventory for a considerable period of time, while the financial pressure on real estate businesses will only increase in the wake of rising land costs in first tier cities. As a result, nearly every real estate enterprise is actively seeking new financing channels in an effort to pull through. In 2015, the real estate market showed signs of moving away from a mainly indirect financing model towards a primarily direct financing model with indirect financing playing a secondary role. A greater number of real estate enterprises began pursuing asset light business models, creating large numbers of private equity real estate funds, setting up real estate investment trusts (REITs), and testing the waters of real estate crowd funding—at present, there is a total of 34 real estate crowd funding platforms throughout China, with 330 real estate crowd funding projects announced in total; 265 of such projects have been successful, thereby obtaining RMB 651.6653 million in financing—while some real estate companies are going as far as directly investing and buying shares in banks, insurance companies and other such financial institutions.

Behind the boom in real estate crowd funding in China, we should also note that presently China lacks the legal norms for and effective control over real estate crowd funding. Therefore, the various business arrangements pertaining to real estate crowd funding projects must effectively address a variety of possible restrictions under existing laws in order to navigate through the existing legal gaps. Otherwise, such projects could be held back by the corresponding laws and regulations, such as the conditions for the pre-sale of commercial housing under the *Urban Real Estate Administration Law* and the *Urban Commercial Housing Pre-sale Administrative Procedures*, which require real estate enterprises to obtain a pre-sale licence[35]; some activities may even run afoul of criminal laws, including illegal fund raising and unlawful issuance of securities.

B. Replacing Business Tax with Value Added Tax in the Real Estate Industry

In 2011, the Ministry of Finance and the State Administration of Taxation obtained approval from the State Council to launch a pilot programme to replace business tax with value added tax ("BT-VAT").[36] As at 2015, the BT-VAT programme had been in place for 4

---

35 Under Article 45 of the Urban Real Estate Administration Law, the pre-sale of commercial housing is subject to the following conditions: …a licence for the pre-sale of commercial housing must be obtained; under Article 6 of the Urban Commercial Housing Pre-sale Administrative Procedures, no one is permitted toengage in commercial housing pre-sale activities without a Commercial Housing Pre-sale Licence.

36 The Ministry of Finance and State Administration of Taxation Circular concerning the Promulgation of the "Pilot Programmes for Replacement of Business Tax with Value Added Tax" (MOF and SAT Circular No. 110 of 2011): http://www.mof.gov.cn/zhengwuxinxi/caizhengwengao/2012wg/wg201201/201203/t20120331_640067.html, accessed on 7 March 2016.

years, yet BT-VAT replacement in the real estate sector continues to be the toughest nut to crack[37]. This is because, presently, under current policies and laws, input tax deductions are not available for land costs that are part of the cost structure of real estate enterprises; while more often than not, building materials suppliers and labour providers are unable to provide official tax invoice ("*fapiao*") for construction and installation costs (or, if such a tax voice is provided, it is not a VAT invoice) as they tend to be small-scale taxpayers, which ultimately impacts businesses' input tax deductions.

Nevertheless, BT-VAT replacement is inevitable in the real estate industry. Real estate developers need to plan for rainy days ahead by adopting reasonable tax planning and making necessary preparations, such as gradually giving up on acquiring high-priced land, choosing construction companies which qualify for VAT taxpayer status, reviewing the various business segments involved in real estate development so as to identify any potential BT-VAT risks, or adjusting product structures, and switching to commercial property projects including commercial real estate, tourism real estate and logistics real estate. Only if businesses proceed with caution will they be able to reduce their tax burden and lower costs during the implementation of the BT-VAT policy.

C. Entry of Collectively Owned Rural Land Into the Market

Along with the advancement of China's urbanisation and rapid growth of the real estate market, collectively owned rural land has become increasingly engulfed by the current of the market in a variety of forms, be they legal, illegal, public or private. However, collectively owned rural land still faces numerous difficulties and issues when entering the market: 1. farmers using collectively owned rural land do not have complete rights to dispose of their land, thereby limiting the circulation of collective owned land; 2. it is highly likely that farmers' incomplete rights to collectively owned land will lead to limited value added benefits once the stock of land enters the market; 3. a uniform land market is yet to be created, meaning that, among other things, both a land trading price mechanism and a trading supervisory mechanism are lacking.

On 21 January 2015, the General Office of the Central Committee and the General Office of the State Council jointly promulgated the *Opinions on Pilot Programmes for Rural Land Expropriation, Market Entry of Collectively Owned Commercial Construction Land and Homestead System Reform*, signifying that the market entry and reform process for collectively owned rural land had officially commenced. Despite the hardships facing the market entry and reform of collectively owned rural land, such reform is of great significance and will need to make steady headway one step at a time.

V. Conclusion

2015 saw a continuation of the relaxed real estate market policy environment of 2014,

---

37 As at the deadline for this review, China's "two sessions" were underway. It was indicated in Premier LI Keqiang's Government Work Report that the BT-VAT Programme will be fully implemented starting 1 May 2016, at which time the real estate industry will also be included in the BT-VAT Programme. http://www.china.com.cn/lianghui/news/2016-03/05/content_37943454.html, accessed on 7 March 2016.

with a number of favourable regulatory policies, laws and regulations introduced one after another. However, with the exception of certain top tier cities and individual central cities in the western region experiencing relatively large population influxes, the real estate market response was lacklustre and overall growth remained sluggish. Presently, China's real estate industry is undergoing a major industry reshuffling and shakeup, and the tide of mergers and acquisitions in the industry continues to come in one after another, while the Internet continues to infiltrate and is attempting to change the real estate industry. New business models such as crowd funding are flourishing, while senior housing real estate and logistics real estate are attempting to establish themselves as the new industry hot spots and growth contributors. In this period of profound industry changes, the efficiency of real estate assets and capital allocation will certainly improve. The outlook for 2016 is that the acceleration of destocking and M&As will continue to be the themes of the real estate industry for some time to come. The financial strain on the industry, as well as the pressure to destock, will compel real estate enterprises, both large and small, to use all of their tricks up their sleeve in an effort to stay competitive with one another. Those real estate companies that are prescient enough will seek opportunities by setting foot in healthcare real estate, senior housing real estate, tourism real estate, logistics real estate, industrial park real estate, overseas real estate, PPP and other types of business. Not only will this lay the seed for new growth, but also a great deal of new disputes.

Annual Review on Energy Dispute Resolution in China (2016) *

ZHANG Libin [1]

I. Introduction

The reform of the oil, gas and power industries remained the key areas of concern in the energy sector in 2015. In addition to the industries aforementioned, other industries which will be addressed in this paper include coal, nuclear power, wind power, solar power, biomass fuels and geothermal energy, etc. The author will highlight the environmental protection issues in the energy sector as what the author did last year, and explore issues on the energy performance contracting. In respect of applicable laws, regulations and policies, the author will outline the upstream, midstream and downstream reform and developments in the oil and gas industry, the reform attempts in the power industry, as well as the legislative progresses in the nuclear power industry.

The author will also introduce and conduct analyses on some landmark cases in the case studies section. Noteworthy is the fact that in some cases, the disputes between the contractual parties were caused by changes in the state policies. From a legal perspective, it is therefore necessary to determine whether such policy changes constituted any force majeure, frustration of a contract or inability to perform a contract. The author will, through these cases, examine various issues concerning energy disputes, especially the ones involving the current laws and policies. This paper aims to draw your attention to the formulation of solutions to these issues.

In addition, the Energy Charter and the "One Belt and One Road" strategy are the two hot issues of the energy sector in 2015. Lastly, this paper will summarise the legislative developments and the current status of dispute resolution in the energy sector in 2015, and will shed lights on the prospects of the future development in China's energy sector and the dispute resolution thereof in 2016.

II. Laws, Regulations and Policies in the Energy Sector

A. Legislation of *the Energy Law*

China has to date not promulgated a basic energy law entitled the *Energy Law of the Peo-*

---

* Translated by Herbert Smith Freehills LLP.

1 Partner, Broad & Bright, Beijing; Deputy Director and Guest Professor of Energy Law and Policy Research Centre, Peking University.

ple Republic of China (the "*Energy Law*"). On 3 December 2007, the office of National Energy Administration (the "NEA") formally released the consultation draft of the *Energy Law* for public consultation. On 21 November 2008, the National Development and Reform Commission (the "NDRC") submitted the review draft of the *Energy Law* to the State Council for review and consideration. In 2009, a working group was formed to review and revise the *Energy Law*. This group later produced a revised draft of the *Energy Law*, after which the legislation of the *Energy Law* was shelved. Not until 2013 was the *Energy Law* officially included in the legislative work plan of the State Council. According to an NDRC report dated 5 August 2015, the *Energy Law* legislation was identified as one of the "priority projects" of the State Council in 2015 for "comprehensively deepening the reform and upholding the rule of law". The latest update provided by the NDRC on 5 August 2015 indicated that a review draft of the *Energy Law* had then been submitted to the State Council for consideration and the relevant legislative review was currently underway in coordination with the Legislative Affairs Office of the State Council. The author is of the opinion that the *Energy Law* should not be reduced to a piece of "window dressing" legislation or to a policy slogan. Rather, it should be a legislation of real substance and practicability, and can provide guidance to and lay the foundation for the reform of China's energy sector. Otherwise the legislative purposes of enacting the *Energy Law* would be frustrated.

B. Legislation in the Oil and Gas Industry

China has to date not promulgated a specialized law on oil and gas, but relevant legislative research on an oil and gas law has been underway. On 11 December 2015, Shi Zihai, the director of the Policy Research Office and the spokesperson of the NDRC, reportedly noted that the *Master Plan of Reform of the Oil and Gas Regime*, preparation of which was led by the NDRC and NEA, had been submitted to the State Council. So far, no consensus has been reached in respect of the oil and gas legislative model: whether oil and gas, and upstream and downstream, should be legislated separately, or whether a unified law should be enacted for the entire industry. The Chinese Government, whilst enacting the *Oil Law*, should also clear up or amend the existing rules which are of lower legislative authority or would block the market access of oil mining rights.

The legislation in the oil and gas industry paced slowly in 2015. Nevertheless, the reform attempts have been ongoing. Relevant to these reform attempts are a number of administrative regulations and department rules promulgated by the relevant authorities. The reform of the oil and gas industry apparently has adopted a progressive approach: once the relevant reform initiatives have been implemented and matured, they will then be institutionalised through legislation. The major development of regulations and policies in the oil and gas industry in 2015 will be discussed below.

1. Invitation for bid in the upstream segment

In 2015, in order to reinforce the development of and investment in oil and gas exploration, and to diversify the base of investment in the upstream oil and gas investors' base, the Ministry of Land and Resources put the oil and gas exploration blocks in Xinjiang out to open tender. It was the first time ever that all qualified domestic enterprises meeting the qualification criteria (including private enterprises) were invited to submit a bid. The invitation to tender was aimed to tap the potential oil and gas resources in Xinjiang on the one hand, and to advance the development of oil and gas energy enterprises and enhance the oil and gas exploration and production technology on the other. There is great room for improvement for the tender result and process. The qualification threshold for bidding enterprises, for instance, should be lowered in China, and consortium bids should be permitted as well in conformity with international practices. In addition, some key issues require further clarification by law or by contract: whether the undertakings made by a successful bidder in the assignment of oil and gas mining rights are of a contractual nature, the liabilities following breach of undertakings by a successful bidder, and how a dispute could be settled.

The open tender for oil and gas blocks in Xinjiang marked the official start in China of the reform of the upstream segment of oil and gas resources. China is expected to break its status quo under which the oil and gas exploration is monopolised by certain state-owned oil conglomerates, which will provide invaluable experience for comprehensively deepening the reform of the oil and gas exploration and production system. In fact, in the upstream oil and gas segment, the China National Petroleum Corporation ("CNPC") and the China Petroleum and Chemical Corporation ("Sinopec") are currently exploring the feasibility of partnering with other central and local state-owned enterprises on specific oil and gas block projects. The models of collaboration and dispute resolution mechanism are all on their agenda.

2. Oil and gas pipelines

The reform of midstream pipeline business has already been partially introduced when China's oil and gas reform plan is just about to be announced. A large number of oil and gas pipeline assets in China are corporate assets of CNPC and Sinopec, and pipelines have not become a stand-alone business. In 2015, the relevant authorities in China promulgated the regulations related to oil and gas pipelines. The implementation of these regulations, however, has been slow. According to an announcement made by CNPC at the Shanghai Stock Exchange on 25 November 2015, China Petroleum Pipeline Engineering Corporation ("CPPE"), a wholly-owned subsidiary of CNPC, acquired all the equity interest in East Pipeline, Joint Pipeline and Northwest Joint Pipeline from CNPC and respective transferors. In return, CNPC and the transferors would receive CPPE's shares or cash as consideration. CNPC, through this consolidation, managed to achieve a clear shareholding structure of the pipeline operators. The reform notion of separating the oil and gas pipeline is in line with the general trend of structural reform of the oil and gas industry.

In terms of the legislation in the midstream oil and gas industry, the NDRC together with five other ministries and commissions promulgated on 27 April 2015 the *Administrative Measures for Concession Operation of the Infrastructure and Public Utilities* (the "Measures for Concession"), which would apply to energy-related infrastructure. As a means to establish public-private partnerships (PPP), private capital (including both domestic and foreign capital), in accordance with the Measures for Concession, is encouraged to enter into concession agreements with certain government authorities regarding the construction and operation of infrastructure or public utilities in seven sectors including the energy sector.

3. Crude oil import

In February 2015, the NDRC issued the *Circular on Issues Concerning the Administration of the Use of Crude Oil Imports* (Fa Gai Yun Xing [2015] No. 253), pursuant to which eligible local refineries are permitted to use crude oil imports subject to conditions of phasing out certain redundant production capacities or developing gas storage facilities. On 23 July 2015, the Ministry of Commerce ("MOFCOM") issued the *Circular on the Application by Crude Oil Processing Enterprises for Non-state Owned Enterprise Import License* (Shang Mao Han [2015] No. 407), which clarified the criteria for non-state-owned enterprises to engage in crude oil import, and also imposed a string of prior procedures. The application criteria in the Circular provided that an enterprise applicant shall be a legal person, shall have carried out the filing and registration for a firm engaged in foreign trade or have obtained the qualification for import and export business, shall have been authorised to conduct the wholesale business of refined oil products, and shall have been equipped with atmospheric and vacuum distillation units with a per unit crude oil processing capacity of more than 2 million tonnes per year. The Circular, in addition, sets out the requirements for energy use in petroleum refining, product quality and production safety.

Apart from Xinjiang Guanghui Petroleum Co., Ltd, which was granted by MOFCOM in 2014 the non-state-owned enterprise license for crude oil import, a number of other enterprises, including Dongming Petroleum & Chemical Group Co., Ltd of Shandong Province, Panjin Beifang Asphalt Fuel Co., Ltd of Liaoning Province, Lijin Petrochemical Plant Co., Ltd, Kenli Petrochemicals Group Ltd, Dongying Yatong Petrochemical Co., Ltd of Shandong Province and Ningxia Baota Petrochemical Group, following promulgation of the relevant policies in 2015, have been issued the licenses upon review and public notification by MOFCOM. The availability of crude oil import license to private enterprises has brought hope for private capital to lift policy barriers and enter the full production chain of the oil and gas industry.

Furthermore, due to the weak domestic demand and the apparent over-capacity, the monopoly once enjoyed by the "Three Barrels of Oil" on export quota of refined oil products has eventually been lifted. On 25 November 2015, Sinochem Quanzhou Petrochemical Co., Ltd, a subsidiary of Sinochem Group, was granted a total export quota of 450,000 tonnes of refined oil products. It is understood that in the future, local refineries are also expected to be allocated an export quota for refined oil products. A local refinery qualified to import crude oil and entitled to use imported crude oil is expected to be well positioned to obtain an export quota.

4. Oil and gas price

On 12 October 2015, the CPC Central Committee and the State Council issued *Certain Opinions on Advancing the Pricing Mechanism Reform* (the "Opinions"). The Opinions set out the extensive requirements for comprehensively deepening a pricing reform, improving the pricing mechanism in key sectors, refining the pricing guidance provided by the government, and strengthening supervision over market price and *Anti-Trust Law* enforcement, so as to create a pricing mechanism suitable for the development of economy and the society as a whole. The Opinions specify the key objectives as follows: by 2017, price controls in competitive sectors and segments will have been substantially removed, and government pricing will be primarily limited to major public utilities, public welfare services and natural monopolies arising out of access to networks; and by 2020, a sound market pricing mechanism will have taken a good shape, a scientific, standardised and transparent price supervision system and an anti-monopoly law enforcement system substantially established, and a price regulation system substantially perfected.

As an important initiative to implement the Opinions, on 21 October 2015, the NDRC issued the amended *Central Pricing Catalogue* (Decree No. 29, 2015), which took effect on 1 January 2016. Compared to the previous version, the pricing categories and the specific pricing items have been reduced in number by approximately 46% and 80% respectively. On 20 November 2015, the NDRC released the *Circular on Reducing the Gate Station Prices of Natural Gas Used for Non-residential Purpose and Further Accelerating the Market-oriented Price Reform* (Fa Gai Jia Ge [2015] No. 2688). It is noted that the NDRC is accelerating the formulation of a special plan on reforming the pricing system, and also advancing the amendments to the *Price Law of the People's Republic of China* (Zhu Xi Ling No. 92). It is true that the natural gas market in China remains relatively monopolised. However, the natural gas market reform, with the ongoing natural gas pricing reform, is expected to embrace a significant breakthrough.

Given that the pricing mechanism for refined oil products has been further improved and the international oil price has dropped drastically, the NDRC, in an effort to further improve the pricing mechanism of refined oil under the new circumstances , suspended twice in December 2015 the price adjustments of domestic refined oil products. At the same time, it held meetings to seek public opinions on further improving the pricing mechanism, in preparation for amending the *Administrative Measures for Oil Prices (For Trial Implementation)*. (The improved pricing mechanism and the new *Administrative Measures for Oil Prices* were both promulgated in January 2016.)

C. Legislation in the Power Industry

The reform of the power industry always goes hand in hand with China's economic reform and opening-up. On 15 March 2015, the new power system reform plan entitled *Certain Opinions of the CPC Central Committee and the State Council on Further Deepening the Reform of the Power System* (Zhong Fa [2015] No. 9, "Circular 9") was promulgated. Circular 9 reiterates the overall direction of deepening the reform of the power industry to "accelerate the construction of a market structure and system with effective competition, and form a mechanism whereby energy prices are mainly determined by the market", and establishes a structural framework for the power industry that "reinforces the supervision and administration of power transmission and distribution network in the "midstream" of the industry, and affords more access for power generation and power sale entities at the two ends, each on the basis of further realising the separation of governmental functions from enterprise management, separation of power plants from power transmission networks, and separation of primary business from sidelines". Circular 9, in terms of specific policies, puts forward a reform notion of "three opening-ups, one deepening and three reinforcements". The "three opening-ups" refers to orderly removing the price control over power in competitive segments other than power transmission and distribution, orderly making power distribution and sale businesses accessible to private investments, and orderly opening up power generation and consumption plans other than those for public welfare and adjustment. The "three opening-ups" extends the spirit in Circular 5 of "constructing a government-regulated power market system where governmental functions are separated from enterprise management, fair competition, being open and orderly, and healthy development", encourages various entities to enter the power market such that the market-driven allocation of power resources may be gradually accomplished. "One deepening" refers to "further deepening the study on the construction of a regional power grid and a power transmission and distribution system suitable for China". "Three reinforcements" refers to "further strengthening government supervision, further reinforcing comprehensive planning for power, and further enhancing the safe and effective operation and reliable supply of power".

The competent state authorities, in order to implement Circular 9 and to provide further guidance on part of the reform, have issued a series of implementing rules such as the *Guidance on the Improvement of Power Operation and Facilitating the Generation of More Clean Energy and the Generation of Clean Energy in Full Capacity*, *the Notice on the Improvement of Emergency Response and the Proper Implementation of Comprehensive Pilot of Power Demand Management in Urban Areas*, *the Notice on the Implementation of the Intention of the Circular Zhong Fa* [2015] *No. 9 and the Acceleration of Reform of Price for Power Transmission and Distribution*, *and the Notice on the Issues Concerning the Pricing Mechanism for Inter-Provincial Power Transactions.* The NDRC and the NEA also promulgated six implementing rules including the *Opinions on Furthering the Implementation of Reform of the Transmission and Distribution of Power Price*, the *Opinions on Furthering the Implementation of the Construction of Power Market*, the *Opinions on Implementing the Construction and Regularised Operation of Power Transaction Agencies*, the *Opinions on Implementing Orderly Opening Up of Power Generation and Consumption Plans*, the *Opinions on Implementing Reform of Sales of Power*, and the *Guidance on Strengthening and Standardising the Supervision and Administration of Fire-Coaled Captive Power Plant.* These rules and regulations primarily served to provide a definite implementation roadmap and measures for carrying out the related work.

With regard to legislation, the National People's Congress ("NPC") deliberated on and adopted the amendments to the *Power Law* on 24 April 2015. The provisions in the *Power Law* that require the AIC registration at the pre-approval stage were amended. The former Article 25.3, which stipulated that "[n]o power vendor may commence business operations unless it have, upon providing its Power Supply Certificate, applied to a competent industrial and commercial department for, and obtained, a business license", was deleted. A Power Supply Certificate is the legal license for a power vendor to supply power to users within the power supply area as approved by competent power administration departments. This policy had been implemented since the promulgation of the *Power Law* in 1996. It is noteworthy that the said amendments to the *Power Law* are not to cancel the approval system of Power Supply Certificates, but instead to change the nature of the original AIC registration from an ex-ante requirement to an ex-post one. Prior to the amendments, a power supplier intending to obtain a business license would have to submit an application to the competent local authority and provide such documentation as the power supplier's company profile, geographic plan of the power supply area, power capacity and distribution map, selling price of power and supporting materials. After obtaining the Power Supply Certificate, an enterprise shall not commence business until it had applied to the competent industrial and commercial department and obtained the business license. In accordance with the amended *Power Law*, however, any market entity intending to engage in power sales may first apply to the competent industrial and commercial department for a business license, and apply thereafter for a Power Supply Certificate. The amendments were made primarily to implement the State Council's reform notion of "license first and certificate to follow" in 2014.

D. Legislation in the Fields of Atomic Energy and Nuclear Power

In the atomic energy industry, there is only one piece of legislation, i. e. the *Radioactive Pollution Prevention Law of the People's Republic of China* ("RPPL"), which was enacted in 2003. In addition, there are a number of administrative laws and ministerial regulations. However, there is no specific enactment in China for the utilisation of atomic energy, in particular for nuclear safety, while it is far from satisfactory to rely solely on the RPPL. The introduction of the *Atomic Energy Law* and the *Nuclear Safety Law* has formed part of the prospective legislation on atomic energy. Since the Fukushima nuclear disaster in Japan, the Chinese Government has become more aware of the importance of the enactment of these two pieces of legislation. As a result, the *Atomic Energy Law was* put on the State Council's Legislation Plan 2011 and categorised as one of the Group 3 projects, for which active further research and assessment are required; the *Nuclear Safety Law* was put on the Legislation Plan of the Standing Committee of the 12th NPC and categorised as one of the Group 2 projects, i. e. "drafts of law that entail intensive work and are to be submitted for deliberations upon fulfilment of relevant conditions". Active legislative work in atomic energy, perfection of the legal bodies related to atomic energy, safeguarding peaceful and orderly utilisation of atomic energy, therefore, are pressing tasks in the field of energy laws.

It is noted that the draft of the *Nuclear Safety Law*, as the umbrella legislation in the field of nuclear power, has been scheduled to be submitted for the NPC's deliberations in mid-2016. [2] Amongst other things, the general public's entitlement to participating in the planning, examination and approval of nuclear power stations is expected to make its way into the forthcoming *Nuclear Safety Law*. The *Nuclear Safety Law* will fill various legislative gaps concerning nuclear safety and security in China, such as damages for nuclear accidents, access to information about nuclear safety and security, public involvements, etc. Examples of public involvement include inviting officials and relevant persons of the place where a new nuclear power station is to be built to visit the completed nuclear power station, and enhancing publicity through public networks. As a matter of law, the prospective *Nuclear Safety Law* will safeguard the right of the general public to participate in the planning and building of nuclear power stations.

E. Legislation Developments on the Environmental Protection in the Energy Sector

Article 58 of the *Environmental Protection Law of the People's Republic of China* stipulates that: for any activities that cause environmental pollution, ecological damage or harm to

---

2 "'Public opinion will determine whether and where to build a nuclear power station' will be incorporated in the Nuclear Safety and Security Law", China Business Journal, http://news.cb.com.cn/html/economy_9_26785_1.html, accessed on 13 January 2016.

the public interest, a social organisation satisfying the following conditions may bring a lawsuit in a People's Court: (1) it has registered with a civil affairs department of a municipal (or above) government of its district; (2) it has mainly engaged in such public interest activities as environmental protection for five consecutive years or more, and has no law violation records. A People's Court shall hear the case filed by the foregoing social organisation that meets the above criteria. The social organisation bringing in the action shall seek no economic gains from the litigation.

On 6 January 2015, the Supreme People's Court issued the *Interpretations of the Supreme People's Court on Certain Issues Concerning the Application of Law in Hearing Environmental Civil Public Interest Cases*, effective on 7 January 2015 (Fa Shi [2015] No. 1, the "Interpretations"). The Interpretations comprises a total of 35 articles covering four major aspects: first, social organisations may bring in an environmental civil public interest action; second, cross-administrative region jurisdiction may apply to such actions; third, a private interest litigation over the same environment pollution may "free ride" on the public interest litigation; and fourth, the plaintiff's burden of litigation cost is lessened.

On 1 June 2015, the Supreme People's Court issued the *Interpretations of the Supreme People's Court on Certain Issues Concerning the Application of Law in Hearing Environmental Tort Liability Cases*, effective on 3 June 2015 (Fa Shi [2015] No. 12). These judicial interpretations, comprising a total of 19 articles and effective on 3 June 2015, elaborate on the issue of application of law in an environmental tort case from 8 aspects. The judicial interpretations apply to private and public interest environmental actions and to environmental pollution cases and an ecological damage cases. They also established the general legal principles applicable to the two types of actions mentioned above. They expressly provide that a polluter should assume tort liabilities for any damages arising from environmental pollution regardless whether the polluter was at fault or not. Any denial of liability by a polluter on the grounds that the emissions were in conformity with the state or local pollutant emission standards would not be sustained by a People's Court.

Since the new *Environmental Protection Law* took effect, it was widely believed in the industry that the floodgate of public interest environmental litigations has been opened. In fact, however, only approximately over 20 cases have since been filed nationwide. Some judicial practices impose strict restrictions on plaintiffs' legal standing in bringing a public interest environmental case, and the proceedings initiated by environmental protection organisations have not always been readily heard by the courts. It is our hope that the acceptance by the courts of the above public interest environmental cases will have a positive impact on advancing the judicial practices of public interest environmental litigation in China.

III. Case Studies in the Energy Sector

A. Oil and Gas

1. Dispute in relation to mining rights of oil and gas

Case 1: Appeal Case between Xing Long Oilfield Services Co., Ltd located in Zhao Yuan County of Da Qing City and Da Qing Shun Wei Energy Development Ltd in relation to Dispute of Confirming Validity of Contract

Background Facts

On 30 June 2002, the Defendant entered into a Min 47 Oilfield Exploration in Jiangxin Island and Oil Production Contract with Jilin Oil and Gas Development Co. , Ltd (hereinafter referred to as "Jilin Oil"), pursuant to which the Defendant was entitled to assign all or part of its rights and/or obligations under the contract to any of its affiliates, provided that the prior consent of Jilin Oil was obtained. On 16 January 2002, the Defendant and the Plaintiff entered into a certain Min 47 Partial Compensable Assignment of Oilfield in Jiangxin Island Contract, whereby all plots south of Xinkai River as specified in the contract were transferred to the Plaintiff. A dispute arose thereafter between the Defendant and the Plaintiff and was submitted to the court for resolution. In the trial of first instance, the People's Court of Zhao Yuan County verified the business scope in the business licenses of both the Defendant and the Plaintiff, and found that Plaintiff entered into the assignment contract whilst not entitled to do so. Specifically, the Plaintiff did not have the qualification according to its business scope to exploit and produce oil. The contract entered into between the Plaintiff and the Defendant, therefore, was formed but did not take effect. The Plaintiff was not satisfied with the judgment and appealed to the Intermediate People's Court of Daqing City, Heilongjiang Province on the ground that it was the operation rights that were assigned under the contract between the parties.

Court's Opinions

The court of second instance noted that according to (i) Article 16 of the *Mineral Resources Law of the People's Republic of China*, the exploitation of oil, gas and special minerals such as radioactive minerals shall be approved by the relevant agencies authorised by the State Council, and a mining license shall be issued; and (ii) Article 37 of the *Interim Administrative Provisions of Assignment of Mining Rights*, the assignee and the assignor shall both apply to the registration authority for approval of the assignment of mining rights of any kind, and upon examination and approval shall proceed with the registration of change in ownership. The parties concerned entered into the contract in dispute without obtaining a mining license, and all plots south of Xinkai River under the Min 47 Oilfield Exploration in Jiangxin Island and Oil Production Contract were transferred to the Appellant without the consent of Jilin Oil. This violated relevant provisions of the *Mineral Resources Law of the People's Republic of China* and the *Interim Administrative Provisions of Assignment of Mining Rights*. As a result, the contract shall be held null and void. The original judgment was not inappropriate and shall be upheld.

Author's Observations

The framework of assignment of mining rights in China (i. e. the system built upon administrative regulations in which assignment of mining rights is "prohibited in principle but permitted in exceptional circumstances") has come into being. The current assignment system is mainly reflected in (i) the *Administrative Provisions of Exploration Rights and Mining Rights* promulgated by the State Council in 1998, (ii) the *Interim Administrative Provisions of Assignment of Mining Rights* promulgated by the Ministry of Land and Resources in 2000, and (iii) the *Mining Rights Trading Rules* (For Trial Implementation) promulgated by the Ministry of Land and Resources in 2011. The *Mining Rights Trading Rules (For Trial Implementation)* sets out two types of mining rights assignment. One is assignment by way of invitation to bid, auction and quotation, and the other is assignment by way of negotiation between the assignee and the assignor. The mining rights assignment contract entered into by way of negotiation is subject to approval and registration of the change in ownership of mining rights. In practice, disputes abound in relation to the assignment of oil and gas mining rights.

In this case, the court did not clarify whether the assigned rights are mining rights or more general exploitation and production rights. Theoretically, a party can collaborate with another that owns mining rights in exploiting and producing oil whereas assignment of mining rights is not necessarily concerned. It is not factually clear in this case whether the contract between Jilin Oil and the Defendant involves assignment of mining rights owned by Jilin Oil. If the Defendant only has exploitation and production rights under the contract, then the contractual rights concerned in this case could be the oil exploitation and production rights. The assignment contract between the Plaintiff and the Defendant was certainly subject to Jilin Oil's consent, which nevertheless was not given in this case. In addition, the court was silent on the fact that the Plaintiff must be the Defendant's affiliate in order for the Defendant to undertake any assignment pursuant to the contract. Lastly, pursuant to the current PRC administrative regulations, any upstream operations of oil and gas shall be approved by the State Council. No industry access approval so far has been granted by the State Council to any company other than Petro China, Sinopec, CNOOC, and Yanchang Petroleum. On that score, the contract concerned was invalid. Unless and until the restriction on access to the upstream market is removed under the oil and gas reform scheme, companies face significant legal risks in entering into invalid cooperation or assignment contracts when engaging in oil exploitation and production.

2. Pricing dispute of a gas supply contract

Case 2: Appeal Case between Jinguang Electronic Ceramics and Electric Appliances Co., Ltd of Wangdu County ("Jingguang") and Wangdu Zhongran Urban Gas Development Co., Ltd ("Zhongran") in relation to the Dispute of a Gas Supply and Use Contract [3]

Background Facts

The Plaintiff, Jingguang, entered into an Urban Gas Supply Contract with the Defendant, Zhongran, on 8 June 2006. It was agreed in the contract that: "Any price adjustment shall, in principle, be made according to the gas price and the timetable approved by the price administration agency, but under the special circumstances where the general cost price of the upstream source gas is adjusted, the price shall be adjusted by applying the new rate effective on the date of adjustment to be specified in the official directives issued by the upstream sector (relevant formalities for the new rate shall be carried out later with the price administration agency)". In 2010, the NDRC and the Development and Reform Commission of Hebei Province ("Hebei DRC") issued, in succession, directives providing that, effective on 1 June 2010, the ex-factory benchmark price of natural gas be raised by RMB 0.23/m^3 and open to a further 10% increase on that basis. Hebei Natural Gas Co., Ltd also adjusted the price of natural gas in the Gas Supply and Use Contract (2010-2011) entered into with Zhongran. Zhongran charged Jingguang RMB 3.15/m^3 and 2.93/m^3 for gas used from July 2010 to the end of January 2011 and from February 2011 to the end of November 2011 respectively. Jingguang raised objections to the price and tariff adjustment clauses. Jingguang's claim was rejected by the court of first instance.

Jingguang was not satisfied and appealed against the decision of first instance. It contended

3 Civil Judgment of the Intermediate People's Court of Baoding City (District), Hebei Province (2015) Bao Min San Zhong Zi No. 275. Date of Judgment: 14 August 2015

that in accordance with the *Measures for Natural Gas Price Administration in Hebei Province*, for natural gas price administration, the government-directed price shall be used as the on-site selling price for gas supplied to non-residential users, and the people's governments of municipalities with districts or authority-enlarged counties (cities) were authorised to fix the price. It also contended that Baoding Bureau of Commodity Prices was the competent department authorised to set prices within this administrative region; that the decision of first instance erred in following the circulars issued by the NDRC, Hebei DRC, PetroChina and Hebei Natural Gas Company on price adjustment of natural gas; that the said adjustment related to the ex-factory benchmark price of natural gas rather than the on-site selling price, to which the price approved by local price administration in accordance with the provisions of the *Price Law* and other relevant laws should apply; and that the relevant price clauses in the contract were invalid on the grounds that natural gas was a crucial commodity relating to national economy and common people's livelihood, therefore, any price adjustment shall be made in compliance with strict legal procedures including hearings. A natural gas company, before the price was set by the price administration agency, shall not raise the price without authorisation, and no price adjustment shall be made prior to an approval.

Court's Opinions

The court of second instance delivered the following opinions. The gas industry was characterised by its nature of an inherent monopoly. The tariffs in the industry have long been subject to government regulation and control. The market mechanism, however, has been gradually introduced to the industry such that all enterprises in the industry should follow market rules. Under Article 3 of the *Price Law of the People's Republic of China*, the State shall introduce and gradually improve a pricing mechanism driven primarily by the market forces under macroeconomic control. A price should accord with the value of the product. Majority of the commodities and services should be priced based upon the market factors. Only a minor fraction of them may adopt prices directed or set by the government. The *Measures for Natural Gas Price Administration in Hebei Province (Pilot)* provide that price administration of natural gas covers natural gas ex-factory price, pipeline transmission price, urban natural gas gate station price, and on-site selling price, etc. The on-site selling price for non-residential users shall adopt the government-directed price. Under the current pricing mechanism, the national and local authorities of price administration use the cost-plus pricing method to set the prices of natural gas irrespective of the ex-factory price, the pipeline transmission price or the end-user price. Under the cost-plus pricing method, the price of natural gas will be determined on the basis of the costs of natural gas plus reasonable profits whilst taking account of affordability. The Measures, meanwhile, also require a correlation mechanism be established between the on-site selling price and the upstream price of natural gas, whereby the on-site selling price may be adjusted in the same direction accordingly to reflect any change in the upstream price or the pipeline transmission price. The price adjustment clause contained in the contract of the parties, therefore, was found to be legal and valid.

Secondly, the price adjustment made by Zhongran during this period did not exceed the price cap imposed by the state administrative authorities. In this price adjustment, the NDRC rules set the upper limit for the on-site selling price for non-residential users at RMB 3.278/m^3, whilst the upper limit for price increase set by Zhongran was RMB 3.15/m^3, which was within the range of price fluctuation required by the government authority. Thirdly, according to the price adjustment clause contained in the Jingguang Natural Gas Sales Contract, it was expressly agreed between the parties that: "Any price adjustment shall, in principle, be made according to the gas price and the timetable approved by the price administration agency, but under the special circumstances where the general cost price of the upstream source gas is adjusted, the price shall be adjusted by applying the new rate effective on the date of adjustment to be specified in the official directives issued by the upstream sector ". The said price adjustment was precisely made in the special circumstances where the general cost price of the upstream source gas was adjusted, which was in conformity with the contractual provisions and based on the document issued by the NDRC, the authority of commodity price administration. The adjustment made by Zhongran of the gas price from RMB 3.15/m^3 to RMB 2.93/m^3 in February 2011 was an exercise of corporate autonomy in line with the company's business strategy and was not prohibited by laws or regulations. In conclusion, the claims made by Jingguang were untenable and rejected.

Author's Observations

The author selected and highlighted this case because the author believes it is a very typical case. The case fully illustrates the policy orientation since the business system reform of the gas industry in mainland China in 2003 towards gradual introduction of market competition and the establishment and improvement of the market-driven pricing mechanism. The ongoing competition in the Chinese gas distribution sector, with a wide variety of non-state owned capital such as private, Hong Kong and foreign investments having entered the competition of the urban gas industry, has gradually led to the end of local monopolies. The Defendant in the case, Zhongran, is an enterprise wholly owned by a legal person from Taiwan, Hong Kong or Macau. The pricing of natural gas also adopts a dual-factor pricing model whereby the government prescribes a referential benchmark price and a price movement range, and the business operator then sets a specific price within the government-fixed range according to the conditions of market demand and supply, and costs of production and operation. On 31 May 2010, the NDRC released the *Circular on Increasing the Ex-factory Benchmark Price of Domestic Onshore Natural Gas* (Fa Gai Dian (2010) No. 211), under which the ex-factory benchmark price of oil and gas sector was raised by RMB 0.23/m^3, the "dual-track" pricing system was simultaneously terminated, and any upward adjustment of the ex-factory benchmark price was capped at 10% with however no limit on downward adjustment. The supplier and the purchaser may negotiate a specific price as long as such price does not exceed the ex-factory benchmark price by 10%, which signals the adoption of the price adjustment policy, and the alignment of the natural gas price with the global oil price to form a correlation mechanism between the upstream and downstream sectors. These policies as unequivocal legal basis have been affirmed in some current judicial practices. The court in this case upheld the price adjustment arrangement that adopted the cost-plus pricing method, as a result of which the gas company could successfully transfer to gas users the risk of price increase by its supplier. The court judgment, nevertheless, did not answer Jingguang's claim that a gas company shall not raise the price before the price was set by the price administration agency or jump the gun by raising the price first and then proceeding to obtain an approval. Jingguang's reason was, with respect to the on-site selling price, natural gas was a crucial commodity that had enormous bearing on national economy and common people's livelihood, and therefore a price adjustment would have such widespread effect and profound impact that would justify going through strict statutory procedures including a hearing. In the instant case, the Court avoided this key issue by holding that the claims advanced by Jingguang had no legal basis. The issue, therefore, remained undecided under Chinese laws.

3. Impacts of changes of policy on performance of contract

Case 3 (i): *Li Qiuqin v He' nan Zhonghe Gas Co. , Ltd*, a dispute arising from a Gas Supply Contract [4]

Background Facts

On 25 October 2002, the Defendant, Zhonghe Gas Co. , Ltd and the housing estate where the Plaintiff, Li Qiuqin, resided, entered into a liquefied gas supply contract whereby the Defendant agreed to, in the housing estate where the Plaintiff resided, build facilities for the supply of liquefied gas and pipes connected to each household, and guaranteed the supply of gas to all the households (including the Plaintiff) in the housing estate. After the contract came into effect, the Plaintiff duly discharged its obligations to pay relevant fees. In 2006, the Housing and Urban and Rural Construction Bureau of Xuchang City prepared A *Request for Direction Concerning Issues in Connection with the Conversion from Liquefied Gas to Natural Gas by Using Pre-existing Urban Pipeline Network* and A *Public Announcement by the Xuchang City People' s Government on the Conversion from Liquefied Gas to Natural Gas by Using Pre-existing Pipeline Network*, which in effect ordered the conversion to natural gas within the municipality and cessation of supply of liquefied petroleum gas after the completion of the conversion. The housing estate where the Plaintiff resided fell within the geographical area of the conversion. On 13 June 2014, the conversion to natural gas was carried out in the housing estate where the Plaintiff resided pursuant to a notice jointly issued by the Xuchang City Utilities Supervision Centre, Yanzhong Community Committee of Qilidian Office of Weidu District, Xuchang City Tianlun Gas Co. , Ltd, Home Owners' Committee of Yanzhong Estate and Xuchang Changyuan Property Management Co. ,Ltd. The above-mentioned parties and the Defendant subsequently agreed that the supply of liquefied gas by pipeline was to be ceased. The Plaintiff alleged that the Defendant had breached the contract, requesting the latter to keep supplying liquefied gas to her household and to pay her RMB 5,000, being the economic losses she suffered from the cessation of liquefied gas supply. The Defendant argued that the contract was incapable of actual performance due to relevant policies, and asserted that the claim for RMB 5,000 in damages by Plaintiff was groundless and should be dismissed.

Court' s Opinions

It was held by the first instance court, i. e. Weidu District People' s Court of Xuchang City, He' nan Province that there was indeed a supply of gas contract between the Plaintiff and the Defendant, who should discharge their respective obligations thereunder. In this case, however, the Defendant, as a supplier of pipeline-carried liquefied gas, ceased the supply of liquefied petroleum gas to the Plaintiff and other home owners of the same housing estate at the request of relevant authorities of the Xuchang City People' s Government and the Assembly of Home Owners of the housing estate where the Plaintiff resided. The said act should be deemed

---

4 Civil Judgment of the Hebei Province Xuchang Weidu People' s Court (2014) Wei Bei Min Chu Zi No. 00385. Date of Judgment: 10 August 2015

to have terminated the gas supply contract by reason of force majeure. There was no apparent fault on the part of the Defendant when it unilaterally terminated the supply of gas contract. It cannot be denied, however, that the Defendant was to some degree negligent whilst performing the conversion in response to the request of other authorities, and had more or less adversely affected the Plaintiff. The Defendant was expected to do a better job in future. The Court dismissed the claims lodged by Li Qiuqin, the Plaintiff.

Case 3 (ii): Appeal Case between Yumen Zhongxin Energy Co., Ltd ("Zhongxin", Appellant), Gansu Sales Branch of Petro China (Respondent) and Gansu Jiuquan Sales Branch of Sinopec (the third party in the trial of first instance) in relation to a lease dispute [5]

Background Facts

On 14 January 2010, a Contract on Lease of Gas Station Assets (North Station) was entered into by and between the plaintiff in the trial of first instance, i. e. the Appellant, Zhongxin, and Gansu Jiuquan Branch of PetroChina. It was agreed that Gansu Jiuquan Branch of Petro China would take out a lease on the north station of Gandianzi Gas Station from 26 May 2014 to 25 May 2022 at an annual rent of RMB 1.2 million. In 2013, to implement the "Silk Road Economic Belt" development strategy formulated by the CPC Central Committee, the Development and Reform Commission of Gansu Province ("Gansu DRC") drew up a plan to set up gas filling stations in highway services areas throughout the province. Pursuant to the "*Reply of Approval from the Development and Reform Commission of Gansu Province regarding the Establishment of the Gas Filling Station in Chijin Service Area of Yumen*", Zhongxin was approved to set up a gas filling station in northern Chijin Service Area of Yumen, with the project site being "Gandianzi Service Area, Chijin Town, Yumen City". Zhongxin demanded to rescind the contract on the grounds that the said policy and approval by Gansu DRC, constituted an unforeseeable non-commercial risk when the Contract on Lease of Gas Station Assets was entered into in 2010, as a result of which the continued performance of the contract would substantially increase the lessor's costs, and Zhongxin would not be capable of completing the construction of the gas filling station within the timeframe stipulated in the Gansu DRC approval. These constituted a change of circumstances and therefore the contract should be rescinded. The court of first instance dismissed the plaintiff's claim for rescission of the contract. The plaintiff appealed to the Gansu Province High People's Court.

Court's Opinions

The court of second instance delivered the following opinions. In accordance with the spirit of "prudently applying the principle of change of circumstances and reasonably reconciling the parties' interests" as set out in the *Guidance of the Supreme People's Court on Certain Issues concerning the Trial of Cases of Disputes over Civil and Commercial Contracts under the Current Situation* (No. 40 [2009] of the Supreme People's Court) and the *Circular of the Supreme People's Court on Correctly Applying the Interpretations II of Certain Issues concerning the Contract Law of the People's Republic of China to Serve the Primary Objectives of the Party and the State* (No. 165 [2009] of the Supreme People's Court), applying the principle of change of circumstances shall be strictly restricted and, when necessary, shall be subject to the review and approval of the Supreme People's Court. It follows that the "*Reply*

[5] Civil Judgment of the Gansu Province High People's Court (2014) Gan Min Er Zhong Zi No. 230. Date of Judgment: 14 April 2015

of Approval from the Development and Reform Commission of Gansu Province regarding the Establishment of the North Gas Filling Station in Chijin Service Area of Yumen" would be a normal commercial risk to be assumed by the Appellant, which would not necessarily lead to the inability to perform the contract. Zhongxin's claim was rejected.

Author's Observations

It is noted that many disputes in the energy industry in 2015 resulted from relevant policy adjustments and changes in the energy sector. Analysing these cases is of great empirical and practical significance to the study of the development of the PRC law, in particular the energy law. These cases raise the questions about whether changes in state policies may constitute force majeure or material change of circumstances, and how a court would handle such cases where policy changes have led to inability to perform a contract. They are issues well worthy of our attention. A combined analysis of Case 3 (i) and Case 3 (ii) is as follows:

With respect to Case 3 (i), Article 94 of the *Contract Law* provides that: "The parties may rescind the contract under any of the following circumstances: (1) the purpose of the contract cannot be achieved due to force majeure…"Force majeure is one of the statutory grounds for rescission of a contract. In this case, the Court held that the contract could be rescinded on the force majeure ground, which arose from the relevant policies promulgated by the Housing and Urban and Rural Construction Bureau of Xuchang City and the government. Article 153 of the General Principles of *Civil Law* and Article 117 of the *Contract Law* define force majeure as the "objective circumstances that are unforeseeable, unavoidable and insurmountable". In the legislative and judicial practices of China, no consensus has been reached on whether changes in state policies constitute force majeure. I believe that we should refocus on the provision of the law that force majeure refers to the "objective circumstances that are unforeseeable, unavoidable and insurmountable," and then take a case-by-case approach in handling the issue at hand. In this case, the policy promulgated by the municipal government of Xuchang amounted to an objective circumstance unforeseeable by the parties and beyond the possibility of being avoided or overcome, and as a matter of fact created a circumstance under which continued performance of the contract became impossible. The Henan court, as a result, held that force majeure occurred and the contract could therefore be rescinded. The author concurs with the court's decision. This case illustrated a positive approach adopted by some judges in applying force majeure clauses to real cases.

The author will then move on to analyse the court's approach in Case 3 (ii), which is in stark contrast to Case 3 (i). The principle of change of circumstances is laid down in Article 26 of the *Interpretations II of the Supreme People's Court of Certain Issues concerning the Application of the Contract Law of the People's Republic of China* as "If, after a contract is reached, any material change of objective circumstances occurs that is unforeseeable when the contract is entered into, not caused by force majeure, nor in the nature of any commercial risks, and if the continued performance of the contract will be manifestly unfair to one party thereto or the purpose thereof cannot be achieved, the parties thereto may apply to the people's court to amend or rescind the contract, and the court shall, in adherence to the principle of fairness and taking into account the facts of the case, decide on whether to amend or rescind the contract". It is evident that the principle of change of circumstances mainly applies to the situation where a material change arises after the execution of the contract and the consequence resulting from such change is manifestly unfair to one party. Although the foregoing as a principle has been laid down in the Chinese law, the Supreme People's Court has imposed stringent restrictions on the application of this principle. The Supreme People's Court, in the *Guidance of the Supreme People's Court on Certain Issues concerning the Trial of Cases of Disputes over Civil and Commercial Contracts under the Current Situation* (No. 40 [2009] of the Supreme People's Court), required that the people's courts have a grasp of the conditions applicable to the principle of change of circumstances in accordance with law, and scrutinise the "unforeseeable" claims put forward by the parties. For contracts of which the subject matter involves bulk commodities with active market conditions and volatile price movements (e. g. petroleum, coke and nonferrous metals) or financial products of inherent investment risks (e. g. shares and futures), the principle of change of circumstances shall be applied even more cautiously". In this case, the relevant policies and approvals presented by Zhongxin were normal commercial risks in the normal course of business, and would not meet the conditions for applying the principle of change of circumstances. The final decision of the court of second instance fully reflected the caution of the people's court in applying the principle of change of circumstances. In judicial practices, where it is unclear whether a certain principle should apply to some cases, the courts are more likely to take a conservative stance in handling such cases by refusing to apply the principle of change of circumstances.

B. Power Industry

Case 4: Appeal Case between Henan Dengfeng Power Supply Company of State Grid and Dengfeng Yangcheng Abrasives Co., Ltd (Respondent) in relation to a Power Supply and Use Contract [6]

Background Facts

On 10 March 2009, a Contract on the Supply and Use of High-voltage Electricity was entered into by and between Henan Dengfeng Power Supply Company of State Grid (the "Power Supplier", i. e. the plaintiff in the trial of first instance and the appellant in the appeal) and Dengfeng Yangcheng Abrasives Co., Ltd ("Yangcheng", i. e. the defendant in the trial of first instance and the respondent in the appeal). It was agreed in the contract that during the term of the contract any adjustment to tariffs and any other charges shall be made according to the requirements of tariff adjustment documents. The Power Supplier shall read the meters at a prescribed date and collect tariffs from Yangcheng periodically. In October 2007, Zhengzhou Bureau of Commodity Prices forwarded the *Circular on Matters Concerning the Regulation of the Quantity and Price of Transferred Electricity of Dengfeng Electricity Group Co., Ltd* (No. 1506) released by the Development and Reform Commission of Henan Province ("Henan DRC"). The circular, effective on 1 May 2007, provided that after the users of the former Dengfeng Electricity Group Co., Ltd switched to Dengfeng Electricity Bureau for power services, the tariff of RMB 365.2/mwh (all governmental charges and surcharges included but excluding urban surcharges) would apply for the time being, and the users' tariffs would be gradually transitioned to those stipulated in the tariff catalogue within three years. In January 2009, Henan DRC also released the *Circular of the Development and Reform Commission of Henan Province on Adjustment of Electricity Price for the Year* 2009 (No. 1976), which pro-

6 Civil Judgment of the Intermediate People's Court of Zhengzhou, Henan Province (2015) Zheng Min Er Zhong Zi No. 1676. Date of Judgment: 18 November 2015

vided that "[t]he tariffs of Central China Grid will be properly raised, electricity supply for business uses (1-10 kVa) will be charged at RMB 0.625/kwh… and the preferential tariffs set by local governments will be revoked". This tariff adjustment took effect from 20 November 2009. On 12 May 2010, the NDRC, the State Electricity Regulatory Commission (SERC) and the NEA, again, jointly promulgated the *Circular on Handling the Preferential Electricity Price for Energy-intensive Enterprises and on Other Issues* (Fa Gai Jia Ge (2010) No. 978), which decided that the preferential tariffs for energy-intensive enterprises be cancelled, and required that all the price discounts be properly adjusted from June 2010.

In this case, the tariff payable by Yangcheng was adjusted to RMB 0.4802/kwh as required by the provincial development and reform commission under Circular 1506. Before 16 May 2010, the defendant company had paid all electricity bills to the plaintiff on schedule. In early June 2010, the Power Supplier claimed that the preferential tariffs provided in Circular 1506 would cease to be valid as at 30 April 2010, and the circular jointly released by NDRC, NERC and NEA (2010 No. 978) had made it impossible to request discounted tariffs from higher authorities. Tariffs would therefore become RMB 0.625/kwh, or a difference of RMB 0.1448/kwh, effective on 1 May 2010 according to Circular 1976 promulgated by the provincial development and reform commission. Yangcheng should make up for the shortfall in tariffs accrued from 1 May to 16 May 2010 in accordance with the contract and the *Contract Law*. The claim was dismissed by the court of first instance. The plaintiff was not satisfied and appealed to the Intermediate People's Court of Zhengzhou, Henan Province.

Court's Opinions

The court of second instance delivered the following opinions. The Power Supply and Use Contract was a civil contract and should comply with the provisions of the *Contract Law* and other relevant civil laws. Article 3 of the *Contract Law* provided that "[c]ontractual parties enjoy equal legal standing and neither party may impose its will on the other". Under Article 6, "The parties shall abide by the principle of honesty and good faith in exercising their rights and fulfilling their obligations". Under Article 78, "A contract shall be assumed not to have been modified if the modifications made to the contract are not clearly agreed upon by the parties". In the instant case, although a Contract on the Supply and Use of High-voltage Electricity was entered into by and between the Power Supplier and Yangcheng, the term of the contract had expired. Nevertheless, Yangcheng continued to deposit tariffs according to the contract whilst the Power Supplier continued to supply power as agreed between the parties, which formed a de facto power supply and use relationship. Neither the Power Supplier nor Yangcheng raised any objection to it. Therefore, such relationship should be validated according to law. In the course of the contract performance, the parties had settled the tariffs for the used electricity, which could be evidenced by the VAT invoices issued by the Power Supplier to Yangcheng. All items set out in the invoices, such as power usage, unit price, amount, tax rate and tax amount, were clear and specific. The Power Supplier claimed that tariffs should become RMB 0.606/kwh from 1 May 2010, but it was not in conformity with the unit price specified in its VAT invoice issued to Yangcheng. Meanwhile, Yangcheng deposited the tariffs in advance, and the Power Supplier issued VAT invoices accordingly, which prove that all rights and obligations set down in the Power Supply and Use Contract had been performed by the parties during this period. Whilst the rights and obligations for the period between 1 May and 16 May 2010 had been fully performed, the Power Supplier's unilateral alteration of the relationship of such rights and obligations lacked factual or legal basis. The original judgment was upheld.

Author's Observations

The author holds that, drawing on its monopoly position in the industry, the State Grid here took a tough position and attempted, on the grounds of the price adjustment policies, to collect tariffs retrospectively on top of what had been paid whilst the rights and obligations of the contract had been fully exercised and fulfilled by the parties. Such taking of tough position had no legal basis. It is a basic legal notion that no additional consideration, under either jurisprudence or the provisions of the *Contract Law*, could be added to a subject matter of a contract that has been performed. In various industries in the energy sector, it is not uncommon to see some large state-owned enterprises in monopoly positions have taken such tough position in relevant transactions. Such dominant position, however, should in no way justify their overstepping the legal boundaries and will not be supported by law.

C. The Coal Industry

Case 5: Appeal Case between Shanxi Lantian Environmental Protection Equipment Co., Ltd and Lanzhou Xinxing Heating Co., Ltd in relation to Dispute of Purchase and Sale Contract [7]

Background Facts

On 28 June 2013, a Contract on Purchase and Sale of Pulverized Coal-fired Boiler Facilities (the "Contract") was entered into by and between Lanzhou Xinxing Heating Co., Ltd (the plaintiff in the trial of first instance and the respondent in the appeal, the "Heating Company") and Shanxi Lantian Environmental Protection Equipment Co., Ltd (the defendant in the trial of first instance and the claimant in the appeal, "Lantian"). It was agreed in the Contract that the Heating Company shall purchase from Lantian a 29MW high-efficiency pulverized coal-fired boiler and a set of ancillary facilities, and that Lantian shall be responsible for all the approval, inspection and acceptance formalities required for the installation of the boiler. On 10 April 2013, the Environmental Protection Bureau of Lanzhou City released the *Circular on Taking the "Double Clearing-up" Action on Coal-fired Boilers in Four Districts*. On 15 July of the same year, the Environmental Protection Administration of An'ning District, Lanzhou issued the *Notice to the Heating Company regarding Boiler Revamp after Inspection*, notifying the Heating Company that natural gas must be used within An'ning District, and requiring the Heating Company to expedite its adjustment plan and revamp the natural gas boiler as soon as possible. Upon receipt of the letter, the Heating Company issued a notice next day to Lantian informing Lantian of the directions the Heating Company from the authorities. The Heating Company claimed that force majeure had occurred, based upon which the Contract on Purchase and Sale of Pulverized Coal-fired Boiler Facilities should be rescinded, and requested Lantian to verify the event of force majeure and return the deposit as soon as possible.

---

7 Civil Judgment of the Intermediate People's Court of Lanzhou, Gansu Province (2015) Lan Min Er Zhong Zi No. 179. Date of Judgment: 18 September 2015

Court's Opinions

The court of first instance supported the Heating Company's claim for rescission of the contract on the grounds of force majeure. It held that Lantian was unable to prove that the losses had resulted from performance of the Contract, and even if such losses did result from performance of the Contract, Lantian was directly responsible for the losses because it blindly commenced production without completing the approval formalities as agreed in the Contract. Lantian appealed against the decision of first instance.

The court of second instance delivered the following opinions. Lantian did not carry out any approval formalities for boiler installation. The Contract, as a result, could not be performed, and the purposes of the Contract could not be achieved. The Heating Company's notification to rescind the Contract complied with the relevant provisions in the *Contract Law*, so the court of first instance rightly supported the claim of the Heating Company. As regards Lantian's claim for damages, Lantian blindly commenced production without completing the approval formalities for boiler installation. Given that it should have had certain assessment and foresight of such risks, Lantian should be directly liable for the losses incurred. The court of first instance did not err, based on the evidence provided by Lantian, in rejecting the counterclaim brought by Lantian. The original judgment was upheld.

Author's Observations

The coal industry in China has in recent years remained stagnant on the whole, as evidenced by the continuing downward movements in coal prices, the severe industry over-capacity, and the ever-increasing inventory among customers. It is widely recognised in the industry that the decrease in demand and the falling coal price are inevitable against the general background in China of phasing out redundant production capacity, restructuring the industry, vigorously promoting sustainable energy and transforming the mode of economic development. Facing the increasing business pressure in the coal industry, coal enterprises are going through a particularly harsh time. A large number of coal enterprises have suffered losses and many small and medium-sized enterprises have ceased production and gone bankrupt. The number of disputes in the coal industry, meanwhile, has been on the rise. Due to the environmental pollution resulted from coal's external costs, the energy regulators in China have required from time to time that coal thermal power facilities be replaced with cleaner energy facilities. Such policies and regulatory requirements of replacement will inevitably affect the performance of executed contracts.

D. Renewable Energy Industry

Case 6: Objection by Xiamen Hot Spring Development Company (the "Development Company") to a Third Party's Acquisition of the Subterraneous mineral rights Owned by the Earth's Surface Use Rights Owner [8]

Background Facts

Xiamen Hot Spring Development Company (hereinafter referred to as the "Development Company") was the land use rights owner of a plot of land. In February 2006, Xiamen Hot

---

8 Yang Yuzhang, "Does the pre-emption of mineral rights hinder fair competition?" The China Land and Resources Newspaper, http://www.qjdtc.com/html/tszs/15/07/4479.html, accessed on 12 March 2016.

Spring Service Centre (the "Service Centre") applied to the Fujian Provincial Department of Land and Resources, which assigned the exploration rights of the subterranean hot water (i. e. geothermal energy and hot spring) within the area of the plot based on a first come, first served basis. The Service Centre obtained the exploration license. In August, the Provincial Department of Land and Resources agreed to grant the mining license to the Service Centre in accordance with the regulations related to the "precedence of exploration rights and conversion of exploration rights to mining rights". In April 2012, the Development Company brought an administrative action against the Provincial Department of Land and Resources as the defendant, and the Service Centre as the third party, to the Court of Gulou District, Fuzhou. The reason was that the Development Company was the owner of land use rights of the plot, which entitled it to operate geothermal energy of the concerned plot. The third party obtained the exploration and mining licenses by lying and concealing the truth, and such licenses should be revoked. The approval given by the Provincial Department of Land and Resources to retain the exploration rights was manifestly illegal and should be nullified. The mining license was granted by the Provincial Department of Land and Resources in violation of the legal procedures and the right to fair competition, and should be revoked as well according to law.

The court of first instance held that the Development Company lacked the legal standing to bring an action and dismissed the claim. The Development Company was dissatisfied and appealed to the Fuzhou Intermediate Court. In July 2013, the Intermediate Court dismissed the appeal and the initial ruling was upheld. The Development Company subsequently lodged a complaint to the Fuzhou Intermediate Court on the grounds that the Provincial Department of Land and Resources and the third party gravely infringed on its right of fair competition. In May 2014, the Fuzhou Intermediate Court decided that the case did not meet the retrial criteria and issued a rejection notice. In December 2014, the Development Company, again, lodged a complaint to the Fujian Province High People's Court on the grounds of "serious infringement of right to fair competition". In June 2015, the Fujian Province High People's Court, upon its review, held that "the Development Company and the Service Centre did not have equal rights and obligations in applying for exploration rights, the right to fair competition as claimed by the Development Company lacked factual and legal basis," and the claims of the Development Company were untenable. Upon deliberation by the judicial committee, a notice of rejection was served, and the Development Company was advised to refrain from bringing any further proceedings or appeals.

Author's Observations

This case concerns the conflict between the overground rights and the subterraneous mineral rights, but unfortunately the issue was never addressed by the court of first instance, the court of second instance and the provincial high court. Under Chinese laws, the state owns overground and underground mineral resources, and any entity or individual can obtain the overground rights and the subterraneous mineral rights only through certain statutory procedures. Mineral rights are a kind of usufructuary right under the *Property Law of the People's Republic of China*, but some scholars consider it as a quasi-usufructuary right, to which the author agrees.

According to Article 3 of the *Law of Mineral Resources*, the state ownership of mineral resources, either overground or underground, do not alter because of different ownership or the right to use the land attached to mineral resources. A Use Right Assignment Contract for the State-owned Construction Land also expressly provides, in the General Provisions, that subterraneous resources and buried objects do not fall within the scope of land use rights assignment. The land use rights and the rights of exploration and mining over one piece of land, therefore, are not necessarily vested in one single entity. Rather, they can be exercised by different entities according to law. The land use rights and the rights of exploration and mining are different usufructuary rights subject to different administrative regimes. Under the current laws and regulations, acquisition of the land use rights does not necessarily come with exploration and mining rights of the mineral resources attached to the land, and vice versa. Owing to the difference in nature of the two rights, the owner of the rights to use the land surface does not necessarily own the mining rights of the underground mineral resources, whilst the owner of the mining rights does not necessarily own the rights to use the land surface. If the two kinds of rights are owned by two different entities, then how do we reconcile the conflicts arising when both rights are exercised? Regrettably, the current Chinese laws are silent on which right shall take precedence over the other except requiring that the parties should settle their disputes through consultations. The author believes that so long as the owner of exploration/mining rights intends to exercise his rights, it is inevitable that the owner of the rights to use the land surface will be disturbed. However, as the law is also silent on whether mineral rights could take precedence over land use rights, immense difficulty has been encountered in real life when using a mining area, which also results in, occasionally, some level of uncertainty in the exercise of mineral rights, and increases the difficulty in dispute settlement.

E. Energy Performance Contracting

Case 7: Appeal Case in relation to the Dispute between Chongqing Chuanran Energy Conservation Technology Co., Ltd and Chongqing Zongshen Power Machinery Co., Ltd [9]

Background Facts

On 20 May 2010, a supply contract was entered into by and between Chongqing Chuanran Energy Conservation Technology Co., Ltd (hereinafter referred to as "Chuanran") and Chongqing Zongshen Power Machinery Co., Ltd (hereinafter referred to as "Zongshen"), under which the parties agreed to implement the project of comprehensive use of residual heat in the die-casting branch of Zongshen Power under the energy performance contracting (EPC) model. The contract provided that the parties share the benefits from energy conservation. Specifically, the benefits owned by Chuanran shall be paid by Zongshen to Chuanran on a monthly basis for a total period of six years. The proportion of allocation was detailed as follows - First year: Zongshen owning 25% and Chuanran 75%; Second Year: Zongshen owning 40% and Chuanran 60%; Third Year and onwards: Zongshen and Chuanran each owning 50%. Until March 2013, Zongshen had never fulfilled its obligations of paying the energy-conservation benefits. Chuanran then sued Zongshen for payment of energy conservation benefits and damages, which claim was supported by the court. In this case, Chuanran claimed that in addition to the aforesaid energy conservation benefits and damages, Zongshen should also pay the predictable energy conservation benefits for a period of 53 months from April 2013 to August 2017 and the corresponding damages. Zongshen argued that Chuanran's claim was groundless both

9 Civil Judgment of the Chongqing High People's Court (2015) Yu Gao Fa Min Zhong Zi No. 0001, Date of Judgment: 26 June 2015

factually and legally, and that Zongshen should not be held liable for the energy conservation benefits and damages. The court of first instance ordered Zongshen to pay RMB 113,495.88 in damages to Chuanran. Neither party was satisfied. Both appealed against the decision.

Court's Opinions

The trial of second instance centred on several issues, the key of which was whether Zongshen should be liable for the expected energy conservation benefits and corresponding damages to Chuanran. The court held that under the *Contract Law*, "[w]here a party causes losses to the other party, the amount of damages payable shall be equivalent to the other party's losses resulting from the breach, including any benefits that may be accrued from performance of the contract". Chuanran, the party providing the energy conservation equipment, would undoubtedly gain energy conservation benefits once the equipment was installed and put into operation, and was indeed allocated the corresponding energy conservation benefits during the 19-month period of performance of contract. Had the parties continued to perform their contractual obligations, Chuanran would have continued to receive the energy conservation benefits until the expiry of the contract. However, Zongshen suspended the use of energy conservation equipment in April 2013 without providing any evidence to show that the suspension was attributable to the quality of the equipment. Zongshen's suspension of the use of equipment inevitably deprived Chuanran of the expected energy-conservation benefits to which it should have been entitled. Zongshen should, after the rescission of the supply contract, compensate Chuanran for the expected benefits arising from the supply contact.

As regards the determination of the losses of expected benefits, the supply contract was silent on the liability for breach of contract and on the method for calculation of the losses in the event of rescinding the contract. Chuanran's expected losses should be those energy conservation benefits it could have received in the remaining period of the contract, exclusive of the necessary costs and expenses however required for Chuanran's performance of its contractual obligations. The court, in reference to Article 19(4) of the supply contract, established the base number of Chuanran's losses of energy conservation benefits to be RMB 1,626,538. It then went on to consider such factors as the remaining term of the supply contract, the contract provisions on allocation of energy conservation benefits, and the necessary costs to be incurred by Chuanran to maintain the equipment in good order. Given the foregoing base number and several factors, the court concluded that Zongshen should be liable for compensating Chuanran for losses of expected benefits in the amount of RMB 400,000, which should be adequate to remedy Chuanran's losses of expected benefits. Chuanran's claim for liquidated damages arising from the late payment of energy conservation benefits was, therefore, dismissed.

Author's Observations

This is the first time the author has selected an EPC case for case study. The EPC industry has a bright prospect in China. However, for the time being, this industry is lightly regulated and lacks mandatory policies and regulations especially systematic laws and regulations in respect of financial management, tax deduction or exemption, financial support and policy support which are suitable for the local markets. The absence of such regulations has not only affected the growth of this industry in China, but also led to numerous disputes, which the current case exemplifies. In EPC disputes, due to the lack of an effective legal regime, it is not uncommon that the party receiving the EPC services would terminate the contract discretionarily, thereby putting the service provider at a disadvantageous position. In this case, the court protected the expected benefits of the service provider, which the author would commend. In addition to the rescission of a contract and the compensation for expected benefits, the author would propose that specific performance of a contract may also be a remedy once the relevant regime becomes more developed, although currently specific performance might still be difficult in terms of enforcement. Regardless, support for an expected benefit claim by a service provider, insofar as the relevant laws and regulations are complied with, is a protection at the most fundamental level, although such protection is not common in judicial practices at present. It is the author's hope that this case may serve as a paradigm for protecting the legitimate interest of service providers and facilitating the healthy growth of the EPC industry.

IV. Hot Issues

Energy Charter and the "One Belt and One Road" Strategy

A delegation led by Mr. Nur Bakri (or Nu'er Baikeli inpinyin), Vice-Director of the NDRC and Head of the NEA, attended an Energy Charter ministerial conference held in the Hague, the Netherlands on 20 and 21 May 2015. On 20 May 2015, Mr. Bakri signed the *International Energy Charter Declaration* on behalf of China, marking the country's transition from an observer by invitation to an "associating state" of the Energy Charter Treaty ("ECT"),[10] and a new leap it takes in the governance of international energy. The significance of China's accession to the *International Energy Charter Declaration* cannot be overrated. Had China not signed the Declaration, it would have no entitlement to participate in amendment of the Declaration in future, and therefore would be made to accept the amendments. All the signatories to the International Energy Charter Declaration, as reported, will be invited to propose amendments to articles of the ECT executed at the European Charter Conference in 1994, and to reach consensus on a new International Energy Charter Treaty.[11]

Effective April 1998, the ECT has had 53 signatories so far. China was invited to become an observer country of the ECT in December 2001. The ECT encompasses all forms of international energy cooperation, including investment, trade, cross-border transportation and energy efficiency, which form the four pillars of the ECT. The dispute settlement mechanism under the ECT applies to each of the four pillars. The ECT, being the first multilateral investment treaty, may very well have made the most innovative contributions to investment protection. In that regard, the ECT aims to provide, in a multilateral context and with respect to the energy arena in particular, the type of protection akin to what was made available in the bilateral investment protection treaties (BITs) negotiated and entered into by member states.[12]

The Treaty provides that a member state is under non-discrimination and non-requisition

---

10 China Energy Web: Energy Charter Treaty: Historical Background, Main Framework and Dispute Settlement(I), translated by ZHANG Libin, ZENG Xuehao. http://mp.weixin.qq.com/s?__biz=MjM5MzgyMTU4MA==&mid=401832522&idx=2&sn=8ae74993209c4885f0c60a0b088f655d&scene=23&srcid=0112vWCewDNkyIVCtWG4Nm9w#rd, accessed on 13 January 2016.

11 News Centre of Energy Storage China: New Opportunities Brought by the Cooperation Between China and Energy Charter and New Discourse Power to be Seized. http://www.escn.com.cn/news/show-243604.html, accessed on 11 July 2015.

12 Graham Coop, Chapter 1, "Investment Arbitration and The Energy Charter Treaty", compiled and edited by Clarisse Ribeiro, 2006.

obligations towards any investments made by investors from other member states. This, from a legal perspective, would mitigate the political risks associated with cross-border investments, assure foreign investors that they will be treated fairly and equally in the host country, and protect foreign investors from unlawful confiscation by the host country. The ECT provides investors with a full-fledged dispute resolution mechanism, and equips a foreign investor with the right to sue a host country directly. To date, a total of 88 arbitral cases have been instituted under the ECT.

The dispute settlement mechanism is the cornerstone of the ECT and is indispensable for protection of the rights set out under the ECT. Pursuant to Article 26 of the ECT, where a dispute arises between an investor and the host country, the investor is entitled to sue the host country. Arbitration may also be deployed by an investor for any violations under Part III of the ECT related to "investment promotion and protection" (Articles 10 to 17 of the ECT). Articles 26(1) and 26(2) provide that, prior to the commencement of any formal proceedings, the investor and the host country shall seek to settle their dispute amicably within a cooling period of 3 months. If the dispute cannot be settled amicably within such period, the investor may choose to resolve the dispute under Article 26(2): (i) in a court or administrative tribunal of the host country; (ii) in accordance with any previously agreed dispute settlement procedures; or (iii) by international arbitration or mediation. In the event that a foreign investor chooses to resolve the dispute by international arbitration, the investor must, under Article 26(4), submit the case to one of the three arbitration procedures: (i) the International Centre for Settlement of Investment Disputes of 1965 ("ICSID") provided that the investor's home country and the host country are both member states to ICSIF; (ii) a sole arbitrator or an ad hoc arbitration tribunal to be appointed or formed under the *Arbitration Rules of the United Nations Commission on International Trade Law* ("UNCITRAL"); or (iii) the Arbitration Institute of the Stockholm Chamber of Commerce. Pursuant to Article 26(3)(a), a member state shall give its unconditional consent to the submission of a dispute to international arbitration. [13]

China and the ECT have in recent years had extensive cooperation by way of mutual visits, seminars, exchanges of information, etc. It is noted that the new International Energy Charter Declaration has extended its coverage over such new areas as relief of energy poverty. China, having already signed the Declaration, will further strengthen its cooperation with the ECT.

The author believes that China's accession to the ECT will bring about a variety of benefits. On the one hand, Chinese companies which have energy investments overseas may seek treaty protection of the transfer of their assets and rights so that more effective protection of China's outbound investments will become available and the energy supply will be stabilized. On the other hand, relying on the ECT provisions of national treatment and the most favourable nation treatment, China can make outbound investments in the international energy sector, enjoy multilateral and binding legal and political protections, reduce all sorts of discriminatory and unjust treatments encountered by its energy companies in certain countries, optimise its imported energy portfolio, broaden the supply base of overseas energy, and improve the demand

---

13 For ECT dispute settlement mechanism, please refer to the article on the China Energy Web: Energy Charter Treaty: Historical Background, Main Framework and Dispute Settlement (II), translated by ZHANG Libin and ZENG Xuehao. http://mp. weixin. qq. com/s? __biz = MjM5MzgyMTU4MA = = &mid = 401832522&idx = 3&sn = 1c3a39bf9e3593cf729b6b921dbf4d72&scene = 23&srcid = 01125z4pvmELJwH7w8p0lsM0#rd, accessed on 13 January 2016.

and supply of energy, so that the country may be more assured of more reliable and adequate supply of energy.

Another benefit to gain from China's accession to the ECT is that the "One Belt and One Road" Strategy to be executed by China[14] will be under the protection of international law. It is noted that eleven months into 2015, China had already invested in 49 countries along the Belt and Road with a total amount of US $ 14.01 billion, representing a year-on-year increase of 35.3%. Over the same period of time, Chinese companies signed 2,998 new project contracts in 60 Belt and Road countries with a total contract value of US $ 71.63 billion, accounting for 43.9% of the total new foreign project contract value of the same period in China and representing a year-on-year increase of 11.2%. More specific projects are expected to materialise under China's "One Belt and One Road" Strategy, which will further help realise the strategy. Nevertheless, the "One Belt and One Road" Strategy is merely a state strategy, and we and other Belt and Road countries have yet to reach any bilateral or multilateral treaties to enjoy the legal protection provided thereunder. The ECT, in this regard, serves to fill this vacuum by providing an existing and effective legal framework for the multilateral protection of investments.

The outbound movements of China's products and capital as well as the liberalisation of trade and investment are relevant to ECT member states. A distinct feature of the ECT is to promote the liberalisation of trade and investment, and to build an energy market that is truly open and non-discriminatory among the member states. The objectives of the ECT and China's "One Belt and One Road" Strategy overlap with each other geographically, and their policy agendas also happen to be compatible with each other. All the Belt and Road countries, except for China, have joined the ECT. In such context, China and other Belt and Road countries may well take advantage of the sophisticated and well-run legal framework of the ECT in their cooperation to reduce the costs of the one-on-one negotiations otherwise required. It cannot be overlooked that, however, there is an acute lack of understanding of the ECT in China amidst the government authorities, the business community, and the academia; the country is relatively unsophisticated on how to resort to international legal mechanism to protect its overseas investments. Apart from that, in-depth research on cases brought and heard within the ECT legal framework remains scarce. Whilst China is hatching and undergoing its energy revolution and energy transformation, law and policy are subject to constant changes during the process of this energy transformation. Such changes in law and policy will usually affect foreign investments in China, thereby increasing the Chinese government's risk of being sued.

V. Conclusion and Prospects

The year of 2015 was a critical year for reinforcing the all-around reform. However, short

14 In September and October 2013, China's President, Mr. Xi Jinping, visited a string of Central Asian countries and Southeast Asian countries and, during his visits, he put forward his major initiatives on the building of the Silk Road Economic Belt and the 21st-century Maritime Silk Road ("the One Belt and One Road"), which has since attracted wide international attention. The One Belt and One Road Strategy will fully rely on the bilateral and/or multilateral mechanisms between China and relevant countries, and take advantage of the existing and effective platforms of the regional cooperation. The One Belt and One Road Strategy is China's top-level strategy at this stage. Whilst attending the 2013 China-ASEAM Expo, China's Premier, Mr. Li Keqiang, stressed that a maritime silk road embracing ASEAM was to be built to gain strategic leverage to promote the development of hinterlands.

of our expectation, the reform in the power industry has failed to make any substantive progress. The reform has entered into a stage of uncertainties where we are faced with many complicated issues, considerable resistance from parties with vested interests and our inadequate knowledge and studies of many issues. As for the oil and gas industry, the oil and gas reform, which is still being blue-printed and pending, has encountered the same difficulties and challenges.

Against such a background, the reform of the power, oil and gas industries has not been fully rolled out, which leads to the sluggish legislative progress in these industries and the lack of substantive development in the legislation of the basic laws in the energy sector. Legal uncertainty remains in the face of the slow reform of the oil and gas and power industries. As a result, when disputes arise, enterprises cannot resort to laws for any sound and definite legal basis. Take the upstream oil and gas mining rights as an example, the definition and legal protection of property rights of mining areas remained inadequate. Investors therefore hesitate to invest in the upstream fields. In the downstream trading field of oil and gas, conflicts still exist in the laws of abusing market position and the *Anti-Monopoly Law*, and many problems will only be resolved gradually with the promulgation of relevant state reform measures and laws and regulations of higher enforceability.

In 2015, the world economy was at a deep post-crisis adjustment phase and was slowing down. China's economic growth has seen further declines, with the official annual GDP growth being 6.9%. The year of 2015 witnessed a fall in the oil price—the price of Brent crude oil dropped to US $36.11/barrel on 22 December 2015, a record low since the 2008 financial crisis. In such circumstances, enterprises engaging in non-renewable fossil energy resources such as oil and gas enterprises and the coal industry have encountered enormous difficulties. When the economy turns sour, disputes arising from investment and trade would increase. The decreasing demand and low oil price reduced the commercial attractiveness of wind power and solar power, which also put pressures on the growth of renewable energy and increased the disputes involving renewable energy.

We should see the reform continue despite some difficulties in the energy sector in 2015. The 2016 general plan for the reform of oil and natural gas structure is soon to be introduced. The deepening reform covering the upstream, midstream and downstream of the oil and gas industry will be gradually rolled out to further alleviate the monopoly and encourage competition. Many enterprises, under the dual pressure of the deepening reform and the extremely depressed oil price, have no choice but to take a series of cost-cutting and efficiency-enhancing measures to create room for its survival and restructuring, including optimizing operations, reducing output, scaling down investments, cutting costs, restructuring assets and renegotiating contracts. During this course, disputes with such stakeholders as business partners, suppliers, service providers, and employees will inevitably increase.

Despite the overall slow progress in the energy sector reform in 2015, there are some highlights. The pilot bidding for the oil and gas exploration blocks in Xinjiang represents a valuable reform attempt and, regardless of some deficiencies, is enormously important. It is important because we can study and improve the transferal system for oil and gas exploration blocks, can explore a competitive transfer system which is suitable for the characteristics of oil and gas exploration and is able to play a definitive role in allocating market resources. It can also stimulate market vitality, can promptly generate experiences which are replicable, transferrable and instrumental to lawmaking, can identify a new mechanism for an open, competitive and orderly market economy, and can provide valuable experiences for deepening an all-round reform of the oil and gas exploration regime.

The three major state-owned oil companies, affected by the depressed oil price and financially strained by the major overseas acquisitions in previous years, will not engage in any major acquisition of overseas oil and gas assets for the time being. However, the Big Three remain the only companies capable of carrying out oil and gas exploration, development and production in China's oil and gas industry. In the meantime, we have noticed that some financially resourceful state-owned enterprises and private enterprises apart from the Big Three are planning to invest in the upstream oil and gas industry. It is expected that the oil and gas reform plan to be promulgated in China will open up the exploration, development and production of China's upstream oil and gas industry and grant market access, which will offer realistic prospect of cooperation among the state petroleum companies as "operator" and "non-operator" investors.

In order to encourage private capital and financial capital to participate in the upstream exploration and development in China's oil and gas sector, we also need to amend relevant laws and regulations, remove market access barriers and innovate the transfer system of oil and gas mining right. We can certainly, for instance, learn from the standard practices in the international oil and gas industry, and allow Chinese enterprises to acquire oil and gas mining rights through consortium bidding. As to the qualification requirements for bidding enterprises, we should distinguish an "operator" entity from a "non-operator" entity, whilst the former should possess technical and operating capabilities and the latter needs only financial capacity. During the course of bidding for oil and gas mining rights, we may encourage different entities to team up for consortium bidding, or to form a joint venture or a limited partnership, or to experiment with a joint operation agreement which is not unusually seen in the world, or we may attempt, to the extent permitted by existing laws, to establish a new model of mixed ownership in China's upstream oil and gas industry.

As the reform of the upstream oil and gas industry is accelerating and private enterprises' entitlement to use imported crude oil and their qualifications for importing crude oil are widening, the reform of the oil and gas industry is in full swing, the structural reform of the power industry is also deepening, laws and regulations related to environmental protection are further developed and refined, and fresh energy-related disputes such as environmental public interest litigation are also mushrooming. These new laws, regulations and landmark cases will play an important role in advancing reform of all industries in the energy sector.

With the Paris Climate Conference being successfully held at the end of 2015, the author believes that, in the near future, China's basic energy law and specialized energy laws, including the *Energy Law*, the *Oil and Natural Gas Law*, the *Power Law*, the *Coal Law*, the *Renewable Energy Law* and the *Nuclear Safety Law*, will be enacted, amended and streamlined. China's regulatory regime of energy resources will also be changed, reform of the oil and gas mining rights system will be further deepened and private capital will have more access to the oil and gas industry; monopoly will be gradually lifted and the oil and gas price will be more attributable to the market forces. Furthermore, structural reform of the power industry will be further deepened. The phasing out of redundant production capacity in the coal industry will speed up. Renewable energy such as hydroelectric power, wind power, nuclear power and solar power will be better utilised. An integrated national market of carbon emission rights will be formed in China, and our low-carbon economy will further grow. China's energy sector will go down the path of sustainable development. As a result, eco-civilization and environmental protection will be substantially boosted. The author believes, the energy supply structure once dominated by fossil fuels will be gradually changed with all of our efforts, and the smog looming over our life will be dispelled eventually. We are looking forward to the great strides that will be made in 2016 in China's energy transformation. With the continued development and improvement of legislation, the enhanced legal certainty will also contribute to the reduction of disputes in the energy sector.

Annual Review on Investment Dispute Resolution in China (2016) *

BAO Zhi, WANG Zekun [1]

I. Overview

The authors have observed that in the year of 2015 for the Chinese market, investment activities remained active while investment disputes have increased significantly. Take Beijing Arbitration Commission as an example, cases related to investment and finance make 27.72% of the total caseload in 2015. As a comparison, in 2014, the ratio was 15.04% and even lower in 2013, at 11.43% [2]. Specifically, cases involving investment, finance and stock buyback in particular have a remarkable increasing rate.

The reasons could be concluded as follows: firstly, due to the economic recession, capital markets have largely slumped, thus the channels for enterprises to issue IPO and re-financing are narrowed. Deterioration of the business environment leads to conflicts among enterprises, founders and investors, generated when allocating interest and responsibilities amongst themselves. Secondly, the new company law and registration capital reform have been gradually enforced, thus start-ups have lower threshold and the capital liquidity are getting higher. Also, due to the macroeconomic condition, more and more economic activities are getting financed through private financing, once one party involved in the private financing is in trouble, this will trigger a ripple effect, and more complicated equity disputes will arise. For the private investors, many of them lack professional background and the informative asymmetry, their rights are easily infringed. Furthermore, the supervision system is not sound enough to deal with the endlessly innovative online financing and hence illegal fund raising, fraudulent fund-raising and illegal absorbing deposit of the public by using the so-called "pseudo fund" frequently occur. In addition, the current legislation of the Chinese investment management system is yet to mature, provisions on restricted or prohibited investment areas scattered in the regulations made by different regulatory bodies, while the negative list of investment entry has not been established. With the increasing investment activities and the gradual expansion of the field of investment, dispute caused by violation of investment entry regulations of certain industry is a noteworthy key issue of this year.

From a transaction structure perspective, more and more investment activities involving

---

* Translated by D. H. Law Associates.

1 BAO Zhi, Partner of Beijing Fenxun law firm; Wang Zekun, Lawyer, Beijing Fenxun law firm

2 See annual report 2013, 2014, 2015 of Beijing Arbitration Commission.

share repurchase, share pledge and other arrangement and methods such as "share in shape but debt in nature", "variable interest entities" and "channel business". Viewed from the type of disputes, apart from the traditional dispute like debt performance sequential order, other issues like transaction requirement satisfaction, price adjustment, company control competition, minority shareholder protection as well as profit sharing have become contentious issues. From the view of the subject of interest, in addition to the traditional industries and financial investors, a considerable number of natural persons are involved in various kinds of investment disputes.

In this article, the authors will go through and summarize the notable cases and legislation updates in 2015 related to investment, and put forward their understanding.

II. Laws, Regulations and Other Normative Documents Publishing Recently

Based on the observation of the authors, legal reform has been carried out in the Investment Law area in 2015, also, as a response to the call from the third plenary meeting of the 18th central committee of the communist party of China, the ongoing tendency of the government is to reduce intervention on the investment market. This year, although new amendments to the Investment Law legislation will still be on the stage of drafts or opinions, the influence brought by this reform will still be noteworthy.

A. Opinions of Enforcing Negative List of Market Entry of State Council

State Council issued *Opinion of enforcing negative list of market entry* on 2 October 2015 (hereinafter referred to as "the Opinions"). The Opinions clearly lists the industries and services that market entities are entitled to invest in or practice in China. It also stipulated what regulatory measures that can be adopted by each level of government.

Enforcing the negative list system is a significant change of the Chinese regulatory framework on investment. All industries, services and business, other than mentioned on this list, can be entered freely by all market entities and such entities have full discretion and autonomy. The opinions further divide the negative list into two methods, one is prohibited items, and another is restricted items. For the prohibited items, the market entities are not allowed to enter and authorities will not grant approval. For restricted items, market entities can file an application to the authority and the authority will give permission according to the law, or in another scenario, once the market entities match all the entry criteria and regulatory standards, the entities can enter the market. For other industries that are not on the negative list, the market entities can enter freely.

The *Opinions* are one part of constructing the negative list system. It also mentioned that this system will be tested under pilot plans in some area from 1 December 2015 to 31 December 2017 to accumulate experience and improve this system gradually. This will also help explore the formation of a unified negative market entry list and the corresponding institutional mechanisms. From 2018 onwards, this negative list system will be officially enforced nationwide in China.

Adoption of the negative list system will stimulate the market's vitality is a significant step to reduce governmental intervention and guarantee entry freedom to market entities, which has great practical significance. The negative list system also accords with the legal principle of "absence of legal prohibition means freedom", which reflects the autonomy of private laws. The market entry freedom is the starting point of regulation over market, if the government is about to impose restriction on market entry freedom, it should have legal basis and give adequate reasoning. Apart from the lawful restricted areas, the market entities can enter freely, they can have full autonomy in deciding their affairs and realizing their lawful interest without any illegal intervention. [3]

It is obvious that the enforcement of the negative list system draws a line between private and public law. It has a significant influence on the validity of contract under public authority interventions. As stipulated in the *Chinese Contract Law*, contracts that contravene the mandatory provisions of laws and administrative regulations will be invalid. Despite this, there remains some uncertainty in this expression that might cause investment activities to incur some risk. Firstly, for the interpretation of "mandatory provision", there is quite large room for interpretation in practice. Though in the current legal practice judges and arbitrators will tend to define "mandatory provisions" as prohibitive provisions, but there is no law that expressly stipulates it. Secondly, according to the Chinese legislation hierarchy, those normative legal documents are below laws and administrative regulations, part of those normative legal documents will obstruct the enforcement of the contract. Thirdly, based on the current approval system, there are certain gaps drawing adverse effects on investment activities. For instance, some industries lack clear legal regulation, supervision as well as entry regulations; the same is not conducive to the normal investment activities. For these above mentioned issues, they have brought obstacles to the investing market activities and legal practice, especially when China is going through economic reforms and various investment areas are emerging, if the legal validity of investing activities cannot be ascertained, then it will be hard for legal risk evaluation and management, also it will be difficult for judicial work and arbitration work.

Chief economist of WTO Patrick Low mentioned in his thesis regarding market liberalization under the GATS agreement that the most prominent advantage of negative list is it can enormously enhance the transparency of market, as those ones that are on the negative list are obvious, if a positive list system is used, then more articles should be introduced. [4] After China has comprehensively enforced the negative list system, on one hand, it will minimize the risk of market entities in engaging investing activities; on the other hand, it will give a clear legal basis when determining the validity of contracts.

B. Foreign Investment Law of the People's Republic of China (Draft for Comment)

On 19 January 2015, Ministry of Commerce of China sought public opinion on the *Draft of Foreign Investment Law* (hereinafter referred to as the "*Draft of Foreign Investment Law*", which has a content that China will rebuild the current foreign investment regime and impose a fundamental change to the current regulatory framework.

As stated by Ministry of Commerce, the *Draft of Foreign Investment Law* is oriented to be

---

3 Wang Liming, "the Negative List Management Model and the Autonomy of Private Law", Chinese law, 5th volume 2014.

4 Lu Zhenhua, "the History of Negative List", the Twenty-first Century Economic Report, January 1, 2014.

a consolidated fundamental law that will manage and boost foreign investment. The word "consolidated" means this law consolidated the related regulations as in *The Law of the PRC on Chinese-Foreign Equity Joint Ventures*, *Law of the People's Republic of China on Foreign-funded Enterprises* and *Law of the People's Republic of China on Chinese and Foreign Contractual Joint Ventures* (hereinafter referred to as the "Three Laws"), it also establishes the uniformed boundary of foreign investment related laws.

The current Chinese FDI legislation took a test driven approach and has features of gradualness and dispersivity, it is gradually formed based on the needs of China enforcing the reform and open up policy. When the new law is enforced, the current three laws on foreign investment will be annulled, thus putting an end to the shattered situation in regulating enterprises with foreign investment. Moreover, the current FDI law regulations are mainly about Greenfield investment, for the M&A sector, Ministry of Commerce and other organs issued various regulations. The content of the *Draft of Foreign Investment Law to Comment* shows foreign investment has been divided into two categories of newly established enterprises and M&A, besides, it also includes long term financing, acquisition of franchise right and real estate, variable interest entities and overseas transactions. In the future, such investments will be uniformly governed by the system established by the *Foreign Investment Law*. On the other hand, according to the statement made by the Ministry of Commerce, regulations such as that on the enterprises' organizational forms and business activities contained in the current three laws on foreign investment are repeated in, or even in conflict with, the *Company Law of the PRC*. The implementation of the new law will gradually remove these repetitions or conflicts. By then, these foreign investors setting up firms in or doing M&A in China need to follow the procedures and fulfill the complacence as stipulated in the *Company Law*, *Partnership Enterprise Law* and the *Sole Proprietorship Enterprise Law*. [5]

Moreover, it is noteworthy that the unification of foreign investment laws further embodies in the stipulation of the fundamental systems in the *Draft of Foreign Investment Law*. Accordingly, seven items including entry management, national security review, investment promotion, reporting, investment protection, complaint coordination, supervision and inspection have been absorbed in the *Foreign Investment Law*.

Based on the *Draft of Foreign Investment Law*, after its enforcement, the following aspects should be worthy noted:

1. About the identification of "Control"

The concept of "control" can be seen in the *Chinese Company Law* and *Anti-Monopoly* law. Article 216 of the *Compang Law* defines "controlling shareholder" and "de facto controller" as below: "controlling shareholder" refers to the shareholder whose capital contribution accounts for 50% or more of the total capital of a limited liability company or whose shareholding accounts for 50% or more of the total share capital of a company limited by shares; or the shareholder whose capital contribution or shareholding is less than 50% but whose voting rights pursuant to such capital contribution or shareholding are sufficient to have a major impact on the resolutions of the board of shareholders or general meeting. "De facto controller" refers

5 Ren Qing, "Three Key Words in the Foreign Investment Law (Draft)", Chinese law review, 3rd volume 2015.

to a person who, although is not a shareholder of the company, is capable of actually controlling the conduct of the company through investment relations, agreements or other arrangements. Instead of making a definition, the *Anti-Monoply Law* uses the concept of "controlling power" and "decisive effect". Ministry of Commerce issued the guiding opinions on the concentrations of undertakings and defines "controlling power", it emphasizes that the identification of controlling power should take both legal and factual factors into consideration such as share holding structure, voting system, constitution of board of directors and its voting system, appointment and removal of high level managerial personnel. Moreover, notice of the general office of the State Council on the establishment of a security review system for foreign investors in the merger and acquisition of domestic enterprises classified the following criteria to judge whether a foreign investor has *de facto* control: 1) foreign investor and its holding parent company or subsidiary in total hold more than 50% shares of the target company after M&A. 2) multiple foreign investors in total hold more than 50% shares of the target company. 3) foreign investor holds no more than 50% shares but it can cast significant influence to the decision making of board of directors and meeting of shareholders. 4) other circumstances that will cause actual controlling power such as financial decision, personnel and technology decision to transfer.

The *Draft of Foreign Investment Law* has combined the above-mentioned points and defines "control" as below: 1) directly or indirectly hold more than 50% shares or similar rights of the enterprise. 2) directly or indirectly hold more than 50% shares or similar rights of the enterprise, but has one of the following powers: directly or indirectly appoint more than a half of the members of board of directors or other decision making body; has the ability to make sure the personnel appointed by itself take more than a half of the members of the board of directors or other decision making body; the voting rights are able to cast a significant influence on the shareholder meeting or board of directors or other decision making bodies. 3) By contract or by trust can impose decisive influence to the enterprise's finance, personnel and technology arrangement.

2. Identification of the foreign investor

Identification of the foreign investor is key to determine whether one investment is foreign investment. The *Draft of Foreign Investment Law* took a dual standard approach of "nationality/registration place plus actual control". Article 11 (1) stipulates that foreign investor means foreign individual, enterprise, government or international organization. Chinese enterprises controlled by these bodies are deemed to be foreign investors. Article 12 stipulates that Chinese investor means enterprises owned by Chinese Individual and Chinese government. Hence, the Chinese domestic enterprises can be divided into the following categories: 1) wholly owned by Chinese individual, directly or indirectly owned by the Chinese government thus foreign investment law will not apply. 2) Foreign investor partially own shares in the enterprises owned by Chinese Individual or Chinese government. The investment activities carried out by the foreign investor should be regulated by *Foreign Investment Law* and fulfill its report duty and obey inspection regulations. 3) Directly or indirectly invested by Chinese individual or Chinese government but controlled directly or indirectly by foreign investors, then not only the foreign investor should fulfill its obligations under *Foreign Investment Law*, but also the enterprise itself should obey *Foreign Investment Law* when doing reinvestment in China. 4) Domestic enterprise funded directly or indirectly by foreign investors also qualifies as foreign invested enterprise and foreign investor.

3. Variable Interest Entities (VIE)

After the *Foreign Investment Law* enforcement, how to handle variable interest entity (VIE) is a key issue drawing great attention when the *Draft of Investment Law* came into effect. The Ministry of Commerce explained that after the new law is enforced, investment through VIE should be governed by *Foreign Investment Law*. But for the VIE prior to the enforcement of the new law, if such entities are classified as restricted or prohibited industries, scholars and practitioners have the following views: 1) foreign invested enterprises with VIE should report to Chinese authorities and if the VIE is controlled by Chinese investors, the VIE can be kept and parties can continue business. 2) Foreign invested enterprises with VIE should report to Chinese authorities and apply for affirmation from the authorities. If the authorities affirm that such enterprises are controlled by Chinese investors then VIE can be kept and parties can continue business. 3) Foreign invested enterprises with VIE should apply for entry approval from authorities, such authorities will make decision by taking various factors such as actual controller into consideration.

In combination with the content of the *Draft of Investment Law*, the behavior of using VIE to avoid entry restrictions will be prohibited by the *Foreign Investment Law* and corresponding responsibilities should be borne. For the VIEs made before the new law, the validity will reply on the further determination and refinement of the contents of the *Draft of Foreign Investment Law*.

4. FDI entry negative list system

Similar to the aforesaid market entry list system, FDI entry negative list system also shows the transformation of government functions of administrative approval to "free of entry when absence of prohibition of law". The starting point of negative list is making national treatment as a guiding principle, all the methods which do not comply with national treatment principle should be listed out in the special administrative measures directory, and this directory will be the unified (or only) regulatory basis for FDI entry management. It is worth noting that all the measures stipulated in this directory should derive from law, administrative regulation or State Council's decision. Nominating the decision of the State Council as the source for special regulatory measures is probably to have reasonable flexibility when measures need to be added or deleted.

For management measures of FDI, according to the *Draft of Investment Law*, foreign investors investing in those industries other than stipulated in the negative list will require no approval for entry and commercial registration, real estate registration, foreign exchange and tax procedures can be made according to relevant laws and regulations.

The relationship between FDI negative list and the aforesaid market entry list should be construed as below: Chinese government makes an independent market entry list while the FDI negative list is a result of bilateral negotiation. In addition, foreign investment should first meet the requirement of FDI negative list, and then it should also meet the criteria set out in the market entry list.

Apart from the above mentioned aspects, there are some other notable changes in the *Draft of Foreign Investment Law* which are: paragraph 3 of Article 15 stipulates that long term shareholder loan falls within the scope of foreign investment, therefore such loan will be regulated not only by *Foreign Investment Law* but also by foreign exchange regulations. The *Draft of Foreign Investment Law* also elaborates rules on national security review, Article 73 stipulates that for the decision on national security review rendered by authority, no administrative reconsideration nor proceedings should be given. Last but not least, according to the Chinese current legal framework, if the *Foreign Investment Law* is officially effective, there will be some coordination issues with other existing laws. For example, Article 47 of the *Sole Proprietorship Enterprise Law of China* stipulates that it will not be applied to wholly foreign own enterprises, such issues are noteworthy in legal practice.

C. Stock Issuing Reform of Adopting "Registration System"

On 27 December 2015, the Standing Committee of National People's Congress released the decision on delegation the State Council to adjust the applicable law of the securities laws of China when enforcing the stock issuing reform and adopted the "registration system" (hereinafter referred to as the "Decision"), which says for the stocks that are planning to be listed in Shanghai Stock Exchange Market and Shenzhen Stock Exchange Market, the State Council can adjust the approval system as stipulated in the *Securities Law of China* and enforce registration system, the detailed plan will be made by the State Council and then submit the same to the Standing Committee of the National People's Congress for record.

Currently, under the current system in China, issuance of stock shares and IPOs are done by approval. The system requires not only mandatory information disclosure, but also the mandatory legal compliance. The securities regulatory commissions will scrutinize the issuer's management structure, business nature, capital composition, development prospect, managerial personal quality and company competitiveness except the formal examination, then it will render a judgment of whether this company is qualified to be listed or not, its guiding principle combines mandatory disclosure and legal compliance. While registration system follows open management principle, in nature, it is a financial disclosure system. The *US Securities Law* is one example that absorbs this principle. It requires the issuer to provide all information that is related to the issuing, and all that information will be recorded in the prospectus. Under the registration system, the securities regulatory body will only review the documents provided by the issuer and see if the issuer has carried out its obligation of information disclosure. The most important feature of this system is it will only do formal examination but no material examination will be carried out.

The enforcement of the registration system shows China will reduce administrative intervention on stock issuing, that is to say, the market will be the final decision maker and public power's decisive role will be changed. The enterprises will have the right to be financed by the stock market. After the registration system is comprehensively enforced, the key issues will be the issuer's information disclosure, arrangers will check the authenticity, accuracy and integrity of such information, securities regulatory body will review on the application document but no material examination, no judgment on its profitability will be carried out, the investors will have the autonomy when buying stock shares and make their own decision.

The aforesaid decision released by the Standing Committee of the National People's Congress is the beginning of the issuing system reform. With the deepening of the reform and improvement of the supporting systems, new legal relationship and disputes will emerge alongside and require more attention. Firstly, as information disclosure is the keystone of enforcing registration system, this sets higher requirements for issuer and intermediaries. If issuer and intermediaries failed to comply with their information disclosure duty and lead to the investors' interest damage, then they will be the people who shall be liable. Secondly, under the premise of issuing registration system, the real regulator will be investors instead of regulatory bodies, the past administrative relationship between regulatory body and issuer will be changed to an equal relationship between issuer and investor. When disputes emerge, certain specific mechanism of redressal should be used. For example, Article 54 of the *Chinese Civil Procedure Law* stipulates that, in class litigation, the several parties have a common object but the number of litigating parties have not been fixed at the time of filing the claim Class litigation is not frequently used in the Chinese legal practice, while with the deepening of the Chinese issuing registration reform, its real value will soon be revealed.

III. Typical Cases

A. "Pseudo Fund": Principal and Profit Return

As mentioned previously, with the flourishing of private financing, all kinds of investment disputes also increased rapidly. Some entities will attract private investors to join the so-called limited liability enterprises as limited liability partners by the name of "investing and financing", further achieve the goal of arranging the "capital pool". Many of such enterprises will end up as "Pseudo fund", when compared with limited liability partner of legitimate private equity fund, these investors lack the ability of risk identification, moreover, due to lacking of knowledge and informative asymmetry, they are in a vulnerable position when doing business. Consequently in legal practice, some judges and arbitrators tend to use the "fair and honest" principle to scrutinize the contractual process and reason whether there is informative asymmetry, they are inclined to offer more protection to investors in vulnerable position.

Case introduction

Individual A, company B and X firm (limited liability enterprise) jointly signed Partnership Agreement in February 2014. The parties agreed that X fund will be set up jointly and then using X fund to invest in Y fund by way of debentures. Individual A is a limited liability partner of X fund and individual B is a general partner and also acts as executive of the fund, B also bears unlimited joint and several liabilities. Under the Partnership Agreement, X fund should allocate profits to A at regular intervals and return the entire principal to A when investment end day comes. In January 2015, company C issued a letter of guarantee to A and promised to take joint and several responsibilities on paying profits and returning principles of Fund X to its investors. In February 2015, Individual E, the actual controller of Fund X disappeared. As Fund X failed to fulfill its obligations of paying profits and returning the principal to A, A as the applicant filed an application to the arbitral tribunal, requested the tribunal to rule that Fund X should pay profits and return principal, also requested Company B and C bear joint and several responsibilities.

Opinions of the arbitral tribunal

In the current case, the tribunal found that the reviewing of the contracting process and the verification of certain legal clauses in the Partnership Agreement are the key to this case.

Proof showed that A was put in an unequal position due to information asymmetry, Company B and staff from Fund X told A that signing the partnership agreement is merely an internal procedure, A can enjoy stable profits. But in the partnership agreement, A as a limited liability partner, will bear the loss of the partnership to the extent of contribution.

The arbitral tribunal reasoned that under the partnership agreement, if fund X fails to allocate profit in a complete and timely manner, then Company B agrees to purchase A's share in the firm. Secondly the agreement says the principal and last installment of profit should be paid to A when termination of investment comes. Moreover, the letter of guarantee shows that Companies should take joint and several responsibilities on paying profits and returning principal to A. Based on the above observations, the tribunal thus ruled that fund X has made a clear promise to A's profit and principal, consequently company B and C should bear joint and several responsibilities.

Observations on this dispute

On 1 June 2007, the revised version of *Partnership Enterprise Law* came into effect. Compared with limited liability companies, limited liability partnerships have advantages of simple incorporation procedures and flexible profit allocation mechanism, consequently LLP is the prevailing organizational form for private equity funds. However, with the rapid development of private funds, some fraudulent firms are using the term of "investing" and "financing" in their names to lure senior citizen and people that lack financial knowledge. In practice, these fraudulent funds will use professional marketing team to market their products, and they will also give a clear yield rate and promise when termination of investment comes, the entire amount of principal with profits will be returned to the investors. Those investors who are lack of financial knowledge will easily misunderstand such terms and think when termination of investment comes, it is 100% secured that the principal and profits will be returned.

In practice, for legitimate private equity funds, if the limited liability partner files suit or arbitration, the court or arbitral tribunal normally will rule accordingly to the limited liability partnership agreement. While for the Pseudo fund dispute, the ruling varies from place to place, some will consider this as financial dispute, some will consider this as private loan dispute and some will consider this as partnership agreement dispute.

For the current case, if we only review the partnership agreement, then as a limited liability partner, should bear the losses to the extent of A's contribution. But based on the information asymmetry of the contractual process, the tribunal thus ruled that A was in a vulnerable position and A's true intent of signing the partnership agreement is to establish a legal relationship that is similar to debtor creditor relationship. Consequently, the tribunal did not classify this case as a case arose out of limited liability partner's responsibility but ruled it as a creditor-debtor relationship thus to protect the investor's interest.

While dealing with such disputes, the authors think that the judge/arbitrator should take the contractual process, information exchange as well as parties' comprehension ability into consideration. Normally speaking, if the general partner shows guarantee to the investor and clearly promises investor that principal and profit will be returned, then this constitutes an obligation and in this scenario the general partner acts as an asset management person. If the general partner fails to do so, he/she should bear the responsibility for breach of contract. Likewise, if a third person offers a guarantee to the investor, the third party person is obliged to fulfill his responsibility. Article 145 of *Securities Investment Fund Law of the People's Republic of China* stipulates that " where, in the course of performing their respective duties, the fund managers or fund custodians violate any provision of this Law or any provision in the fund contracts, thus causing losses to the fund assets or the holders of fund units, they shall bear their respective responsibilities for their own acts and pay compensation in accordance with law; and where losses are caused to the fund assets or the holders of fund units as a result of the joint acts of the fund managers and the fund custodians, they shall bear joint and several responsibility to pay compensation." Article 153 stipulates that "this Law shall apply to the securities investment activities of a company or partnership formed through public or nonpublic capital raising for the purpose of engaging in securities investment activities, the assets of which are managed by a fund management institution or the general partners." Consequently if parties including fund managers breach the contractual duties and cause direct damages to the investors, they are liable to compensate."

B. Identification on Share Repurchase Responsibility and Compensation

In recent years, share repurchase gradually becomes a typical method for enterprises to get external financing. Generally speaking, the external investors that offer financing have the target of financial investment and will rarely participate to the daily operation of the enterprises and consequently it is hard for them to monitor the operational risks. As a safeguard measure, the external investor will ask the enterprise, the controlling shareholder or actual controller to promise that if certain conditions are met, such aforesaid person should repurchase the shares owned by the external investors at the agreed price and terms. Compared to pledge and real estate mortgage, the arrangement of share repurchase has disadvantage in liquidation order, but repurchase of shares does not require registration process and it is comparatively flexible, also it can have a balanced risk and profit sharing mechanism so it is quite popular and in practice, venture capital and equity capital tend to put share repurchase arrangement in equity financing transactions. Currently, some debt financing will also use the so-called "share in shape but debt in nature" arrangement and set share repurchase terms in such arrangements. In practice, in practice, there are discrepancies between the judicial courts and arbitration institutions in the endorsement of such arrangements.

Case introduction

In January 2012, fund A and Company B and B's shareholder Company C jointly signed a share transfer and capital increase contract with B's actual controller D, the parties agreed that A can purchase B's share from C, also A can invest money to B and B will issue shares to A.

According to the agreement, firstly, after the investment is done and until B gets listed, B should annually issue cash dividend to the shareholders and the ratio will be no more than 30% of its allocable profit. Secondly, if any of the following three conditions is met, A will have the option to do swing trade: 1) B's annual net profit is no more than 70% of the promised net profit. 2) B failed to get listed on Chinese stock market before December 31, 2013. 3) B's subsidiaries failed to get mining approval before June 30, 2012. Based on the terms stipulated in this agreement, B, C and individual D should repurchase the shares owned by A, the amount should be A's investment with an annual compound return rate of 15%. Thirdly, if B, C or Individual D failed to do swing trade, for the outstanding amount, they should pay interest to A at a compound interest rate of 15%.

A filed an arbitration application in September of 2015 and claimed: 1) B should pay A dividend of 2014. 2) B should repurchase shares held by A at agreed price. 3) B, C and individual D should pay damages to A with a compound interest rate of 15%. B, C and Individual D claimed 1) A as a shareholder of the company has the right to dividend but the annual audit report of 2014 is not available yet so the amount payable to A cannot be confirmed. 2) *Company Law* does not allow share repurchase under this case's scenario. 3) When contracting this agreement, the parties are in unequal position and some terms of this contract are also biased. Investment activities are a combination of profit making and risk taking. Since A has already received dividend in the previous years, such income has already accrued and must not be included in the share repurchase money and damages that claimed by A. 4) The difference between A's investment and repurchase amount is big enough to make up A's investment return and damages (not to include the dividend that has been distributed to A).

Opinions of the arbitral tribunal

Parties have no dispute over A claiming cash compensation against B's shareholders and its actual controllers (C and individual D). However, the focus of the dispute is the share repurchase responsibility of B. Moreover, the repurchase and compensation amount is also a question to be decided by the tribunal.

For whether B can repurchase the shares owned by A, most of the arbitrators, including the authors believe that this case does not meet the criteria that are stipulated in the company law. For the repurchase and compensation amount, the arbitrators unanimously believe that they should not be bound only by the agreement terms but also need to take other facts like the market yield rate, investors' expected return, whether the investor has acquired income and so on. In other words, the actual dividend paid to A and the difference between the investment principal and the money that has been paid back to A should also be considered. The parties reached a settlement and A will be paid in these two installments.

Observations of dispute

The compensation responsibilities of the companies for external investors include cash compensation. In 2012, the Supreme People's Court ruled in the final judgement of Suzhou Industrial Park Haifu Investment Company v. Gansu Ganheng Non-ferrous Resources Recycling Company that the promoters are liable to compensate investors in cash, but denied that the company itself is liable to compensate the investor in cash. In some similar cases ruled by X arbitration centre, the tribunal ruled that the actual controller of the company was liable to repurchase the shares owned by the investors according to the terms agreed. It also did not uphold the contention that the company was liable to repurchase the shares owned by the investors although the investors have claimed the same.

For the arrangement of company repurchases the shares, from a jurisprudential point of view, the typical ground of opposition is, such arrangement will harm the interest of company's creditors, and thus it should be void. The authors believe that in order to protect the creditors' interest, company law has minimized the possibility that the creditors' interest will be harmed by imposing notification and guarantee procedures. Consequently, if the companies have fulfilled the mandatory notification and guarantee procedures, then this aforesaid ground will no longer be valid. From the practical perspective, the legal restrictions are found in company law article 74: "Under any of the following circumstances, a shareholder, who votes against the resolution of the shareholders' meeting, may request the company to purchase its stock rights at a reasonable price: (1) The company that has made profits for five consecutive years has failed to distribute any dividends to the shareholders for 5 consecutive years and conforms to the profit distribution conditions as prescribed in this Law; (2) The company is going to merge with others, to be split up, or transfer the major properties of the company to others; (3) When the business term as specified in the bylaws expire or other reasons of dissolution as prescribed in the by laws occur, the shareholders' meeting makes the company exist continuously by adopting a resolution to modify the bylaws." and article 142: "A company shall not purchase its own shares except under any of the following circumstances: (1) To decrease the registered capital of the company; (2) To merge with another company holding shares of this company; (3) To award the employees of this company with shares; or (4) It is requested by any shareholder to purchase his shares because this shareholder objects to the company's resolution on merger or split-up made by the assembly of shareholders." Apart from these legal obstacles, when it comes to the enforceability of the arbitral award, it is quite hard to make the relevant changes to the company registration if company is ruled to take the share repurchase responsibility. To conclude, it is hard to support the argument that the company should bear the share repurchase responsibility under the present legal conditions in China.

As regards the quantum of share repurchase, especially the compound rate of return, the authors think it is reasonable and it should be supported in principle. This is because, for external investors, in particular small shareholders or financial investors, they lack access to information compared to the actual controller of the company, considering the high risk of the external investors, a balanced system, namely an incentive and responsibility restraint mechanism is necessary. In other words, when parties reached an agreement based on autonomy and no third party's interest is harmed and no mandatory law is violated then share repurchase and compound return rate should be supported. However, some scholars argue that under such arrangement external investors enjoy treatment more than normal shareholders. External shareholders have equal right of participating company's profit allocation, so they also should fulfill the shareholders' duty to the company (to face investment risk with other shareholders together). From this angle, the compound return rate claimed by the applicant should be properly reduced.

Bearing in mind the principle of fairness and reasonableness and the lawfulness of the content, arbitrators must treat with cautious when faced with the following share repurchase arrangement: First is when the return rate is much higher than the market's standard, which is also against the normal yield and company's business profit. Under these circumstances, such share repurchase terms and yield rate should be adjusted. Second, some arrangements are trying to avoid governmental regulation. In some sectors where foreign investments are involved, considering the industrial policy, some external investors will sign certain agreement with share repurchase clauses; such arrangement will probably be reasoned as void.

C. Identification on the Validity of the Contracts that Breach FDI Policies

As stated above, investment activities in China are gradually expanding into various areas while a comprehensive market entry and FDI entry negative list system has not been established yet. Some investment activities may violate restrictions in certain sector or industry, which will add uncertainty to the legality of such investment activities. Therefore, take FDI as an example, if FDI contravenes sectorial or industrial regulations, then the court or arbitral tribunals should reason the validity of such investment activities.

Case introduction

Limited liability partnership A and company B and B's subsidiary C jointly signed a Share Transfer Agreement with individual D in September of 2012, the parties agreed that A can purchase C's share from B and A will become a shareholder of C. Parties should work together to make sure C will get listed before December 31, 2014. If C fails to get listed or makes a false statement, then B and D should repurchase the shares from A according to the agreement. On the same day A and B signed a separate Capital Contribution Agreement and B transferred the shares it holds of C to A. Later C was suffering from loss under the operation of B and D, moreover C made a false statement thus C failed to get listed on time. A as applicant, requested the tribunal to rule that B and D should repurchase the shares according to the Share Purchase Agreement and bear the responsibility of paying damages to A. B and D argued when contracting the agreement A deliberately concealed that it is a company with foreign investment, while C is in an industry that foreign investment has restricted entry, so the Share Transfer Agreement and the Capital Contribution Agreement should be void as it contravenes with the mandatory laws.

Opinions of the arbitral tribunal

During the trial of this case, the tribunal found the identification of the validity of the share transfer agreement is the center of the dispute and the key for the tribunal to solve this case. According to the *Regulations of the People's Republic of China on the Administration of Security Services* and *Measures of the Public Security Organ for the Implementation of the Security Service Management Regulations*, security companies with foreign investment are not allowed to offer security services to enterprises and organizations that are related to national secrets. However, C's main business is to offer security service for such enterprises and organizations. The tribunal reasoned that while the laws regulate the legal relationship between the security service company and the enterprises that are receiving such services, they will not regulate the share repurchase relationship between A and B. Also, accordingly to the Catalogue of Foreign Investment Industries (amended in 2015), security service industry is not the restricted and prohibited industry. Moreover, even though A has foreign investment, but after B transfers C's share to A, C will not be qualified as a foreign invested company. The tribunal hence reasoned the Share Transfer Agreement is valid.

Observations of dispute

Before the negative list system is comprehensively enforced, FDI related issues and its validity would still be the difficult problem for courts and arbitral tribunals. For such issues, the judges and arbitrators are generally in favor of dividing mandatory regulations into managerial regulations and regulations about effectiveness. In other words, if laws and administrative regulations do not clearly stipulate that violation of such laws will lead to nullity, and violation of such laws will not harm the public interest or the national interest but only harm the party to the contract's interest, then they are managerial regulations. If laws and regulations clearly stipulate that violation will lead to nullity or even the laws are silent on this but enforcing such contract will harm the public interest or the national interest, then they are regulations about effectiveness. In the current case, administrative laws and regulations do not prohibit the content of the share transfer agreement and capital contribution agreement, consequently the agreement should not be deemed as invalid for violation of certain administrative laws. There is also no proof showing enforcement of the share transfer agreement and capital contribution agreement will harm the public interest and the national interest, the agreements are hence valid.

In any case, in the current arbitration practice, the validity of contracts involves a complex interpretation process and a distinction between prohibitive and managerial regulations. Apart from the interpretation process, the validity of similar contracts remain uncertain underthe current legal framework. Therefore, we are looking forward to the official implementation of the negative list system and it will be a significant progress in the Chinese judicial practice.

IV. Summary and Prospect

Investment disputes, unlike the conventional commercial disputes, have the following traits: complexity in legal relationship, interest entity diversification, governmental intervention and public policy consideration. We believe that, on the long run, such traits will still exist.

In 2015, we observed cheerful achievements both on the legislation level and the law enforcement level in terms of deregulation, fostering innovation and entrepreneurship and respect to parties' autonomy. In the dispute resolution sector, some typical behaviors such as "Pseudo fund", "equity buyback", "stock in shape and debt in real" have triggered hot debate among legal practitioners and scholars. With the deepening of the discussion, all sectors of society have developed an objective approach when analyzing typical investment activities and its legal relationships.

We firmly believe that with contributions made by the legislation organ, the legal practitioners as well as the academic circle, the foundation for a solid development of the Chinese investment market and its dispute resolution system will be laid down.

Annual Review on International Trade Dispute Resolution in China (2016) *

WANG Xuehua , LIU Jing [1]

I. Overview

With the steady development of economy, China's Gross Domestic Product (GDP) in 2015 has reached CNY 67.6708 trillion, representing 6.9% increase from the previous year. [2] With respect to international trade, the total value of China's imports and exports in 2015 is CNY 24.5849 trillion, which has decreased 7.0% from 2014. Among them, the total value of exports has decreased 1.8% to CNY 14.1357 trillion; while the total value of imports has declined 13.2% to CNY 10.4492 trillion. The trade surplus has risen 56.7% to CNY 3.68648 trillion.

2015 has witnessed the inauguration of the "One Belt One Road" initiative. Regarding economic and trade cooperation, in order to further deepen collaboration with Eurasia countries, China has actively promoted the reconstruction of the silk road economic belt and Eurasia countries are playing increasingly important roles in China's foreign economy and trade. From January to November in 2015, the trade value between China and the 25 Asian countries has reached USD 1.1 trillion, accounting for approximately one third of China's total foreign trade value [3]. From January to October in 2015, the value of trade in goods between Russia and China has reached USD 52.53 billion. [4]

By the end of 2015, China has signed 14 free trade agreements with 22 countries and areas from Asia, Latin America, Oceania and Europe whilst actively negotiating for several free trade zones. [5] In April 2015, China (Guangdong) Pilot Free Trade Zone, China (Tianjin) Pi-

---

* Translated by Beijing Huanzhong & Partners.

1 Introduction of authors: Dr. Wang Xuehua, partner of Beijing Huanzhong& Partners; Ms. Jing Liu, partner of Beijing Huanzhong & Partners. The attorneys and assistants at the International Trade Department of Beijing Huanzhong& Partners including Yuan Xing, Haitao Li, Xue Zhao, Yi Yang and Jingjing Liu also make substantial contributions to this Report.

2 See PRC National Statistic Website: http://www.stats.gov.cn/tjsj/zxfb/201601/t20160120_1306759.html, accessed on 29 January 2016.

3 See MOFCOM: http://www.mofcom.gov.cn/article/ae/ai/201601/20160101244094.shtml, accessed on 29 January 2016.

4 See MOFCOM: http://countryreport.mofcom.gov.cn/new/view110209.asp? news_id=47590, last vision on March 2nd 2016.

5 See MOFCOM: http://www.mofcom.gov.cn/article/ae/ag/201512/20151201212556.shtml, accessed on 29 January 2016.

lot Free Trade Zone and China (Fujian) Pilot Free Trade Zone were established. [6]

However, the overall environment for developing international trade is not favorable. Although the global economy is in recovery, the strength and speed are not as expected. The complicated international situation is still challenging for China, whose domestic restructuring and upgrading are in the key phase.

In 2015, most of the international trade disputes in China arose from trade in goods. Therefore, this report will mainly focus on the disputes over trade in goods in addition to provide some coverage of the disputes resolution of trade in other forms.

II. Hot-button Issues of International Trade and New Legislation

A. Speeding up the Process of the Free Trade Agreement (FTA) Negotiations

1. China and ROK have signed the free trade agreement

Chinese and the South Korean governments officially signed the *Free Trade Agreement between the Government of the People's Republic of China and the Government of the Republic of Korea* in Seoul Korea on 1 June 2015. The FTA officially took effect on 20 December 2015 when the first round tax deduction was also implemented. The second round tax deduction came into force on 1 January 2016.

China-Korea FTA covers the broadest range of issues and involves the biggest trade volume among FTAs signed by China so far. The FTA concerns trade in goods, services and investments. It will deepen the collaboration of economy and trade between China and Korea, and provide impetus to the growth of economy of both counties and lay solid foundation of mutual benefits to comprehensively improve the strategic partnership of China and Korea. [7]

2. China-Australia FTA has become effective on 20 December 2015

Chinese and Australian government signed the *China-Australia Free Trade Agreement* in Canberra, Australia on 17 June 2015. The FTA officially took effect on 20 December 2015 and the first round tax deduction was initiated meanwhile. The second round tax deduction commenced on 1 January 2016.

The China-Australia FTA covers over ten areas including goods, services and investments, and it is one of the highest level FTAs that China has ever signed with other countries concerning trade and investment liberalization so far. The China-Australia FTA is an important free trade agreement that China has signed with an important economy in Asia-Pacific region following the China-South Korea FTA which is significant for promoting the regional comprehensive economic partnership ("RCEP") and Asia-Pacific Free Trade Zone ("FTAAP") and for accelerating Asia-Pacific regional economic integration to realize regional common development and prosperity. [8]

---

6 See MOFCOM: http://tzswj.mofcom.gov.cn/article/e/201504/20150400950588.shtml, accessed on 29 January 2016.

7 See MOFCOM: "China and ROK sign free trade agreement" http://www.mofcom.gov.cn/article/ae/ai/201506/20150600996379.shtml, accessed on 28 January 2016.

8 See MOFCOM: "China- Australia FTA Officially Signed" http://www.mofcom.gov.cn/article/ae/ai/201506/20150601015183.shtml, accessed on 28 January 2016.

3. China and ASEAN have concluded to upgrade bilateral FTA and signed relevant agreement

On 22 November 2015, China and the Association of Southeast Asian Nations ("ASEAN") signed *The Protocol to Amend the Framework Agreement on Comprehensive Economic Co-Operation and some Underneath Agreement between the People's Republic of China and the Association of South East Asian Nations* ("Protocol") which is the achievement of the negotiation of upgrading the FTA.

The Protocol is the first upgraded agreement based on the free trade zones that China has formed by far and it covers a wide range of areas including trade in goods, trade in services, investment, economic and technological cooperation. The execution of the Protocol will provide fresh momentum for economic development of both China and ASEAN. The Protocol will foster a closer China-ASEAN community with common destiny, and contribute to the achieving the total value of trade reaching 1 trillion US dollars by 2020 and promote the negotiations on the *Regional Comprehensive Economic Partnership* and the establishment of Free Trade Area of the Asia-Pacific. [9]

4. China and the UK have signed the *Memorandum of Understanding on Local Trade and Investment Cooperation and Memorandum of Understanding on Development Cooperation*

On 21 October 2015, China and the UK signed the *Memorandum of Understanding between the People's Republic of China Ministry of Commerce and the Department of Business, Innovation and Skills of the United Kingdom of Great Britain and Northern Ireland on Strengthening Bilateral Local Trade and Investment Cooperation* and the *Memorandum of Understanding between the People's Republic of China Ministry of Commerce and the Department of International Development of the United Kingdom of Great Britain and Northern Ireland on Strengthening Development Cooperation and the Effectively Implementing Partnership with the Goals of Sustainable Development.* Memorandum of Understanding on local cooperation is the first Memorandum signed by China and EU countries on strengthening local economic and trade cooperation.

Upon execution of the above Memorandums, the Ministry of Commerce will set up the long-term mechanism of collaboration regarding bilateral local cooperation with the British Department of Business, Innovation and Skills, and will establish the joint work group of China-UK local cooperation under this mechanism. Its goal is to further strengthen the communication and cooperation between the local governments of the two countries and to promote and deepen the trade and investment cooperation between the enterprises. [10]

---

9 See MOFCOM: "China and ASEAN seals deal to upgrade bilateral FTA" http://www.mofcom.gov.cn/article/ae/ai/201511/20151101191508.shtml, accessed on 28 January 2016.

10 See MOFCOM: "China and UK Sign Memorandum of Understanding on Local Trade and Investment Cooperation and Development Cooperation" http://www.mofcom.gov.cn/article/ae/ai/201510/20151001144400.shtml, accessed on 28 January 2016.

5. The second phase of the China-Pakistan FTA Negotiations continues, and the *Banking Business Service Protocol of the China-Pakistan FTA Service Trade takes effect*

In 2015, the third, fourth, and fifth meeting of the second phase of the China-Pakistan FTA negotiations were held in Beijing and Islamabad respectively. On 20 April 2015, the *Banking Business Service Protocol of the Service Trade of the Free Trade Area between the Government of the People's Republic of China and the Government of the Islamic Republic of Pakistan* was jointly signed by China and Pakistan, which took effect on 11 November 2015 upon internal review and approval by each country. The effectiveness of the Protocol will further enhance the liberalization of the China-Pakistan FTA service trade, provide more financing convenience for the enterprises of the two countries and offer guarantee for the smooth implementation of major projects such as the China-Pakistan economic corridor. [11]

6. Other Free Trade Agreements under Negotiation

(1) Initiation of the China and Georgia negotiation of free trade agreement

On 10 December 2015, China and Georgia executed the *Memorandum of Understanding Launching China-Georgia Free Trade Agreement Negotiations between the Ministry of Commerce of the People's Republic of China and the Minister of the Economic Affairs and Sustainable Development of Georgia* which officially initiated the negotiation of free trade agreement. China is the third largest trade partner and Georgia's second largest importation partner. In March 2015, China and Georgia announced to start the feasibility study of the FTA negotiations. [12]

(2) First round negotiations on China-Maldives Free Trade Area was held in Maldives

The first round negotiations on the China-Maldives Free Trade Area was held in Male, capital of Maldives, on 21-22 December 2015. The two parties negotiated on topics of scope and areas of the negotiation, groups of negotiation, methods of pushing the negotiation forward, trade data, information exchange and tax reduction. The two counties reached agreement on the document of scope and duty and initially agreed that the second round of negotiations shall be conducted at Beijing in March 2016. [13]

B. The Negotiations and Conclusions of Economic and Trade Cooperation Documents between Hong Kong, Macao and Mainland China

1. Liberalization of service trade between Mainland and Hong Kong since June 2016

With the approval of the State Council, Vice Minister of Commerce Shouwen Wang and

11 See MOFCOM: "The 2nd Phase of China-Pakistan FTA Negotiations continues" http://www.mofcom.gov.cn/article/ae/ai/201510/20151001139730.shtml, accessed on 28 January 2016.

12 See MOFCOM: "China and Georgia Officially Launch the Free Trade Agreement Negotiations" http://www.mofcom.gov.cn/article/ae/ai/201512/20151201207622.shtml, accessed on 28 January 2016.

13 See MOFCOM: "First round negotiations on China-Maldives Free Trade Area held in Maldives", http://fta.mofcom.gov.cn/article/zhengwugk/201512/29974_1.html, accessed on 28 January 2016.

Director of the Department of Finance of Hong Kong Special Administration Region Government John Tsang Chun-Wah signed the Mainland and Hong Kong Clo*ser Economic Partnership Arrangement Agreement on Trade in Services in Hong Kong* (hereinafter referred to as "Hong Kong CEPA") on 27 November 2015. The agreement will be officially implemented on 1 June 2016, which will basically realize the liberalization of service trade between Mainland and Hong Kong.

The agreement is the first free trade agreement which allows the whole Mainland to fully open trade in services areas through pre-access national treatment with a negative list and it is also a symbol of the liberalization of trade in services between Mainland and Hong Kong. In addition to the historical level of openness, the agreement clearly stated that Hong Kong is given the most preferential treatment in the Mainland. It means that Hong Kong is entitled to receive all of the treatment included in all free trade agreements that China signs with other countries and regions which is more preferential than that in the Hong Kong CEPA. [14]

2. *Mainland and Macao Closer Economic Partnership Arrangement Agreement on Trade in Services* was signed in Macao

With the approval of the State Council, vice Minister of Commerce Shouwen Wang and Secretary for Administration and Justice of Macao Special Administration Region Government Leong Vai Tac signed *Mainland and Macao Closer Economic Partnership Arrangement Agreement on Trade in Services in Macao* (hereinafter referred to as "Macao CEPA") on 28 November 2015.

The agreement signifies that the whole Mainland and Macao basically realize the liberalization of trade in services. The highlights of the agreement are listed as follows: firstly, it is more open at higher levels. Secondly, it is clearly stated that Macao will enjoy the most preferential treatment in the whole Mainland. It means that Macao is entitled to receive all of the treatment included in all free trade agreements that China signs with other countries and regions which is more preferential than that in the Macao CEPA. Thirdly, it will further establish and perfect the ancillary administration system, which adapts to the negative list model, to facilitate Macao business to enter into the Mainland market. [15]

C. Developing Pilot Free Trade Zones (FTZ) and Sharing Experiences[16]

1. Negative List for FTZs

On 8 April 2015, the State Council issued the *Special Administrative Measures of China Pilot Free Trade Zones for Admittance of Foreign Investments* ("FTZ Negative List"), which took effect on 8 May 2015. The List is applicable to the four pilot free trade zones in Shanghai

14 See MOFCOM: "Mainland and Hong Kong Closer Economic Partnership Arrangement Agreement on Trade in Services", http://www.mofcom.gov.cn/article/ae/ai/201511/20151101196064.shtml, accessed on 28 January 2016.

15 See MOFCOM: "Mainland and Macao Closer Economic Partnership Arrangement Agreement on Trade in Services Signed in Macao", http://www.mofcom.gov.cn/article/ae/ai/201511/20151101196707.shtml, accessed on 28 January 2016.

16 See China Free Trade Service Website: http://fta.mofcom.gov.cn/index.shtml, accessed on 28 January 2016.

Municipality, Guangdong Province, Tianjin Municipality, and Fujian Province. It is no doubt that the rules and policies prescribed about the FTZ will create a new administration system on a national level, and set a good example for the eventual abandonment of the case by case review and approval currently applied for foreign investments.

2. *Framework Plan for Furthering the Reform and Opening up for China (Shanghai) Pilot Free Trade Zone*

On 8 April 2015, the State Council approved *Framework Plan for Furthering the Reform and Opening up for China (Shanghai) Pilot Free Trade Zone*. After the expansion of the Pilot Free Trade Zone, centered on institutional creativity, the Pilot Free Trade Zone reforms continue to explore the administration mode of national treatment plus negative list for foreign investment before admission, deepening systematic reform of administration, and improving the supervision ability and level during and after the event. This plan focuses on accelerating transformation of governmental function, deepening and enlarging corresponding institutional reform regarding administration of investment, speeding up reforms in trade supervision system, deepening reforms in financial system, as well as enhancing legal and policy assurance.

3. Three New Free Trade Zones were set up in Guangdong, Tianjin, and Fujian

In order to further the reforms inaugurated by the Shanghai Pilot Free Trade Zone and to provide comparison with and supplementation to it for the purpose to verify the creative institutional reforms and the feasibility of expanding the reform to establish more test zones for opening up, China decided to establish three new Pilot Free Trade Zones in Guangdong, Tianjin, and Fujian respectively. On 20 April 2015, the State Council issued the Framework Plan for the Pilot Free Trade Zones in Shanghai, Guangdong, Tianjin, and Fujian and the Negative List and measures for national security review of foreign investment which are uniformly applied to all Pilot Free Trade Zones.

4. State Council issued *Several Opinions of the State Council of the People's Republic of China on Accelerating the Implementation of the Pilot Free Trade Zone Strategy*

In order to speed up the implementation of the strategy for pilot free trade zones, the State Council issued *Several Opinions of the State Council of the People's Republic of China on Accelerating the Implementation of the Pilot Free Trade Zone Strategy* on 17 December 2015. This is the first strategic and comprehensive document since China has initiated the progress of establishing the pilot free trade zones, and it is a "top-tier design" for further development of the pilot free trade zones. Meanwhile, this opinion ascertained the short term and mid-to-long term targets in accelerating the implementation of the pilot free trade zone strategy. [17]

---

17 See China Free Trade Website: http://fta.mofcom.gov.cn/article/zhengwugk/201512/29896_1.html, accessed on 28 January 2016.

D. Implementing the "One Belt One Road" Strategy

1. National Development and Reform Commission, Ministry of Foreign Affairs, and Ministry of Commerce of the People's Republic of China together issued the *Vision and Actions on Jointly Building Silk Road Economic Belt and 21st-Century Maritime Silk Road*

In order to advance the initiatives with regard to the "One Belt One Road" Initiative and to reinvigorate it to intensify the connections among Asian, European and African countries and to promote the collaboration for mutual benefits to a record level, the Chinese government has drafted and published the *Vision and Actions on Jointly Building Silk Road Economic Belt and 21st-Century Maritime Silk Road* on 28 March 2015. The document stipulated that investment and trade cooperation is a major task in building the "One Belt One Road", and we should integrate investment and trade, and promote trade through investment.[18] The One Belt One Road Initiative is a systematic project, which should be built up according to the principles of "joint-negotiation, joint establishment and joint sharing", to actively integrate the development strategies of the countries along the Belt and Road.

2. The National Council issued *Guiding Opinions of the State Council of the People's Republic of China on Promoting International Capacity and Equipment Manufacturing Cooperation*

China's equipment manufacture industry has rapidly developed in recently years. The scale of the industry, the technology and competitiveness on the international wide have all substantially improved. The industry has played an important role internationally which witnesses the effectiveness of collaboration on international capacity and equipment manufacture.[19] In order to take advantage of the opportunity and to further the collaboration, on 13 May 2015, the National Council issued the *Guiding Opinions on Promoting International Capacity and Equipment Manufacturing Cooperation.* The *Opinion* pointed out that it is imperative to advance the ability and level of "going-out" of Chinese enterprises, to strengthen the governmental guidance and promotion, to provide more policy support and safeguard against risk.

E. Adoption of Ancillary Administration Rules and Regulations on Implementation of FTAs[20]

1. On 7 December 2015, the General Administration of Customs issued Decree No. 228, 2015, the *Administration of Country of Origin for Goods Imported under the China-Australia Free Trade Agreement* which took effect on 20 December 2015.

---

18 See MOFCOM: Vision and Actions on Jointly Building Silk Road Economic Belt and 21st-Century Maritime Silk Road, http://www.mofcom.gov.cn/article/ae/ai/201503/20150300928878.shtml, accessed on 28 January 2016.

19 See MOFCOM: "Guiding Opinions on Promoting International Capacity and Equipment Manufacturing Cooperation", http://www.mofcom.gov.cn/article/b/g/201507/20150701061179.shtml, accessed on 1March 2016.

20 See PRC General Custom Website: http://www.customs.gov.cn/publish/portal0/, accessed on 28 January 2016.

2. On 7 December 2015, the General Administration of Customs issued Decree No. 229, 2015, the *Administration of Country of Origin for Goods Imported under the China-ROK Free Trade Agreement* which took effect on 20 December 2015.

3. According to *Agreement between the Mainland and Macao Closer Economic Partnership Arrangement and Agreement between the Mainlandand Hong Kong Closer Economic Partnership Arrangement* and the supplementary agreements thereunder, the General Administration of Customs issued *Standard Place of Origin Form of Newly-added Zero-Tariff Goods under Hong Kong CEPA from* 1 *January* 2016 *and Standard Place of Origin Form of Newly-added Zero-Tariff Goods under Macao CEPA from* 1 *January* '2016, and *Standard Place of Origin Form of Newly-added Zero-Tariff Goods under Macao CEPA* from 1 January 2016, all of which took effect on 1 January 2016.

F. WTO Events

1. China Accepted the *Protocol of WTO's Trade Facilitation Agreement*

The Chinese Ambassador to the WTO, Jianhua Yu submitted the book of acceptance to the Director-General of WTO on 4 September 2015, marking that China has completed the domestic ratification procedures of accepting the *Protocol of Trade Facilitation Agreement* (hereinafter referred to as "TFA") and become the 16th member to accept the protocol. According to the WTO rules, TFA will come into effect after it is accepted by over two thirds of WTO members.

TFA is the first multilateral agreement of trade in goods that China has been engaged in and reached after joining the WTO. The effectiveness and implementation of TFA will not only conduces to the modernization of the comprehensive administration system of China's ports, but will also improve the trade facilitation level with China's major trading partners universally to promote China's exports by creating more convenient custom clearance environment. [21]

2. The 10th WTO Ministerial Conference Concluded Successfully and Achieved Historic Results

The 10th WTO Ministerial Conference was held in Nairobi, Kenya on 15-19 December 2015. This is the first time for WTO to hold the Ministerial Conference in Africa. Over 3,000 representatives from 162 members attended the conference.

The conference approved the *Nairobi Ministerial Declaration* and 9 decisions, and promised to further promote Doha Round. The conference has gained fruitful achievements. Firstly, the WTO members promised to comprehensively cancel the agricultural export subsidies for the first time, and reached new multilateral disciplines on issues such as export financing support, cotton and international food aid. Secondly, the conference reached the first WTO tariff concession agreement of the last 18 years, the *Expansion of Information Technology Agreement*, covering the international trade valued US $ 1. 3 trillion. Thirdly, the conference agreed to give the least developed countries preferential treatments in terms of preferential rules of origin and service immunity mechanism. Fourthly, the conference officially approved Afghanistan

21 See MOFCOM: "China Accepted the Protocol of WTO's Trade Facilitation Agreement", http://www.mofcom.gov.cn/article/ae/ai/201509/20150901103603.shtml, accessed on 28 January 2016.

and Liberia to join the WTO. [22]

III. Selected Cases

A. Whether the Seller has Completed Delivery When the Buyer Picks Up the Goods without the Original Bill of Lading?

1. Facts of the Case

On 30 July 2014, company A (hereinafter referred to as the "respondent") as the buyer and company B as the seller signed a Sales Contract, stipulating that company B would sell 43, 500 WMTs of iron ore powder to company A. According to the contract, the seller would arrange transportation of the goods and the latest shipment date was 21 August 2014. The term of price was CFR and the payment was Letter of Credit. Subsequently, the parties executed a Supplementary Agreement I to adjust the discount amount.

On 31 July 2014, the ship loaded with the subject goods departed and the vessel owner signed and issued clean bill of lading. On 8 August 2014, the respondent presented a guarantee to company B for unloading the goods without the original bill of lading, which indicated that delivery of goods should be made to company C. On 13 August 2014, the goods arrived at the destination port and company C accepted the goods.

On 18 August 2014, company D (hereinafter referred to as the "claimant"), company B and the respondent signed a tripartite agreement, which provided that all the rights and obligations of company B under the Sales Contract and Supplementary Agreement I would be transferred to the claimant. It also provided that company B should transfer the original bill of lading to claimant.

Subsequent to C's acceptance of the goods upon instruction from the respondent, the respondent completed formalities for the mandatory inspection and quarantine and customs declaration in the name of the owner and partially resold some goods without making payment. The claimant applied for arbitration according to the contract, demanding the respondent to pay the goods, interests, other fees and losses.

2. Issues and Opinions of the Arbitral Tribunal:

(1) On whether the Arbitration Committee has jurisdiction over the case

The respondent held that the dispute raised from unloading of goods without the original bill of lading, thus the dispute shall be submitted to the British High Court or the maritime court in accordance with the guarantee, rather than submission for arbitration according to the Sales Contract.

The tribunal found that the claimant requested the payment of goods, interests and losses according to the Sales Contract, Supplementary Agreement I and the Tripartite Agreement and consider that the illegal unloading without bill of lading did damage the interests of the claimant as the holder. Therefore, the disputes constituted a concurrence of liability from breach of contract and tort liability. In accordance with the Article 122 of the *Contract Law of People's Re-*

---

[22] See MOFCOM: "The 10th WTO Ministerial Conference Concluded Successfully", http://www.mofcom.gov.cn/article/ae/ai/201512/20151201214369.shtml, accessed on 28 January 2016.

public of China, the claimant was entitled to claim either contractual or tortious liability against the respondent. The claimant chose the contract as the basis for his claim, in which the arbitration clause was legal and valid. Thus the arbitral tribunal has jurisdiction over this case. In addition, the tribunal held that the arbitration provision stayed valid to the assignee when all or part of the rights and obligations were transferred.

(2) On whether the claimant had completed delivery according to the contract

The respondent argued that the claimant neither delivered the bill of lading which represented the ownership of goods to the respondent nor did it actually deliver the goods. The filing for customs declaration by the respondent could not prove that the respondent had received the goods when the claimant did not provide any evidence of delivery of goods.

The tribunal found that the claimant had submitted the guarantee for unloading without the original bill of lading, the Weight Certificate and the Quality Certificate of CIQ Inspection and Quarantine which indicated the respondent as the consignee, company B as the shipper and the clean bill of lading indicating the goods had been shipped. The tribunal further held that these documents complemented with each other and found that the goods of the bill of lading were the objects of the Sales Contract, which had been declared and taken away by the respondent. Therefore, Company B had fulfilled its responsibility of delivery under the Sales Contract. As a result the claimant had fulfilled the responsibility of delivery too as the assignee.

3. Dispute Observation:

In this case, the buyer's taken delivery of the goods without the original bill of lading has damaged the seller's rights as the holder of the original bill of lading and constitutes a concurrence of contractual liability and tortious liability. The seller is entitled to request the buyer to undertake the responsibility due to its breach of contract. In addition, in the case when the whole or part of the rights and obligations were transferred, the arbitration clause is binding upon the assignee. Thus the arbitration clause in the Sales Contract is binding to all of the parties. When the buyer completed the CIQ inspection and quarantine and customs declaration formalities in the name of the owner and resold some goods, the buyer shall be deemed to have accepted and actually controlled the goods and the seller has completed delivery. The buyer's defense for non-payment since it has not received the original bill of lading was untenable.

B. On Whether the Principle is Bound by the Dispute Resolution Clause in the Contract Entered into by and between the Agent and the Third Party[23]

1. Facts of the case

On 12 November 2012, China National Minerals Co., Ltd (hereinafter referred to as "National Minerals") and Xincheng Co., Ltd (hereinafter referred to as "Xincheng") entered into a sales contract, of which the Article 14 prescribed that any controversy or claim arising out of this contract and its enforcement shall be settled by amicable negotiation between the two parties. If no settlement could be reached, the dispute shall then be submitted for arbitration in

23 See the full text of China National Minerals Co., Ltd v Xincheng Co., Ltd on http://www.court.gov.cn/zgcpwsw/content/content?DocID=ff14bf87-ff7c-46ce-a7dd-a999df68bda8, accessed on 30 January 2016.

Hong Kong International Arbitration Centre (hereinafter referred to as "HKIAC") in Hong Kong and governed by the Arbitration Rules of HKIAC. On the same day, Shanghai Chenglong Import and Export Co., Ltd (hereinafter referred to as "Chenglong") signed an agency agreement with National Minerals, stating that National Minerals acted as the agent of Chenglong to import the iron ore from Xincheng, and entered into import contract in accordance with Chenglong's intent. The agency agreement also provided that the sales contract was the integral part of it, besides, the Article 7 of the agency agreement prescribed that either party shall bring any dispute relating to the agency agreement before the people's court where the plaintiff was located.

Afterwards, Chenglong sued Xincheng for its non-performance of the obligation to deliver the goods according to the above-mentioned sales contract and agency agreement.

2. Issues and Court's Opinions

The issue of the case is whether HKIAC or the people's court in Mainland China has jurisdiction over the dispute between Chenglong and Xincheng?

Chenglong claimed that the scope of the agency under the agency agreement between Chenglong and National Minerals was only confined to such substantive rights and obligations as the content of the transaction and the corresponding liability of breach of contract, excluding the manner to resolve the dispute. Therefore, the arbitration clause under the sales contract between National Minerals and Xincheng was beyond the scope of the agency. As a result, Chenglong was not bound by the arbitration clause without its recognition even though it had knowledge of such arbitration clause.

The court of first instance held that the sales contract entered into by and between Xincheng and National Minerals on behalf of Chenglong, the pleading submitted by Chenglong and the objection of jurisdiction filed by Xincheng confirmed as a whole that at the time of execution of the sales contract, Xincheng had been aware of the agency relationship between National Minerals as the agent and Chenglong as the principal. In accordance with the Article 402 of the *Contract Law of the PRC* (hereinafter referred to as "the *Contract Law*"), the sales contract shall be binding directly on Chenglong and Xincheng. Chenglong was bound by not only the substantive clauses but also the arbitration clause for dispute resolution under the contract. Therefore, the dispute shall be submitted for arbitration and the court cannot exercise its jurisdiction over the case.

The court of appeal was of the opinion that although Chenglong did not directly contract with Xincheng in terms of arbitration, neither did it introduce any evidence to establish that the entrusted matters have excluded explicitly the selection of dispute resolution, nor raise any objection to Xincheng on the arbitration clause under the sales contract after National Minerals and Xincheng had entered into such contract. Therefore, in light of the Article 63 clause 2 of the *Contract Law*, the arbitration clause under the sales contract, which was based on the power of attorney granted by Chenglong, was binding on Chenglong.

3. Dispute Observation

The Article 402 of the *Contract Law* prescribes that where the agent, acting within the scope of authority granted by the principal, enters into a contract in its own name with a third party who is aware of the agency relationship between the principal and agent at the time of execution, the contract is directly binding upon the principal and such third party, except where there is conclusive evidence establishing that the contract is only binding upon the agent and such third party. In this case, considering the third party's knowledge of the agency relationship any action within the scope of authority, including the arbitration agreement with the third party, shall be binding on the principal. Whether the agent has authority to agree upon the method of dispute resolution with the third party when the entrusted matters under the agency agreement are "substantive rights and obligations in addition to corresponding liability of breach of contract"? The court hearing the case held that generally the agency shall have the authority to negotiate and enter into agreement about dispute resolution, where there was no evidence establishing that the negotiation on dispute resolution was excluded from the entrusted matters, or the principal raised no explicit objection on such agreement.

C. Which Party Shall Bear the Loss When the Inspection is Impossible to Determine Whether the Goods Delivered in Compliant with Contract due to Damage of the Goods Caused by Delay of Custom Clearance?[24]

1. Facts of the Case

On 26 February 2013, Z&J (U. S. A) Corp. (hereinafter referred to as "Z&J Company") entered into a sales contract with Ningbo Oriental Jiuzhou Foods Industrial Co., Ltd (hereinafter referred to "Jiuzhou Company"), stating that Z&J Company would buy low sugar canned orange with snap lids from Jiuzhou Company in three installment, with Ningbo as the port of shipment, and Montreal as the destination.

Afterwards, Jiuzhou Company delivered the first shipment of 6,900 boxes in three containers, and Z&J Company made corresponding payment. However, after the first shipment arrived in the destination, the client of the Z&J Company found that the goods were in bad quality. For example, some of the cans got rusty and shrunken, and the boxes got wet. After negotiation, Z&J Company and Jiuzhou Company signed an agreement on return of the 2,873 boxes of the goods of the first shipment, and agreed that the two parties would open the boxes in the place of Jiuzhou Company to examine the quality of the goods, and then negotiate on the subsequent issues.

The returned goods, however, were stacked up in the Port of Ningbo for nearly three months without being picked up by any party. The Ningbo Customs disposed the goods later on as they were abandoned goods. Therefore, Z&J Company filed a lawsuit to the court of first instance, claiming that Jiuzhou Company shall return the fund paid for the returned goods and compensate for its consequential losses such as sea freight, customs clearance charge, charge for picking, travelling expenses and lodging fee. After hearing the case, the court of first instance ruled to sustain most of the claims of Z&J Company. Then Jiuzhou Company appealed the case to the Higher People's Court of Zhejiang Province. The court of appeal sustained the judgment by the court of first instance.

---

24 The ruling of this case is sourced from China Judgment Online, http://www.court.gov.cn/zgcpwsw/content/content?DocID=f6c6eab5-f2ea-4626-974b-504a86c8d0c0, accessed on 30 January 2016.

2. Issues and Court's Opinions:

(1) On which party is obliged to complete the import custom clearance for the returned goods

In this case, there was no contractual provision on which party shall take the duty to complete the import custom clearance for the returned goods. The court of appeal opined that, in light of the relevant provisions issued by the General Administration of Customs, the returned export goods should be imported with original state. Since it was Jiuzhou Company that declared to the Customs when the cargo in question were exported, and the consignee stated in the declaration form was Jiuzhou Company as well, it was the obligation of Jiuzhou Company to complete the import custom clearance formalities for the returned goods. Taking into account the application for returned goods dated 24 February 2014 which was made by Jiuzhou Company, and a statement on 6 March 2014 submitted to the Customs by Jiuzhou Company, both specified in detail the number of the declaration form, the name, the quantity, and the value when the goods were exported. These documents indicated that Jiuzhou Company was aware that it was the declarant to the Customs when the goods were exported. Therefore, it was also obliged to complete custom clearance for the returned goods.

(2) On which party shall bear the loss when the inspection is impossible to determine whether the goods delivered in compliant with contract due to damage of the goods caused by delay of custom clearance

The court of first instance concluded that Jiuzhou Company should take the risk because it did not go through the import custom clearance without justifiable reason after receiving notice to accept the returned goods, which eventually resulted in abandonment of the goods by the Customs thus impossible to conduct inspection. It is therefore assumed that the goods were defective as claimed by Z&J Company. Jiuzhou Company was obliged to return the corresponding payment and compensate Z&J Company for consequential losses as sea freight. The court of appeal ruled that the court of first instance made no mistake in terms of fact finding and the application of law when hearing the case, thus sustained the judgment by the court of first instance.

3. Dispute Observation

In this case, the two parties did not stipulate which party shall be responsible to complete the custom clearance for returned goods. Article 57 of the *Rules of the Customs of PRC for the Administration of the Levying of Duties on Imported and Exported Goods* stipulates that the taxpayer shall complete the import customs declaration for the returned exported goods which are imported again with original state. By reference to the provision above, it is certain that the taxpayer, i. e. ,the seller, shall be responsible to go through the import custom clearance for the returned goods. This case is referential when it comes to the problem of "returned goods" in the international trade in goods. Furthermore, the seller did not pick up the goods after they are returned, which resulted in the abandonment of the goods by the Customs and it was impossible to determine whether the quality of the goods was conformed to the contract. Considering that the seller did not perform its obligation, the court concluded that the seller shall take the risk of the impossibility of examination and further assumed that such returned goods were defective. Thus it can be seen that both the buyer and the seller in international trade shall perform the obligation of managing the goods appropriately in order to minimize the loss.

D. How to Determine the Competency as a Party in Arbitration If a Hong Kong Firm Entered into An International Sale of Goods?

1. Facts of the Case:

On 2 April 2014, company C, a branch of Hong Kong company A (hereinafter referred to as "claimant"), and Jiangsu company B (hereinafter referred to as "respondent") signed the international sales of goods contract which stipulated that the respondent bought instruments from company C with the total price of $293,000. It further provided that 50% shall be paid by letter of credit at sight immediately when the contract became effective, and 50% shall be paid through ECD upon signature of the receipt of delivery.

After execution of the contract, company C performed its contractual obligations according to the respondent's requirements and the terms of the contract by shipping the instrument within the time specified. Upon arrival, the respondent signed the receipt of the instrument and the inspection certificate after inspection of the goods. The respondent failed to make the 50% payment within the period required while neither raised any objection to the quality of the instrument nor provided any inspection report required for quality objection. The claimant submitted the dispute for arbitration when it requested payment but with no avail, claiming that the respondent shall make the payment for the goods delivered, any losses from delay of such payment and the costs incurred from the arbitration.

2. Issues and Tribunal's Opinions:

(1) Application of Law

There are two aspects of the application of law in this case, i. e. the law applicable to the contract of international sales of goods and the law applicable to the competency of the claimant.

As to the law applicable to the contract, according to Article 41 of *Law of the Application of Law for Foreign-related Civil Relations of the People's Republic of China* (hereinafter referred to as "*Law of the Application of Law*"), the contracting parties may choose the laws applicable to contracts by agreement. If the parties do not choose, the laws at the habitual residence of the party whose fulfillment of obligations can best reflect the characteristics of this contract or other laws which have the closest relation with this contract shall apply. In this case, the parties did not have agreement on the applicable law to disputes, given to the claimant's place of business, the destination of goods and the place where the arbitration institution is located are all in People's Republic of China, the arbitral tribunal held that the laws of People's Republic of China should be applied.

With regard to the law applicable to determine the competency of the claimant, the tribunal found that the claimant is a company incorporated under Hong Kong law. In accordance to Article 14 of *Law of the Application of Law*, Hong Kong law should be applied to determine the claimant's competency.

(2) Whether the claimant is competent in this case

The arbitral court noted that the claimant was not a party to the sales contract, but company C which is a branch of the claimant is a party.

The legal opinion provided by the claimant was issued by a Hong Kong law firm indicated that in the light of Hong Kong law, the claimant is a limited company registered in Hong Kong. However, company C is not a legal entity and has no independent legal personality but only a business establishment used by the claimant. As the company C is only a business establishment instead of a legal entity, it has no independent status in litigation, thus any liability arising from the business conducted in the name of company C should be borne by the claimant. The contract in dispute was signed by the claimant by using of the business establishment of company C with the respondent. Therefore, the tribunal held that in line with Hong Kong law, Hong Kong Company A has competency as a party in the ongoing arbitration.

(3) The performance of both parties

The tribunal found that on the basis of the certificate of receipt of goods, bank statements and other evidences, the respondent had received the goods delivered by the claimant without raising any objection about delay in delivery and any other defective performance. In this case, the claimant fulfilled its delivery obligation under the sales contract. On the contrary, the respondent did not pay for the 50% contract price which became payable upon the receipt of goods by the final user, and should be liable for breach of the contract. Accordingly, the tribunal awarded in favor of the claimant.

3. Dispute Observation

The core issue of the case is whether the claimant is competent as a party in the arbitration. Article 14 of *Law of the Application of Law* provides that "The laws at the locality of registration shall apply to such items as the civil rights capacities, civil acts capacities, organizational institutions, rights and obligations of shareholders, etc., of a legal person and its branch …" The tribunal of this case confirmed the place of registration of the claimant and correctly applied Hong Kong law to determine its competency.

E. On Whether It Constitutes Fraud under the Letter of Guarantee (hereinafter referred to as "L/G") When the Beneficiary Asks the Guarantor for Payment without Proving the Breach of the Underlying Contract by the Applicant

1. Facts of the case

On 16 January 2010, a real estate developer, Oriental Homes & Real Estate Co., Ltd (hereinafter referred to as "Oriental Homes"), entered into a construction contract together with Anhui Waijing Construction (Group) Co., Ltd (hereinafter referred to as "Waijing Group") as the contractor and China Anhui Waijing Central America Co., Ltd (hereinafter referred to as "Waijing Central America") as constructor. Afterwards, Waijing Group applied to Anhui Provincial Branch of China Construction Bank ("CCB") for a Performance Bond, with the Bank of Costa Rica as reissuing bank and Oriental Homes as beneficiary. On 28 May 2010, the Bank of Costa Rica issued a Performance Bond numbered G051225, with Anhui Provincial Branch of CCB as the guarantor, Waijing Group as the principal and Oriental Homes as the beneficiary. The amount guaranteed was 2,008,000 USD. At the same time, Anhui Provincial Branch of CCB issued a Counter Guarantee numbered 34147020000289 to the Bank of Costa Rica, promising to pay the fund under the Performance Bond within 20 days after receiving the notice from the latter.

On 7 February 2012, Waijing Central America filed an application for arbitration to Costa

Rica Centre for Dispute Resolution of the Union of Architects and Engineers on the ground that it constituted material breach of contract that Oriental Homes delayed to pay the project funds and the corresponding interest. On 10 February, the Bank of Costa Rica sent electronic message to Anhui Provincial Branch of CCB, stating that Oriental Homes claimed for the payment of 2,008,000 USD under the No. G051225 Performance Bond. On 23 February, Waijing Group brought a lawsuit to Hefei Intermediate People's Court of Anhui Province on the ground of fraud under the L/G and required to suspend the payment under No. G051225 Performance Bondand No. 34147020000289 Counter Guarantee. The court ruled on such suspension on 27 February. On 29 February, Anhui Provincial Branch of CCB sent electronic message to notify the Bank of Costa Rica of the court's ruling, together with the copy of the verdict by the court which was received by the Bank of Costa Rica on 5 March. On 16 March, the Bank of Costa Rica communicated with Anhui Provincial Branch of CCB by telecom, stating that it decided to suspend the payment under No. G051225 Performance Bond till the dispute was resolved, and required Anhui Provincial Branch of CCB to extend the term of the No. 34147020000289 Counter Guarantee till such dispute was settled by the court in Mainland China. On 20 March, Anhui Provincial Branch of CCB prolonged the expiration date of the No. 34147020000289 Counter Guarantee and promised that "we will pay to the Bank of Costa Rica once we are ordered by the court in China to pay the fund under No. 34147020000289 Counter Guarantee". The Bank of Costa Rica paid to Oriental Homes the fund under No. G051225 Performance Bond on 21 March. On 9 July 2013, Costa Rica Centre for Dispute Resolution of the Union of Architects and Engineers ruled that the Oriental Homes had materially breached the contract during its performance of the construction contract.

2. Issues and Court's Opinions

The primary issue in this case is whether the action of Oriental Homes constitutes fraud under the L/G.

The court of first instance held that, the Performance Bond has prescribed that the Uniform Rules for Demand Guarantees ("URDG") shall be applied in this case. In accordance with URDG, the independent L/G is formalized document, which means that when the guarantor examines reasonably and cautiously the documents submitted by the beneficiary, the scope of such examination shall be only confined to the conformity with the provision of the L/G and the internal consistency of such documents, without examination of performance of the underlying contract excluded. In light of the principle of utmost good faith established by industrial practice and international conventions which meanwhile recognizes independency of L/G, however, any fraudulent claim will be viewed as a vital defense of the guarantor to decline the payment on the occasion of the *prima facie* consistency of the documents, i. e., fraud exception principle. Therefore, when hearing the case relating to fraud in the L/G the court shall examine where necessary the performance of the underlying contract, particularly when the validity of the underlying contract has been recognized by oversea judicial institutions in its effective ruling or award. In such case, the facts discovered by such ruling or award can be referred to as evidence about performance of the underlying contract. Based on the facts found by Costa Rica Centre for Dispute Resolution of the Union of Architects and Engineers, Oriental Homes had materially breached the contract, for which it was obliged to pay the project funds and corresponding interest to Waijing Central America. In this case, the purpose of the Performance Bond was to insure that Waijing Central America fully performs the construction contract. Oriental Homes, who was aware of the fact that Waijing Central America had already submitted the dispute for arbitration but introduced no evidence establishing that Waijing Central America had materially breached the contract, had abused its right of claim under the L/G and violated the fundamental principle of utmost good faith, which constituted fraud under the L/G.

The court of appeal was of the opinion that the award rendered by Costa Rica Centre for Dispute Resolution of the Union of Architects and Engineers did not ruled on the material breach of contract of Waijing Central America. Besides, in light of the construction contract, Waijing Central America was entitled to suspend the construction without any liability before Oriental Homes paid the project funds. Therefore, the claim of Oriental Homes to the Bank of Costa Rica for the payment under the Performance Bond was fraudulent and had no reasonable ground.

3. Dispute Observation

In accordance with URDG, when examining the documents submitted by the beneficiary, the guarantor shall bear unconditional payment obligation provided that such documents fully conform with the L/G and the documents are consistent with each other, without examining the authenticity and validity of the documents or the performance of the underlying contract. The independency of L/G as formalized document, however, makes it possible for the beneficiary to raise fraudulent claim. In light of the principle of utmost good faith, the fraud exception principle is adopted in international practice and convention in case of any fraudulent conduct under the L/G. Therefore, the court in this case ruled that the guarantor was obliged to examine the performance of the underlying contract with necessary effort.

Besides, the applicant, for issuing the L/G, shall bear the burden of proof on the fraudulent conduct of the beneficiary when filing a lawsuit to the court on the ground of fraud under the L/G. If the applicant is able to prove that it has already fully and duly performed the obligations under the underlying contract or its breach of contract arises from the intentional misconduct of the beneficiary, then the claim for payment of beneficiary can be ruled as fraud. If the applicant, however, only enable it to prove that the beneficiary breached the contract but failed to prove it has fully and duly performed its obligations under the contract, then such claim for payment of the beneficiary cannot be viewed as fraud.

IV. Hot Theoretical Issues

The hot-button theoretical issues regarding dispute resolution in international trade in 2015 have displayed several characters, including keeping closed eyes on the hot issues on economy and trade, diversity of research objectives and concentrating on international trade and Pilot Free Trade Zones.

A. Research on Judicial Safeguard in Pilot Free Trade Zones

Pilot Free Trade Zones have assumed the role of "test field" for further promoting the reform and open-up in China and renovation of its economic system. On 29 September 2013, China (Shanghai) Pilot Free Trade Zone was founded. On 24 March 2015, the Political Bureau of the Central Committee of the CPC adopted a general plan regarding Pilot Free Trade

Zones in Guangdong, Tianjin and Fujian. With the expansion of Pilot Free Trade Zones and the commencement of their operation, how to cultivate good legal environment for the Pilot Free Trade Zones has become a concern of the relevant communities. Particularly, how to improve and structure the dispute resolution system to provide internationalized, flexible and professional dispute resolution services is imperative to the smooth development of the Pilot Free Trade Zones.

Mr. Li Zhiqiang and Mr. Tian Xiaoming at Jin Mao Partners have published an article, *The Jurisdiction of Dispute Resolution in China's Pilot Free Trade Zones.* [25] In this article, the authors believe that as the methods of choice for disputes resolution, in the context of Pilot Free Trade Zones, litigation and arbitration shall follow the current trend and point out that jurisdiction is priority for all commercial disputes in the Pilot Free Trade Zones. The article firstly summaries the status quo of jurisdiction in litigation within the four Pilot Free Trade Zones, and then analyzes the necessity and feasibility of establishing centralized jurisdiction in litigation in the Pilot Free Trade Zones. The authors conclude that through centralized jurisdiction for cases related to Pilot Free Trade Zones to achieve uniform application of law and improvement of dispute resolution system upon expansion of the Pilot Free Trade Zones is critical for providing vigorous judicial safeguard for the sustainable development of Pilot Free Trade Zones. Secondly, the article also reviews the status quo of cases involved Pilot Free Trade Zones and the chronology and resolution of the disputes about arbitration jurisdiction in the Pilot Free Trade Zones. The authors hold that professionalization and internationalization in adjudication of cases involved Pilot Free Trade Zones, improvement of disputes resolution system including litigation and arbitration, determination and internalization of jurisdiction would provide potent judicial safeguard to achieve internalization and legalization of the Pilot Free Trade Zones and would promote them to become world-renowned centers of international commercial disputes resolution.

Dr. Xu Kai, assistant research fellow at the East China University of Political Science and Law, and research fellow at Legal Research Institute of Pilot Free Trade Zones at the East China University of Political Science and Law analyzed the judicial safeguard in China (Shanghai) Pilot Free Trade Zone in his publication, The *Prospective Study of the Judicial Safeguard in China (Shanghai) Pilot Free Trade Zone.* [26] Dr. Xu proposed that upon the adjustment and revise of the legislation in China (Shanghai) Pilot Free Trade Zone, the issues about judicial safeguard are becoming more and more prominent, including the form of adjudication institution, jurisdiction and application of law. As to the jurisdiction in Pilot Free Trade Zones, Dr. Xu believed that for the jurisdiction of the courts in Pilot Free Trade Zones, adoption of exclusive jurisdiction is infeasible. On the contrary, actions regarding expansion of jurisdiction, centralization of jurisdiction and judicial interpretation should be adopted to define the jurisdiction of cases involved Pilot Free Trade Zones. With respect to application of laws to litigation cases in China (Shanghai) Pilot Free Trade Zone, Dr. Xu believed that it was necessary not only to recognize the uniqueness of the two systems applicable in and outside the Pilot Free Trade Zone, but also to be clear that on essence the Pilot Free Trade Zone is not an independ-

---

25 See generally, Li Zhiqiang, Tian Xiaoming "The Jurisdiction of Dispute Resolution in China's Pilot Free Trade Zones". Annual Meeting of China Academy of Arbitration Law 2015.

26 See generally, Xu Kai, "The Prospective Study of the Judicial Protection in China (Shanghai) Pilot Free Trade Zone", Jiangxi Social Science, Issue No. 1 of 2015.

ent jurisdiction. Therefore, methods adopted as to the application of law for foreign-related cases involving Pilot Free Trade Zones shall be distinguished from that for cases involving Pilot Free Trade Zones outside the zones.

B. Research on Transfer of Risk in International Sale of Goods

Sale of goods has been playing an important role in international trade. Consequently, disputes arising from international sale of goods have also been representing substantial part in international trade relevant disputes. Transfer of risk is a hot-button issue among all of the disputes.

In the *Transfer of Risk in The International Sale of Goods* written by Professor Gaoqiang Cai and Ms. Lu Chen at the Xiangtan University Law School[27], the authors started from the theory of the risks underlying international sale of goods and the theory of transferring, and divided transfer of risks in international sale of goods into four circumstances, i. e. , transfer of risks under normal conditions, transfer of risks for floating cargo, transfer of risks when the buyer was in breach and the transfer of risks when the seller was in breach and analyzed each circumstance in detail.

The authors were of the opinion that the transfer of risks under ordinary conditions could be further divided into two situations. First, when the goods are not delivered to carriers for transportation, the risks shall be transferred from the buyer to the seller when the buyer accepts the goods at the buyer's place of business. Second, when the goods are delivered to carriers for transportation, three principles shall apply respectively regarding the transfer of risks, i. e. , the principle of delivery to carriers, the principle of delivery to carriers at particular place and the principle of delivery at destination. For the floating cargo, the risk shall be transferred to the buyer from the seller upon execution of the contract for sale of goods. When the buyer was in breach, the risk shall be borne by the buyer; when the seller was in breach, the risk shall be borne by the seller.

C. Introduction and Research on Principles, Rules and Application of Interpretation of Contracts under English Contract Law

The legal principles of international economy and trade have still been dominated by Anglo-American laws. Among the principles, contract law and commercial law have played a crucial role. As a continental law country, China has no common law tradition and has limited understanding of the Anglo-American contract law and commercial law. This situation cannot satisfy the ongoing increase on the needs of international trade thus has spurred widespread interest in learning and researching English contract law.

Mr. Yang Liangyi series works have provided in-depth review of English contract law. For example, for determination of contractual damages under English contract law, Mr. Yang Liangyi has provided substantial review in his book, the Contractual Damages and Remedies which was published in 2013.

As the cornerstone of commercial activities, how the contract is construed under the Anglo

---

27 Gaoqiang Cai and Ms. Lu Chen, "Transfer of Risk in The International Sale of Goods", Xiangjiang Law Review, Issue No. 1 of 2015, pp. 278 - 289.

-American law and how the principles of construction and interpretation are applied in practice?

In the *Construction of Contract: Rules and Application* written by Mr. Yang Liangyi which is revised on the basis of the *Construction of Contracts* published in 2007[28], by drawing on the latest development of the law and the published cases, it has introduced the general principles of contract construction and their application in practice and has presented unique views on many disputed issues. Mr. Yang starts from fundamental principles of construction of contracts, and introduces meeting of minds of the parties and contents of contracts, and the principles relating to internal construction, external construction, implicitly, conditions, good faith negotiation, context, time provision, delay and general provisions. There are also relevant cases arbitrated in Hong Kong in the last chapter of the book.

IV. Summary and Prospect

In the past year, Chinese government signed Free Trade Agreement (FTA) with South Korea and Australia separately, entered into the upgraded protocol of the FTA with ASEAN, and has been negotiating with Pakistan, Maldives and Georgia on FTA and EU on the Investment Treaty. In terms of the cross-strait economic and trade cooperation, the CEPA Agreement on Trade in Services between Mainland and Hong Kong and the CEPA Agreement on Trade in Services between Mainland and Macao have come into effect, which means that the trade in services between the whole Mainland and Hong Kong and Macao will be almost liberalized from 1 June 2016. Besides, the expansion of domestic Pilot Free Trade Zone (FTZ) and the application of the first negative list to all the FTZs symbolize that China has determined to deepen the reform and opening-up policy, innovate the economic system and facilitate the investment and trade.

The measures facilitating the investment and trade will require corresponding safeguard and support from the legal system. It is predictable that the foreign-related civil and commercial disputes and disputes relating to investment will increase in appropriation to the extent of implementation of the policies and strategies aforementioned. Considering commercial arbitration has become the preferred manner to settle the foreign-related disputes in aspect of economy and trade, the system of commercial arbitration in Mainland China is far from keeping up with the trend when the scale of disputes relating to the economy and trade is steadily enlarged. It is by no means incidental for the establishment of representative office by Hong Kong International Arbitration Centre and Singapore International Arbitration Centre, nor the cases involving mixed arbitration clause or the dispute resolved in Mainland China by overseas arbitration institution. All of the situations will affirmatively contribute to the revision of *Chinese Arbitration Law* and the perfection of the arbitration system in Mainland China. In fact, what we expect is, that *Chinese Arbitration Law* as well as the courts, arbitration institutions and lawyers in Mainland China are able to provide the domestic and foreign clients with internationalized arbitration service in reconcile with the more facilitating investment and trade system and with the rapidly increasing civil and commercial disputes.

---

28 See generally, Philip Yang, Construction of Contract: Rules and Application, 1st edn, Law Press, March 2015.

Annual Review on Financial Dispute Resolution in China (2016) *

TAO Xiuming [1]

I. Overview of the Financial Markets and Disputes in China in 2015

A. The Financial Markets in China in 2015

In 2015, China's overall economic situation was complicated and China's economy experienced a series of major changes, some expected and others not. Taken as a whole, the previous development model of China's economy has turned out to be unsustainable. The annual economic growth is clearly slowing down and the country's economy has been in a downward cycle on the whole. The irrational aspects of the economic structure have become increasingly apparent. There is an urgent need to cut down the massive traditional production over-capacity. It is difficult to maintain the high levels of debt leverage and financing costs. The Chinese economic growth has stalled and the risk factors have increased in its financial markets.

In 2015, China's financial markets were subject to the impact of very complex domestic and international market factors. As far as monetary policy is concerned, the main task was to prevent and control systemic risks, while making efforts tostabilize and at the same time stimulate economic growth. In other words, priority was given to the monitoring of total money supply, the maintenance of a certain credit scale and the guarantee of market liquidity while taking restricted and targeted measures to stimulate economic growth and restructure the economy. More specifically, the People's Bank of China (the "Central Bank") had cut interest rates continually to lower financing costs in the market. The local governments reorganised their debts by replacing bank loans with long-term bonds thus reducing the burden of debt to prevent an outbreak of default risks. The Central Bank made use of monetary tools in the money market and reserve requirement ratio cuts to ensure the supply of base currency and market liquidity. There was an appropriate level of intervention in the RMB exchange rate market in order to proactively respond to excessive offshore RMB short-selling and control panic capital outflows. It was the diversity of the Central Bank's monetary policies and the flexibility in using these tools that led to the Central Bank being called on to strengthen its dialogue, communication and interaction with the market.

---

* Translated by Linklaters LLP.

1 TAO Xiuming is a founding partner of Jun Ze Jun Law Offices

In 2015, there had been unprecedented and repeated intensive fluctuations in China's capital markets, mainly composed of the stock market, making the majority of investors fully appreciate the risks of the stock market. The severe stock market crash fully exposed the serious defects in the structure of the market, the lack of regulatory capability and the inappropriateness of certain regulatory measures, and once again led to discussions on the reform of the existing financial regulatory regime, characterized by the application of separate regulations to separate business sectors, to create a single super financial regulatory authority. The regulatory reform was imperative.

However, there were still some highlights in China's capital markets in 2015, notwithstanding the above mentioned stock market disasters. It is particularly worth mentioning that the NEEQ (National Equities Exchanges and Quotations) market flourished. Given the extreme difficulty in IPO financing in the main board market, the Chinese government significantly expedited the construction and expansion of the NEEQ market in 2015 in order to facilitate direct financing of small and medium-sized enterprises. As indicated by the NEEQ data, the total number of the NEEQ listed companies surpassed 5,000 by the end of December 2015 and more than 3,000 companies were listed in 2015 alone. It is expected that the total number of the NEEQ listed companies will reach 10,000 by the end of 2016. There have been great expectations for the NEEQ market. It serves as an important channel for small and medium-sized and innovative enterprises to raise funds in the capital markets, a linking point of strategic significance between China's real economy and capital markets, as well as an important market for private equity investments and M&A transactions. It will become an important component of China's overall capital markets.

Furthermore, the establishment of the China-initiated Asian Infrastructure Investment Bank and the inclusion of RMB in IMF's Special Drawing Right basket with effect from 1 October 2016 are two historic events in China's financial markets development process in 2015.

B. Financial Disputes in 2015

In 2015, it was precisely because of the impact of China's continuing economic slowdown, the existing high debt levels, high leverage, excess capacity and economic restructuring, the fierce fluctuations in the capital markets, the proliferation of private financial activities and the imperfection of government regulation and other factors, that default-related disputes increased significantly in the financial and capital markets. In short, as indicated by statistics from China's several major domestic commercial arbitration institutions alone (apart from the data from the court system), there was a significant increase in both the number of cases and total amount of money in dispute in connection with financial investment disputes. Moreover, in addition to the increased number of cases, there was an obvious trend towards the specific forms of financial disputes becoming more diversified and complicated. It should be noted that financial investment disputes have increasingly become a major part of the disputes administered by China's major arbitration institutions.

II. Major Changes in the Regulatory System in respect of the Financial Markets

In 2015, on one hand, the overall financial regulatory regime was further relaxed and the financial markets were further liberalised. On the other hand, the regulatory authorities began to regulate specific financial businesses which had been developing very rapidly but chaotically, in particular the Internet-based finance.

Major changes in the laws and regulations are as below:

A. Removal of the Loan-to-Deposit Ratio (LDR)

On 29 August 2015, the Standing Committee of the National People's Congress adopted, upon resolution, the *Decision on Revising the Commercial Banking Law of the People's Republic of China* removing the 75% cap on LDR as a regulatory requirement which had been in force for more than 20 years and changing LDR from a statutory regulatory requirement to a monitory indicator of liquidity. The revision took effect on 1 October 2015. The removal of LDR as a statutory regulatory requirement has a far-reaching impact on commercial banks. Firstly, it adds capacity for banks to provide loan facilities, which is conducive to the development of the real economy and eliminates from the system the root cause of difficulties in obtaining facilities. In particular, the removal will effectively add capacity for granting facilities by banks of small or medium size, focus on increasing the support to agriculture, rural areas and farmers as well as small and micro businesses, and improve efficiency in the use of funds and optimise the economic structure. Secondly, it is conducive to putting off-balance sheet and "channel" businesses back on the balance sheet so as to reduce the cost of funds, thereby effectively addressing the problem of high financing costs. Thirdly, it is conducive to reducing the cost of the banks in respect of their liabilities and mitigating the pressure from the increase in the cost of liabilities faced by banks in the course of interest rate liberalisation, which is in turn helpful for commercial banks to properly respond to the impact of interest rate liberalisation. Fourthly, it helps commercial banks remain steadfast in the reform towards market liberalisation and facilitates the perfection of the operational system of banks.

B. Introduction of the Deposit Insurance Fund

The *Regulations on Deposit Insurance* became effective on 1 May 2015, marking a milestone for the Chinese financial reforms. According to the *Regulations on Deposit Insurance*, where the total sum of the principal of all the insured deposits maintained by a depositor with an insurance institution and the interest thereon is RMB 500,000 or less, it shall enjoy full insurance coverage, and any amount exceeding such total sum shall be covered by the remaining assets after the liquidation of the insurance institution according to law. As surveyed and estimated, such maximum limit is higher than the protection offered in most countries in the world and it can provide full protection to 99.63% of the depositors in China. After the implementation of the *Regulations on Deposit Insurance*, banks should make contributions to the deposit insurance fund at the rate determined by the deposit insurance institution. This may increase the cost of operation for the banks. It also means that the complete liberalisation of interest rates will take place marking an end of an era in which the banks rely on State policies to secure deposits at a low cost and make profit by simply taking advantage of the traditional spreads without making any effort. It also means that the Chinese government will (at least nominally) no longer provide any endorsements for the banks. Commercial banks will have to bear the operational risks completely on their own, and where necessary, will directly face the risk of bankruptcy.

In response to the above, the *Interim Measures for the Administration of Certificates of Deposit of Large-denomination* were promulgated by the Central Bank in June 2015, pursuant to which certificates of deposit of large sums as general deposits are also covered by the deposit insurance. Many countries in the world issued certificates of deposit of large sums as an important means of promoting reform in the course of deposit rate liberalisation. The introduction of certificates of deposit of large sums is conducive to the orderly expansion of the scope of market price of debt products and the perfection of the mechanism for generating market interest rates. It also strengthens the independent pricing ability of financial institutions and nurtures the concept of market pricing on retail market participants such as corporations and individuals, which gathers valuable experience in the continuous promotion for the deposit rate liberalisation. Meanwhile, by gradually replacing wealth management products and other high-rate debt products with the certificates of deposit as regulated and liberalized, it is of positive significance to promoting the reduction of financing costs.

C. Optimisation and Reform of the Issuance of Corporate Bonds

In January 2015, the *Administrative Measures on Issuance and Trading of Corporate Bonds* were promulgated by China Securities Regulatory Commission (CSRC). The *Measures* make breakthroughs in terms of expansion of the scale and term of issuance, establishment of a full system for private placement, increase in bond exchanges, cancellation of the sponsorship system and the Public Offering Committee system, establishment of an investor suitability administration system and restrictions on retail investors to participate in the dealings in corporate bonds, all of which adapt to the new situation of the reform and development of the bond market. They are conducive not only to promoting the transformation of bond market regulation and improving the ability of the bond market to serve the real economy, but also to strengthening market regulation and investor protection.

The bond offering market in China has been segmented with different competent authorities for each segment, amongst which, the National Development and Reform Commission regulates corporate bond offerings, the size of which remain very small whereas the National Association of Financial Market Institutional Investors (NAFMII) under the Central Bank is responsible for other financial instruments such as CPs(Commercial Papers), SCPs(Secured Commercial Papers), MTNs(Medium Term Notes), PPNs(Private Placement Notes), ABNs (Asset Backed Securities), PRNs(Project Revenue Notes) and SMECNs(Small and Medium Collective Notes). In recent years, hundreds of billions worth of offerings of such financial instruments have been registered with NAFMII each year. The innovation of financial instruments by NAFMII does not only play a significant role in promoting the development of the bond market in China but also it has a significant effect on the share of the markets subject to the regulation of these regulatory authorities. Therefore, the *Administrative Measures on Issuance and Trading of Corporate Bonds* promulgated by CSRC also has a competition implication.

D. Regulation of Internet-based Finance

Internet-based finance is an industry approved and encouraged by the Chinese government. On 18 July 2015, the Central Bank together with ten other ministries and commissions issued the *Guiding Opinions on Promoting the Healthy Development of Internet-based Fi-*

nance. Under the *Opinions*, the legitimate status of Internet-based finance is officially recognized and the nature of information for Internet-based finance is also clarified. With the general requirements of "encouraging innovation, preventing risks, drawing on advantages while avoiding disadvantages and ensuring sound development", the *Opinions* clearly define the scope of responsibility of the model of several Internet-based financial businesses such as equity crowd-funding, P2P online loans and online payment, and are described as the first comprehensive "basic law" for the Internet-based financial industry which provides regulatory support to, and identifies the direction of, the innovation and development of the Internet-based financial industry.

After the *Opinions* were issued, relevant auxiliary regulations and detailed rules have been promulgated and become effective gradually. For example, China Insurance Regulatory Commission issued the *Interim Measures for the Regulation of Internet-based Insurance Businesses* which regulate Internet-based insurance business whereas the Central Bank promulgated the *Administrative Measure on Online Payment Services Provided by Non-Bank Payment Institutions* which will take effect on 1 July 2016.

III. Selected Financial Dispute Cases in 2015

Case Study I: The First-ever Equity Crowd-funding Case [2]

[**Facts**]

On 21 January 2015, Beijing Fit Network Technology Co., Ltd (hereinafter referred to as "Fit") and Beijing Naomi Catering Management Co., Ltd (hereinafter referred to as "Naomi") entered into an Entrusted Financing Service Agreement ("Service Agreement"), under which Naomi entrusted Fit to raise RMB 880,000 (inclusive of the RMB 176,000 payable by Naomi) through "www.renrentou.com", a platform operated by Fit, for the establishment of a limited partnership which will open a restaurant to be known as "Paigu Naomi Get Healthy Quick Trendy Restaurant (排骨诺米多健康快时尚餐厅)". Following the execution of the Service Agreement, Naomi paid RMB 176,000 toYee Pay.com, a cooperative partner of Fit, pursuant to the Service Agreement, and carried out such work as project locating and execution of a lease. Fit also performed its contractual obligations to raise RMB 880,000 by the required deadline. However, as their co-operation proceeded, the platform "www.renrentou.com" identified a number of rather significant issues concerning Naomi, including its premises being an apartment instead of a bungalow as agreed in the Service Agreement, its failure to produce a building title certificate and a rather big difference between the rent for the property and the rents for the other properties in the neighborhood. The parties subsequently held a meeting with the investors, but were unable to find a solution.

On 14 April 2015, Fit received a notice of contract termination from Naomi, which terminated the Service Agreement with immediate effect, demanded a refund of the amount raised from Naomi and claimed for RMB 50,000 for losses. On the same day, Fit also sent Naomi a notice of contract termination terminating the Service Agreement on the grounds of a default by

---

2 For details of this case, see "First Instance Judgment Pronounced on the Country's First Crowd-funding Case", http://rmfyb.chinacourt.org/paper/html/2015-09/16/content_102835.htm?div=-1, accessed on 2 March 2016.

Naomi and claiming for liquidated damages and compensation for losses from Naomi. The parties later took the case to court. Fit, as the plaintiff, demanded: 1. a payment by Naomi of RMB 44,000 as financing commission to Fit; 2. a payment by Naomi of RMB 44,000 as liquidated damages to Fit; 3. a payment by Naomi of RMB 19712.5 as compensation for the economic losses suffered by Fit. Naomi, as the claimant in the counterclaim, demanded: 1. a refund of RMB 176,000 and payment of interest thereon by Fit; 2. a payment by Fit of RMB 50,000 as compensation for the losses suffered by Naomi.

The People's Court of Haidian District, Beijing, held in its judgment of first instance that: 1. Naomi, the defendant, pay Fit, the plaintiff, RMB 25,200 as financing commission and RMB 15,000 as liquidated damages within ten days of the date on which the judgment became effective; 2. Fit, the respondent in the counterclaim, refund the capital contributed by Naomi, the claimant in the counterclaim, in the amount of RMB 167,200 within ten days of the date on which the judgment became effective; 3. other claims made by the plaintiff be rejected; 4. other claims made by the claimant in the counterclaim be rejected.

On 23 December 2015, Beijing First Intermediate People's Court rejected the appeal filed by Naomi and affirmed the original judgment made in the first instance.

[**Court's Opinions**]

The court finds that there are two core issues in dispute in this case:

1. the legal effect of the Service Agreement and the legal relationship between the parties to the agreement;

2. whether the parties to the agreement have breached the agreement and what liability they shall assume for such breach.

On the first issue, the court finds that, first of all, the basis for the adjudication of the legal effect of the Service Agreement is the mandatory provisions of current laws and administrative regulations which govern validity, the main provision in question being Article 10 of the *Securities Law of the People's Republic of China* (the "*Securities Law*"). Considering that all investors in this case are members of the crowd-funding platform "www.renrentou.com" who have had their real names verified by the platform, and that the total number of investors has not exceeded the maximum of 200, the court, based on the gist of normative documents such as the *Guiding Opinions on Promoting the Healthy Development of Internet-based Finance* jointly promulgated by ten ministries and commissions, including the Central Bank, and for the purpose of encouraging innovation, finds that the crowd-funding transaction in this case does not amount to a "public offering of securities" and that the transaction is not in contravention of Article 10 of the *Securities Law*. Moreover, China has not yet issued any specific administrative regulations or departmental rules on crowd-funding. Other relevant documents are primarily the *Guiding Opinions on Promoting the Healthy Development of Internet-based Finance* and the *Measures for the Administration of the Filing of Over-the-Counter Securities Business for Record* issued by the Securities Association of China, neither of which prohibits or negates the kind of crowd-funding activity that this case concerns. Furthermore, on the capacity of Fit as a party to the agreement, Fit conducts business after it has obtained a business license, a telecommunications and information service operating license and other permits, and no legal obstacle currently exists in this regard. In view of the above, the court finds the Service Agreement valid.

On the definition of the legal relationship between the parties to the Service Agreement, the court finds that the legal relationship between the parties is primarily that under a contract for brokering services. However, the court also makes it clear that its definition of the legal relationship between the parties represents a rather generalized view of the disputes in this case; considering that crowd-funding is a new financial business model and that the continuous innovation, change and adjustment of and to the services provided by crowd-funding platforms and their functions is on-going, the specific legal relationship will vary in accordance with the facts of each case.

On the second issue, the court finds that the parties ceased their respective performances of the contract in this dispute due to the conflict between the parties regarding such issues as the form and status of the property provided for the operation of the financing project. The associated certificates provided by Naomi failed to fully eliminate the potential risks, which directly led to the loss of trust between the parties to the transaction. Therefore, Fit has a valid reason to terminate the contract in accordance with Clause 7.1 of the Service Agreement. After considering the full process of contract performance, the court finds that Naomi shall bear a larger part of the liability for the non-performance of the contract.

[**Observation**]

In this case, the court affirms the legal effect of the form of transaction which entails Fit providing a financing service to Naomi via the crowd-funding platform "www.renrentou.com", thus leaving room for the development of Internet-based crowd-funding business.

The court strictly limits the legal basis for affirming the validity of the contract to the mandatory provisions in laws and administrative regulations and, when laws and regulations governing Internet-based crowd-funding business are not yet fully in place, affirms the validity of the contract in this case in accordance with the gist of the *Guiding Opinions on Promoting the Healthy Development of Internet-based Finance* and the provisions of laws at a higher level, such as the *Securities Law*, thus giving due respect to the innovation of business models by market players. Such adjudication approach should be the correct one to take when dealing with financial innovation which is not yet regulated by any specific law. If we take the traditional perspective of financial industry regulation, financial business is a business subject to vigorous regulation and may only be conducted after financial business licence has been obtained; currently there is no licensing system applicable to Internet-based financial business.

In the present case, the court defines the legal relationship between the Internet-based crowd-funding platform and the financing party as that under a "contract for brokering services", thereby providing guidance for the determination of the legal status of such platforms and for the design of contracts. The court also emphasises that its definition of such legal relationship is based on a rather generalised overview of the facts of this case and may not be applicable to other cases. When dealing with specific cases, the particular set of facts of those cases will need to be analysed. This has also fully reflected the prudent approach the court has taken when faced with the reality that laws and regulations always fail to keep up with the endless stream of business innovation in the Internet-based financial industry and the continuous exploration of new transactional models by the market, leaving the adjudicators with no law or regulations that they can apply directly.

In this case, when expounding on whether Fit as the financing platform and Naomi as the financing party have breached the contract, the court interprets the obligations which the financing party and the investors are required to perform. The court finds that Naomi has disclosed untrue information, as there may be defects in the property leased for the project, and that Naomi has breached the warranty that all material information it provides is true, accurate and complete. The court also finds that the platform "www. renrentou. com" has the obligation to verify the authenticity of the financing information provided by the project sponsor. The above acts by Naomi are sufficient to give Fit the right to terminate the contract.

Another issue which demands our attention is that Naomi claims that in accordance with the *Limited Partnership Law of the People's Republic of China* ("*LP Law*"), a limited partnership may have 2 to 50 partners, yet Fit has sourced investment from 86 investors via the platform "www. renrentou. com"; under the Service Agreement, these investors will form a partnership with Naomi for the operation of "Paigu Naomi Get Healthy Quick Trendy Restaurant (排骨诺米多健康快时尚餐厅)", which is in contravention of the legal requirements with respect to the number of partners a partnership may have. Fit argues that the problem of exceeding the maximum number of investors stipulated in the *LP Law* can be properly solved within the existing legal framework, namely, the project sponsor may form a limited partnership A with some of the investors (with the project sponsor acting as the general partner of limited partnership A). Limited partnership A will then form limited partnership B with the remaining investors (with limited partnership A acting as the general partner). As a result of this, the number of investors of both A and B will remain within 50. The court does not expound on the legality or compliance of such transactional structure, probably because the court does not consider the issue to be a core issue of this case. Therefore, whether the number of partners in a limited partnership is subject to a look-through remains to be tested by the judiciary.

Case Study II: Claim in Respect of Insider Trading of Securities[3]

[**Facts**]

At 11 : 05 a. m. on 16 August 2013, due to error of its system, Everbright Securities Co., Ltd (hereinafter referred to as "Everbright Securities") mistakenly placed a massive RMB 23.4 billion worth of purchase orders for stocks, of which RMB 7.27 billion were concluded, in its strategic trading system when effecting the subscription, redemption and arbitrage transaction of an Exchange Traded Fund (hereinafter referred to as "ETF"). When the market reopened for trading at 1 : 00 p. m. the same day, Everbright Securities hedged the transaction exposure resulting from the orders mistakenly placed through the short-selling of stock index futures and selling the ETF, without disclosing the above information. At 2 : 22 p. m. on the same day, Everbright Securities published an announcement stating that "the proprietary trading business of the strategic investment department encountered problems when using the independent arbitrage system."

In November 2013, the CSRC made a decision to impose regulatory sanctions on Everbright Securities and found that the conversion of stocks it held in the ETF and selling of the ETF, as well as the short-selling of stock index futures before the publication of insider information by Everbright Securities constituted insider trading, and imposed certain sanctions on Everbright Securities which included, among others, confiscation of profits and a fine totalling RMB 520 million. Since December 2013, certain cases were filed by investors against Everbright Securities with respect to its liabilities for its insider trading, by using insider informa-

3 For details of this case, see "Judgement Pronounced for 8 Claims by Investors Against Everbright Securities In Respect of Insider Trading, 6 Investors Won" at http://www. chinacourt. org/article/detail/2015/10/id/1722908. shtml, accessed on 2 March 2016.

tion relating to certain securities and futures, and were submitted to Shanghai No. 2 Intermediate People's Court.

Shanghai No. 2 Intermediate People's Court issued the first-instance judgement on 30 September 2015 in connection with 8 relevant cases and supported all or part of the claims filed by Zhang and 5 other investors. Zhang and 5 other investors received civil compensation in the range between RMB 2,220 to RMB 200,980 but the claims from Wang and another investor were dismissed.

Everbright Securities and certain investors lodged appeals later. On 20 January 2016, Shanghai High People's Court pronounced the formal judgement for two of the appeal cases. Shanghai High People's Court rejected the appeal and upheld the original judgement in respect of these two cases, which were the case where the Xu (the plaintiff) and Everbright Securities (the defendant) refused to accept the first-instance judgement with respect to the dispute regarding liabilities in connection with the insider trading of futures and their relevant appeals; as well as the case where Everbright Securities (the defendant) refused to accept the first-instance judgement with respect to the dispute with Qin (the plaintiff) regarding liabilities in connection with the insider trading of futures and its relevant appeal.

[**Court's Opinions**]

After the review, the court is of the opinion that the CSRC's administrative sanctions and the effective judgement of relevant administrative proceedings have found that the conversion of stocks it held in the ETF and selling of the ETF, as well as the short-selling of stock index futures before the publication of insider information by Everbright Securities constituted insider trading, and such administrative sanctions and administrative proceedings may be admitted as the basis for judgement in this case. Everbright Securities is found to be at fault by carrying out the so-called hedging operations to avoid losses without disclosing the relevant information. The fact that its internal "Business Management Rules of Strategic Investment Department" may not violate the legal requirements against insider trading will not have any impact on the determination of the fault committed by Everbright Securities.

With respect to determining the causal relationship, during the period of insider trading being committed by Everbright Securities where those investors who are plaintiffs effected trading of 50ETF, 180EFT and its constituent stocks, IF1309 and IF1312 in a reverse direction against the trading direction of the insider trading of Everbright Securities, then it was presumed to constitute the causal relationship, and Everbright Securities shall provide compensation in respect of the losses incurred by investors which stemmed from Everbright Securities' fault. As to the calculation of the amount of losses, the losses shall be reasonably calculated in light of the actual trading of the investors after taking into consideration the difference between the trading price and the benchmark price as well as the different circumstances of each investor. Where those investors who are plaintiffs carried out trading outside the period of insider trading, such investors were considered as bandwagon investors and Everbright Securities shall not be liable for the losses incurred by those investors. No causal relationship was found in this case so the investors shall bear the investment risks on their own.

[**Observation**]

This is the first case in China in which the plaintiffs won the claims for civil compensation in respect of insider trading, while in all other similar previous cases in China, including in the claim for civil compensation in 2012 in respect of insider trading by Huang Guangyu, none of the plaintiffs won their cases. This case brings a new remedy for investors who claim for civil compensation for losses resulting from insider trading by listed companies.

The court first uses the CSRC's decision on imposition of administrative sanctions on Everbright Securities as the basis and finds that Everbright Securities commits insider trading. Despite the fact that the determination by a court of whether a relevant entity has committed misconduct is not conditional upon the decision made by a regulatory authority (and as a matter of fact, there are different views in the market and the legal profession as to the fact-finding undertaken and administrative sanctions imposed by the CSRC in respect of the Everbright Securities case), and that investigating the facts and determining the nature of the conduct of the party concerned shall be one of the duties and responsibilities of the judicial authority, if a judgement has been made by the relevant regulatory authority, the judicial department shall respect the effective conclusion made by the competent authority in accordance with the procedures required by laws.

The court then makes its determination as to whether Everbright Securities has subjective fault. The court is of the view that, pursuant to the relevant provisions of the *Securities Law*, a listed company shall immediately disclose any of its major events which may have significant impact on the share price. The court also provides its interpretation of the term "immediately" and interprets it as "at once" and "right away", and determines that Everbright Securities has subjective fault in failing to immediately disclose the inside information after taking into consideration the probability and feasibility for Everbright Securities to disclose such inside information.

In respect of Everbright Securities' assertion that the hedging transactions are a trading strategy to stop losses under the then circumstances and are in compliance with its business management rules, the court is of the view that hedging transactions are not illegal in nature, but in this case where the mistakenly placed orders have given rise to inside information, Everbright Securities should have exercised a higher standard of duty of care to ensure the legality of its conduct and should not only have acted pursuant to its internal regulations.

On this basis, the court analysed whether a causal relationship exists between the economic losses suffered by the plaintiff and the insider trading. The court is of the opinion that the causal relationship in the securities market is different from traditional civil causal relationship. First, the securities market has a large number of players with rapid trading speed and high trading volume. Most of the securities transactions are concluded by match-making by the exchange house in the manner of call auctions and continuous auctions, and the party which commits insider trading and the victims of insider trading do not have direct connections or contact with each other. Therefore, stocks traded by investors cannot be completely identical with stocks traded by the party which commits insider trading. Second, damages to the investors in the securities markets are mainly caused by the rise or fall of prices of securities, which however may be affected by a large number of factors and the volatility of securities prices are often the result of a combination of several factors. Therefore, it is nearly impossible for investors to prove the causal relationship in insider trading, and this makes the penalty system for insider trading impracticable and contravenes the intention of the legislations. At present, China's laws and regulations and judicial interpretations do not have particular provisions in respect of the determination method of causal relationship in respect of insider trading, in which case, the court refers to the rules for the determination of misrepresentations, which are: "The people's court shall determine that the causal relationship exists between a misrepresentation and the resulting injury if: (1) the securities in which the investor invests are directly connected to the misrepresentation; (2) the investor purchases the securities on or after the date on which the misrepresentation is made and before the date on which the same is exposed or corrected; and (3) on or after the date on which the misrepresentation is exposed or corrected, the investor incurs a loss as a result of the sale of the securities or is incurring a loss as a result of his continuing to hold the securities." The causal relationship will be presumed to exist at law if the above three conditions are met. In this case, the court adopts the principles for presumption of causal relationship and is of the view that insider trading behavior shall be presumed to have an effect on the variety and price of the investment products invested in by the investors and will further cause losses to the investors. In particular, to the extent that insider information is price sensitive, during the period when insider trading is carried out by the party who commits insider trading, if an investor makes a securities investment in a reverse direction against the main trading direction of the insider trading, and the investor deals with the securities, securities derivative products or future contracts directly relating to the insider information and hence suffers losses, then it will be presumed that the insider trading and the losses suffered by the investor have a causal relationship. If, eventually, this principle is commonly recognized in the judicial practice, then the burden of proof on investors will be significantly mitigated.

In conclusion, we can see from this case that courts are conducting intensive study on the securities markets and have a deep understanding of the legislation governing insider trading. This case not only brings a new way for civil remedies for investors to claim for compensation for losses resulting from insider trading by listed companies, but also provides guidance on the method of determination of the nature and quantity of insider trading, subjective fault, causal relationship and calculation of losses. I believe that, after the conclusion of this case, more and more investors will rely on this judicial channel to protect their interests and listed companies will become more compliant and diligent in terms of their operations.

Case Study III: Dispute on Forced Close-out by Trust Company [4]

[**Facts**]

The plaintiff Ye Chuanlin and the defendant Xiamen International Trust Co., Ltd entered into the Fund Trust Contract for Investment in Structured Securities, pursuant to which the plaintiff, as the general principal, would contribute RMB 5 million and entrust the defendant to invest in stock and other securities products. The plaintiff lodged a lawsuit with the Xiamen Intermediate People's Court of Fujian Province and requested a court order to be granted for cancellation of the Fund Trust Contract for Investment in Structured Securities, return of the principal and compensation for the loss of RMB 1 million. The plaintiff requested to cancel the contract on the grounds that the trust documents violated the provisions of *Contract Law of the People's Republic of China* on fraud, material misconception and apparent unfairness. Such violations were mainly reflected in the following aspects: 1. The contract was concluded as a result of material misconception. The plaintiff purchased the product based on the commitment

4 See "Civil Judgement of First Instance on the Trust Dispute between Ye Chuanlin on one hand and Xiamen International Trust Co., Ltd on the other hand" at http://wenshu.court.gov.cn/content/content? DocID=c6ae77c8-6043-466d-a602-b278d769fbfe&KeyWord=Xiamen International Trust Co., Ltd, accessed on 5 March 2016, for the detailed information about this case.

given by the sales person of China Galaxy Securities Co. , Ltd (hereinafter referred to as "Galaxy Company") (the custodian of the trust contract) on free purchase and sale and automatic close-out by computer once the warning level was reached. The contract was executed by way of post and the contract submitted by the defendant was inconsistent with the original one. 2. The defendant did not fulfil the duty of honest disclosure. The defendant neither informed the plaintiff of the special account number, nor sent the written materials on unit net value by post or disclosed the information about preferred principals and preferred beneficiaries, in accordance with the contract, resulting unapparent unfairness and fraud. 3. There was over RMB 1 million remaining after the forced close-out, but the defendant only returned slightly more than RMB 300,000 when due. This was obviously unfair and fraudulent. 4. It was obviously unfair and fraudulent that the defendant did not file the trust products with the local banking regulatory bureau. 5. There were certain problems existing in the defendant's operating software. This was obviously unfair and fraudulent.

[**Court's Opinions**]

The court finds that, with respect to material misconception, the plaintiff did not submit proof establishing the false promotion made by Galaxy Company's sales person with respect to the free purchase and sale and automatic close-out by computer at the warning level; despite the inconsistency in the details of the handwritten parts, such as the time of signing of the trust documents submitted by the plaintiff and the defendant, the provisions of the contracts are consistent with each other, further, the words "I have carefully read and fully understood the trust documents and other reference documents and I agree to be bound by the aforesaid legal documents and I am willing to bear all risks arising from the investment in this trust plan" manually transcribed by the plaintiff in the risk disclosure statement are adequate to prove that the plaintiff Ye Chuanlin has read and fully understood the contents of the trust documents and therefore the court finds the plaintiff's argument of concluding the contract as a result of material misconception baseless.

With respect to apparent unfairness and fraud, the court finds that, according to the trust documents, the trust shares are classified into a senior tranche and a junior tranche and trust revenue will be distributed to the plaintiff after deducting the preferred principal's gains, compensation for trust services and custodian fee and other trust fees; and that the pre-warning level and close-out level are also set out in the trust documents, the defendant is entitled to a forced close-out when the price is lower than the close-out level, and the balance after close-out will be distributed to the plaintiff after the preferred principal's gains and other relevant fees are firstly deducted therefrom. Therefore, the plaintiff bears the risk commensurate with his gains, and based thereupon, the court finds that the plaintiff does not have grounds to argue that it is apparently unfair and fraudulent as a result of only slightly more than RMB 300,000 being returned out of over RMB 1 million remaining after the forced close-out.

The plaintiff's argument that the defendant did not provide the number for the special account opened for the plaintiff, did not send the written documents on unit net value by post, and did not disclose the information about the preferred principals and the preferred beneficiaries and that there are certain problems existing in the operating software is only relevant with respect to whether or not the defendant has any fault in the performance of the contract, and does not serve as a legal ground for exercising the right of contract cancellation. The plaintiff may institute a separate lawsuit in respect of the defendant's performance of the contract. In addition, whether or not the trust products under the lawsuit needed to be filed with the banking regulatory authorities shall only relate to the exercise of regulatory power by a regulatory authority and shall not serve as a legal ground for exercising the right of contract cancellation.

In light of the above, the court makes a verdict rejecting the claims made by the plaintiff for cancelling the trust contract and other relevant matters.

[**Observation**]

This case is an example of how the plummeting stock market impacted the secondary market in 2015. As a result of the stock market collapse, the pre-warning and close-out mechanism was triggered in respect of many asset management products in the investment securities market and some investors suffered enormous losses. And hence, these investors initiated judicial proceedings and demanded that the asset management product trustees or administrators pay compensation to them to cover their partial losses.

In this case, the plaintiff adopted a litigation strategy claiming that the trust contract might be cancelled on such grounds as material misconception, material unfairness and fraud. On the basis of the facts alleged by both parties and the provisions of the trust contract, the court made a prudent determination on the existence of the grounds for cancelling the contract or not and emphasized that the investor shall bear the investment risks if and to the extent that the trust contract and risk disclosure statement have expressly specified and disclosed the close-out triggering conditions and consequences as well as the risk and loss on investment, which shows the court's full respect for the autonomy of will of both parties and promotion of the legal force of contracts. Moreover, the court indicated in this case that the issue of trust product filing, in its opinion, was a matter of compliance and related only to the exercise of regulatory power by a regulatory authority and was not a subject matter to be ruled on by the court in commercial disputes.

This case is a warning to all investors to carefully read the investment documents, fully understand the investment risks therein and prudently make their investment decision, instead of expecting to be compensated by way of reversing the provisions of the contract in the event of suffering a loss on an investment. At the same time, this case serves as an alert that trust companies and other asset management institutions shall provide full disclosure of the risks when designing their contracts, comply with all regulatory regulations, strictly perform all provisions of a contract and diligently fulfil their duties as trustees in a professional way.

Case Study IV: Determination of the Effectiveness of Unlawful Futures Trading and Contracts

[**Facts**]

Client A and Company B enters into a Client Agreement, under which they would conduct on-exchange spot precious metals trading and spot precious metals trading on a deferred settlement basis. Client A believes that the trading between them is futures trading on a platform provided by the relevant exchange and in accordance with the *Administrative Regulations on Futures Trading*, futures trading shall be conducted on a lawfully established futures exchange or other exchanges approved by regulators. As the exchange designated by the parties in this case is not a lawfully established futures exchange, their trading is illegal, and the contract executed between them is invalid as a result of breach of the mandatory regulations. Accordingly, Client A asserts that Company B shall return the investment principal and the interest thereon. Company B believes that the trading between them is spot trading, and that the exchange designated by them is a lawfully established institution, approved by the provincial local government and registered with the administration for industry and commerce, of which Company B is a lawful member. Therefore, their contract is lawful and valid.

Following its analysis, the tribunal opines that the trading between the parties is not futures trading, and that the exchange in question is not an illegal futures exchange. The contract in this case represents the true intention expressed by the parties to it, and has not violated any mandatory provisions in any law or administrative regulations. Therefore, it is lawful and valid. Consequently, the claim made by the arbitration applicant was rejected by the tribunal.

[**Tribunal's Opinions**]

With respect to one of the core issues in this case, i. e., whether the trading in this case is futures trading, the tribunal finds that the primary features of futures trading is on-exchange call auction and the use of standard contracts; however, none of the trading products in this case included such features. With respect to the other core issue, i. e., whether the exchange in this case is lawful, the tribunal finds that, due to the terms of reference for the tribunal being to hear and determine the dispute between the parties rather than determining and judging a third party's behaviour, it is not in a position to pass a judgement on the trading model and lawfulness and compliance of the exchange. Moreover, the exchange has never been banned by any approval authority or regulatory authority, and it remains lawfully existing.

Meanwhile, in the tribunal's view, Company B has also fulfilled its obligations to fully disclose the trading risk in performing the Client Agreement, and has never engaged in fraud or abuse of its dominance. Client A, as a party to the trading, has confirmed that it has the corresponding experience in the trading of financial products, and has expressly acknowledged in a handwritten document its full awareness of the trading risk involved in this case and its intention to bear any potential trading losses.

Therefore, the tribunal believes that the Client Agreement is the true intention expressed by the parties, has not violated the mandatory provisions of any law or administrative regulations, and therefore is lawful and valid.

[**Observation**]

From the perspective of product classification, characterization and regulation of the financial markets, there exists a variety of products and innovation continues relentlessly in the financial markets. In addition, many products bear different names and are subject to the regulation of different regulatory authorities and regulatory regimes, but they have similar economic effects and trading mechanisms. On the one hand, academic and/or legislative and regulatory efforts have always been made to characterize and classify all kinds of transactions; on the other hand, innovations in the market often leave legislation and regulations behind. Moreover, certain transactions come into being and develop in the absence of a complete or appropriate legal and regulatory regime and even evolve into popular products or transactions in the market. The financial markets follow a route of "trading innovation regulation—new innovation". If a trading product ("Product A") is similar to an existing (traditional) product (Product B) in terms of economic effects or trading features, it is inappropriate to determine that Product A is Product B or a disguised form of Product B based on such similarity alone, as this could easily lead to regulatory confusion and disturb the market order.

Therefore, it is inappropriate to classify a newly created derivative product or a derivative product with unique characteristics into traditional products which are usually subject to relatively systematic or stricter regulation. Instead, we should give a certain room (in respect of both naming and characterization) to newly created derivatives for them to exist. It is irrefutable that there are defects in the Chinese financial markets, in particular, the derivatives market. The regulatory regime governing qualifications for trading parties and trading rules, etc., is not systematic and clear enough, and investors are not well aware of the trading mechanisms and risks when participating in trading. As a result, significant losses and disputes arise from such trading. If non-standard transactions are simply determined to be invalid without comprehensive and prudential analysis, it obviously contravenes the spirit of contract law and the principle of good faith, and in the long run, will not benefit the stability and development of the Chinese financial markets.

In addition, as an adjudicator of an individual case, the tribunal is not in a position to analyse and pass judgement on the trading model, lawfulness and compliance of the exchange. This is because, on the one hand, the exchange is not a party to this case and, on the other hand, objectively, not all the necessary market information is in the possession of the tribunal. The tribunal is unable to determine the lawfulness of the exchange beyond the scope of the case to be heard. It is appropriate to determine the lawfulness of the trading only based on the characteristics of the trading itself.

Case Study V: Effect of Government's Undertaking Letter[5]

[**Facts**]

The appellant, Bank of China (Hong Kong) Limited (hereinafter referred to as "BOC"), states that according to the application of China Liaoning Limited (hereinafter referred to as "CLL"), an affiliate of Liaoning Provincial Government in Hong Kong, the former Sin Hua Bank Hong Kong Branch (it was merged into BOC later and its rights and obligations was assumed by BOC) issued No. G-01-R-01679 and No. G-01-R-01680 documentary letters of credit on 13 May 1999 and 15 May 1999 respectively, in the amount of USD 3.5925 million and USD 2.85 million, respectively. Thereafter, CLL issued to the former Sin Hua Bank Hong Kong Branch a Trust Receipt confirming its receipt of the documents evidencing the ownership of the goods under the two letters of credit. However, so far CLL has not paid the principals and the interests under these two letters of credit. On 9 February 1996, the appellee, Liaoning Provincial Government, issued an Undertaking Letter to the former Sin Hua Bank Hong Kong Branch, agreeing to the provision and/or continued provision by the former Sin Hua Bank Hong Kong Branch to CLL of a quota of HK $ 50 million for ordinary issuance of letters of credit (including a quota of HK $ 50 million for taking delivery on trust), and indicating that it will endeavor to maintain the existence and normal operation of the borrower, do its best to procure that the borrower will fulfill its liabilities and obligations, and if the borrower is unable to repay its debts, assist in resolving the debt issue of the borrower and hold the bank harmless against any economic loss. The appellant sued requesting the appellee to assume the liability of the guarantee and to pay the principals and the interests owed

5 For details of this case, see the "Civil Judgement of Second Instance on the Dispute over the Guarantee Contract between Bank of China (Hong Kong) Limited on one hand and The People's Government of Liaoning Province and Huludao Zinc Smelter Factory on the other hand" at http://www.court.gov.cn/wenshu/xiangqing-4793.html, accessed on 2 March 2016.

by CLL to the appellant.

Both the court of first instance and the court of second instance held that there was no agreement on the guarantee between the appellant and the appellee because the Undertaking Letter, judging by its meaning, does not constitute a guarantee under law and the letter issued by the appellant's lawyer did not require Liaoning Provincial Government to assume the liability of paying the debts on behalf of the debtor.

[**Court's Opinions**]

Regarding whether the Undertaking Letter issued by Liaoning Provincial Government constitutes a guarantee contract as provided in the *Security Law of the People's Republic of China* ("*Security Law*"), the court of first instance is of the opinion that Article 6 of the *Security Law* provides that "Guarantee referred to in this Law means that the guarantor agrees with the creditor that when the debtor fails to discharge the debt, the guarantor shall discharge the debt and assume the liability in accordance with the agreements." Judging by the name of the Undertaking Letter, the intent to provide a guarantee has not been reflected. Judging by the contents of the Undertaking Letter, such statements as "endeavor to maintain the existence and normal operation of the borrower", "assist in resolving", "hold you harmless against economic loss", etc. show no express intent to assume guarantee liability or to repay the debt on behalf of the debtor. The two letters sent by BOC'scounsel King & Wood Shenzhen Office to Liaoning Provincial Government on behalf of BOC only required Liaoning Provincial Government to honor its promise and hold BOC harmless against economic loss, and did not require Liaoning Provincial Government to satisfy the debt of CLL on its behalf, while Liaoning Provincial Government also did not make any expression of the intent to assume the guarantee liability or to repay the debt on behalf of CLL. In addition, according to Article 8 of the *Security Law*, except for on-lending for the purpose of use of the loans of foreign governments or international economic organizations upon the approval of the State Council, a State organ shall not be a guarantor, thus Liaoning Provincial Government has no civil legal capacity to act as a guarantor in this case. Finally, before bringing a lawsuit to a mainland court, BOC only required Liaoning Provincial Government to assist in resolving the issue of unpaid debt owed by CLL and did not require Liaoning Provincial Government to assume the guarantee liability or to repay the debt on behalf of CLL. In conclusion, the Undertaking Letter issued by Liaoning Provincial Government to BOC does not constitute a security in the form of a guarantee as provided in the *Security Law*, and there is no security contract between BOC and Liaoning Provincial Government.

The court of second instance agreed with the aforesaid opinion in principle and dismissed BOC's appeal on 22 December 2014 according to law and upheld the original judgement.

[**Observation**]

It is not uncommon that local governments provide endorsements for corporate financing in practice. In addition to the bank facility in this case, in practice, there are also circumstances where the financing platforms of local governments set up, through trust companies, trust schemes to conduct financing, i. e. "Government-Trust Cooperation", etc. These local governments will issue undertaking letters to provide credit enhancement for the repayment by enterprises. The effect of these letters is of great concern in the legal profession.

In this case, the court opines that two conditions precedent are required to be met for a local government's undertaking letter to constitute a security provided by that government for the discharge of debt: (i) it can be inferred from the expression in the undertaking letter that the government has made an expression of the intent to assume the guarantee liability or to repay the debt on behalf of the debtor, and (ii) when claiming for its rights, the creditor must expressly point out that it requires the government to discharge the liability of repayment on behalf of the debtor. Therefore, not all undertaking letters issued by local governments constitute lawful and valid security and, in judicial practice, judgement should be made based on the specific circumstances of each case. On the other hand, it can be inferred from the logic of the court's reasoning that not all undertaking letters are comfort letters (i. e. documents without legal effect) and, if the undertaking letter meets certain conditions, the security documents issued by the government as a guarantor may be recognized by law, though of course it shall also meet the regulatory requirements formulated by the relevant regulatory authorities.

IV. Review of Hot Issues and Analysis of the Current Regulatory Regime in the Financial Markets

A. Vitality and Risks in Private Finance

In recent years, private financial activities have thrived. In addition to micro-loan companies and guarantee institutions that have been subject to regulation, a large number of wealth management and investment institutions, P2P institutions and internet finance institutions have emerged in the market, and "finance for all people" has become a common practice. However, due to the lack of essential regulation, market risks have gradually emerged. Based on rough estimates, by the end of 2015, the accumulated amount of transactions in the P2P sector all around the country reached almost RMB 1,500 billion and there were more than 3,400 P2P lending platforms (only including those having online business), out of which around 1,000 platforms disappeared after having raised funds (e. g. the Ezubao event at the end of 2015) [6]. Except for a few, most of the remaining P2P institutions have also encountered financial problems which led to significant hidden social risks, which have attracted intense attention from the Chinese government.

The reason why P2P institutions often encounter problems is that such institutions are engaged in financial business while most of them fail to meet the basic rule of conduct and risk control requirements applicable to financial business. They simply seek and match funds resources and demands and charge fees from such match-making. Most P2P institutions are unable to evaluate and manage borrowing and lending risks and credit standing of borrowers and lenders. Meanwhile, P2P institutions are unable to control risks and they lack integrity. For the purpose of developing their business, P2P institutions normally obtain funds by "undertak-

6 Ezubao was established on 25 February, 2014, with a registered capital of RMB 100 million. According to the platform data, it has realized a transaction volume of more than RMB 73 billion and attracted 4.9 million investors within less than two years. The yield of the products on its platform was 9% -14.6%, far higher than that of the wealth management products at banks. Ezubao sold its products through offline physical stores and even set up physical stores in third-tier, fourth-tier and fifth-tier cities. It conducted promotions in a way similar to pyramid selling. Its promotion advertisements went out at prime time on various media. At the beginning of 2016, the relevant personnel of Ezubao were investigated by the public security authority and arrested as approved by the procuratorate authority for the crime of illegally absorbing public deposits.

ing" to generate high yields for the investors who are not sufficiently capable of making investments, and have small and scattered investment channels. Then the institutions lend such funds to small and medium enterprises, start-ups or individuals who are unable to obtain funds through normal channels due to deficiencies in their management and operation, lack of financial capability to repay debts or existence of apparent operational risks. In the absence of financial regulation, such institutions, for the purpose of continuing their business, set up cash pools which eventually become "Ponzi schemes". They keep borrowing new debts to repay old debts until their capital chain breaks and they run away.

In 2015, risk incidents took place frequently in the area of private finance involving funds ranging from hundreds of millions of RMB, several billions of RMB to even tens of billions of RMB. In many cases, intermediary agencies often co-mingled assets of different projects due to their negligence in management and, in some cases, intermediary agencies even misappropriated investors' funds for their own benefits. The related issues are very complicated. Such incidents have not only led to many civil disputes, but also triggered class actions. Some have involved financial crimes or have been dealt with as financial criminal cases by the authorities.

It is worth mentioning that under the current Chinese legal framework, there is no applicable regulatory regime and there exist many obstacles in legal proceedings with respect to the resolution of risk incidents related to group private financing caused by intermediary agencies. It is common that when such incidents take place, the intermediary agencies have disappeared. On the one hand, relevant business materials, notably the investors' information, fundraising documents, post-fundraising conditions of invested projects, investment files and such evidentiary materials that are crucial to the resolution of such event, are likely to be improperly kept, incomplete or even destroyed; on the other hand, the investors may not initiate legal proceedings against the assets of the invested institutions or projects directly in their own names as they entrusted the intermediary agencies to carry out such investment and financing activities. As such, the invested projects are not monitored by any person and the investors do not have recourse against them. With respect to the debt disputes which have triggered class actions, even if the relevant governmental agencies, public security authorities and judicial bodies participate in the resolution, it is still impossible to manage or liquidate the invested projects and assets by themselves or through third party institutions due to the lack of a clear legal mechanism and authorization. Considering the emergence and significance of such issues, the market has called for the formulation of a custody law to regulate such situations.

B. Regulated Management of Private Financing

1. Regulation of P2P business

In recent years, the P2P online lending business has been developing rapidly in the absence of effective regulatory rules so that many risk incidents have occurred, as mentioned above. For the purpose of regulating online lending, the China Banking Regulatory Commission researched and drafted together with such other departments as the Ministry of Industry and Information Technology, the Ministry of Public Security and the State Internet Information Office the *Interim Measures on Managing the Business of Online Intermediary Agency of Lending Information (Draft for Comments)* in December 2015, providing further details in respect of the spirit indicated in the *Guiding Opinions on Promoting the Healthy Development of Internet-based Finance* and regulating the risks and problems existing in the operation of online lending platforms. The *Interim Measures* have defined the meaning of online lending, clarified their application scope and the basic principles of online lending activities, and restated the legal status of online lending institutions as intermediary agencies for information. However, the models of self-financing and creditors' rights transfer currently adopted by most online lending institutions have obviously violated such requirements. Therefore, after the *Interim Measures* officially take effect, platforms adopting the models of self-financing and creditors' rights transfer as their main business models will have to withdraw from the market and such platforms are of a high number.

Nevertheless, as mentioned above, where there appears any breach in the borrowing and lending transaction matched by an online lending platform, it is still very difficult for the investors to seek remedies through judicial channels due to the operational characteristics of online lending platforms and the current system for bringing lawsuits. However, new regulatory requirements would also give rise to new problems. In terms of the subjects of lawsuits, according to the new regulatory requirements, online lending platforms are only intermediary agencies for information and may not provide investments or financing guarantees, and as such, platforms are not qualified to initiate lawsuits against borrowers as the borrowing and lending relationship arises between investors and borrowers. In addition, investors on online lending platforms are scattered. One project may often have investors around the country and the amount invested by each single investor may be very small. In such cases, firstly, it is difficult to gather all the investors scattered around the country in one court, especially if the investors make investments only in very small amounts; and, secondly, as each case may involve dozens or hundreds of investors, the workload of adjudication institutions will increase significantly. Furthermore, as all the transactions take place virtually on the internet and there is no physical evidence proving the process from contract execution to capital disbursement, it is difficult for investors to obtain evidence and they may even be unable to obtain loan contracts. This would no doubt increase investors' lawsuit cost. In short, if online lending platforms may not participate in cases and may not initiate lawsuits against borrowers for and on behalf of investors or through assuming creditors' rights from investors, it will be extremely difficult for investors to protect their own rights and interests in their own name through judicial channels. Therefore, in the face of the disputes arising out of the private finance sector, which is developing rapidly and involves intermediary platforms, one or two administrative measures are inadequate and a complete set of specific substantive laws and procedural laws must be formulated.

2. Regulations on private borrowing and lending

The relatively imperfect financial legal system in China has always been confounding the judicial adjudication profession with respect to such issues, regarding private borrowing and lending, as how to determine the level of interest rates protected by law and the legitimacy and validity of the borrowing and lending between non-financial enterprises. In August 2015, the Supreme People's Court promulgated the judicial interpretations on the *Several Issues concerning the Application of Law in the Trial of Private Lending Cases*, regulating and clarifying private borrowing and lending from the following aspects.

First of all, according to the *Some Advice on the Trial of Loan Cases by the People's Courts* promulgated in 1991, the General Rules on Loans promulgated by the Central Bank in 1996 and the *Measures for Banning Illegal Financial Institutions and Illegal Financial Activities* promulgated by the State Council in 1998, the borrowing and lending between enterprises is normally held by courts to be invalid on the basis that such borrowing and lending violates the financial regulatory rules of the State. Such judicial adjudication has always been criticised by the market and the legal profession. According to the above judicial interpretations, borrowing and lending between enterprises to satisfy their needs in production and operation should be protected from the judicial aspect. It will help enterprises carry out independent operation, alleviate such recurring problems as "difficult to obtain financing" and "expensive to obtain financing" and satisfy the needs of enterprises in respect of their own operations. It is also conducive to the regulation of the private lending market, promoting steady economic development of the State and unifying adjudication standards and regulating the criteria for civil litigations.

Secondly, P2P platforms are regulated under the *Several Issues concerning the Application of Law in the Trial of Private Lending Cases*. According to the provisions of the judicial interpretations, with respect to the borrowing and lending relationship arising between lenders and borrowers through P2P online lending platforms, providers of P2P online lending platforms are not required to assume liabilities of guarantee if they only provide intermediary services. In contrast, the people's courts may order providers of P2P online lending platforms to assume liabilities of guarantee at the request of lenders if such providers explicitly indicate through web pages, advertisements or other media that they will provide a guarantee in respect of the lending, or there is other evidence to establish this.

In addition, the annual interest rate for private lending was also adjusted under the *Several Issues concerning the Application of Law in the Trial of Private Lending Cases* from "no higher than four times the interest rate for bank loans" to 24%. An interest at a rate of 24%–36%, if already actually paid, will also be acknowledged and protected by the courts while an interest at a rate higher than 36% will not be protected.

The promulgation and implementation of the *Several Issues concerning the Application of Law in the Trial of Private Lending Cases* will play a critical role in simultaneously regulating and promoting, and properly guiding, the private lending market. The legalisation of borrowing and lending between enterprises may allow enterprises to take full advantage of their idle funds for conditional lendings and thus establishing a normal inter-enterprise financing channel. In addition, financing favouring such organizations as small and micro businesses and sole traders may be developed and thus further developing the real economy in a healthy manner. However, the author is of the view that it is a big problem in the *Several Issues concerning the Application of Law in the Trial of Private Lending Cases* that the legitimate level of interest rates is fixed at a certain figure. 24% may not be too high for the economic activities during inflation periods, but may be extremely high for those during deflation periods. When fixing the level of interest rates at a certain figure, the legislators apparently gave no consideration to the changing elements of market interest rates, which indicates that legislation is divorced from the market.

V. Conclusion

Finance is undoubtedly the core of modern economy and the degree of "financialisation" of China's economy has been progressing year after year. There exists a huge intrinsic need for reform and development in China's financial markets, especially in such regards as how to reduce the cost of capital in the market, render more support to the development of the real economy, improve the regulatory system, control systematic risks and maintain the relative stability of the RMB, etc.

Compared to other economic sectors, the financial markets require stricter regulation. From a legal perspective, financial products or transactions are the subject matters of transactions which entail the most legal elements, in a sense that financial products are legal and contractual arrangements with respect to cash flow and risks of underlying assets. The author is of the view that in relation to the resolution of financial disputes, based on the features of China's financial markets, adjudicatory bodies and adjudicatory personnel should attach particular weight to the following issues:

1. The issue of legality and compliance in respect of financial innovation. As financial innovation is a means of circumventing or breaking through financial regulation to a certain extent and involves complex structuring of legal rights and obligations, it will naturally give rise to the issue of how to determine the nature of, and how to classify, the transactions and how the relevant laws shall apply, i. e. how to judge the legality and compliance of an innovative financial transaction. A consensus that has already been reached in the industry is that violation of regulations will not necessarily result in the illegality or invalidity of the transaction. However, how to determine the liability of such violation is frequently an issue in dispute, despite that it is the regulatory authorities' duty other than that of the civil adjudicatory bodies to impose regulatory sanctions. What the adjudicatory bodies need to consider is whether a financial institution, which has stronger bargaining power in the transaction, should assume the liability for the losses suffered by the counterparty as a result of transactions in violation of regulations, and how to determine the causation between the violation of regulations and the incurred losses. This requires analysis based on the particulars of each case.

2. The importance of protecting the stability of transactions. For the cases regarding disputes with respect to innovative financial transactions or abnormal patterns of financial transactions which are rather widely conducted, in the absence of explicit laws which are capable of being directly applied, it is not advisable to simply declare its invalidity by mechanically applying existing laws, which may not be suitable for the case at hand. Instead, emphasis should be put on maintaining the stability of the transactions in the market, including completed transactions, and protecting the transactions based on good faith as well as the fairness in respect of different interests. In this regard, the arbitration bodies, which have more discretionary power than the courts, may achieve real fairness and justice through their adjudication.

3. The features of the transactions to be understood for accurate determination of the genuine intent of the parties to the transactions. In practice, due to the complicated structure of a financial transaction and the design of transaction documents, it is sometimes difficult to understand the genuine intent of the parties to the transaction and the changes in the course of executing the transaction simply based on what was agreed on in the transaction documents. In order to truly achieve fair adjudication and dispute resolution, the adjudicators should avoid over-reliance on the literal meaning in the documents and should understand the nature and the logic of the transaction as well as the genuine arrangement of interests on the basis of the features of the transaction so as to make a proper adjudication.

4. Sufficient attention to be paid to quantitative analyses. Given that the formula used for calculating prices, revenue, interest payment, liquidated damages or losses in respect of a transaction is usually determined in advance, attention should be given to quantitative analysis in addition to qualitative analysis when handling a financial dispute. Exercising discretion or making a compromise should be avoided as far as possible.

5. Attention to be paid to adjudication efficiency. The intrinsic nature of financial disputes is monetary interests and time is of the essence. Timely adjudication is relevant not only to a transaction and the liquidity of the financial assets but also the calculation of the daily cost of funds or liquidated damages. Therefore, any delay in adjudicating will certainly increase the costs of transactions as well as the burden on the breaching party especially. Where the underlying transaction amount is significant, the cost will increase daily and will become considerable. Therefore, adjudication should be made in a timely manner.

In connection with the above issues which require attention in the adjudication of financial disputes, the author believes that the mainstream commercial arbitration institutions in China have a relatively adequate number of professional arbitrators and a good foundation in the selection of arbitrators as well as case management and progression. Besides, there is still room for improvement. As such, arbitration will be a good option for resolution of financial disputes in China.

Annual Review on Intellectual Property Dispute Resolution in China (2016) *

XIE Guanbin, JIAO Shan, CHE Luping [1]

I. Introduction

In 2015, the number of patent, trademark and copyright registration applications increased, whilst the number of intellectual property cases accepted by the courts has also increased. As for dispute resolution mechanisms, there was greater diversification and innovation in this area. The Justice Bureaus and the Intellectual Property Offices around the country have actively cooperated with industry associations to explore internal mechanisms to resolve intellectual property disputes.

A. Main Data

On 14 January 2016, the State Intellectual Property Office published the 2015 data on invention patents applied for and licensed. Altogether 1,102,000 invention patent applications were considered in 2015, 18.7% more than the preceding year. This is the first time this number has exceeded one million and the fifth time China has ranked No. 1 globally in terms of having the highest amount of invention patent applications submitted. There were also 359,000 invention patents licensed. Among them 263,000 were licensed in China, 100,000 and 61.9% more than the preceding year. By the end of 2015, there were 872,000 effective invention patents licensed in China (excluding Hong Kong, Macao and Taiwan). [2]

On 17 February 2016, the National Copyright Administration published the 2015 data on nationwide copyright registrations [3]. Copyright registrations have increased, totalling 1,641,200 million in 2015, 35.49% more than the previous year. Copyright registrations for artistic works numbered 1,348,200. Computer program registrations numbered 292,400 and registered security over patents numbered 606. 35.9% more artistic works were registered in 2015 than in 2014 and photographical works accounted for 38.74% of artistic registrations. Also included within artistic works registered were literature works, works of art, films and TV pro-

---

* Translated by Wragge Lawrence Graham & Co.

1 The authors are lawyers from the Beijing Lifang Law Firm.

2 The State Intellectual Property Office, "Press Conference on Application and Licence of Patent Inventions 2011", http://www.sipo.gov.cn/twzb/2015ndzygztjsj/ , accessed on 21 January 2016.

3 The National Copyright Administration, "The Registration of Copyright Keeps Increasing in 2015", http://www.sipo.gov.cn/mtjj/2016/201602/t20160217_1240222.html , accessed on 29 February 2016.

grams, sound recordings, dramas and dance choreographies. There were approximately 300,000 computer programs registered in 2015 which is 30.63% more than the preceding year.

On 23 February 2016, the Trademark Office published the 2015 statistics with regards trademark applications and registrations in all provinces, autonomous regions and municipalities [4]. In 2015, there were 265,874 trademark applications and 2,077,037 effective trademark registrations. By the end of 2015, there were 9,204,015 total effective trademark registrations.

In 2015, courts in Beijing concluded 246,000 intellectual property cases, 24.4% more than the preceding year; and Courts in Shanghai considered 9,077 intellectual property cases, whilst 8,254 of them were concluded. [5]

In 2015, the State Business and Industry Administrations investigated and dealt with 34,000 cases involving violations of intellectual property rights and 20,700 cases involving misleading promotion and representation. [6]

B. Intellectual Property Dispute Resolution Institutions

In June 2015, the Beijing Justice Bureau and Beijing intellectual Property Office signed the *Co-operation Agreement on Promoting the Establishment of Expertise-Based, Industry-Wide People's Organisations for Intellectual Property Dispute Resolution*, under which the First People's Committees for Intellectual Property Dispute Resolution were set up by six industry associations, including the National Electronic Standardization Association and the Beijing Software and Information Services Association. Upon receiving an application by the parties, the Committees are authorised by judicial and executive bodies to resolve a wide range of intellectual property disputes. [7] On 14 January 2016, the long-awaited Intellectual Property Committee of the Beijing People's Dispute Resolution Association was set up, making it the first specialised committee of the Association.

On 8 December 2015, six institutions in Guangzhou, namely the Intellectual Property Office, the Guangzhou Justice Bureau, Guangzhou Customs, Huangpu Customs, the Guangzhou Arbitration Association of the People's Republic of China and the Guangzhou Industry Association Union on Border Protection of Intellectual Property Rights, signed the *Cooperation Agreement on Promoting the establishment of the People's Committees for Intellectual Property*

---

4 Trademark Office of the State Administration for Industry and Commerce, "Statistics on Trademark Applications and Registrations in All Provinces, Autonomous Regions and Municipalities", http://www.sipo.gov.cn/twzb/2015ndzygztjsj/ , accessed on 29 February 2016.

5 China Council for the Promotion of International Trade, "Intellectual Property Cases Accepted and Decided by Courts in Beijing and Shanghai in 2015", http://www.ccpit.org/Contents/Channel_3586/2016/0127/573513/content_573513.html, accessed on 29 February 2016.

6 The State Intellectual Property Office, "The National Industrial and Commercial Administrations Completed Thirty Four Thousand Intellectual Property Cases", http://www.sipo.gov.cn/mtjj/2016/201601/t20160120_1231103.html, accessed on 29 February 2016.

7 Beijing Intellectual Property Office, "Beijing People's Mediation Association Establishes the Board for Intellectual Property", http://www.bjipo.gov.cn/zwxx/zwxxgzdt/201601/t20160119_34751.html, accessed on 21 January 2016.

Dispute Resolution [8]. This agreement aims to enhance the capabilities of all industry associations, exhibition organisers and other non-governmental organizations to resolve intellectual property disputes under applicable laws and regulations.

II. Newly Enacted Laws, Regulations or Other Regulatory Documents

In 2015, new laws and regulations (whether procedural or substantive) have demonstrated China's resolution and determination to protect intellectual property rights, based on the legislative spirit to effectively protect the legitimate rights and interest of intellectual property rights holders. They have laid a strong foundation for healthy market competition and have enormously enhanced the confidence and enthusiasm of rights holders seeking protection in China.

A. Intellectual Property Trial Procedure

On 26 February 2016, the Supreme People's Court published *Interpretation of the Supreme People's Court on Several Issues Concerning the Application of Law in Handling Cases on Conduct Preservation in Disputes over Intellectual Property and/or Competition* (*Consultation Paper*) [9] to solicit public opinion on how to best regulate conduct in intellectual property and competition cases. The *Consultation Paper* provides that before a court decision or arbitration verdict takes effect, the parties can apply for preliminary relief such as a for preservation order, with the intention of ordering the respondent to the application to act or refrain from acting in a certain manner. The *Consultation Paper* also covers jurisdictional issues, letters of application, time limits and procedural requirements of court investigations. The *Consultation paper*, which incorporates the *Civil Procedural Law* and General principles of *Civil Law*, provides a detailed explanation of a number of areas including guarantees, release of guarantees, non-performance, application errors and application fees.

Articles 7 and 8 of the *Consultation Paper* provide directions for the Courts with regards to how to investigate and adjudicate upon an application for a preservation order. Specifically, Article 7 lists the factors to be considered in determining the necessity of preservation of evidence, namely, the applicant's possibility of success in the action, whether the applicant will suffer irreparable harm, whether any harm suffered by the respondent will exceed that suffered by the applicant and whether public interest will be harmed. Article 8 provides examples of when "irreparable harm" may and may not apply. There will likely be "irreparable harm", where the preservation applied for will significantly reduce the harm suffered by the applicant and make it impossible for the respondent to adequately compensate the applicant. Two other examples where "irreparable harm" might occur in intellectual property or in competition cases are when the competitive activities will significantly reduce the competitive advantage of the

---

8 Guangzhou Intellectual Property Office, "The Signing Ceremony of the Cooperation Agreement on Jointly Promoting the Organisation of People's Intellectual Property Mediation Institutions successfully held in Guangzhou", http://www.gz.gov.cn/gzgov/s5855/201512/d90cbd654a174974848fe458fdeefb71.shtml, accessed on 21 January 2016.

9 The Supreme People's Court, "Interpretation of the Supreme People's Court on Several Issues concerning the Application of Law in the Review of Cases Involving Conduct Preservation for Intellectual Property Right and Competition Disputes (Consultation Draft)", http://www.chinacourt.org/article/detail/2015/02/id/1557854.shtml, accessed on 18 January 2016.

applicant, and when the evidence to be preserved might infringe the rights of the applicant. It is likely there will not be "irreparable harm" when the applicant deliberately delays judicial remedies or fails to exercise its intellectual property rights without legitimate reasons, or when the damage suffered can be quantified. Thus it can be seen that the *Consultation Paper* provides more detailed guidance on handling intellectual property and competition cases based on Article 101 of the *Civil Procedural law*.

However, there is still room for discussion before the publication of the *Consultation Paper*. Firstly, what if there exists both a situation where "irreparable harm" is likely to occur and one where it is not likely to occur as outlined in the scenarios contained in Article 8, e. g. when the conduct to be preserved will significantly reduce the competitive advantage of the applicant but at the same time be quantifiable, how should the courts define such conduct? Secondly, evidence preservation may not apply in cases that involve reducing the competitive advantages of the applicant by overtaking its market share or forcing it to adopt irreversible low-price measures (as specified in Section 8 of Article 1). This is because fluctuating market shares is common business practice in a healthy market and it is not seen as "irreparable harm" therefore justifying conduct preservation [10]. Lastly, the guidance regarding what facts and evidence the parties shall submit when applying for a preservation order appears to be too broad.

B. Copyright

1. *Amendments to Measures for the implementation of Copyright Administrative Punishment (Consultation Paper)* by the National Copyright Administration

On 8 September 2015, the National Copyright Administration published *Amendments to Measures for the implementation of Copyright Administrative Punishment (hereinafter referred to as "Consultation Paper")* to solicit public opinion on the Consultation Paper and the existing and suggested penalties under *Copyright law*[11]. These measures have not been revised since the revision of *Copyright Law* in 2010. This *Paper* has suggested updates to the measures as required by the revised *Copyright Law* of 2010 and suggests refinement of the procedures of administrative punishment. Examples are: in the case of heavy fines the parties are entitled to apply for a public hearing, a "heavy fine" is 250,000 RMB and above and there is no distinction between individuals and legal entities; and if a party fails to apply for a public hearing within three days of being notified then that party is deemed to have waived its right to a public hearing. The *Consultation Paper* has also suggested some provisions in terms of Internet copyright administrative sanctions. Internet service providers are to be punished if they clearly know of any infringement or fail to take measures to remove infringing material after receipt of the copyright owner's notice and as a result this is considered to have harmed the public interest.

---

10 ABA, "Joint Opinions of ABA on Interpretation of the Supreme People's Court on Several Issues concerning the Application of Law in the Review of Cases Involving Conduct Preservation for Intellectual Property Right and Competition Disputes (Consultation Draft)", http://www.aiweibang.com/yuedu/20353800.html, accessed on 18 January 2016.

11 Legislative Affairs Office of the State Council, "The Notice of the National Copyright Administration to Seek Public Opinions on the Measures of Implementing the Copyright Administrative Penalties (Revision Draft for Consultation)", http://www.chinalaw.gov.cn/article/cazjgg/201509/20150900478945.shtml, accessed on 18 January 2016.

The *Consultation Paper* also suggests that Internet copyright administrative sanctions are extended to include disseminating works of other people resulting in views of more than 25,000; or if you disseminate the work and you are a registered member of a website with views of over 500; or lastly if you are a member of a website and receive views of 250 other members and you make a profit of more than 1,250 RMB. The Amendments refined many detailed judicial practices in *Copyright Law* and strengthened the *Administrative Law* enforcement in this area. Generally speaking, the *Consultation Paper* has to some extent boosted the development of administrative protection of copyright and enhanced the confidence of copyright holders seeking government protection.

2. *Answers to Questions concerning Trial of Copyright Dispute over Variety Programs* by the Higher People's Court of Beijing[12]

Recently, there have been an increasing number of Chinese variety shows that are adapted from foreign variety shows. It is common for the Chinese TV stations to "imitate" foreign variety shows without their permission. It is hotly debated whether variety shows fall under copyright protection and if so how they should be protected. In response to this, on 15 April 2015, the Higher People's Court of Beijing issued *Answers to Questions concerning Trial of Copyright Disputes over Variety Programs* (hereinafter referred to as the "*Answers*") to be implemented by the Beijing Intellectual Property Court, the intellectual property divisions of Beijing's district courts and the Zhuang Guan Cun Division of the Haidian District Court. The *Answers* categorise original variety programs as movie-like works or video recordings under copyright and neighbouring rights protection. The *Answers* also address such other issues as ownership of the variety programs, rights of the performers, identification and indemnification of infringements. Furthermore, the *Answers* confirm that the basic premise and idea behind a variety program is not protected by *Copyright Law*, but a variety program's written scripts, stage designs, music etc. do indeed constitute "artistic works" and shall be protected. The contract covering the introduction of program models therefore should cover a wide range of issues such as copyright licensing, technical services etc. Thus it can be seen that the *Answers* turns to the "originality" standard in determining copyright protection for variety programs while singling out individual cases for extra analysis. The *Answers* also emphasise fact-based damages to guide and encourage the parties to actively produce evidence.

C. Patents

The State Intellectual Property Office commenced the legislative process of revisingpatent law in November 2011, passing the *Amendment to the Patent Law of the People's Republic of China* (hereinafter referred to as "*examination draft*"), which was relayed to the State Council in January 2013. After an inspection of patent law enforcement during the first half of 2014, the Standing Committee of the National People's Congress provided its opinions on the draft in terms of a number of areas including patent quality, patent protection, patent implementation and public service. The State Intellectual Property Office revised the 2013 draft accordingly,

---

12 China Economy, "Beijing Higher Court for the first time released decisions of variety show copyright cases", http://www.ce.cn/culture/gd/201504/16/t20150416_5124952.shtml, accessed on 18 January 2016.

and on 1 April 2015 issued the *Amendment to the Patent Law of the People's Republic of China (consultation draft)* with corresponding interpretation documents[13]. On 2 December 2015, the Legislative Affairs Office of the State Council issued the *Amendment to the Patent Law of the People's Republic of China* (hereinafter referred to as "*Examination Draft*") to solicit public opinion[14].

The *Examination Draft* contains thirty-three substantively revised articles, one added chapter entitled "Implementation and Application of Patents", 18 articles revising current provisions, 14 added articles and one repealed article. The relevant revisions on the production of evidence relate to: general improvements to evidence rules (Article 68); determination of effects of mediation agreements (Article 61); addition of punitive damages against intentional infringement (Article 68); increasing penalties against group infringement, repetitive infringement and other intentional infringement (Article 60); passing off (Article 66); improvements to the means of administrative law enforcement (Article 67); specifying indirect liability (Article 62); liability of internet service providers (Article 63); establishing the credit profiles for copyright protection (Article 74); and refinement of the procedures and principles of patent re-examination and invalidation (Article 41 and Article, 46).

D. Anti-Monopoly

In line with the agenda of the Anti-Monopoly Committee of the State Council, in June 2015 the legislative process of six guideline documents for anti-monopoly law was commenced, which included the *Anti-Monopoly Guideline on Abuse of Intellectual property Rights* and five other guidelines which relate to anti-monopoly in the automotive industry, the lenient treatment for monopolistic agreements, exemption procedures for monopolistic agreements, suspension of investigation and calculation of fines. On 31 December 2015, the Price Supervision and Anti-Monopoly Bureau of the National Development and Reform Commission issued on its website the *Anti-Monopoly Guideline on Abuse of Intellectual property Rights* (hereinafter referred to as "*Consultation Paper*")[15] to solicit public opinion. The *Paper* defines the *Anti-Monopoly Law* and the Intellectual Property regime as aiming to promote competition and innovation, enhance economic efficiency, protect consumers' interests and enhance social welfare. The *Anti-Monopoly Law* does not focus on the exercise of intellectual property rights but rather focuses on such exercises that may inhibit competition or innovation. The *Consultation Paper* provides guidelines for the means to evaluate intellectual property agreements that may exclude/inhibit competition or innovation and intellectual property-related conduct that may constitute abuse of a dominant market position. The *Consultation Paper* looks at a range of other issues including joint inventions, patent pools, cross licensing, standard setting, price

---

13 The State Intellectual Property Office, "Notice on Seeking Public Opinion on Revision of Patent Law of People's Republic of China (Consultation Draft)", http://www.sipo.gov.cn/tz/gz/201504/t20150401_1095939.html, accessed on 28 January 2016.

14 Legislative Affairs Office of the State Council, "Notice on Seeking Public Opinions on Revision of Patent Law of People's Republic of China (Consultation Draft)", http://www.gov.cn/xinwen/2015-12/03/content_5019664.html, accessed on 28 January 2016.

15 National Development and Reform Commission, "Seeking Public Opinions on Anti-Monopoly Guidance regarding the Abuse of Intellectual Property Rights", http://jjs.ndrc.gov.cn/fjgld/201512/t20151231_770233.html, accessed on 28 January 2016.

limits, exclusive grant-back, no-challenge clauses, exemption by agreement, unfairly high license fees, refusal to license, tying, discriminatory treatments and injunctive relief.

III. Major Cases

A. The Idea and Expression Dichotomy in Copyright Law

The Supreme Court in April 2015 issued the *Annual Report on Intellectual Property Cases*, in which the Court concluded that intellectual property disputes have been returning to deal with some of the most basic and fundamental principles of *Intellectual Property Law*, such as dealing with the concept of copyright ownership[16]. This was shown in the case Chen Zhe v. Yu Zheng, Hunan eTV Culture Media Co., Ltd, Dongyang Huanyu Film and Television Culture Co., Ltd, Wanda Media Co., Ltd and Dongyang Xingrui Film and Television Culture Media Co., Ltd (copyright infringement)[17]. This case concerned an appeal to the Beijing Higher People's Court, who on September 16th 2015 affirmed the judgment of the court of first instance and upheld the way it distinguished ideas from the expression of ideas. *Copyright Law* does not protect ideas but only the expression of an idea. The Beijing Higher Court held that when the designs of characters and scenes within a television show are so specific that they reflect the author's "creative choices and judgments", the scene selections, structural arrangement, and transitional designs will constitute the expression of ideas and be afforded copyright protection. The appellate court emphasised that a comparison needs to be made with a view to identifying substantive similarities. Even though according to the public domain principle, some plots are public domain materials, this does not affect the originality of the complete work which might combine such plots with other non-public domain plots; and even though the infringing work slightly differs from the original work, this does not affect the identicalness of the two works in their inner logical development. Both parties to the case submitted large volumes of evidence and the Court compared the two works in detail. This case provides practical guidance on distinguishing between expression and ideas and in protecting copyright subject matters.

B. The Copyright Subject Matters in Internet

In 2015, internet-related intellectual property issues were at the centre of public attention. Emerging online industries and new online technology have provoked debate about new copyright subject matters.

Beijing Ledong Zhuoyue Technology Co., Ltd v. Beijing Kunlun Yuexiang Internet Service Co., Ltd et al (copyright infringement and unfair competition)[18]. This case involved

---

16 The Supreme People's Court, "Abstract of the Supreme People's Court' Annual Report (2014) on Intellectual Property Cases", http://www.chinacourt.org/article/detail/2015/04/id/1600446.shtml, accessed on 16 February 2016.

17 Trial of the first instance: the Third Intermediate People's Court of Beijing (2014) San Zhong Min Chu Zi No 07916; trial of the second instance: the Higher People's Court of Beijing (2015) Gao Min (Zhi) Zhong Zi No. 1039.

18 Beijing Intellectual Property Court (2014) Jing Zhi Min Chu Zi No. 1.

the protection of business rights in mobile games. The Court did not grant copyright protection for the game names and character names but did grant copyright protection for the characters themselves which were regarded as adapted works. However, while comparing *I am MT with Super MT* (the games which were the subject of the dispute), the Court found them not to be substantively similar and thus there had been no copyright infringement. There was also a claim of unfair competition. The Court held that, since the plaintiff had released its game earlier and the game had gained considerable fame, the defendant's failure to avoid using the game name and character name constituted infringement of a well-known internet product/service, as well as false advertising. This case provides a useful example of a party seeking to protect their mobile game. This case teaches us that game characters are capable of being afforded copyright protection if they satisfy the "originality" condition and even if game names and character names are not protected under *Copyright Law*, a party might be able to successfully protect their mobile game through *Unfair Competition Law*.

Shanghai Fuluo Stationery Co., Ltd v. Shanghai Yixiang Stationery Co., Ltd (copyright infringement)[19]. This case provides a new insight into webpage copyright protection. The Court held that the colour, text, layout and motion effects of webpages may be sourced from public domain materials, but the arrangement of these features which generates visual beauty and is original and duplicable shall be regarded as "works" within the meaning of copyright law. This case confirms that webpages can be afforded copyright protection.

Sina Internet Information Service Co., Ltd v. Tianying Jiuzhou Internet Technology Co., Ltd (copyright protection)[20]. This case involved the long-debated issue of copyright in sports matches. The Court considered that a pre-recorded broadcast of a sports match differed to a sports match being shown live. Pre-recorded broadcasts may be produced by selecting, rearranging, commentating, replaying, and featuring some or all parts of a live match which has been recorded by multiple machines. Therefore, so long as the pre-recorded broadcast is "original" it is afforded copyright protection. In this case the court held that the broadcast in question satisfied the originality requirement and so constituted a copyright work. To broadcast another's copyrighted broadcast of a sports match does not constitute a breach of the right of dissemination via information networks but only a breach of "other rights enjoyed by the copyright owner". This case answered the much discussed question of whether a broadcast of a sports match could enjoy copyright protection, whilst usefully stating the factors to be considered in determining whether a broadcast satisfies the originality condition required in order for copyright protection to be afforded.

C. Protection of the Right to Network Dissemination of Information with the Rise of Technology

With new technologies becoming so prominent in our everyday lives, copyright protection, which developed in relation to traditional media, has struggled to keep pace and be fit for purpose. For example, one hotly debated recent issue relates to how the breach of right of dis-

---

19 Trial of the first instance: Minxing District People's Court of Shanghai (2014) Min Min San (Zhi) Chu Zi No. 154; trial of the second instance: Shanghai Intellectual Property Court (2015) Hu Zhi Min Zhong Zi No. 4.

20 Chaoyang District Court of Beijing (2014) Chao Min (Zhi) Chu Zi No. 40334.

semination through information networks applies in the context of the development of TV set-top boxes and mobile devices.

Hunan Happy Sunshine Interactive Entertainment Media Co. , Ltd v. Tong Fang Co. ,Ltd (infringement of the right of communication through information networks)[21]. The adjudicating court held that determination of dissemination through information networks should be based on the "server principle". The "rabbit video" apps pre-installed within Tong Fang set-top boxes contained links to a number of online video websites, which the Court considered constituted active directional linking. Because of this active directional linking, Tong Fang had a duty of care to inspect the content authenticity of the videos broadcast by the linked webpages. Therefore, the court held Tong Fang Co. , Ltd to be liable. This case provides new insights into dealing with infringement of the right of communication via information networks in regard to set-top boxes.

CCTV International Network Co. , Ltd v. Beijing Douguo Information Technology and Beijing Douguo Yangtian Internet Technology Co. , Ltd (infringement of the right of communication through information networks)[22]. The point at issue in this case was whether the mobile app in question directly offered online video watching or offered the links only. The Court was of the opinion that the mobile app did direct users to other pages. However, users remained within the app and the app's pages when doing so. For example rather than being directed to Sohu (a third party video posting website), the user remained within the app but with what only appeared to be a Souhu page. The Court concluded that Douguo Co. , Ltd offered direct online watching and it was found to be liable.

D. Fair Use of Trade Mark

Fair use of a trade mark can be a strong defence in trade mark disputes. Published court cases in 2015 provide new insights for parties seeking trade mark protection.

Kai De Fu International Trading (Shanghai) Co. , Ltd v. Kuosheng Plumping Co. , Ltd for trademark (infringement and false advertisement (appeal))[23]. This case involved a trade mark infringement claim. The adjudicating Court delivered its opinion from two perspectives, namely mens rea and legitimacy of trade mark uses. It considered that the expression "Jie shui" (the trade mark registered in Chinese characters) in Kuosheng's slogan was merely objectively descriptive of its distributor, and that it was used in good faith and wouldn't cause confusion. Therefore, it was decided that the symbol "Jie Shui" was being correctly used as a trade mark and did not constitute trade mark infringement. The Court adopted the "three elements" approach established in Guccio Gucci S. P. A. v. Jiaxing Panduofu Trading Co. ,Ltd (appeal) (trademark infringement and unfair competition)[24]. The three elements are good faith, no use of a trade mark belonging to another for one's own goods/services and use of a trade mark belonging to another simply to describe the business of who owns this trade mark.

---

21 China Court, " Happy Sunshine Suing Tong Fang for Infringing Dissemination Right of Happy Camp", http://www.chinacourt.org/article/detail/2015/09/id/1710144.shtml, accessed on 21 January 2016.

22 Jianghua Times, "A Bite of China 2 Infringed by Douguo, CCTV Claiming Millions for Damages", http://tech.ifeng.com/a/20150604/41100234_0.shtml, accessed on 21 January 2016.

23 Shanghai Intellectual Property Court (2015) Hu Zhi Min Zhong Zi No. 161.

24 Yangpu District People's Court of Shanghai (2013) Yang Min San (Zhi) Chu Zi No. 574.

Beijing Northern Sport Co. Ltd v. Xi'an Peidong Urban Construction Investment Development Co., Ltd (trademark infringement)[25]. This case was an appeal relating to the trade mark "Mud" (registered in Chinese characters) in the name of a Mud baby competition for ecological muds. The Court held that the sign "Mud" in "Mud Football" (registered in Chinese characters) and "Mud Football Baby" (registered in Chinese characters) was not noticeably displayed and the name of the organiser was explicitly specified and so the trade mark use was simply descriptive. Therefore, the Court decided that the symbol "Mud" was being correctly used and did not constitute trade mark infringement.

In Lais Anti-Prolifery International Co., Ltd v. Pujiang Yahuan Locker Co., Ltd (trade mark infringement)[26]. In this case, the Supreme Court defined the nature of trade mark use in an Original Equipment Manufacturer (OEM) for export. The Court found that applying signs and marks to OEM products is merely to physically mark the OEM and since the products do not circulate in Chinese markets, such signs and marks bear no such function as identifying the source of the product. Therefore, applying signs and marks to OEM exports should not be regarded as trade mark usage. In this case, the Supreme Court re-emphasised the test for infringement, i. e., the infringing activity inhibits the identification function of the trade mark. If an act does not enable a trade mark to be distinguished, it shall not be regarded as trade mark use within the meaning of *Trade Mark Law*. Nor is there any point discussing the similarities or sameness of the trade marks or products.

E. Protection of Prior User's Rights and Interests in Cases Concerning Trade Mark Granting and Confirmation

With the addition of the prior use defence in the new *Trade Mark Law*, courts of all levels now pay more attention to the balance between a prior user's rights and interests and the disputed trade mark in handling trade mark disputes. In many cases the courts have strictly adhered to Article 1 of *Opinions of the Supreme People's Court on Several Issues Concerning Trial of Administrative Cases over Trademark Right Granting and Confirmation*, which states that "the People's Court shall accurately apply the legislative spirit of *Trade Mark Law* in coordinating the protection of the rights and interests in prior business signs with the maintenance of market order … with the emphasis placed on maintenance of the market order now achieved."

Kai Luan (Group) Co., Ltd v. the Trademark Review and Adjudication Board of the Trademark Office under the State Administration of Industry and Commerce[27]. The plaintiff requested to invalidate the trade mark of a third party called Zhang Hongbin, alleging that the disputed trade mark "Kai Luan" infringed one of the prior trade mark rights of Kai Luan Co., Ltd for the following reasons: the name "Kai Luan" bore the business reputation and relations established by the plaintiff over time; the plaintiff's business operations extended to those under the distributed trade mark "Kai Luan" and thus constituted similar or identical goods/services; and the third party clearly knew or should have known the trade mark "Kai Luan". For

---

25 The Higher People's Court of Shanxi (2015) Shan Min San Zhong Zi No. 00031.

26 Trial of the first instance: the Intermediate People's Court of Ningbo, Zhejiang (2011) Zhe Yong Zhi Chu Zi No. 56; trial of the second instance: the Higher People's Court of Zhejiang (2012) No. 285, retrial: the Supreme People's Court (2014) Min Ti Zi No. 38.

27 Beijing Intellectual Property Court (2014) Jing Zhi Xing Chu Zi No. 193.

these reasons the Court concluded that the trade mark was filed in bad faith. The Court stopped the pre-emptive registration by the third party and protected the rights of the prior trade mark owner as well as upholding the market order of fair competition.

Guizhou Tongji Pharmaceuticals Co. , Ltd v. the Trademark Review and Adjudication Board of the Trademark Office under the State Administration of Industry and Commerce (TRAB)[28]. The Court found that compared to the two trade marks cited by the TRAB, the disputed trade mark in question was actually more similar to a prior trade mark owned by the applicant, the business reputation of this earlier mark distinguished it from the two TRAB cited trade marks. Also, the Court found that the prior trade mark already registered to the applicant had become known by the public through years of use, and that it may cause public confusion due to the possibility of people associating similar trade marks filed for registration with the prior trade mark used in connection with similar kinds of goods/services. In this instance the later trade mark might steal the reputation and popularity of the prior trade mark. The Court's stance with regards to taking unfair advantage of the reputation of prior trade marks is to protect the stability of the market, whilst also protecting the normal business operations of the trade mark owner. This case is useful as a reference for when dealing with similar cases in the future.

In Qian Cheng v. Beijing Hall of Music for infringement of exclusive use of registered trademark[29]. The Court discussed the conditions required for the prior user rights defence to be applied. The Court found that the prior user rights defence raised by the defendant was valid on the grounds that the defendant was the prior user of the sign "Open the Door of Music" and everyone who had used the sign in public campaigns qualified as the defendant to the case, and that the campaign in which the defendant used the sign was in some degree popular among relevant groups of the public. In this case, the Court protected the brand name which had been owned by the Beijing Hall of Music for decades and thus effectively balanced the interests of prior users and rights holders.

F. Application of Statutory Compensation in Infringement Cases

Statutory compensation was a hotly discussed issue during the latest amendment process of *Intellectual Property Law*. The upper limit of statutory compensation shows that China is determined to strengthen the protection of intellectual property rights. However, there is still uncertainty over how to apply the statutory compensation in judicial practices. In Castel Group v. Li Daozhi and Shanghai Ban Ti Wines Co. , Ltd for trade mark infringement (retrial)[30], the Supreme Court reduced the compensation award from 33,374,000 RMB, which was awarded by the appellate court, to the statutory maximum of 500,000 RMB that should have been applied in accordance with *Trade Mark Law* (revised in 2011). The huge difference between amounts awarded in these two decisions attracted much scholarly attention. The compensation awarded by the court at first instance, which was affirmed by the appellate court, was based on the profit rates of the representative company Zhang Yu Co. , Ltd, which operated in the wine industry, as well as the wine importer which was the owner of the trade mark-in-suit, Jian Fa Co. , Ltd. However, the Supreme Court, in contrast to the first instance and appellate court,

---

28 Beijing Intellectual Property Court (2014) Jing Zhi Xing Chu Zi No. 182.

29 Retrial, Beijing Intellectual Property Court (2014) Jing Zhi Min Zhong Zi No. 00134.

30 Retrial, the Supreme People's Court (2014) Min Ti Zi No. 25.

ruled that Zhang Yu Co. , Ltd and Jian Fa Co. , Ltd were not parties to the dispute nor did they have any interest with the other parties to the case, and so they were different business operators from the defendant. Therefore, determination of the profitability of the defendants based on Zhang Yu Co. , Ltd or Jian Fa Co. , Ltd's profit rates lacked any legal basis. Furthermore, in the absence of bad faith on the part of the defendants, it was difficult for the Court to determine the cause and effect relationship between the profits made by the defendant and the infringed trade mark. Therefore, given that both plaintiffs and defendants submitted evidence regarding the sales of the infringing commodities or reduction of sales of the right holder, the Supreme Court found that it was difficult to calculate the profits gained by the infringing party or the loss of profits of the rights holder. This meant the Supreme Court ordered an award for the statutory maximum amount of compensation to be applied in these proceedings. Upon comprehensive consideration of the parties' historical disputes and their negotiations, the format and subjective intentions of the infringing activity, the use and reputation of the right holder's trade mark, the reputation of the defendant's product and the licence fee of the disputed trade mark, the Supreme Court awarded damages of 500,000 RMB to the trade mark proprietor.

G. Implementation of a Standard Defence in Patent Litigation

In precedents involving infringement of Standard-Essential Patents, the alleged infringing party usually raises the implementation of standard defence to establish non-infringement. This defence originates from the conflict between the exclusivity of a patent and the universality of Standard-Essential Patents[31]. In Zhang Jingting v. Hangshui Ziya River Construction Engineering Co. , Ltd (patent infringement)[32], the Supreme Court found that the preface of the relevant Standard explicitly limited the patent in connection with the plaintiff (with address and telephone number attached) and indicated that anyone using the patent should contact the plaintiff in advance. Therefore, the implementation methods in the defendant's implementation standard constituted patent infringement. This case shows that whether patent information is specified in a particular Standard is a crucial element in deciding the validity of the alleged infringing party's implementation Standard defence for using the Standard without the patent holders' permission.

In Beijing Yingtelai Technology Co. , Ltd et al v. Shanghai Senlin Special Type Steel Door Co. , Ltd (patent infringement)[33], the parties did not dispute that the alleged infringing products were subject to patent protection. However, the defendant claimed that the alleged infringing products were manufactured according to the national Standard, co-designed by Yingtelai and thus did not constitute infringement. The appellate court found that the national Standard only covered specifications, sizes and materials, but not the technical methods used to produce the products. Thus, even if the infringing products (which were co-designed by the plaintiff) were manufactured according to the national Standard, this in itself is not a valid de-

---

31 Li Jiang, "Development of Judicial Practices of Standard-Essential Patents in China", the speech in the international symposium on "Law Refinement of Standard-Essential Patents".

32 Civil judgment of the Supreme People's Court (2012) Min Ti Zi No. 125.

33 Civil judgment of trial of the second instance of the Higher People's Court of Beijing (2015) Gao Min (Zhi) Zhong Zi No. 1040.

fence against infringement. The decision indicates that in patent infringement cases involving the implementation of the Standard defence, the courts should first consider whether the patent-in-suit is essential to the relevant Standard. This depends on whether the Standard covers specific technical methods and, if it does, whether protection for the methods and the patent-in-suit overlaps. When it is established that the patent-in-suit is a Standard-Essential Patent, the court shall then evaluate the patent information disclosed alongside the intentions of the alleged infringing party to decide whether the implementation of the standard defence is valid.

H. Eliminating and/or Restricting Competition Activities as an Element of Abuse of Dominant Market Position

The Supreme People's Court pointed out in (2013) Min San Zhong Zi No. 3, which was a case involving the abuse of a dominant market position, that "even though the alleged operator enjoys dominant market position, to establish abuse of a dominant market position and to determine the legitimacy of such activities requires a comprehensive evaluation of their negative or possibly positive impacts on consumers and competition." Tonghua v. China Mobile Communications Corporation Shanghai Co., Ltd[34] is the first case to have cited the above precedent. The Shanghai Higher Court held that in China the effect of eliminating and/or restricting competition constitutes an abuse of a dominant market position. While evaluating this element, the Court considered whether the alleged activities eliminated and/or restricted competition and whether this affected consumer choice. The Court concluded in this case that there had been no abuse of a dominant market position and thus there was no need to define the boundaries of the relevant market. The monopoly claim was dismissed.

In Gu Fang v. China Southern Airline Co., Ltd (denial of trade)[35], the Guangdong Higher Court interpreted "refusing to trade" (which is contained in Section 3 of Article 17 of the *Anti-Monopoly Law*) as meaning when operators with a dominant market position refuse to trade with a relevant trading counterparty without justification and for reasons to achieve the purpose or effect of eliminating and/or restricting competition. The court was satisfied that the defendant had justified reasons in committing the alleged actions and had no intention to eliminate and/or restrict competition. The Court also concluded that the defendant's actions did not have such an effect of eliminating and/or restricting competition. Therefore, the defendant's actions did not constitute an abuse of a dominant market position within the meaning of *Anti-Monopoly Law*.

IV. Hot Issues

A. Evidence Preservation and Conduct Preservation in Disputes Involving Computer Software Infringement

The biggest barrier for right holders seeking protection against computer software infringe-

34 Civil judgment of trial of the second instance of the Higher People's Court of Shanghai (2014) Hu Gao Min San (Zhi) Zhong Zi No. 105.

35 Civil judgment of trial of the second instance of the Higher People's Court of Guangdong (2014) Yue Gao Fa Min San Zhong Zi No. 1141.

ment by end users is that the computer devices involved are under the possession of the infringer, which makes it difficult to obtain evidence in connection with the infringing activities and difficult to determine the actual losses suffered by the right holder. Therefore, in computer software disputes, it is a common practice for rights holders to request evidence preservation prior to or during the litigation and for the courts to carry out evidence preservation at the alleged infringer's premises. However, on 9 September 2015, the Supreme People's Court published *Typical Cases Decided by the Intellectual Property Courts in Beijing, Shanghai and Guangzhou*[36], which listed "the case of Autodesk and Adobe applying for evidence preservation before litigation"[37]. The twelve typical cases[38] published on the first anniversary of the Beijing Intellectual Property Court on 9 November 2015 included "Adobe and Autodesk v. Dongfang Fengxing (Beijing) Media Co., Ltd and Dongfang Fengxing (Beijing) Trading Co., Ltd which related to evidence preservation for computer software copyright"[39]. To list computer software infringement disputes involving evidence preservation as typical cases demonstrated the advancing protection of intellectual property in china and the willingness to encourage evidence preservation to achieve timely and effective judicial remedies. This may greatly facilitate the ability of rights holders to protect their rights, whilst sending a warning to infringers.

Additionally, the Supreme People's Court in *Typical Cases Decided by Intellectual property Courts in Beijing, Shanghai and Guangzhou* cited the case of "Baoxue Entertainment Co., Ltd and Shanghai Wang Zhi Yi Internet Technology Co., Ltd which related to applying for conduct preservation"[40]. In this case, the Guangzhou Intellectual Property Court organised a hearing among the parties upon receipt of the motion for a preliminary injunction. After hearing the pleadings of both parties, the Court found that the applicants were very likely to win and that the defendant's activities would cause irreparable harm to the applicants' legitimate interests, and further that the applicant's security had been provided for by the applicant. The Court thus granted the preservation order. The Court basically complied with the investigation requirements of preservation motions as contained in the *Interpretation of the Supreme People's Court on Several Issues Concerning the Application of Law in the Review of Cases Involving Behaviour Preservation for Intellectual Property Right and Competition Dispute* which was issued by the Supreme People's Court in February 2015. The Court effectively protected the rights of rights holders and balanced this with the interests of all the parties. The re-

---

36 The Supreme People's Court, "Typical Cases Decided by the Intellectual Property Courts of Beijing Shanghai and Guangzhou", http://www.court.gov.cn/zixun-xiangqing-15370.html, accessed on 20 January 2016.

37 Autodesk v. Shanghai Feng Yu Zhu Exhibition Co., Ltd for copyright infringement of computer software, Shanghai Intellectual Property Court (2015) Hu Zhi Min Chu Zi No. 194; Autodesk v. Shanghai Feng Yu Zhu Exhibition Co., Ltd for copyright infringement of computer software, Shanghai Intellectual Property Court (2015) Hu Zhi Min Chu Zi No. 192.

38 Jing Fa Wang Shi, Beijing Court Live, "One-Year Anniversary of Beijing Intellectual Court, 12 typical Cases Published", http://www.iprlawyers.com/ipr_Html/31_02/2015-11/11/20151111152959157.html, accessed on 20 January 2016.

39 Autodesk v. Dongfang Fengxing (Beijing) Media Co., Ltd for copyright infringement of computer software, Beijing Intellectual Property Court (2015) Jing Zhi Min Chu Zi No. 55; Autodesk v. Dongfang Fengxing (Beijing) Trading Co., Ltd for copyright infringement of computer software, Beijing Intellectual Property Court (2015) Jing Zhi Min Chu Zi No. 56.

40 Ifeng, "Baoxue won the fight, World of Warcraft suspended", http://games.ifeng.com/yejiehangqing/detail_2015_03/12/40747397_0.shtml, accessed on 21 January 2016.

sult is to develop the confidence of rights holders within the creative industries.

However, dealing with end user infringement of computer software continues to be impeded by difficulties in obtaining technical evidence. For example, in the context of evidence preservation of server software there are two issues: firstly when it is deleted it is hard to restore it; and secondly it can be difficult to get server owners and operators who are not party to the litigation to assist in providing evidence. This is to say that aside from the effective and timely enforcement of the court, there are also many technical obstacles remaining with regardsto protection of computer software.

B. Patent Protection of Computer Software

At the end of 2015, Sogou lodged altogether 17 patent infringement claims in the Beijing Intellectual Property Court, Shanghai Intellectual Property Court and Shanghai Higher People's Court alleging that Baidu Keyboard, which is an app allowing users to set their device language to either Chinese or English, infringed its patent rights and they claimed damages of 260 billion RMB. One of the claims was against the patent CN 1920754 B, which is for a method and system to input WordArt and shapes to apps, which was first applied to keyboard systems by Sogou to enable the use of emoticons created by a combination of multiple characters. Sogou claimed 100 billion RMB in damages in respect of this claim. The total amount claimed and the individual claims both set new records for claimed damages in patent disputes in China and marked the start of a new era where the internet industry effectively uses patent rights to gain greater online protection.

In 2015 the issue of computer software patents attracted extensive attention and sparked heated discussion within the legal profession. In a forum held by the State Intellectual Property Administration and the Ministry of Industry and Information Technology, experts discussed the hot issues of computer software patents, specifically the issue of interpreting the patent features with functional restrictions and proof of infringement. With regard to the interpretations of the features of software patents with functional restrictions, an outstanding problem is the inconsistency between the provisions of the existing *Patent Review Guidance* and Article 4 of *Interpretations of the Supreme People's Court* 2009. According to the definition in the *Patent Review Guidance*, if a patent feature with functional restrictions is supported by the instruction book, protection of it shall extend to all means of implementation for the purpose of achieving that function; whereas Article 4 limits the protection of patent features with functional restrictions to only the means of implementation and equivalent restrictions. In the current retrial of Nokia v. Huaqin, Nokia at the time of writing are trying to make a breakthrough in the administrative review of software patents, i. e. , to limit the scope of protection to the functional restrictions of a software patent. As seen in the dispute between Sogou and Baidu, in which Baidu has filed an invalidation application, it can be foreseen that more of these problems will occur. Also, in software patent disputes, another problem facing rights holders is how to obtain evidence to prove infringement. This is especially difficult when Sogou chose not to sue manufactures of the end devices pre-installed with Baidu keyboards but only the owner of the infringing software, which usually requires inspection of the functions of the software to prove that the infringing software's underlying algorithm reads onto the protection of the patent-in-suit.

C. Hot Issues Regarding the Patent Law Revision

On 2 December 2015, the Legislative Affairs Office of the State Council issued *The Revision of the Patent Law of the People's Republic of China (Draft for Review)* which has been widely discussed within the legal profession. In particular, attention of the general public has been drawn to such *Patent Law* issues as the declaration of invalidity, spoliation inference and statutory compensation.

The *Draft for Review* tries to improve the patent invalidation declaration rules to solve various problems relating to patent protection such as that of circular litigation and lengthy trial proceedings. As the biggest amendment, the *Draft for Review* deleted the indirect provision in Article 60 of the *Consultation Draft* relating to when invalidation declarations take effect. This in fact repealed the changes made to the invalidation declaration rules in the current *Patent Law*. The general response toward the said changes made by Article 60 of the *Consultation Paper* is negative. Specifically, some experts[41] recommended changing the term "third party" in Article 46 of the current *Patent Law* so that the Patent Re-examination Board of SIPO can no longer be a defendant to administrative cases for patent invalidation.

Section 3 of Article 68 of the *Draft for Review* added the principle of spoliation inference. If the infringing party fails to provide evidence, the court can determine the compensation amount based solely on claims and evidence presented by the rights holder. On the one hand this rule will to some degree alleviate the right holder's burden of proof. However, the application is limited to compensation[42]. Some commentators have also suggested adopting the document evidence rule as provided for in judicial interpretations of *Civil Procedural Law* to issue court orders requesting submission of evidence. Another change made by the Draft for Review to the *Consultation Draft* is that the statutory compensation range is increased from a range of 10,000 RMB to 1,000,000 RMB to a new range of 100,000 RMB to 5,000,000 RMB. This is to provide stronger protection for rights holders and will increase the average compensation amount awarded in patent cases. According to a sample survey conducted by legal scholars, among all the cases which involved patent infringement in Beijing, Shanghai, Guangdong, Jiangsu, Zhejiang and Zhongqing, only 1.67% of them adopted a non-statutory estimation of damages; for those adopting statutory compensation, the average amount of compensation for invention patents was 143,300 RMB. 68.57% of the cases had damages of over 100,000 RMB, the average compensation amount for utility models was 114,400 RMB and 20.91% of cases have damages over 100,000 RMB[43]. These statistics show that raising the bottom statutory compensation amount will enhance the average compensation level especially for appearance design patents and at the same time it will ensure better compensation for the loss suffered by owners of high-value patents by lifting the upper limit of statutory compensation.

---

41 Li Jian, "Direction and Focus of the Development of Patent Laws", http://www.zhichanli.com/article/9089, accessed on 12 January 2016. Wan Mi, "Focuses on and Controversies over the Fourth Revision Draft for review of the Patent Law," http://www.cqlsw.net/legal/legislation/2015122818340.html, accessed on 21 January 2016.

42 Li Jian, "Direction and Focus of the Development of Patent Laws", http://www.zhichanli.com/article/9089, accessed on 12 January 2016.

43 Xu Yingcong, "Practices and Reflections of the Patent Law Statutory Compensation in China", Hebei Law Review, 2014 (12), pp. 60-72.

However, on the other hand, there have been abuses of statutory compensation in judicial practices in China. This revision will confer greater discretion on the courts, which may lead to different decisions being reached for similar cases[44] and the elevated statutory compensation level will generate unreasonable expectations from patent owners and the public, undermining the credibility of patent laws[45]. Therefore the imperative of judicial protection of patent rights is to set compensation levels for patent infringement back to the normal level but strengthen the application of evidence rules in civil procedures[46].

V. Conclusions

Generally speaking, intellectual property dispute resolution in 2015 both diversified and specialised and has balanced different interests. Intellectual property courts and arbitration tribunals were established in 2014 and intellectual property mediation also commenced in 2015 which further diversified dispute resolution mechanisms. In terms of intellectual property laws and regulations, procedural conduct preservation, substantive administrative *Copyright Law* enforcement, the revision of *Patent Law* and anti-monopoly guidance, have all reflected years of effort in developing intellectual property dispute resolution. Judicial dispute resolution has also become more advanced and specialised. As for dispute resolution results, the typical cases in 2015 have all encountered the challenge raised by applying new technologies to traditional subject matters of *Intellectual Property Law*, as well as the extensive controversies over the seemingly different decisions on similar cases. However, judgments overall have been the result of individual case analysis based upon specific facts combined with the effort to balance the interests of rights holders and other competitors from the same industry. From the hot issues in 2015, we can see that the internet will continue to be a breeding ground for intellectual property disputes. Intellectual property dispute resolution mechanisms are advancing both the degree and scope of protection for rights holders, whether it is from a procedural or substantive perspective. However, along with that comes the unavoidable problem of increasing conflicts and disputes among different interests. Rights holders are still complaining of narrow protection mechanisms while competitors are still not happy with what they perceive as harsh punishments. How to balance the interests of all parties while at the same time encouraging innovation provides both the greatest challenge and opportunity for 2016.

44 Ruan Kaixin, "Some Thoughts on Raising the Statutory Compensation by the Revision of Patent Law", http://www.zhichanli.com/article/20705, accessed on 12 January 2016.

45 Sun Yuanzhao, "My Suggestions on Revision of Patent Law (Draft for Review)", http://www.zhichanli.com/article/22531, accessed on 12 January 2016.

46 Li Fushan, "Review (the Third in a Series) of the Fourth Revision of Patent Law: Pros and Cons of Patent Protection", http://www.zhichanli.com/article/6669, accessed on 12 January 2016.

Annual Review on Film and TV Dispute Resolution in China (2016)

XU Bo [1]

I. Introduction

In 2015, frequently driven by government agencies and market players, the film and TV industry achieved sustained development and prosperity through close cooperation with investors, coordination among the broadcasting networks and stations, and integration of the industrial chain.

This article focuses on analyzing the disputes as well as detecting and observing the hot issues exposed in the industry in 2015 by probing into the development of films, TV series, TV programs and web series in the same year.

A. Overview on China's Movie Industry in 2015

In 2015, the total movie box office receipts in China was RMB 44.069 billion, an increase of 48.7% over the previous year, marking the highest annual increase during the period of the Twelfth Five-Year Plan. [2] RMB 27.136 billion or 61.58% of them were contributed by domestically produced movies, [3] which generated an overseas sales income of RMB 2.77 billion, an increase of 48.13% over the previous year. [4]

In 2015, 686 feature films were produced in China. 383 new films were released, of which 320 were domestically produced. [5] 81 films, including 47 domestically produced ones, received a box office of over RMB 100 million. A total of 51 animated films were produced and 44 were released, increasing by 9 over 2014, with a total box office of RMB 1.989 billion, representing a year-on-year increase of over 75%.

---

1 Director and Senior Partner, Beijing Tianchi Juntai Law Firm

2 Sohu Entertainment, "National Total Box Office Receipts Reached RMB 44.1 Billion, with Number of Screens Increased to Nearly 32,000, Catching up with That in North America", http://yule.sohu.com/20160101/n433223812.shtml, accessed on 1 January 2016."

3 Central government portal, "Total Movie Box Office Receipts in China in 2015 Jumped to RMB 44.069 billion", http://www.gov.cn/xinwen/2015-12/31/content_5030030.htm, accessed on 31 December 2015.

4 WeChat account ctvcc01 of China Alliance of Radio, Film and Television, "2015 Film Market Reminder", 18 January 2016.

5 Sohu Entertainment, "National Total Box Office Receipts Reached RMB 44.1 Billion, with Number of Screens Increased to Nearly 32,000, Catching up with That in North America", http://yule.sohu.com/20160101/n433223812.shtml, accessed on 1 January 2016."

The global box office for 2015 was USD 38 billion. About USD 11 billion or 29% was contributed by the United States, and USD 6.78 billion or 18% was contributed by China.[6]

In 2015, cinemas in urban areas received 1.26 billion film viewers, an increase of 51.08% over the previous year, and the average annual number of films viewed by each urban resident was 1.8. The national average attendance rate was 17.5%, slightly increasing from the 15% in 2014.[7]

In 2015, 1,200 new cinemas were built and the number of screens rose by 8,035, showing an average daily increase of more than 22. There were over 6,000 cinemas nationwide, with a total of 31,627 screens, only 7,000 less than those in North America, the world's largest market. At the county level, there were 3,241 cinemas with 12,777 screens.[8]

---

6 WeChat account ctvcc01 of China Alliance of Radio, Film and Television, "2015 Film Market Reminder", 18 January 2016.

7 Sohu Entertainment, "National Total Box Office Receipts Reached RMB 44.1 Billion, with Number of Screens Increased to Nearly 32,000, Catching up with That in North America", http://yule.sohu.com/20160101/n433223812.shtml, accessed on 1 January 2016."

8 ibid.

2015 Box Office Ranking [9]

Rank	Name	Type	Annual Box Office (RMB 10,000)	Annual Ticket Price (RMB 10,000)	Average Number of Viewers Per Show	First-week Box Office (RMB 10,000)	Share of First-week Box Office	Country and Region	Distributor	Format
1	Monster Hunt	Fantasy/Comedy	243944.4	37	42	66975	27	China	EDKO (Beijing) Distribution Co., Ltd	2D/3D/IMAX
2	Fast & Furious 7	Action/Crime/Thriller	242654.8	38	42	39872	16	US/Japan	China Film Group Corporation	2D/3D/IMAX
3	Lost In Hong Kong	Comedy	161314.1	32	40	68414	42	China	Beijing Enlight Pictures Co., Ltd	2D/IMAX
4	Avengers: Age of Ultron	Science Fiction/Action/Adventure	146437.6	40	29	96658	66	US	China Film Group Corporation	2D/IMAX
5	Goodbye Mr. Loser	Comedy/Love/Teen	144133.4	32	34	25837	18	China	Wuzhou Film Distribution	2D
6	Jurassic World	Action/Adventure/Science Fiction/Thriller	142065.9	38	33	60645	43	US	Universal Studios	2D/IMAX
7	Mojin - The Lost Legend	Thriller/Adventure	137112	36	45	60001	37	China	Huayi Brothers Media Corporation	2D/3D/IMAX

9 Source: EBOT, http://www.cbooo.cn/year? year=2015.

Rank	Name	Type	Annual Box Office (RMB 10,000)	Annual Ticket Price (RMB 10,000)	Average Number of Viewers Per Show	First-week Box Office (RMB 10,000)	Share of First-week Box Office	Country and Region	Distributor	Format
8	Jian Bing Man	Comedy/Love	116014. 2	32	39	43163	37	China	Wuzhou Film Distribution	2D
9	The Man From Macau II	Action/Comedy	97473. 6	39	37	27409	28	China	Bona Film Group	2D/3D
10	Monkey King: Hero is Back	Animation/Action	95632. 4	34	34	8669	9	China	Beijing Juhe Yinglian Media Co. ,Ltd	2D/3D
11	Mission: Impossible – Rogue Nation	Action/Adventure/Thriller	86953. 9	32	26	55278	64	US/China	Paramount Pictures Corporation	2D/IMAX
12	The Hobbit: The Battle of the Five Armies	Fantasy/Adventure/Action	76607. 7	39	30	31254	41	US/New Zealand	China Film Group Corporation	2D/IMAX
13	Dragon Blade	Action/Costume/War/Love	74409. 7	40	38	34732	47	China	Eastern Mordor	2D/3D/IMAX
14	Terminator: Genisys	Science Fiction/Action/Adventure	72522. 1	36	24	16808	23	US	Paramount Pictures Corporation	2D/IMAX

Rank	Name	Type	Annual Box Office (RMB 10,000)	Annual Ticket Price (RMB 10,000)	Average Number of Viewers Per Show	First-week Box Office (RMB 10,000)	Share of First-week Box Office	Country and Region	Distributor	Format
15	Wolf Totem	Feature/Adventure	69968	39	34	15732	22	China/France	China Film Group Corporation	2D/3D/IMAX
16	Chronicles of the Ghostly Tribe	Action/Thriller/Fantasy/Adventure	68268.3	34	30	42356	62	China	Le Vision Pictures (Beijing) Co., Ltd	2D/3D
17	Ant-Man	Science Fiction/Action/Adventure	67171.1	36	22	27257	41	US	China Film Group Corporation	2D/IMAX
18	San Andreas	Disaster/Thriller/Action/Adventure	62967.4	37	24	31881	51	US	China Film Group Corporation	3D
19	Devil and Angle	Comedy	59644	29	46	50918	79	China	Beijing Enlight Media Co., Ltd	2D
20	The Martian	Science Fiction/Action/Adventure	58644.6	36	24	31020	53	US	Twentieth Century Fox Film Corporation	2D/IMAX

B. Overview on China's TV Series Industry in 2015

In 2015, TV series producers of various types in China produced and obtained approval for distribution of 1,146 TV series with 43,077 episodes. The proportions of themes are as follows:[10]

A total of 676 series with 24,367 episodes were on realistic themes, respectively accounting for 58.99% and 56.57% of the total. Among them, 614 series with 22,214 episodes were on contemporary themes, respectively accounting for 53.58% and 51.57%; and 62 series with 2,153 episodes were on modern themes, respectively accounting for 5.41% and 4.998%.

470 series with 18,710 episodes were on historical themes, respectively accounting for 41.01% and 43.43% of the total. Among them, 287 series with 10,796 episodes were on themes of early modern times, respectively accounting for 25.04% and 25.06% of the total; and 183 series with 7,914 episodes were on themes of ancient times, respectively accounting for 15.97% and 18.37%.

A total of 17 series with 577 episodes were on major themes and approved for project launching. 14 series with 445 episodes of them were on major revolutionary themes and 3 with 132 episodes were on major historical themes.

---

10 Source: The Notification of State Administration of Press, Publication, Radio, Film and Television on Public Disclosure of Filed TV Series Produced in January – December 2015, http://dsj.sarft.gov.cn/tims/site/views/applications.shanty?appName=note, accessed, on 4 March 2016. On 27 February 2016, Li Jingsheng, Director General of the Department of Teleplay, State Administration of Press, Publication, Radio, Film and Television said at the 2015 annual meeting of TV series industry that 1,274 TV series with over 47,277 episodes were publicly disclosed and filed. http://dianshiju.cntv.cn/2016/02/28/ARTIJoPrjwmNYkG9yIH0eq2r160228.shtml, accessed on 4 March 2016.

2015 Top Prime-time TV Ratings (CSM50 4+) [11]

Rank	Name	Channel	Viewership Rate (%)	Market Share (%)	Rank	Name	Channel	Viewership Rate (%)	Market Share (%)
1	The Empress Of China	Hunan TV	3.060	8.139	26	Legend of Dare Stone	Shandong TV	1.096	3.002
2	Legend of Mi Yue	Shanghai Oriental TV	2.677	6.884	27	Royal Romance	Zhejiang TV	1.041	2.936
3	Legend of Mi Yue	Beijing TV	2.614	6.720	28	Yangko Dance	Jiangsu TV	1.030	2.754
4	Cruel Romance	Hunan TV	1.993	5.554	29	Youth Aseemble	Hunan TV	1.030	2.963
5	The Disguiser	Hunan TV	1.932	5.603	30	Yangko Dance	Tianjin TV	1.008	2.692
6	Legend of Fragrance	Hunan TV	1.891	5.213	31	Diamond Lover	Zhejiang TV	0.996	2.972
7	Hero Dog	Hunan TV	1.764	4.963	32	Swan Dive for Love	Zhejiang TV	0.988	2.628
8	The Wife's Lies	Hunan TV	1.695	4.898	33	Nursing Our Love	Hunan TV	0.986	2.755
9	Destined to Love You	Hunan TV	1.557	4.636	34	My Baby	Jiangsu TV	0.980	2.935
10	The Chinese Old Peasant	Beijing TV	1.537	3.990	35	Second Child Time	Shanghai Oriental TV	0.979	2.752
11	SWAT	Hunan TV	1.472	4.363	36	Left Hand Cleaver	Beijing TV	0.962	2.706
12	Ice and Fire of Youth	Hunan TV	1.414	4.193	37	The Legendary Broadsword	Shandong TV	0.955	2.482
13	The Empress Of China	Zhejiang TV	1.401	3.719	38	Silent Separation / My Sunshine	Shanghai Oriental TV	0.953	2.454

11 Tvtv.hk, "Hunan TV Topped 2015 Ranking List of TV Ratings, with "The Empress of China" Outperforming "The Legend of Mi Yue", http://www.tvtv.hk/archives/2853.html, accessed on 5 January 2016. Note: This list only covers the prime-time shows, and the viewership rate for cross-year series is counted from 1 January 2015.

Rank	Name	Channel	Viewer ship Rate (%)	Market Share (%)	Rank	Name	Channel	Viewer ship Rate (%)	Market Share (%)
14	The Chinese Old Peasant	Shandong TV	1.364	3.540	39	Pretty Wife	Jiangsu TV	0.945	2.445
15	Tiger Mom	Shanghai Oriental TV	1.336	3.915	40	MUM GO GO GO	Shandong TV	0.945	2.828
16	My Mother Tian Xiaocao	Shandong TV	1.333	3.452	41	Three Actual Detectives	Jiangsu TV	0.925	2.386
17	Nursing Our Love 2	Hunan TV	1.312	3.552	42	Ex-husbands	Hunan TV	0.911	2.751
18	Diamond Lover	Zhejiang TV	1.249	3.557	43	Anti-terrorism Special Forces	Shanghai Oriental TV	0.910	2.422
19	Beautiful Secret	Hunan TV	1.247	3.399	44	Swan Dive for Love	Beijing TV	0.909	2.404
20	Silent Separation / My Sunshine	Jiangsu TV	1.230	3.163	45	Fishing Island in a Fury	Shandong TV	0.903	2.496
21	Gold Female Thief	Jiangsu TV	1.228	3.268	46	If Love Can Be Repeated	Zhejiang TV	0.900	2.488
22	Best Get Going	Jiangsu TV	1.199	3.575	47	You are My Sisters	Shandong TV	0.897	2.681
23	The Step-father	Shandong TV	1.152	2.975	48	Three Dads	Zhejiang TV	0.895	2.474
24	Mother Like Flowers	Jiangsu TV	1.150	3.175	49	Xiucai Encountered Soldiers	Beijing TV	0.892	2.560
25	Good Time	Shanghai Oriental TV	1.136	3.130	50	The Graduates	Jiangsu TV	0.877	2.481

Ranking List of Online Viewership of TV Series for January 1– August 9, 2015[12]

Rank	Name	Aired Date	Number of Clicks	Rank	Name	Aired Date	Number of Clicks
1	The Journey of Flower	Tuesday, June 9, 2015	108.6	25	The Duke of the Mount Deer	Saturday, December 20, 2014	15.9
2	The Empress Of China	Sunday, December 21, 2014	107.1	26	Tea Love	Friday, May 22, 2015	15.2
3	Silent Separation / My Sunshine	Saturday, January 10, 2015	80.7	27	Walking on the Blade	Sunday, December 28, 2014	14.2
4	Tiger Mom	Sunday, May 3, 2015	57.6	28	Grow Up	29, 2015	13.7
5	Gold Female Thief	January 28, 2015	54.5	29	Medical Library Detectives	January 28, 2015	13.1
6	The Four (2015)	Tuesday, March 17, 2015	52.9	30	The Legendary Broadsword	Saturday, January 17, 2015	12.9
7	Cruel Romance	Tuesday, March 3, 2015	51.7	31	Best Get Going	Friday, July 17, 2015	12.6
8	SWAT	Tuesday, April 28, 2015	43.5	32	Lron Walnut	Friday, March 20, 2015	11.5
9	The Wife's Lies	Sunday, March 29, 2015	41.4	33	The Chinese Old Peasant	Monday, December 22, 2014	11.4
10	Legend of Fragrance	Wednesday, February 4, 2015	38.8	34	Think Before You Marry	Wednesday, April 15, 2015	11.0
11	The Investiture of the Gods	Thursday, February 19, 2015	37.3	35	Pretty Damn Cool Dad	Monday, April 13, 2015	10.8
12	Destined to Love You	Tuesday, June 16, 2015	35.1	36	The Next Station is Marriage	Monday, May 4, 2015	10.4
13	The Condor Heroes (2014)	Thursday, December 4, 2014	34.8	37	My Baby	Friday, July 3, 2015	10.3

12 Zongyijia.com, "Top 50 TV Series with the Most Online Viewership", http://www.zongyijia.com/News/News_info?id=41382, accessed on 11 August 2015.

Rank	Name	Aired Date	Number of Clicks	Rank	Name	Aired Date	Number of Clicks
14	Double Life	Friday, June 12, 2015	25.4	38	Dare To Love	Thursday, March 12, 2015	10.1
15	Diamond Lover	Wednesday, July 22, 2015	24.5	39	My Elder Brother My Sister-in-law	Monday, March 23, 2015	10.0
16	You are My Sisters	Sunday, June 14, 2015	22.1	40	Boss & Me	Tuesday, July 8, 2014	9.9
17	The Cage of Love	Tuesday, May 26, 2015	20.4	41	Heroes of Sui and Tang Dynasties 5	Sunday, February 22, 2015	9.9
18	The Legendary Sniper	Wednesday, December 24, 2014	19.4	42	Hua Xu Yin: City of Desperate Love	Thursday, July 9, 2015	9.6
19	Legend of Dare Stone	Sunday, February 15, 2015	18.8	43	Wang Dahua's Revolutionary Career	Wednesday, April 1, 2015	9.4
20	The Ordinary World	Thursday, February 26, 2015	18.1	44	Endless Love	Wednesday, June 17, 2015	8.9
21	City of Angels	Saturday, March 28, 2015	17.8	45	Red Flowers Red Flames	Monday, December 22, 2014	8.8
22	Ice and Fire of Youth	Sunday, July 12, 2015	17.8	46	Master of Destiny	Thursday, May 28, 2015	8.6
23	Detectives and Doctors	Saturday, January 10, 2015	16.3	47	Hey Daddy	Thursday, March 26, 2015	8.5
24	New Ghost Stories	Tuesday, May 5, 2015	16.2	48	Empresses in the Palace	Monday, March 26, 2012	8.3

C. Overview on China's Variety Shows in 2015

215 variety shows were launched in 2015.[13]

A total of 35 variety shows presented by satellite TV channels were with a viewership rate of over 1%, including 3 weekly broadcasts and 32 season broadcasts.[14]

By channels, 3 programs presented by Zhejiang TV were with a viewership rate of over 4%, 1 program with that of over 3%, 1 program with over 2% and 4 with over 1%, and all these programs were season broadcasts. 4 programs presented by Hunan TV were with a viewership rate of over 2% and 5 were with that of over 1%. Among them 7 were season broadcasts and 2 were weekly broadcasts. 2 programs presented by Shanghai Oriental TV were with a viewership rate of over 2% and 5 with over 1%, and all of them were season broadcasts. 1 program presented by Jiangsu TV was with a viewership rate of over 2% and 5 were with that of 1%. Among them 1 was weekly broadcast and 5 were season broadcasts. 3 programs of Beijing TV were with a viewership rate of over 1%, and all of them were season broadcasts.[15]

---

13 China Social Science Network, "215 Variety Shows Launched in 2015, with Serious Homogeneity in Reality Shows", http://pic.cssn.cn/wh/zy/zyzx/201601/t20160111_2820342.shtml, accessed on 11 January 2016.

14 Tvtv.hk, "Ranking List of Variety Shows with Top Ratings for 2015: All the Top Four Were Presented by Zhejiang TV" http://www.tvtv.hk/archives/2815.html, accessed on 1 January 2016.

15 ibid.

Ranking List of Average Viewership Rate of Evening Programs of Provincial Satellite TV Channels for 2015 (CSM50 4+)[16]

Rank	Program	Channel	Aired Time	Viewership Rate (%)	Market Share (%)	Rank	Program	Channel	Aired Time	Viewership Rate (%)	Market Share (%)
1	The Voice of China 4	Zhejiang TV	Third Quarter	4.865	16.007	26	The Goddesses' New Clothes	Shanghai Oriental TV	August–October	1.175	3.950
2	Running Man 2	Zhejiang TV	Second Quarter	4.756	15.550	27	Documentary on the Production of Legend of Mi Yue	Beijing TV	December	1.101	3.317
3	Running Man 3	Zhejiang TV	Fourth Quarter	4.310	14.432	28	Real Hero	Jiangsu TV	Third Quarter	1.082	4.200
4	Running Man 1	Zhejiang TV	January	3.763	11.390	29	Dream Maker	Beijing TV	First Quarter	1.081	3.170
5	I Am A Singer Season 3	Hunan TV	First Quarter	2.723	12.532	30	We Are In Love	Jiangsu TV	Second Quarter	1.080	5.360
6	Original Comedy Show	Shanghai Oriental TV	Fourth Quarter	2.320	7.660	31	Masked Singer	Jiangsu TV	Third Quarter	1.070	5.046
7	Dad, Where Are We Going? Season 3	Hunan TV	Third Quarter	2.262	10.749	32	Takes A Real Man	Hunan TV	Second Quarter	1.030	4.850
8	Happy Camp	Hunan TV	Weekly Broadcast	2.195	6.110	33	Sisters Over Flowers	Shanghai Oriental TV	March–May	1.017	3.564

16 Tvtv. hk, "Ranking List of Variety Shows with Top Ratings for 2015: All the Top Four Were Presented by Zhejiang TV", http://www.tvtv.hk/archives/2815.html, accessed on 1 January 2016.

Rank	Program	Channel	Aired Time	Viewership Rate (%)	Market Share (%)	Rank	Program	Channel	Aired Time	Viewership Rate (%)	Market Share (%)
9	Go Fighting	Shanghai Oriental TV	Third Quarter	2.151	7.023	34	China Star Dream Star	Shanghai Oriental TV	Fourth Quarter	1.011	3.720
10	Challenger Alliance	Zhejiang TV	Fourth Quarter	2.118	6.000	35	The 12 Front	Zhejiang TV	Third Quarter	1.000	4.320
11	Super Brain Season 2	Jiangsu TV	First Quarter	2.102	6.846	36	Super Team	Jiangsu TV	First Quarter	0.994	3.370
12	Up Idol	Hunan TV	August–October	2.026	9.760	37	X-Fire	Zhejiang TV	Fourth Quarter	0.983	4.181
13	You Are the One	Jiangsu TV	Weekly Broadcast	1.770	5.826	38	Super Diva	Shanghai Oriental TV	Second Quarter	0.976	3.450
14	Wonderful Friends	Hunan TV	First Quarter	1.699	7.580	39	Duets	Beijing TV	Second Quarter	0.976	2.980
15	Day Day Up	Hunan TV	Weekly Broadcast	1.544	4.279	40	Dancing With The Stars	Shanghai Oriental TV	First Quarter	0.936	2.980
16	Inheritors	Beijing TV	Fourth Quarter	1.477	4.510	41	Warriors	Yunnan TV	June–September	0.925	2.772
17	Hidden Energy	Zhejiang TV	February–May	1.432	4.479	42	I am Speaker Season 2	Beijing TV	September–December	0.923	3.110
18	Dad Came Back	Zhejiang TV	Second Quarter	1.430	4.130	43	Jin Xing Show	Shanghai Oriental TV	Weekly Broadcast	0.915	4.014

Rank	Program	Channel	Aired Time	Viewership Rate (%)	Market Share (%)	Rank	Program	Channel	Aired Time	Viewership Rate (%)	Market Share (%)
19	Fight For Her	Jiangsu TV	Second Quarter	1.356	3.951	44	Son in Law Came	Jiangsu TV	Fourth Quarter	0.898	2.540
20	I Love Challenge	Shanghai Oriental TV	Third Quarter	1.306	6.230	45	The Adventure of the West	Zhejiang TV	Fourth Quarter	0.878	2.299
21	Top Funny Comedian	Shanghai Oriental TV	Second Quarter	1.276	4.044	46	Let's Go	Sichuan TV	July–November	0.877	2.400
22	Freshman	Hunan TV	Fourth Quarter	1.259	5.840	47	Off To School	Shanghai Oriental TV	Third Quarter	0.865	3.652
23	Inheritors	Beijing TV	Fourth Quarter	1.258	3.370	48	Run for Time	Hunan TV	Fourth Quarter	0.854	3.750
24	Divas Hit the Road	Hunan TV	Second Quarter	1.251	6.600	49	The Exploration of The World	Jiangsu TV	Second Quarter	0.851	3.494
25	Along the Way with You	Zhejiang TV	First Quarter	1.230	3.679	50	Perhaps Love	Hubei TV	Third Quarter	0.839	2.980

In terms of web variety shows, as of 16 December 2015, 26 new variety shows were launched online during the year, with a total of 6.306 billion views. Among them, 10 were reality shows of general people and 2 were reality shows of stars, with the emergence of diversified new themes in music, creation of idols, etc. [17]

As of mid-December 2015, the top 20 web variety shows were viewed for a total of 7.349 billion times, doubling the figure for 2014, and the average play times for a single show reached 367 million. Among them, 9 variety shows produced by iQIYI. COM were viewed for 3.402 billion times, accounting for 45% of the top 20 and with the top market share; 6 shows produced by Tencent Video account for 30% of the top 20; YoukuTudou and LETV. COM respectively took a share of 10% with 2 shows and Sohu Video took 5% with 1 show. [18]

Top 20 Most Viewed Web Variety Shows for 2015 [19]

Rank	Program	Platform	Playback Times (100 million)
1	We 15	Tencent Video	8.75
2	Off To School	iQIYI. COM	6.97
3	Let's Talk 2	iQIYI. COM	6.63
4	Wow	Tencent Video	5.99
5	My Best Singer	iQIYI. COM	5.40
6	Meet Your Dream Star	Tencent Video	5.19
7	Are You Normal 2	Tencent Video	5.01
8	X-Fire	Tencent Video	3.70
9	I, Supermodel	iQIYI. COM	3.40
10	iQIYI Films	iQIYI. COM	3.36
11	Xiaosong Pedia	iQIYI. COM	3.15
12	Hello, Mr. Right	LETV. COM	2.54
13	Sexy Beast	Tencent Video	2.54
14	King of Pop	iQIYI. COM	2.44
15	Star Moon Private Talk Show	LETV. COM	1.80
16	Big Brother	YoukuTudou	1.50
17	I, Supermodel 2	iQIYI. COM	1.46
18	Dapeng Talk Show	Sohu Video	1.25
19	Big Pair of Trump Card	iQIYI. COM	1.21
20	Age of Ambition	YoukuTudou	1.20

17 NetEase News, "iQIYI. COM Obtains Highland of 2015 Online Variety Shows with Top Market Share" http://news.163.com/15/1230/10/BC301HF400014AED.html, accessed on 30 December 2015.

18 ibid.

19 ibid.

D. Overview on China's Web Series in 2015[20]

In 2015, totally 355 web series were aired, among which 31 were IP web series (the series adapted from works with copyrights), accounting for 8.7% of the total. 7 of the top 10 most viewed web series in 2015 were IP web series. They were: The Lost Tomb, The Journey of Flower 2015, Darker II, Wu Xin, The Monster Killer, Beauty Queen's Personal Expert, Love Me If You Dare and Concubinage Record. All the top three were IP web series, with The Lost Tomb topping others with 2.75 billion times of view.

Top Ten Web Series for 2015[21]

Rank	Name	Platform	Playback Times (100 million)
1	The Lost Tomb	iQIYI. COM	27.54
2	The Journey of Flower 2015	iQIYI. COM	15.38
3	Darker II	Tencent Video	14.28
4	Diors Man	Sohu Video	11.48
5	Falling Down	PPTV, Sohu Video	10.80
6	Wu Xin The Monster Killer	Sohu Video	10.25
7	Beauty Queen's Personal Expert	iQIYI. COM	9.75
8	Soul Ferry	iQIYI. COM	9.46
9	Love Me If You Dare	Sohu Video	9.12
10	Concubinage Record	PPTV	7.61

The number of IP web series in 2015 increased by 15 or 93.8% over 2014. The web series adapted from novels saw the fastest growth, with an increase of nine over 2014; those adapted from games increased by one over 2014; and new forms of IP adaptation from novel derivatives, audiobooks, theater dramas, books and comic books began to appear. Among the top ten IP web series, nine were adapted from novels and one was adapted from derivatives. In terms of platforms, five out of the top ten IP web series were produced by iQIYI, one was by Tencent Video, two were by Sohu Video and one by PPTV and LETV respectively.

20 Guduo media, "IP Web Series in 2015: Which Are the Top Ten?", http://www.guduomedia.com/4756.html, accessed 16 December 2015.

21 ibid.

Top Ten IP Web Series for 2015[22]

Rank	Name	Platform	Original IP	Playback Times (100 million)
1	The Lost Tomb	iQIYI. COM	Novel The Lost Tomb	27.54
2	The Journey of Flower 2015	iQIYI. COM	Extra episode of TV series The Journey of Flower	15.38
3	Darker II	Tencent Video	Novel The Death Notice	14.28
4	Wu Xin The Monster Killer	Sohu Video	Novel Wu Xin The Monster Killer	10.25
5	Beauty Queen's Personal Expert	iQIYI. COM	Novel Beauty Queen's Personal Expert	9.75
6	Love Me If You Dare	Sohu Video	Novel Love Me If You Dare	9.12
7	Concubinage Record	PPTV	Novel Concubinage Record	7.61
8	Psychological Sin	iQIYI. COM	Novel Psychological Sin	5.67
9	The Four Horsemen	iQIYI. COM	Novel The Four Horsemen	5.33
10	Naughty Princess	LETV. COM	Novel Naughty Princess	4.80

II. New Relevant Laws, Regulations and Other Regulatory Documents

In 2015, government authorities such as the General Office of the Central Committee of the Communist Party of China, the State Council, the Ministry of Finance and the State Administration of Press, Publication, Radio, Film and Television (the "SARFT") issued the *Opinions on Accelerating the Construction of a Modern Public Cultural Service System*, the *Plan on Implementing* the *Opinions on Accelerating the Construction of a Modern Public Cultural Service System*, the *Notification on Further Strengthening the Management of the Use of Radio and Television Hosts and Guests*, the *Notification of the State Copyright Administration on Standardizing Copyright Order in Network Disk Services*, the *Notification on Strengthening the Management of Reality Show Programs*, the *Guiding Opinions of the State Council on Accelerating the Construction of the New Supportive Platform for Public Entrepreneurial and Innovation*, the *Opinions of the General Office of the State Council on Intensifying the Fight against Infringement and Counterfeiting in the Field of Internet and other notifications* and opinions concerning the film and television industry. Among them the important ones include:

A. *Notification on Reporting Information on Overseas Films and TV Plays Broadcast Online*

On 21 January 2015, The General Office of SARFT issued the *Notification on Reporting*

22 ibid.

Information on Overseas Films and TV Plays Broadcast Online (Xin Guang Dian Ban Fa [2015] No. 14). According to the *Notification*, websites must report their import plans and fill out the relevant information for the overseas films and TV plays they import in 2015 on the "Platform for Unified Registration of Information on Imported Overseas Films and TV Plays Broadcast Online"; the quantity of overseas films and TV plays allowed to be imported by websites is restricted to not more than 30% of the quantity of domestically produced films and TV plays they purchase and broadcast (with episode as a unit, each counted as 45 minutes); and the episodes broadcast after 1 January 2015 as part of uncompleted series shall be included in the quota for the planned import of overseas series in 2015. [23]

On 1 April 2015, the *Notification of the State Administration of Press, Publication, Radio, Film and Television on Further Implementing Relevant Provisions on the Management of Overseas Films and TV Plays Broadcast Online* (Xin Guang Dian Fa [2014]204) issued by SARFT on 2 September 2014 was officially implemented.

After that, various video sites started to change their ways of importing overseas films and TV series. Tencent Video cooperated with HBO and exclusively put online 20 classic American series including Game of Thrones, with 739 episodes in total; LETV. COM purchased the copyright of House of Cards Season 3, which was shot in one take by Netflix; and Youku purchased the copyright of the shooting while broadcasting Walking Dead Season 5 and promoted its "classic series library" by importing the completed US series such as 24 Hours, Desperate Housewives and Heroes. [24]

This caused a plummeting of the purchase prices of South Korean series, which previously hit new record highs. HE&M, the producer of Mizuki SBS drama "Hyde, Jekyll and I", received a proposal of "USD 100,000 for the copyright of each episode" from an online video site in China, which was 2/3 less than the expected price of over USD 300,000 per episode. Park Mi-hee, representative of HE&M, believed that the plummeting price was attributable to the restrictive policies of the Chinese government. [25]

B. *Rules on Marketing and Sales of Film Tickets*

On 8 July 2015, China Film Distribution and Exhibition Association and China Film Producers Association (hereinafter referred to as the "Two Associations") issued the *Rules on Marketing and Sales of Film Tickets*. According to the Rules, e-ticketing service providers shall sign consignment/settlement contracts; the retail prices shall not be lower than the agreed prices; in promotional activities, the discounts from the agreed prices shall be compensated by the organisers of the activities; e-sellers of tickets shall indicate the ticket price and the services fees on the face of the tickets; and automatic ticketing equipment shall not withdraw funds from the ticket prices.

---

23 Chinese Cultural Industry Association: "Notification on Reporting Information on Overseas Films and TV Plays Broadcast Online Issued by General Office of the State Administration of Press, Publication, Radio, Film and Television", http://www.chncia.org/2015/0122/3818.html, accessed on 22 January 2015.

24 Xue163.com, "How to Watch US Series under Restriction on Overseas Plays: Video Sites May Replay Classics", http://www.xue163.com/news/1214/12141703.html accessed on 10 January 2016.

25 Zongyijia.com, "Royalties for South Korean Series Plummeted with SARFT's Order on Restricting Overseas Plays", http://www.zongyijia.com/News/News_info?id=32128, accessed on 23 January 2015.

After the issuance of the Rules, some argue that the Rules may violate the *Anti-Monopoly Law of the People's Republic of China*. In response, the Two Associations said that the Rules are for the purpose of ensuring the healthy and orderly development of the film industry, strengthening the self-discipline mechanism for the industry and creating a good environment for the development of the industry. The contents of the Rules do not violate the *Anti-Monopoly Law* as the Rules are not intended to organise business operators to carry out any act prejudicing competition, and the implementation of the Rules will not hamper competition or harm the interests of consumers. [26]

As for the impacts of the Rules on cinemas, Internet businesses and consumers, analysts believe that the interests of cinemas will not be affected as the number of film viewers will still increase though the ticket prices will be push up to some extent. Internet ticketing companies can still subsidise consumers by points, vouchers or other forms of benefit, and consumers can still enjoy preferential treatments. [27]

C. *Measures for Levy, Use and Management of National Special Funds for Film Industry Development*

On 31 August 2015, the Ministry of Finance and the SARFT issued the *Measures for Levy, Use and Management of National Special Funds for Film Industry Development*, according to which the scope of use of the special funds for film industry shall cover: cinema building and renovation and upgrading of cinema equipment; dubbing of the films in ethnic minority languages; construction and development of key film bases; production, distribution and exhibition of excellent domestic films; distribution and exhibition of films with cultural characteristics and artistic innovations; construction and maintenance of the integrated film ticketing information managing system; and other expenses for the development of film industry approved by the Ministry of Finance or provincial financial authorities. National and provincial management committees for film special funds shall be set up respectively at central and provincial levels. The for-profit film exhibitors with business registration shall pay 5% of their box office revenue to the film special funds, and the funds shall be paid into the central and provincial treasury at a ratio of 4 : 6.

Compared with the *Measures for Management of National Special Funds for Film Industry Development* implemented on 1 July 2006, the new *Measures* cover a more extensive scope of leviers and add new contents in the use and management of the special funds by setting a separate chapter of "legal liabilities" and explicitly providing that "those suspected of committing a crime shall be transferred to judicial authorities".

---

26 China Film Distribution and Exhibition Association, "Explanations on the Rules on Marketing and Sales of Film Tickets", http://www.chinafilm.org.cn/Item/Show.asp? m=1&d=8339, accessed on 7 August 2015.

27 Yao Lei, "Who Will Suffer from the Issuance of Rules on Marketing and Sales of Film Tickets, Cinemas or Consumers?", Sohu Finance, http://mt.sohu.com/20150713/n416686521.shtml, accessed on 13 July 2015. Gold line: "With Rules on Marketing and Sales of Film Tickets Issued, Cheap Tickets May Become the Past", http://news.cnfol.com/chanyejingji/20150720/21126606.shtml, accessed on 20 July 2015.

D. *Law of the People's Republic of China on Promotion of Film Industry (Draft)*

On 1 September 2015, the executive meeting of the State Council adopted the *Law of the People's Republic of China on Promotion of Film Industry (Draft)*. From 1984 when the Law was first drafted to 1 September 2015 when it was adopted, it took over 30 years. The draft law on film promotion integrates the development of film industry into the national economic and social development planning; encourages enterprises to engage in film making business by streamlining procedures and lowering the thresholds of market access; makes provisions on concealing box office and cinema advertising; and incorporates film education into the compulsory education program. [28] Aiming at promoting the development of China's film industry, the Law will lay a solid foundation for the sustained, healthy and stable development of China's film industry and provide an institutional guarantee for building China into a country with a strong film industry. The effects of the implementation of Law are yet to be observed and studied.

E. *Professional Ethics Self-discipline Convention for Press, Publication, Radio, Film and Television Practitioners*

On 15 September 2015, 50 associations in the press, publication, radio, film and television sectors signed in Beijing the *Professional Ethics Self-discipline Convention for Press, Publication, Radio, Film and Television Practitioners* (hereinafter referred to as the "*Self-discipline Convention*"), which requires that the film and television practitioners should not produce, endorse or disseminate false advertisements; should not plagiarise the creative ideas and achievements of others; should not disparage the reputation and works of others; and should not involve in "pornography, gambling and drugs" and the behaviours in violation of public order and morals.

The *Self-discipline Convention* extensively applies to the practitioners in the government authorities, enterprises, non-profit institutions and associations in press, publication, radio, film and television. Its relevant contents are incorporated in the articles of association of the signatories and in the employment contracts and relevant cooperation contracts of the members of the signatories to ensure the actual binding effect of the Convention. [29]

F. *Notification of the Ministry of Finance and the State Administration of Taxation on Applying Zero VAT Rate on Film, Television and Other Export Services*

On 30 October 2015, the Ministry of Finance and the State Administration of Taxation is-

---

28 China Press Publication Radio Film and Television Journal, "State Council Adopts Draft Law on Promotion of Film Industry: What Will the First Law on Film Bring to Us?" http://toutiao.com/i6203208625525637634/, accessed on 8 October 2015.

29 SARFT, "50 Associations in Press, Publication, Radio, Film and Television Sectors Sign Professional Ethics Self-discipline Convention for Practitioners", http://www.sarft.gov.cn/art/2015/9/18/art_114_28494.html, accessed on 18 September 2015.

sued the *Notification of the Ministry of Finance and the State Administration of Taxation on Applying Zero VAT Rate on Film, Television and Other Export Services* (Cai Shui [2015] No. 118), which provides that from 1 December 2015 onwards, zero VAT rate shall be applied on the taxable services of production and distribution of radio, film and TV programs (works) provided by the organisations and individuals within the territory of China for overseas organisations.

Concerning item 6, Article 7, Annex 4 of the original policy, the *Notification of Ministry of Finance and State Administration of Taxation on Integrating Rail Transport and Postal Industries into Pilot Project of Replacing Business Tax with Value Added Tax* ([2013] No. 106), the 2015 *Notification* changes the distribution services of radio, film and television programs (works) from being exempted from tax to being subject to zero tax rate; and divides the export services such as the film and television services provide by organizations and individuals within China into two categories by types of enterprises: one eligible for tax refund (exemption) and the other for tax exemption. [30]

G. *Notification of the Film Bureau of the State Administration of Press, Publication, Radio, Film and Television on Strictly Cracking down on Illegal Infringements Including Bootleg Recording of Films* and *Notification of the Film Bureau of the State Administration of Press, Publication, Radio, Film and Television on Strictly Protecting Film Copyrights by Strengthening the Application of Digital Watermarking Technology*

In October 2015, SARFT Film Bureau issued the *Notification of the Film Bureau of the State Administration of Press, Publication, Radio, Film and Television on Strictly Cracking down on Illegal Infringements Including Bootleg Recording of Films* (Ying Zi [2015] No. 578) and the *Notification of the Film Bureau of the State Administration of Press, Publication, Radio, Film and Television on Strictly Protecting Film Copyrights by Strengthening the Application of Digital Watermarking Technology* (Ying Zi [2015] No. 581). The two *Notifications* points out that to regulate the film market order and strictly crack down on the bootleg recording films and other illegal infringements, it is required to track the cinema in which the recording was made and the time of the recording by using digital water-making technology; and film post-producers, when undertaking digital copy processing and key making for films, should inform the entrusting party to enable the digital water-making function, so as to ensure that the film is with relevant information when exhibited in cinemas.

On 21 December 2015, SARFT Film Bureau issued the Announcement of the Film Bureau of the State Administration of Press, Publication, Radio, Film and Television on *Strictly Cracking Down on Bootlegging Films and Other Infringements* (Ying Zi (2015) No. 681), which reported to the whole industry the bootleg recording of films by five cinemas and required that the two Committees should suspend the supply of films to members with repeated incidents of bootleg recording.

---

30 Wang Wenqing, Li Yong, "Interpretation of Document Cai Shui [2015] No. 118: How to Carry out Tax Refund as Export Services of Film, Television, etc. Shift from Tax Exemption to Zero Tax Rate?", China Taxation News, http://www.shui5.cn/article/21/83341.html#0-tsina-1-66633-397232819ff9a47a7b7e80a40613cfe1.

In addition to the above mentioned relevant laws, regulations and other regulatory documents, the *Copyright Law of the People's Republic of China* (*Revised Draft for Considerations*) and the *Measures for Management of Audio and Video Programs Disseminated Through the Internet and Other Information Networks* (*Revised Draft for Comments*) are still in the process of revision and are to be observed after their official implementation.

III. Typical Cases

A. Dispute on the Authorship of the Script of "the Legend of Mi Yue" [31]

1. Basic facts

On 7 April 2015, Jiang Shengnan, the author of the novel "Legend of Mi Yue", filed an action against Wang Xiaoping, the scriptwriter stated in the promotional materials of the TV series Legend of Mi Yue, and Dongyang Flower Film & TV Culture Co. Ltd (hereinafter referred to as the "Dongyang Flower Company") for breach of copyright, requiring an apology and claiming for a mental damage compensation of RMB 1.

Jiang Shengnan stated that "the Legend of Mi Yue" was a work solely completed by her. In 2012, she signed with Dongyang Flower Company a Contract on TV Script Writing, and by the end of March 2014, she delivered by installments the adapted scripts for all the 53 episodes of the TV series Legend of Mi Yue to Dongyang Flower Company, and the Company paid all the fees for the script writing to her. In August 2014, Dongyang Flower Company began to claim in promotional activities that Wang Xiaoping was the "chief scriptwriter" or "scriptwriter" of the TV series Legend of Mi Yue. Jiang Shengnan believed that she was the author and owner of copyright of the novel "Legend of Mi Yue", which was the original work of the script and TV series Legend of Mi Yue, and that she was the scriptwriter of the TV series, and legally had the right of authorship to the script. The acts of Dongyang Flower Company and Wang Xiaoping violated her copyright interests.

The People's Court of Lucheng District, Wenzhou City People's Court accepted the case and heard it at first instance on 21 August 2015. During the proceedings, as the TV drama "Legend of Mi Yue" was still in post-production, with the date of broadcast undetermined, and given the involvement of business secrets and the fact that the script "Legend of Mi Yue" was not yet filed to SARFT for recording, the case did not meet the conditions for infringement analysis. Thus, the Court of Lucheng District ruled to suspend the trial.

On 19 November 2015, Dongyang Flower Company filed a lawsuit to the People's Court of Chaoyang District, Beijing against Jiang Shengnan.

Dongyang Flower Company stated that in August 2012, Beijing Star Granada Television Culture Communication Co., Ltd (hereinafter referred to as the "Star Granada Company") entered into a Contract on TV Script Writing with Jiang Shengnan, which specified the agreed matters on Jiang's creation of "Legend of Mi Yue" on the commission of the Star Granada Company. In the same year, the two sides signed a Supplemental Agreement, under which

31 Wenzhou Network, "First Instance Hearing of Jiang Shengnan vs. Dongyang Flower Film & TV Culture Co. Ltd. Will Be Resumed", http://news.66wz.com/system/2015/11/26/104646486.shtml, accessed on 26 November 2015.

Jiang Shengnan promised that she would not publish or distribute the original novel in print or online before the broadcast of the TV series "Legend of Mi Yue", and that she agreed to transfer the relevant rights and obligations to the third party.

In June 2013, Dongyang Flower Company signed with Star Granada Company the Agreement on Transfer of the Copyright of TV Script "Legend of Mi Yue" and the Supplemental Agreement, under which Star Granada Company transferred its relevant rights and obligations under the Agreement on TV Script Writing and the Supplemental Agreement which it signed with Jiang Shengnan to Dongyang Flower Company.

Dongyang Flower Company believed that Jiang Shengnan published without permission the novel "Legend of Mi Yue" before the broadcast of the TV series Legend of Mi Yue and distributed parts of the novel (I, II and III) even after the Company sent a lawyer's letter on 2 September 2015. This behaviour not only violated legal provisions and contract agreements, but also seriously affected the Company's plan for the distribution and promotion of the TV series, causing significant losses. Therefore Dongyang Flower Company claimed an immediate stop of the publication and distribution of the novel "Legend of Mi Yue" and a public apology.

Jiang Shengnan argued that on 17 July 2014, in the presence of the director Zheng Xiaolong and others, the producer expressly agreed that the novel "Legend of Mi Yue" may be published and distributed at the end of June 2015.

2. Court decisions[32]

The People's Court of Chaoyang District, Beijing held that: According to the Contract on TV Script Writing, the Supplemental Agreement and the Power of Attorney between Jiang Shengnan and the Star Granada Company, Jiang Shengnan bears the obligation not to publish the original novel in print or online before the broadcast of the TV series. Jiang Shengnan failed to provide valid evidence that the producer consented to the publication of the novel in late June 2015 or that the publication and distribution of the novel was authorised by the Dongyang Flower Company. Therefore Jiang's publication and distribution of the novel "Legend of Mi Yue" prior to the broadcast of the TV series constituted a breach of contract and Jiang shall bear the corresponding legal liabilities. As apology is not a way of bearing liabilities for breach of contract specified in the *Contract Law*, and the two parties did not agree on such a way of bearing breach liabilities, the People's Court of Chaoyang District, Beijing did not support the claim for apology from the Dongyang Flower Company.

Therefore, on 24 November 2015, the Court of Chaoyang District Court ordered Jiang Shengnan to immediately stop the publication and distribution of the novel "Legend of Mi Yue" and rejected other claims of Dongyang Flower Company.

On the same day of that judgment, the People's Court of Lucheng District issued the Notification on Evidence Production within Limited Time to Dongyang Flower Company, requiring that the Company provide the shooting script and broadcast tapes of the Legend of Mi Yue and other evidence within 10 days for the Court to conduct infringement analysis. The

---

32 CNR network, "First Instance Decision on the Dispute on Legend of Mi Yue: the Scriptwriter Shall Immediately Stop Publishing and Distributing the Novel of the Same Name", http://china.cnr.cn/xwwgf/20151124/t20151124_520586951.shtml, accessed on 24 November 2015.

People's Court of Lucheng District said that the trial on the copyright infringement case of Jiang Shengnan v. Dongyang Flower Company and Wang Xiaoping would soon be resumed.

3. Observations on the dispute

As more and more online literature and original works are adapted for films, TV dramas, cartoons, games and other new works, the disputes between the original authors and the writers of adapted scripts are increasing. To solve the problem of unclear boundary between the original and adapted works, in terms of the contents of works, the two parties should agree in their contract with details such as the plot in the original work that cannot be modified and the name of the adapted work, so as to prevent any arbitrary revision of the theme of a work; and in terms of the sequence of authorship, it is necessary to explicitly state in contract that "no person shall have his/her name appear as scriptwriter", so as to avoid losing the first place in the sequence of authorship due to the participation of others. In addition, the case also exposed the weak legal awareness of practitioners and lack of copyright agents in the industry.

B. Dispute on Income Distribution of Three Shots of Surprises[33]

1. Basic facts

Concerning the income distribution of the film Three Shots of Surprises (hereinafter referred to as the "Three Shots"), Zhang Yimou filed a lawsuit against Beijing New Picture Film Co (hereinafter referred to as "New Picture Film"), claiming RMB 15 million of the income.

On 7 July 2015, the People's Court of Chaoyang District, Beijing publicly heard the case at first instance.

Zhang Yimou stated that, in June 2009, he signed a Memorandum of Agreement with New Picture Film and Hong Kong Films Ltd (hereinafter referred to as "Edko"), under which the following matters were agreed on the cooperative shooting of the film Three Shots: Edko shall be responsible for the investment, New Picture Film shall be responsible for everything concerning the publicity and distribution of the film within China, and Zhang Yimou shall serve as the director of the film. All income from the distribution of the film in Chinese Mainland, with the costs for promotion and distribution paid by the defendant deducted, shall be shared equally among the three parties, that is, each of the three parties shall have a share of at least RMB 15 million (temporarily counted) from the income. However, after receiving the entire box office share, New Picture Film never paid any share of the income to Zhang Yimou until then.

The lawyer representing New Picture Film stated that the company has transferred by remittance over RMB 12.53 million to Chen Ting, wife of Zhang Yimou, by 13 installments in 2010 and 2011 as the share of income and performed the tax payment obligation on behalf of

---

33 Xinhua News Agency, "Zhang Yimou's Claim for RMB 15 million against New Picture Film Co. Heard at First Instance: What are the Implications of Disputes in Film and TV Circle?", http://news.xinhuanet.com/legal/2015-07/07/c_1115847003.htm, accessed on 7 July 2015. China News, "Zhang Yimou's Claim for Film Income Share Heard at Second Instance in Beijing", http://www.bj.chinanews.com/news/2016/0111/49666.html, accessed on 11 January 2016. Phoenix, "Zhang Yimou vs. New Picture Heard at Second Instance Today", http://news.ifeng.com/a/20160111/47025276_0.shtml, accessed on 11 January 2016.

Zhang. Therefore there was no non-payment issue.

The representative of Zhang Yimou stated that the over RMB 12 million received was the remunerations of Zhang Yimou for his serving as director in five films including Hero and House of Flying Daggers, but not the share of the income from Three Shots.

On 15 September 2015, the first instance court decided that New Picture Film shall pay Zhang Yimou RMB 15 million as the share of the income from Three Shots. New Picture Film considered the decision as erroneous and appealed to the No. 3 Intermediate People's Court of Beijing. The case was heard at second instance on 11 January 2016.

New Picture Film stated that Zhang Yimou received the remunerations for the five films including Hero and House of Flying Daggers as early as in 2005. The time when the company paid the over RMB 12 million coincided with the time when Three Shots was released. In addition, the case has exceeded the statute of limitations, and as for the amount of money, the share of income paid by New Picture Film to Zhang Yimou was equal to that paid by it to Edko.

The lawyer representing New Picture Film stated that the evidence on Zhang Yimou's receipt of remunerations was filed during the first instance proceedings, and new evidence was filed during the second instance proceedings to prove that Zhang Yimou received the remunerations for the films including Hero in January 2005.

Zhang's side argued that in the first instance both parties recognised that New Picture Film paid over RMB 12 million to Zhang's wife, but the two parties had a dispute on whether the amount concerned was the remunerations for Three Shots or other films, and the first instance court had reviewed and made a finding on such dispute. The amount of the remunerations for Three Shots was a conservative estimate that they made without obtaining any box office receipt, as New Picture Film refused to provide any such receipt. The evidence submitted by New Picture Film to the court was not within the legally provided scope. Even if it was proved that someone received over RMB 5 million as remunerations for the films including Hero and House of Flying Daggers and signed the name of Zhang Yimou, this could not prove that Zhang Yimou personally received the money.

Currently the second instance decision was not issued yet.

2. Observations on the dispute

Disputes on film income distribution occurred more than once in recent years. To avoid similar disputes, the partners should clarify the ways and ratios of box office distribution in written agreements and make comprehensive communications, so as to prevent disagreements resulted from lack of evidence or different understandings of parties.

In addition, the emphasis on human relationships rather than the law in the film and television industry is also an important factor causing disputes. In the film and television industry, the signing of written agreement is not as valued as in other industries, and oral and written agreements are unclear, lacking important provisions, ignoring details and follow-up remedies. These are the causes of disputes. Further, the varying degrees of strictness in performing agreement by different parties will also lead to disputes.

C. Case on Infringement of the Name of Jiangsu TV Program You Are the One[34]

1. Basic facts

On 16 February 2009, Jin Ahuan applied to the Trademark Office of the State Administration for Industry and Commerce for the trademark registration of "You Are the One" in traditional Chinese (非誠勿擾). On 7 September 2010, he received the Trademark Registration Certificate No. 7199523 for "You Are the One", with authorised services of category 45, including "dating services, marriage agency", etc. Subsequently, he opened a marriage agency named "You Are the One". On 15 January 2010, Jiangsu TV began to broadcast its dating show "You Are the One". This point of time was after Jin Ahuan's application for the trademark registration of "You Are the One" but before "You Are the One" was officially approved and registered.

In 2013, Jin Ahuan sued Jiangsu TV, stating that it violated his trademark. In December 2014, the People's Court of Nanshan District, Shenzhen heard the case at first instance. The Court held that the name of Jiangsu TV program "You Are the One" was the same as the word trademark "You Are the One" of Jin Ahuan, and the use of "You Are the One" by Jiangsu TV was a use as a trademark. But "You Are the One" of Jiangsu TV was a TV show, which was in a service category different from that authorised for the trademark of Jin Ahuan. The two were commodities (services) in different categories and Jiangsu TV did not constitute infringement. Accordingly, the Court rejected the claim of Jin Ahuan. Jin Ahuan appealed against the decision.

2. Court decisions

The Intermediate People's Court of Shenzhen heard the appeal in December 2015. It held that, in determining whether the case constitutes an infringement of trademark rights, one should consider not only the form of TV broadcast of "You Are the One" but also the contents and purposes of the TV program, and should objectively determine whether the two services are the same or similar. Judging from the purpose, contents, form and recipients of service, the program "You Are the One" of Jiangsu TV was to provide marriage and dating services, which were the same as the authorised services specified in the Trademark Registration Certificate No. 7199523 for the trademark "You Are the One" of Jin Ahuan, i. e. "dating and marriage agency". As Jin Ahuan's No. 7199523 trademark "You Are the One" has been put into commercial use, the behaviour of Jiangsu TV affected the normal use of the trademark. The visibility of Jiangsu TV and its promotional activities for the program led to reverse confusion among the public. Jiangsu TV received a large amount of advertising fees through the broadcast of the program You Are the One, and made profits through receiving text messages in the later stage of the program. This was sufficient evidence to prove the for-profit commercial use,

34 Net Ease News, "Jiangsu TV Fails in the Case on Trademark Infringement of You Are the One and Is Ordered to Immediately Stop the Use of 'You Are the One' ", http://news.163.com/16/0106/07/BCKO3IB500014AEE.html, accessed on 6 January 2016. China Intellectual Property News, "TV Marriage Program 'You Are the One' Is Sued for Trademark Infringement ", http://www.iprchn.com/Index_NewsContent.aspx?newsId=52339, accessed on 24 October 2012.

which constituted trademark infringement.

Therefore the Court ruled that Jiangsu Provincial Radio and Television Station shall immediately stop the infringement on Jin Ahuan's No. 7199523 registered trademark "You Are the One" and that Jiangsu TV channel shall immediately stop using the program name "You Are the One".

3. Observations on the dispute

The case plays a positive role in raising the awareness of the protection of intellectual property rights among TV programs. For example, it helps to improve the copyright awareness of producers and to know that trademark registration is needed before the promotion and production of a film or TV program, authorisation from the relevant right owner should be obtained through formal channels, and a professional in *Intellectual Property Law* should be hired for professional legal guidance in this field.

When creating a new TV program, it is advisable to consult a lawyer specialising in intellectual property for professional legal advices on whether the name of the program has legal risks, how to protect the reputation of the brand of the program, etc.

D. Arbitration on Brokerage Contract Dispute between Film and TV Production Company A and Performer B

1. Basic facts

Film and TV production company A as the applicant and performer B as the respondent signed on 15 December 2012 a Sole Agency Contract on Performance Brokerage Services (hereinafter referred to as the "Contract"), in which the respondent entrusted the applicant as the respondent's exclusive worldwide broker and the two parties agreed on various brokerage-related matters. The Contract specified that any dispute between the two parties shall be settled through arbitration by Beijing Arbitration Commission. In 2015, a dispute arose between the parties on the nature and performance of the Contract, and the applicant applied to Beijing Arbitration Commission for arbitration.

2. The arbitration award

The arbitral tribunal held that although certain provisions of the Contract could indeed reflect the existence of the principal-agent relationship between the parties, the comprehensive services provided by the applicant for the respondent and the power of the applicant to manage the respondent were beyond the scope of agency appointment contracts as specified in Chapter 21 of the specific provisions of the *Contract Law*. Therefore, the Contract was an atypical unnamed contract.

As for the performance of the Contract, the tribunal found that the evidence submitted by the applicant could prove that the applicant already fulfilled its obligations as a brokerage firm and did not violate the Contract. While the preconditions for the right to rescind the Contract were not met, the respondent rescinded the Contract by unilaterally sending a letter on March 1, 2014 and signed an agreement with a third party to star in a role. These behaviours constituted a breach of contract. Considering that a performance brokerage contract is personal and matters for the artistic career of the respondent as a performer, and that more disputes will arise and will affect long-term career development of the respondent if the validity of the Contract is maintained despite the existence of intense conflicts, the arbitral tribunal therefore ruled that the Contract shall be rescinded and the respondent shall pay the corresponding penalties for breach of contract.

3. Observations on the dispute

The root causes of disputes on performance brokerage between brokerage firms and performers are as the following: First, since the two parties to a brokerage contract are not on an equal status, the stronger party will often develop some unequal clauses; Second, when becoming famous, performers are no longer willing to accept the low proportion of commissions agreed in the original brokerage contract and want to start all over again; Third, some performers failing to become well-known are dissatisfied with their brokerage firms for not trying hard to find performance opportunities for them; Fourth, performers and brokerage firms disagree with each other on arrangements, income distribution and loss compensations.

Currently, there are not yet any specific laws, regulations or industry standards regulating performance brokerage contracts. The nature of such contracts remains controversial. Some view them as agency appointment contracts, while others believe that they are contracts covering multiple legal relationships such as agency, brokerage, copyright and employment.

E. Arbitration on Dispute between Copyright Investment Company A and Culture Communication Company B Concerning Contract on the Right of Communication Through Information Network

1. Basic facts

In July 2013, copyright investment company A as the applicant and culture communication company B as the respondent signed an Agreement on Authorising Exclusive Right of Communication through Information Network (hereinafter referred to as the "Agreement"), in which the respondent authorised the applicant the exclusive right of full communication of a series through information network within the territory of People's Republic of China, and the parties agreed on matters such as the relevant rights and interests. Under the Agreement, the applicant shall pay RMB 120,000 per episode to the respondent as the minimum license fee, and when income is generated from the distribution of the series, the applicant shall be entitled to receive first the amount equivalent to the minimum license fee and then 30% of the total income. In 2015, a dispute arose between the parties on the share of the income from the distribution of the series, and the applicant applied to Beijing Arbitration Commission for arbitration.

2. The arbitration award

The arbitral tribunal held that after paying RMB 4.8 million as minimum license fee, the applicant obtained the right of full communication through information network concerning the series. Therefore it was not possible that the respondent entrusted the right of communication through information network concerning the series to the applicant again for the distribution of the series, and thus it was not possible that the applicant failed to complete the matter entrusted by the respondent.

As for whether the Agreement was rescinded, the respondent failed to produce any evidence that it sent to the applicant a relevant notification, and the evidence it produced could not prove that the parties had a conversation and reached an agreement on the termination of the Agreement. Therefore, the applicant shall be entitled to receive the share of income from the distribution of the series in accordance with the Agreement.

3. Observations on the dispute

Rescission of a contract, as a way of terminating the civil and commercial transactions between the parties to an agreement, is of great importance to the parties. The parties need to exercise their statutory or agreed right of contract rescission under different circumstances. In the absence of written evidence, the court or arbitral tribunal cannot determine whether an agreement has been rescinded. Therefore, both parties to an agreement should pay attention that when rescinding the agreement, they need to sign a written agreement or send a letter on the rescission to secure documentary evidence.

In addition, some cases in 2015 are still at the stage of lawsuit filing or trial and need continuous observations. They include: Beijing IQIYI Science and Technology Co., Ltd v. Dreamer Film (Tianjin) Co., Ltd concerning the dispute on the cooperation agreement over The Ghost Blows: Absolutely Fine City; Zhang Muye v. China Film Co., Ltd and Lu Chuan concerning the dispute on the copyright and infringement of The Ghost Blows: Chronicles of the Ghostly Tribe; Beijing Happy Twist Film Co., Ltd, New Classics Media Corporation, scriptwriter Peng Anyu (pen name: Peng Damo) and scriptwriter Yan Fei v. Yang Wen concerning the reputation infringement dispute on Goodbye Mr. Loser; and Wang Xiaodi (pen name: Jiu Ye Hui) v. Sohu Video concerning the copyright infringement dispute on Long Time No See.

IV. Hot Topics

A. The Film and Television Industry Becomes a Comprehensive Investment and Financing Platform

In 2015, the film and television industry was more closely connected with commercial and financial capitals. On the one hand, film and television industry has become a new platform for competition of multiple stakeholders and capitals. Funds both within and outside the industry poured into the production of films and TV programs in 2015. This was not only because the capital market was attracted by a rapid growth in box office revenues, but more importantly, the explosive growth of film and TV products in recent years can bring great profits to investors. Moreover, by attracting public attention through investment in the film and TV industry, investors can get more benefits in addition to the financial profits in the industry and meet their multiple needs of interests.

On the other hand, the influx of capitals and investors promoted the development of the industry. Driven by capital investment, the industry takes content production, industrial standards and international operations as new focal points, enables and expands the whole industry chain operations with IP as the core and makes an industrial layout. As a result, the industry will be more comprehensive and economically important.

Finally, it should be noted that the many or excessive speculations in capital operations began to trigger concerns about bubbles in the film and TV industry. Further observations and studies are needed on how to allow the film and TV industry and the commercial and financial industries to promote the healthy development of each other while they are in closer cooperation.

B. IP-based Whole Industry Chain Operations and Market Competition

IP, literally intellectual property, means in the film and television industry the original works such as online novels, games and comics. Driven by IPs, companies in the industry began to expand to the upper, middle and downstream industrial chain.

Currently, online literature at the top end of the industry chain has a scale of ten billion Yuan, the market of films and TV plays in the middle stream is growing from a hundred billion to several hundred of billion RMB, and the derivatives market in the downstream has an even larger size. The competitiveness of a company in the industry chain lies on the one hand in its control of high-quality IP resources, and on the other hand in its extension to the downstream industry chain. A company will have a log of advantages if it extends to the upper, middle and downstream industry chain and continuously develops contents based on high-quality IPs. [35]

Currently, the competition in the market of IP-based films and series mainly focuses on IP resources and profitability. Film and TV companies in China represented by Ciwen Media, Huace Film & TV, H&R Century Pictures and Enlight Media not only have strong production and marketing capabilities, but also reserve a large number of high-quality fiction resources. Take Ciwen Media as an example, it has reserved copyrights of more than 40 works, including the adaptation right of 19 original novels. The premiere of TV series The Journey of Flower adapted from a novel brought the company an income of RMB 168 million. [36]

C. Websites and TV Stations are Connected and Video Sites are to Catch up With TV Stations

As new media platforms such as video sites and IPTV become increasingly active, while the traditional TV media are seriously affected, they also take this opportunity to converge with network platforms such as video sites and develop together with them. Typical practices include: the dual-platform resource utilisation of Hunan TV and Mango TV, the in-depth cooperation between Anhui TV and Tencent Video in the investment, production, promotion and broadcast of TV series, and the broadcast of the programs of Jiangsu TV on various video sites. Thus, it is a trend in the future cooperation between websites and TV stations to break the traditional boundary between television and new media, integrate contents in different forms into a unified platform for planning, collection, production and broadcast and release them at different media platforms, so that different media may converge with and infiltrate each other in terms of organisations, processes and mechanisms and the resources integration, interactions

---

35 76hui.com, IPs Become a New Darling in Film and TV Industry and Whole Industry Chain Operations Are the Most Important: Credit Analysis on the Industry of IP-based Film and TV Play Production, http://www.minshang.org.cn/hqsy/201511/27/1286.html, accessed on 27 November 2015.

36 ibid.

and coordination among all media forms may be achieved.[37]

In addition, video sites also began to reversely transfer some contents to TV stations. For example, Youku's "Full Video Night" chose to cooperate with Anhui TV. The event was exclusively broadcast live by Youku, and a fine cut version was broadcast at Anhui TV during the Spring Festival. On 22 September 2015, iQIYI. COM launched the global exclusive premiere of The Legend of S with a paid model, and on 16 January 2016, the series was renamed "The Legend of Swordsman" and broadcast in Anhui TV.

In addition, the above mentioned overall situation of China's TV series industry in 2015 shows that the traditional TV media like TV stations are no longer the only channel for the sale of TV series. The billions of views online of TV series can create more profits for the producers. This trend of video sites catching up and surpassing TV stations is subverting the original "order" of content presentation and will change the production mode of TV series.

D. Internet + and China's Films and TV Programs[38]

The integration and collision between "Internet +" and the film industry in China promoted the horizontal integration and vertical reshaping of the industry. On the one hand, in terms of contents, the emerging forms of digital films, such as micro-films and mobile films, have generated brand new narratives and aesthetic characteristics in the Internet era, and the traditionally produced films, with the assistance of IP theme development and big data analysis, fit better the tastes of the younger audiences born in the Internet age. On the other hand, in terms of the operations of the industry, such as the integrated film marketing, "Internet +" brings comprehensive changes to the traditional film industry, such as the above mentioned film crowd-funding, online marketing and ticketing, cooperation between video sites and TV stations, extension of industry chain and cross-platform development. On 21 January 2016, Juyinghui, the first O2O sharing and trading platform in China's film industry, which is committed to providing services for all parts of the industry chain and enabling effective and optimal allocation of film resources in advance, released its 2016 annual plan and announced that its film and website and China's first film assessment centre were formally launched and put into operations.

In the future, the Internet will further change the modes of production, marketing and profit making of films in China, promote the transformation of the development of China's film industry from quantity and capital driven to quality and creativity driven, and achieve optimal allocation of film resources in China. With the Internet-thinking influencing every aspect of the film industry, the endogenous driving force with creativity at the core will be enhanced, making it possible to realise the industrial integration, long tail economy of films, development of derivative value and formation of large international entertainment media groups.

---

37 Sina Media, "Media Convergence: BRTN Creates All Media Strategic Partners Advertising Model", http://news.sina.com.cn/m/2014-12-01/161331229263.shtml, accessed on 1 December 2014.

38 Film Benchmark, "'Internet+' and Upgrading of China's Film Industry", http://www.wtoutiao.com/p/id3IQ5.html, accessed on 16 July 2015. Li Yan, "China's First Film Assessment Center Formally Launched", chinaxwcb.com, http://book.chinaxwcb.com/media/news/2016/0121/44110.html? from=message&isappinstalled=0, accessed on 21 January 2016.

E. Sino-foreign Cooperation in Films and TV Programs

As of January 2016, China has signed film co-production agreements with 13 countries including Canada, Italy, Australia, France, New Zealand, Singapore, Belgium, South Korea, Spain, the UK, India, Malta and the Netherlands. 94 Sino-foreign projects of film co-production were launched in 2015. Among them, the number of the projects of co-production with the United States, South Korea and Britain increased significantly. [39] In January 2016, China and Egypt signed the Memorandum of Understanding on Film Cooperation and negotiated on the signing of the Agreement on Cooperative Film Production between the two sides.

The cooperation between China and South Korea is the closest among the Sino-foreign cooperation in film and television. This is reflected in: the sales of copyrights of TV series between the two countries; Korean actors and actresses starring in Chinese films and TV series; excellent and dedicated production teams from South Korea participating in the production of Chinese films and TV programs; other creative staff participating in the creation of works; introduction of the mode of South Korean variety shows into China and mergers and acquisitions of South Korean producing institutions. To deepen the China-ROK cooperation in film and television, the two countries can make more in-depth communications and cooperation in cultural contents based on the intersections of their cultures.

F. VAM Agreements in the Film and TV Industry

VAM (Valuation Adjustment Mechanism) agreements in the film and TV industry are mainly in two types:

One is the performance-based VAMs. For example, the VAM agreement on the acquisition of Dongyang Flower Company by LETV specifies that Dongyang Flower Company shall make a net profit of RMB 63 million, 81 million and 103.2 million respectively in 2013, 2014 and 2015. This kind of VAM is generally with harsh conditions and has a term of three to five years. If the performance fails to meet the requirement, the acquiree will usually pay a compensatory consideration or reduce its equities or cash. For acquirers, VAM can help them keep their listing qualifications, take the high growth cultural industries as their new profit generators, or carry out capital arbitrage after improving their market capitalisations through acquisitions. For acquirees, VAM can bring them great profits within a short period. As film and TV companies are mostly with a light asset model, they have volatile performance but higher valuations in acquisitions. Therefore secondary market investors should make rational choices in investment and pay attention to risks.

The other is the viewership rate based VAMs. In this form of VAM, the parties to the agreement determine the purchase price of films or TV programs on the basis of viewership rates. If the rate reaches or exceed the agreed points, the purchase price will be increased by a certain percentage; and if the rate fails to reach the agreed points, the price will be reduced by a certain percentage. Depending on the presence or absence of the minimum purchase price,

---

39 WeChat account ctvcc01 of China Alliance of Radio, Film and Television, "2015 Film Market Reminder", accessed on 18 January 2016.

viewership rate based VAMs can be divided into guaranteed VAMs and non-guaranteed ones. A problem in the viewership rate based VAMs is: the objectivity of the rate is challenged as the rating technology is not objective and the ratings companies are in monopoly positions.

There are not yet prohibitive legal provisions on VAM agreements and the effects of the performance of such agreements need further observations.

G. Establishment or Acquisition of Performance Brokerage Firms by Film and TV Companies

Performers constitute the core strength in the development and operations of the film and TV industry. Payments to performers account for the most part of the costs afforded by film and TV companies when producing films and TV programs. Out of the considerations on reducing costs, for the purpose of developing a new generation of talented performers and in line with the strategies of extending to upper stream of the industry chain, film and TV companies have began to establish or acquire performance brokerage firms. For example, on October 22, 2015, Huayi Brothers announced the acquisition of Zhejiang Dongyang Haohan Pictures Entertainment, which was just established for one day and had the development and operations of derivatives of performers as one of its main business; On 25 January 2016, Huayi Jiaxin announced its subscription of 12.62% of the shares of SIGNAL Entertainment Group, a South Korean company, and became the Group's largest sole shareholder. The Group is a representative integrated entertainment business in South Korea mainly engaged in performers brokerage and management, singers (K-pop) brokerage and management, production of variety shows and production of films and TV series.

In 2015, M&As for listing and cross-border M&As continued in the film and TV industry in China; many stars became shareholders of listed companies; crowdfunding began to be used for integration of promotion and marketing resources; e-commerce companies joined competitions in the film and TV industry; and the construction of film bases began to transform towards cultural properties. Currently, domestic films still have a huge room for development in overseas sales.

V. Summary and Outlook

A. Rulings and Penalties in the Film and TV Industry

The disputes in the film and TV industry are mainly copyright disputes and other contract disputes relating to such industries. The specific data on the disputes have not been released by authoritative institutions.

B. Disputes between Broadcasters and Producers

Given the high input costs, long payback period and cash flow constraints in the TV series industry, the disputes between TV stations and producers began to appear. There are two main types of disputes:

One is the contract disputes or debt disputes arising from the delay of payment by TV stations to producers. The cause of such disputes is that the funds of TV stations to purchase television dramas mainly come from the TV advertising revenue, but due to the economic downturn in 2015, the advertising revenue of TV stations fell sharply. Data show that in 2015, the total volume of TV advertising decreased for the first time. The TV advertising rate in the first quarter fell 5.5% over the same period in the previous year, and the number of brands with advertising costs of over RMB 5 million fell to the level five years ago.[40] For the first three quarters of 2015, the Chinese advertising market shrank by 3.5% year on year. In particular, the traditional advertising market including TV advertising shrank by a staggering 7.3%.[41] Affected by this, TV stations became less capable of paying the programs purchase prices, resulting in a large number of delayed payments. It is reported that some TV stations have delayed the payment of hundreds of millions of RMB of programs purchase price.

The other is the infringement disputes arising from the failure of TV stations to broadcast TV series according to agreements. When TV stations cut off the starting and ending parts of programs instead of fully broadcasting them as they are delivered by the producers according to programs purchase agreements, the authorship of some main creators of the programs will be infringed as a result and thus disputes will be caused between the producers and creators. TV stations do that because they want to save time to broadcast ads and increase income.

A small part of the above mentioned disputes are settled through legal channels such as litigation and arbitration, but most of them are still hidden or solved through non-litigation channels.

C. Lack of Standards in the Film and TV Industry

Industry standards are of great importance for the development of an industry. They regulate the development of the industry by clarifying the direction of development, promoting technological progress, facilitating the formation of the core competitiveness of the industry, and becoming the basis of technology, management, work and procedures to be adhered to by the whole industry. They play the role of maintaining the quality of the products in the industry, increasing the credibility of the market, promoting the circulation of commodities and ensuring fair competitions.

Although China's film and TV industry is developing fast, there are still no standards specifically applying to the industry. From a macro perspective, the lack of standards is not conducive to the maturity and progress of the industry as a whole, and from a micro perspective, the disputes between producers and scriptwriters and among producers on the preparation of scripts, special effects, texts and sounds and on the production quality are exactly because there is no industry standard for determining whether the quality of preparation or production meets requirements and standards. And once any dispute occurs, the discretion of the court instead of the judgment of a professional authentication institution is often relied on for its resolution. Such discretion sometimes causes losses of varying degrees to both parties of the litigation as it is not in line with the characteristics of the industry.

---

40 Website of China Advertising Association, "TV Media Market in 2015 and Future Trends", http://www.cnadtop.com/focusNews/2015/11/19/a632fe85-cdaa-41b4-ac61-3952a3e70ee5.htm, accessed on 19 November 2015.

41 evaad.com: "-3.5% for First Three Quarters 2015: Things Go Wrong in China's Advertising Market!", http://news.evaad.com/2015/11/20/6e5b9b81db68ebb5.shtml, accessed on 20 November 2015.

D. The Ways of Dispute Resolution Should be Consistent With the Characteristics of the Film and TV Industry and Follow the Legal Principle of Matching Rights With Responsibilities

Take the TV series Palace 3 the Lost Daughter as an example, in addition to the questions on the standard and legal identification of plagiarism and infringement of film and TV scripts, the infringement and law violation of some creators in the film industry chain and the share of legal liabilities (among investors and producers) in the whole films or TV dramas attracted more attention.

Therefore the industry needs judicial decisions to fit the transaction practices in the industry, respect the characteristics of the industry, distinguish the legal responsibilities of different industry players and not easily impose joint and several liabilities.

In the book publishing industry, in which copyright is also taken as the core competitiveness, after years of trial practice in *Copyright Law*, judicial interpretations and judicial precedents have made legal treatments that both comply with the law and respect the characteristics of the industry, requiring different industry players to bear different legal consequences according to their respective liabilities for infringement and imposing joint and several liabilities in a prudent and restrictive way:

First, book sellers will not bear the liability of compensation for copyright infringement if they can prove that they purchase the books from legitimate sources.

Second, book publishers will not bear the liability of compensation for copyright infringement if they can prove that they have fulfilled their obligations of reasonable care.

Third, generally it will not be ruled to stop publication and distribution if the contents involved in infringement are small in quantity and the circumstances are minor.

Fourth, judicial activities will be carried out to promote settlement between the parties and transform the confrontation into authorisation and cooperation.

These dispute resolutions adapted to the trading habits and characteristics of an industry can be extended to the trials in film and TV industry.

E. Share of Liabilities Arising From the Suspension of Broadcast Caused by the Violations of Main Creators of Film or TV Works Against Laws or Disciplines and the Insurance Mechanism in the Film and TV Industry

In recent years, some practitioners in radio, film and TV such as scriptwriters, directors and performers receive administrative and criminal punishments for drug abuse, prostitution and other illegal activities. In response, SARFT required suspending the broadcast of the films, TV series, web series, micro-films and various radio and TV programs that involve those with illegal activities in their production as well as the advertising programs endorsed by them. This affects the investors and producers in the film and TV industry as the film and TV works painstakingly produced by them cannot be distributed, which makes it hard to make profits and even impossible to cover the costs.

Currently, investors and producers prevent this kind of incidents mainly by adding in agreements the clauses on compensations for the losses caused by the violations by main creators against laws or disciplines or by signing industry self-regulation conventions. But it is hard to achieve the goal. Even if the clauses on compensation are performed, the amount of the compensation cannot cover the actual losses occurred to the investors and producers. Thus, the occurrence of such incidents will promote two solutions: First, separate the violations by the creators of film and TV works against laws and disciplines from the works. Otherwise it will be a breach of the principle of matching legal rights with responsibilities. Second, introduce an insurance system to protect the rights and interests of the investors, producers and performers. Investors, producers, performers and trade associations can all buy the insurance as insurers. In the event of serious incidents affecting the release of a film or TV program, such as the main creators receiving administrative or criminal punishments due to violations against laws or regulations, insurance companies can assume the insurance liability within the insurance coverage and thus reduce the loss of all parties to some extent. The industry is considering the introduction of the insurance system which has long been used in Hollywood film industry to reduce the risk of damages. The insurance covers the delays caused by performers' injuries or inability to perform, poor weather, equipment damage, film damage and other factors.

F. The Trade Associations in Film Industry to Play a Management Role

Trade associations as social intermediary organisations between companies and the market and between companies and the government are responsible for self-regulation of the industry. With the development of the film and TV industry, there have been over 30 voluntarily established trade associations governed by the SARFT, the local Civil Affairs Bureaus and China Association for Science and Technology in the industry, including China Alliance of Radio, Film and Television, China Film Distribution and Exhibition Association, China Film Producers Association, Capital Radio & TV Program Producers Association, China Society of Motion Pictures and Television Engineers, and China Science Film and Video Association. These associations represent the common interests of all their members and provide services for their members in communication, coordination, supervision and rights protection. They also bear the responsibilities for rule-making, managing and regulating of the order of the industry.

G. Numbers of Institutions and Individuals Specialised in the Legal Affairs Related to the Film and TV Industry are Increasing

With the development of the film and TV industry, the institutions and individuals providing legal services for the industry increase. They include internal corporate legal staff and external lawyers.

Overall in 2015, China's film and TV industry had a remarkable performance in the spotlight. As the methods of financial capital operations are gradually used in the film and TV industry and the Internet brings new models of cooperation and partners, the film and TV industry is going through a process of optimal allocation of resources as well as the establishment, revision and improvements of industry rules to adapt to the market. The emergence of a lot of disputes is not only an embodiment of that process, but also help to the industry in detecting problems and finding effective solutions to them. Film and TV industry, as one of the most comprehensive and complex industries in the society, will see more diverse disputes in the future.

Annual Review on General Aviation Dispute Resolution in China (2016)

DONG Nianqing [1] *ZHANG Qihuai* [2]

I. Introduction

2015 was an unusual year for general aviation. In this year remarkable achievements were made in aircraft manufacturing. Unmanned aerial vehicles (UAV) as a dark horse stood out in the field of general aviation. Many domestic and foreign investors were optimistic about the UAV industry and invested in UAV manufacturers. The civilian UAVs produced by the manufacturers in China accounted for seventy percent of the global total production. Cases on UAV disputes sharply increased and became a new type of cases for courts and arbitration institutions. The safe operations and regulation of UAVs is not only a hot topic in the industry, but also a concern of the whole society and the world. Although China did not issue laws and regulations with significant impacts on the industry, the policies and regulatory documents that were developed in the year still brought great confidence.

A. Great Achievements Were Made in Aircraft Manufacturing

In 2015, China's civil aircraft manufacturing industry saw a fruitful year with great results: On 2 November 2015, the large passenger aircraft C919, which was independently developed by China, rolled off final assembly line in Shanghai at Commercial Aircraft Corporation of China Ltd (COMAC), marking a new era of China's manufacture of large aircraft; and on 29 November 2015, the first domestically produced regional jet ARJ21 was successfully delivered to the launch customer Chengdu Airlines Co., Ltd (Chengdu Airlines).

1. China-made large passenger aircraft C919 rolled off the assembly line

On 2 November 2015, C919, the first large passenger aircraft independently developed by China, rolled off the assembly line in the new plant of Pudong Base of COMAC's Final Assembly & Manufacturing Center in Shanghai after 7 years of design and development. C919 large passenger aircraft is China's first trunk civilian aircraft developed in accordance with the latest international airworthiness standards. Its development began in 2008. It has 158 seats for

---

1 DONG Nianqing is Professor of Law and Director of Research Center for Aviation Law at Civil Aviation Management Institute of China.

2 ZHANG Qihuai is Founder and Managing Partner of Lanpeng Law Firm.

basic mixed-class layout, 168 for all-economic class layout and 174 for high-density layout, with a standard range of 4,075 km and an extended range of 5,555 km. This not only marks the completion of the assembly of major components and the installation of airborne systems of the first C919 aircraft, which is ready for ground tests, but also marks the achievement of the R&D of the C919 large aircraft project and lays a solid foundation for the aircraft's maiden flight in the next step. The new technology, materials and processes adopted in the large passenger aircraft C919 have a radioactive effect and play an important role in driving the economic and technological development, the progress in basic disciplines and the development of the aviation industry in China. The C919 aircraft has far-reaching significance for the development of China's civil aircraft industry, improvement of basic industrial strength and development to a manufacturing power. Building on the C919 large passenger aircraft, there will also be a series of products including the lengthened, shortened, extended-range cargo type and business type aircraft. [3]

2. China-made ARJ21 aircraft received three certificates

On 30 December 2014, the Civil Aviation Administration of China (CAAC) issued to COMAC in Beijing the certificate of up-to-standard model for ARJ21-700 aircraft. This symbolizes that China's first regional jet received the up-to-standard model certification from the CAAC and that the design of the aircraft meets the basic requirements to ensure safety. On 29 November 2015, CAAC and other relevant authorities issued to Chengdu Airlines the nationality registration certificate, airworthiness certificate and radio station license for ARJ21-700, which is the first new regional jet designed by COMAC in accordance with the internationally applied *Airworthiness Standards: Transport Category Airplanes* (CCAR-25) and produced with independent intellectual property rights. The ARJ21-700 indicates that for the first time there will be a domestically produced regional jet in the domestic flight routes and that China has completed the whole process of the design, prototype, test, trial flight, certification, production and delivery of regional jets and has acquired the ability to develop regional jets and have them receive airworthiness certification. The delivery of the first ARJ21-700 aircraft for commercial use is an important milestone in the process of building China into a civil aviation power and the development of China's high-end manufacturing industries. [4] The issuance of the three certificates means that the ARJ21-700 aircraft can be put into normal commercial operations [5].

3. The meteoric rise of UAV production

Currently, China has become a major developer and producer of civil UAVs in the world. Incomplete statistics show that there are over 400 organizations in China engaged in the R&D, production and sales of UAVs. China has led the world in civil UAVs, especially consumer

---

3 China-made Large Aircraft C919 Rolls off Final Assembly Line in Shanghai" http://news.xinhuanet.com/local/2015-11/02/c_128384700_7.htm), accessed on 20 January 2016.

4 CAAC Issues Three Certificates to First ARJ21 Delivered" http://www.caac.gov.cn/A1/201512/t20151201_83464.html), accessed on 20 January 2016.

5 Paragraph 1, Article 37 of the Civil Aviation Law of the People's Republic of China provides that "A civil aircraft with the nationality of the People's Republic of China shall not fly unless it holds the airworthiness certificate issued by the civil aviation authority under the State Council".

UAVs. China produces seventy percent of the civil UAVs in the world. The data from Shenzhen Customs show that in the first eight months of 2015, the exports of UAVs in Shenzhen valued at RMB 1.57 billion, a 23.1-fold upsurge over the same period last year. They are mainly exported to the markets of China's Hong Kong, the United States and the EU. In the *Shenzhen Aerospace Industry Development Plan* (2013- 2020), the city explicitly gives priority to the development of UAVs, proposes the "UAV Takeoff Project", focuses on supporting UAV industry bases and encourages enterprises to actively explore the domestic and international markets. [6]

In addition, in terms of the manufacturing of general aircraft, domestic manufacturers keep releasing new models and products independently or in cooperation with foreign producers. For example, on 6 February 2015, Rui Xiang RX1E electrically-powered two-seater light aircraft, as China's first manned electric aircraft with independent intellectual property rights, received the up-to-standard model certification by CAAC and will enter the stage of mass production. [7] On 18 October 2015, Tecnam an Italian general aviation manufacturer announced its exclusive agreement with Liaoning United-Air Shenyan Aircraft Company, under which it authorized Liaoning United-Air Shenyan Aircraft Company to produce in China three Tecnam aircraft models. [8] On 28 November 2015, two light sport aircraft assembled by Liaoning Shanhe Navigable Services Limited officially rolled off line in Jilin City, Jilin Province. The brand of these light sport aircraft, Aurora, is the first national brand in Chinese Mainland that received an airworthiness certificate for light sport aircraft from CAAC. [9]

B. General Aviation Fleet and Enterprises Continued to Grow

In 2015, the numbers of general aviation aircraft and companies kept growing. In terms of general aviation fleet, by the end of 2013, China had had a total of 1,654 registered aircraft in the general aviation fleet. By the end of 2014, the total number had been 1,952, representing an increase of 298 or 18% over 2013. By the end of 2015, the figure had been 2,127, an increase of 175 or 8.9% over 2014. In terms of general aviation enterprises, as of the end of 2013, there were 208 general aviation enterprises actually owning aircraft. As of the end of 2014, that number was 257, an increase of 49 or 24% over 2013. As of the end of 2015, the number was 298, an increase of 41 or 16% over 2014. [10]

---

6 Xiong Li, "Seventy Percent of Global Civil UAVs Are Made in China", Economic Daily, 7 January 2016.

7 "China's First Manned Electric Aircraft Receives Up-to-Standard Model Certification", 7 February 2015, see the website of Xinhua News Agency (http://news.xinhuanet.com/politics/2015-02/07/c_127468497.htm), accessed on 22 January 2016.

8 "United-Air Shenyan Authorized to Produce Airplanes of Tecnam Models in China", 18 October 2015, see Civil Aviation Resource Net (http://news.carnoc.com/list/326/326511.html), accessed on 22 January 2016.

9 "Two Light aircraft of Jilin Shanhe Navigable Services Rolled off Line in Jilin Economic Development Zone", 28 November 2015, see the website of Xinhua News Agency (http://www.jl.xinhuanet.com/2013jizhe/2015-11/28/c_1117291202.htm), accessed on 22 January 2016.

10 Source: "2015 Year-end Review of General Aviation", see General Aviation Resource Net (http://www.garnoc.com/2015tonghang/pc/), accessed on 20 January 2016.

Table:2013–2015 Changes in General Aviation Fleet and Enterprises

	Total number of registered GA aircraft	Year–on–year increase	GA enterprises actually owning aircraft	Year–on–year increase
end of 2013	1654		208	
end of 2014	1952	18%	257	24%
end of 2015	2127	8.9%	298	16%

II. New Laws, Regulations or Other Regulatory Documents

In 2015, the laws and regulations on general aviation were not issued as expected by the industry and the society. But this did not mean that there was nothing worth mentioning in this aspect. The fact is, general aviation appeared for the first time in the document of CPC Central Committee and the construction of a general aviation infrastructure network was lifted to an unprecedented height. Similarly, the documents of the State Council further proposed the industrialization of general aircraft. In addition, CAAC issued the *Interim Measures for Administration on Operations of General Aviation Charter Flights (Short Distance Transport)*. In response to the rapid development of UAVs, a rule on UAV operations and a standard on UAV industry were issued. They will play an important role in regulating the safe operations and production quality of UAVs.

A. *CPC Central Committee's Proposal for Formulating the 13th Five–Year Plan for Economic and Social Development*[11]

In Part 3 of the *CPC Central Committee's Proposal for Formulating the 13th Five–Year Plan for Economic and Social Development* (hereinafter referred to as the "*Proposal*"), "Adhere to Innovative Development and Focus on Improving the Quality and Benefit of Development", it was proposed to "expand the space for infrastructure construction. Implement major public facilities and infrastructure projects; implement the Internet power strategy and accelerate the construction of the next–generation information infrastructure with high speed, mobility, security, ubiquitousness; accelerate the improvement of infrastructure networks of water conservancy, railways, highways, waterways, civil aviation, general aviation, pipelines, postal facilities, etc." The lack of infrastructure is one of the bottlenecks faced by the development of general aviation. The *Proposal*'s focus on this outstanding issue and obvious weakness and explicit proposal to speed up the improvement of the network of general aviation infrastructure are of great significance for the development of general aviation. More importantly, the *Proposal* lifted general aviation to an unprecedented height by separating it from civil aviation and listed it in parallel with railways, highways, waterways and civil aviation. This sufficiently reflected the importance of general aviation to the promotion of economic development. It is foreseeable that during the 13th Five–year Plan period there will be a great progress in the con-

11 Adopted on 29 October 2015 at the Fifth Plenary Session of the Eighteenth CPC Central Committee and published on 3 November 2015, see people.cn (http://politics.people.com.cn/n/2015/1103/c1001-27772701-3.html), accessed on 10 January 2016.

struction of general aviation infrastructure such as general aviation airports, flight service stations and aviation gasoline supplies.

B. *Made in China* 2025 [12]

On 8 May 2015, the State Council issued the *Made in China* 2025, which is the first 10-year action plan for China's implementation of its manufacturing power strategy. In the third part of the document "Strategic Tasks and Priorities, "aviation equipment" was taken as a key area for breakthrough development: "Aviation equipment; speed up the development of large aircraft, start the development of wide-body passenger aircraft at an appropriate time, encourage international cooperation in the development of heavy helicopters; and promote the industrialization of trunk and regional aircraft, helicopters, unmanned aerial vehicles and general aircraft; make breakthroughs in the technology of engines with high thrust-weight ratio and advanced turboprop (shaft) and turbofan engines with high bypass ratio, and establish an industrial system for independent development of engines; develop advanced airborne equipment and systems and form a complete independent aviation industry chain." For general aviation, the "industrialization" and "industry chain" proposed in *Made in China* 2025 pointed out the direction and objectives of the development of general aviation and the entire aviation industry. If the Proposal was to address the lack of infrastructure for the development of general aviation, the *Made in China* 2025 was to address another element for the development - the manufacturing of general aircraft. China has laid some basis for the manufacturing of general aircraft, but there is still considerable room for development in aspects such as production scale, technical capabilities and quality. *Made in China* 2025 proposed "industrialization of general aircraft", which aims at forming a complete industry with the R&D, manufacturing, and maintenance of general aircraft, achieving the transformation from quantitative integration to qualitative upheaval, and truly making general aviation an important part of national economy. The manufacturing of general aircraft and the development of general aviation are both part of the aviation industry. In addition, to "form a complete independent aviation industry chain" was a higher requirement for the aviation manufacturing industry.

C. *Interim Measures for Administration on Operations of General Aviation Charter Flights (Short Distance Transport)* [13]

General aviation charter flights refer to the irregular services of passenger and cargo transport that general aviation enterprises provide for users by using civil aircraft with less than 30 seats (excluding primary category aircraft) according to the times, origins and destinations specified in the contracts signed with users. In such service, no ticket is available to the general public, no flight schedule is published in advance, and flight frequency is to be decided on the basis of needs. The *Interim Measures for Administration on Operations of General Aviation Charter Flights (Short Distance Transport)* provides a rule for general aviation charter flights to follow, especially the short-distance charter transportation of less than 500 km. It is a posi-

12 No. 28 document of State Council, 2015

13 Issued by CAAC on 28 September 2015 and implemented on trial basis on 1 December 2015.

tive exploration and will promote the normalization of short-distance transport.

D. *Provisions on the Operations of Light and Small Unmanned Aircraft (Trial)* [14]

This is the first regulatory document on the operations of UAVs issued in China. In recent years, the production and application of civil UAVs are flourishing at home and abroad. In particular, the number of low-altitude, low-speed, micro, light and small UAVs is increasing rapidly and accounts for the most of civil UAVs. In order to regulate the operation of such civil UAVs, CAAC Department of Flight Standard issued the *Provisions on the Operations of Light and Small Unmanned Aircraft* (Trial) in accordance with CCAR-91 (hereinafter referred to as the "*Provisions*"). The *Provisions* applies to the following three types of UAVs: those that are available for visual line of sight (VLOS) operations or beyond VLOS operations and are with an empty weight of not more than 116 kg and a takeoff gross weight of not more than 150 kg; those for plantation protection that are with a calibrated air speed of not more than 100 km/h, a take off gross weight of not more than 5,700 kg and a flight height of not more than 15 m above the spray surface; and unmanned airships with an inflated volume of 4,600 m^3. The *Provisions* specifies the responsibilities and rights of the captains of civil UAVs and makes detailed provisions in 14 aspects, including the requirements to be met for qualifying as civil UAV pilots.

E. *General Technical Standard on Civil Unmanned Aircraft Systems* [15]

The *General Technical Standard on Civil Unmanned Aircraft Systems* (hereinafter referred to as the "*Standard*") was jointly drafted and developed by "Civil UAS common technical standards" by China (Shenzhen) UAV Industry Alliance together with Northwestern Polytechnical University and UAV manufacturers such as Seahawks Aviation General Equipment Co., Ltd and Shenzhen Dajiang Innovation Technology Co., Ltd. The *Standard* covers seven parts: scope of application; classification and codes; composition and main technical parameters; test methods; inspection rules; and packaging, transport and storage. The establishment and implementation of the *Standard* marks the end of the history when there was no industry standard for the civil UAV industry in China for a long period of time. The issuance of the *Standard* fills the gaps in the field of UAV in China. It is of extensive and far-reaching significance for both promoting the progress and development of the UAV industry and expanding the applications of unmanned aircraft systems.

III. Major Cases

Compared with previous years, disputes on UAV sales and purchase contracts account for a larger proportion. Among them the disputes caused by ambiguousness or no agreement on quality are the most prominent, reflecting the rapid development of the industry and the lack of

---

14 Issued by CAAC Department of Flight Standard on 29 December 2015 and effective as of the date of issuance.

15 Issued on 17 June 2015 by China (Shenzhen) UAV Industry Alliance.

relevant laws, regulations and industry standards. Meanwhile, in terms of general aviation, outstanding issues include the lawsuits between the seller and the buyer in the sales and purchase of general aircraft for the inability to achieve the purpose of the contract due to the failure to obtain the airworthiness certificate, and the disputes between the parties involved in the operations and services of general aviation caused as one of the parties does not have the legal business qualification. These disputes show strong characteristics of the industry. Even though an aircraft sales and purchase contract complies with the contract law and other basic legal provisions, if the requirements in the laws, regulations and rules on general aviation are not met, it is still possible that the purpose of the contract cannot be achieved and the transaction cannot be smoothly carried out. Therefore, before signing a contract, the parties to the transaction need to pay more attention to the legal provisions in the field of general aviation, so as to facilitate the transaction and reduce disputes.

A. On Quality Standards for UAV Products

Zhuhai Poly Technology Co., Ltd (plaintiff and appellant) v. Zhuhai Special Economic Zone Green R/C Model Airplanes Co., Ltd (defendant and appellee) on UAV sales and purchase dispute[16]

[**Basic facts**]

On 5 December 2012, the plaintiff and the defendant signed an Equipment Purchase Contract, under which: the plaintiff shall buy from the defendant a first-generation unmanned MAV Tianyan-X4 at the price of RMB 220,000; the plaintiff shall pay the defendant RMB 100,000 after the acceptance of goods and the normal installation, commissioning and operation of the equipment; the place of delivery shall be in the location of the plaintiff and the time of delivery shall be before 8 December 2012; and the defendant shall be responsible for training personnel for operations and maintenance free of charge, with the contents of the training covering the basic principles, operations and maintenance of the aircraft. The defendant promised to replace the first-generation aircraft with a second-generation one within 2 months from the date of delivery, and the plaintiff shall pay the remaining amount upon the replacement. In the event of the failure of the defendant to deliver the aircraft on schedule, unless the failure was caused by force majeure, the defendant shall pay the plaintiff a breach penalty for the delay in delivery, which shall be 0.3% of the contract price per day. On the next day of the signing of the contract, the defendant delivered to the plaintiff an unmanned MAV Tianyan-X4, and the plaintiff made a payment of RMB 100,000 to the defendant on 7 December 2012. On 1 March and 20 March 2013, the plaintiff believed that the purchased MAV Tianyan-X4 had problems during use, and requested the defendant to provide solutions. The defendant made a written reply in response to the issues raised by the plaintiff. The plaintiff required the defendant to continue the performance of the contract through Express Mail Service (EMS) on 15 April 2013, and required through EMS to rescind the contract and pursue the breach liabilities on 15 May 2013. On 8 July 2013, the plaintiff filed a lawsuit, claiming rescission of the contract. As of the date on which the lawsuit was filed, the defendant failed to deliver the second-generation

---

16 See Civil Judgment (2013) Zhu Xiang Fa Min Er Chu Zi No. 1281 of the Poeple's Court of Xiangzhou District, Zhuhai City, Guangdong Province.

MAV Tianyan-X4 to the plaintiff. The plaintiff requested the court to order that: (1) the Equipment Purchase Contract should be rescinded, with the defendant repaying the purchase price of RMB 100,000; (2) the defendant should pay to the plaintiff a breach penalty of RMB 99,000 (counted from 8 February 2013 to the effective date of the judgment); and (3) the defendant should pay all the costs of litigation. The defendant did not agree to rescind the contract but agreed to deliver the second-generation MAV Tianyan-X4 to the plaintiff.

[**Opinions of the court**]

The original court held that the focus of the dispute was whether the defendant constituted a fundamental breach of contract. According to the plaintiff: the first-generation MAV Tianyan-4X delivered by the defendant had quality problems, and the defendant failed to replace the first-generation aircraft with a second-generation one within the agreed time limit, thus leading to the failure to achieve the purpose of the contract. Therefore the defendant constituted a fundamental breach of contract. Based on the facts found, the court held that the parties had no agreement on the quality of the MAV Tianyan-X4, and that the defendant did not acknowledge the quality problems of the aircraft listed by the plaintiff and made a reasonable explanation on such problems stated by the plaintiff. As for the failure of the replacement for a second-generation aircraft, the delivery was delayed because the parties had been negotiating on the matters of their cooperation, which was proved by the correspondence provided by the defendant. Therefore, the court held that the claim of the plaintiff that the defendant constituted a fundamental breach of contract could not be established, and that the requests of the plaintiff for rescission of the contract, repayment of purchase price and payment of breach penalty had no legal and factual basis and therefore the court would not support such requests.

The plaintiff refused to accept the court decision and made an appeal on the grounds of unclear fact finding and erroneous application of law by the original courts. The second instance court[17] held that: The appellant argued that the first-generation aircraft did not meet quality standards, but did not provide evidence on the specific quality requirements on the aircraft. The handwritten contents of the appellee in the "Solution" column of the "Existing Problems in Tianyan-X4 (first-generation) Aircraft" were only a plan for the parties to solve problems through negotiation and did not contain any expression that the appellee admitted the existence of quality problems in the first-generation aircraft. Therefore, the claim of the appellant that the first-generation aircraft failed to meet quality requirements could not be established. According to Paragraph 2 of Article 5 of the Equipment Purchase Contract between the two parties, the appellee shall replace the first-generation aircraft with a second-generation one within 2 months after the delivery (i. e. before 7 February 2013), otherwise the appellee shall pay a breach penalty at 0.3% of the contract price per day. This showed that the replacement with a second-generation aircraft was a contractual obligation of the appellee, and as the appellee did not fulfill this obligation, the appellant was entitled to rescind the contract in accordance with law. The Appellee stated that the failure of the replacement was because of the negotiations of the two parties but did not provide evidence on that statement, and the appellant did not recognize it. Therefore this statement of the appellee could not be an established defense. Given the EMS detail lists provided by the appellant and the context of the "Demand Letter for Contract

17 See Civil Judgment (2014) Zhu Zhong Fa Min Er Zhong Zi No. 32 of the Intermediate People's Court of Zhuhai City, Guangdong Province.

Performance", the contract was rescinded 15 days after 16 April 2013 when the appellee received the Demand Letter. Thus, the court of second instance confirmed that the sale and purchase contract concerned in the case was rescinded on 1 May 2013.

The court of second instance decided on 6 May 2014 that: (1) the civil judgment of the original court shall be revoked; (2) the Equipment Purchase Contract between the two parties shall be rescinded on 1 May 2013; (3) the appellee shall pay the appellant a breach penalty (counted at 0.3% of RMB 220,000 as the base per day from 8 February 2013 to 1 May 2013); and (4) the appellant's claim for the repayment of RMB 100,000 of purchase price from the appellee shall be rejected.

[**Observations on the dispute**]

The case reflects common concerns of the entire UAV industry, in particular the quality standards of UAVs and their components. According to the *Contract Law of the People's Republic of China* (hereinafter referred to as the "*Contract Law*"), where the parties have no clear agreement on quality in their contract and cannot clarify it in accordance with the provisions in Article 61 of the *Contract Law*, the contract shall be performed in accordance with national or industry standards; and where there is no national or industry standard, the contract shall be performed in accordance with the generally held standards or specific standards in line with the purpose of performing the contract. In the UAV industry, both national and industry standards are in absence. During the second instance of the case, the appellee claimed in its defense that "UAVs are new industrial products and there is no standard on them. The products of Green R/C Model Airplanes Co., Ltd have no quality problem." This typically illustrates the status quo of the UAV industry with no standards. As mentioned above, some research institutions and UAV manufacturers in China jointly developed the *General Technical Standard on Civil Unmanned Aircraft Systems*, but this standard alone cannot yet covers all aspects of UAV production. As for the "generally held standards" and "specific standards" under the *Contract Law*, the contracting parties need to clearly agree on them in their contracts, otherwise, disputes are inevitable. The present case is a typical example. In short, in the contracts on the sales and purchase of UAVs and their components, the lack of quality standards is a prominent issue, which also affects the acceptance and delivery. In the absence of national and industry standards, refining and improving the terms and conditions of the contract is an effective way to avoid disputes.

B. Inability to Achieve the Purpose of Contract due to Absence of Airworthiness Certificate for General Aircraft

Pang Wenku (plaintiff) v. Guangzhou Sino-German Light Aircraft (SGLA, defendant) on light sport aircraft sale and purchase dispute[18]

[**Basic facts**]

Under the Contract on Sale of Light Sport Aircraft between the plaintiff and the defendant: Pang Wenku shall buy a light sport aircraft sold by SGLA as an agent; the subject matter shall be a CAVALON airplane manufactured by AUTOGYRO, a German company, at the total

18 See Civil Judgment (2015) Yue Gao Fa Min Er Shen Zi No. 504 of the Higher People's Court of Guangdong Province.

price of RMB 1.3 million; SGLA shall ensure the quality, design and necessary equipment accessories of its airplane products; and SGLA shall provide for Pang Wenku a general light sport aircraft meeting the airworthiness requirements and relevant technical advices.

[**Opinions of the court**]

The Higher People's Court of Guangdong Province held that: the airworthiness requirements agreed in the contract shall be construed as being eligible to apply for airworthiness certificate in China. However, the basic facts of the case showed that the aircraft concerned in the dispute was not qualified for the procedures of applying for airworthiness in China, could not receive an airworthiness certificate in China and thus could not legally fly in China. Therefore, as SGLA violated the contract by providing for Pang Wenku a light sport aircraft that did not meet the airworthiness requirements, leading to the inability of Pang Wenku to achieve the purpose of the contract, Pang Wenku shall have the right to request rescission of the contract. After the rescission of the contract, Pang Wenku shall have the right to request for restitution, adoption of other remedies and compensations concerning the part that had been performed according to the performance and the nature of the contract. Therefore Pang Wenku's claims for rescission of the Contract on Sale of Light Sport Aircraft with SGLA and for the repayment of the purchase price of RMB 1.3 million for the CAVALON light sport aircraft and the relevant interest by SGLA to Pang Wenku were reasonable and lawful, and were supported in the second instance judgment. The fact finding was clear, the application of law was correct and there was no improper handling. The Higher People's Court of Guangdong Province made a civil judgment on 15 June 2015, rejecting the application of SGLA for retrial.

[**Observations on the dispute**]

According to the *Civil Aviation Law of the People's Republic of China* and the *Regulations of the People's Republic of China for the Administration of the Airworthiness of Civil Aircraft*[19], "Civil aircraft may engage in flight operations only when they have possessed an Airworthiness Certificate issued by the CAAC. The Airworthiness Certificate issued by the CAAC shall specify the type(s) of activities the aircraft is (are) suitable for, the period of validity of the Certificate, and other conditions and restrictions required for ensuring safety"[20]. It is also required to obtain the certificate of up-to-standard model, manufacturing permit and nationality registration certificate before applying for the airworthiness certificate[21]. Where a civil aircraft of any model and its engines, propellers and on-board equipment produced by a foreign manufacturer are imported into China for the first time, such foreign manufacturer shall file an application with the competent civil aviation authority under the State Council for Validation of Type Certificate. A Validation of Type Certificate shall be issued if the aircraft is found qualified through examination"[22]. Detailed provisions on the specific procedures for ap-

---

19 Issued by the State Council on 4 May 1987 and implemented on 1 June 1987.

20 See Article 37 of the Civil Aviation Law of the People's Republic of China and Article 9 of the Regulations of the People's Republic of China for the Administration of the Airworthiness of Civil Aircraft.

21 See Articles 6, 34 and 35 of the Civil Aviation Law of the People's Republic of China and Articles 6 and 7 of the Regulations of the People's Republic of China for the Administration of the Airworthiness of Civil Aircraft.

22 See Article 36 of the Civil Aviation Law of the People's Republic of China and Article 12 of the Regulations of the People's Republic of China for the Administration of the Airworthiness of Civil Aircraft.

plication are contained in the *Validation Procedures for Imported Civil Aviation Products and Parts*[23] and the *Procedures for Model and Design Approval of Light Sport Aircraft*[24].

The light sport aircraft bought by Pang Wenku was imported from Germany and had to obtain an airworthiness certificate before flight. To obtain an airworthiness certificate, an application should be made for Validation of Type Certificate and nationality registration certificate, because "Civil aircraft that are to fly within the People's Republic of China must possess Nationality Registration Certificates. Civil aircraft that have been registered in the People's Republic of China shall bear the nationality of the People's Republic of China and shall be issued Nationality Registration Certificate by the CAAC"[25]. According to the cited legal provisions, the certificate of up-to-standard model and airworthiness certificate shall be applied for by the manufacturer of the aircraft. Failure to obtain an airworthiness certificate means inability to fly. This was the situation facing Pang Wenku in the present case. Thus, in the sale and purchase of aircraft, obtaining airworthiness certificates is of vital importance and must be explicitly specified in the contract. The sale and purchase of an aircraft are different from the sale and purchase of general commodities. Many people take it for granted that all they have to do is to buy the aircraft, but they do not know that the purpose of purchasing the aircraft will not be achieved if the airworthiness certificate cannot be obtained.

C. Impact of no Qualification for General Aviation Business on the Effectiveness of Contracts

Suzhou Gusu International Travel Service Co., Ltd (plaintiff, appellant) v. Suzhou Ruohang Transportation Development Co., Ltd (defendant, appellee) on aerial sightseeing service dispute[26]

[**Basic facts**]

The plaintiff (Party B) and the defendant (Party A) signed an Exclusive Agency Agreement on 24 September 2014, under which Party A shall authorize Party B as the exclusive agent of Party A's products and projects in Chinese Mainland (including the aerial tour of modern Suzhou Industrial Park and the aerial tour of Suzhou cultural relics) within the period from the date of signing the agreement to 10 October 2015. The standard price for the aerial tour of modern Suzhou Industrial Park was RMB 860 / person and that for the aerial tour of Suzhou cultural relics was RMB 1,660 / person. Article 6 of the Contract specified that "Party B shall pay a total amount of RMB 2 million as annual deposit. This Contract shall enter into force af-

23 The document was issued by the Aircraft Airworthiness Certification Department of the former General Administration of Civil Aviation of China (CAAC now) and was effective on 1 January 2000, with file No. AP-21-01R1. For the contents of the document see the official website of the CAAC (http://www.caac.gov.cn/E1/E2/SHSDL/200707/P020070720349086269267.pdf), accessed on 22 January 2016.

24 The document was issued on 6 February 2015 by the CAAC Aircraft Airworthiness Certification Department, with file No. AP-21-AA-2015-37R1. For the contents of the document see the official website of the CAAC (http://www.caac.gov.cn/E1/E2/SHSDL/201504/P020150430326874949890.pdf). From the date of issuance, it replaced the Procedures for Model and Design Approval of Light Sport Aircraft which entered into force on 26 January 2014 (AP-21-AA-2014-37), accessed on 22 January 2016.

25 See Article 11 of the Regulations of the People's Republic of China for the Administration of the Airworthiness of Civil Aircraft.

26 See Civil Judgment (2015) Su Zhong Shang Zhong Zi No. 01307 of the Intermediate People's Court of Suzhou City, Jiangsu Province.

ter Party B pays such amount to Party A within 3 working days after the signing of this Agreement". Article 8 of the Contract specified that Party B should design and produce advertisements for the aerial sightseeing tours and bear the advertising costs. The Contract took effect immediately after both parties signed it and the defendant received the deposit paid by the plaintiff and was valid until 15 October 2015. After the signing of the Contract, the plaintiff paid the defendant RMB 2 million as contract deposit. The plaintiff sold tickets of the aerial sightseeing tours to customers based on the contents specified in the Contract and the ticket buyers were arranged by the defendant to actually experience the flight service of the tours. The court also found that the plaintiff sent a legal letter on 2 February 2015 to the defendant, requesting the defendant to provide the General Aviation Business License and the Certificate for Commercial Non-transportation Operators. On 18 March 2015 the plaintiff sent another legal letter to the defendant, stating that the defendant did not have the appropriate qualification for air operations and therefore the Cooperation Agreement signed between the parties should be invalid, and requesting for the refund of the deposit of RMB 2 million and the payment of the corresponding interest loss by the defendant to the plaintiff. The defendant acknowledged that it received the above letters from the plaintiff and that it had not obtained the qualification for a commercial (non-transportation) air operator, but it explained that it commissioned other companies with the appropriate qualifications to undertake the fight tours in the aerial sightseeing tour projects developed by it.

[**Opinions of the court**]

The original court held that: The validity of a contract is its legal effect and refers to the legally binding force of an established contract on the parties to it. A valid contract is legally binding on the parties and is protected by the national law, while an invalid contract is not legally binding. According to legal provisions, a lawfully formed contract is effective upon its formation. The parties may agree to attach conditions to the validity of the contract, and a contract with such conditions attached is effective upon the satisfaction of the conditions. In the present case, the Exclusive Agency Agreement signed between the parties specified that "Party B shall pay a total amount of RMB 2 million as annual deposit. This Contract shall enter into force after Party B pays such amount to Party A within 3 working days after the signing of this Agreement", and this was the condition for the validity of the contract agreed by the parties. Both parties acknowledged during the trial that the plaintiff had paid in full the deposit of RMB 2 million to the defendant. Therefore the condition for the entry into force of the contract agreed between the parties was met. It was found that both parties had the capacities for civil rights and civil conduct required for signing a contract. The contents in the Exclusive Agency Agreement signed between the parties were negotiated and confirmed by both parties and were an authentic declaration of the intentions of the parties. In addition, there was no circumstance for invalidation of the contract. Therefore the Exclusive Agency Agreement between the parties was valid and had entered into force. As for the statement of the plaintiff that the qualification for operating the aerial sightseeing tour in the Exclusive Agency Agreement was the cause for the invalidation of the contract, according to the law, the circumstances for the invalidation of a contract include: (1) either party enters into the contract by means of fraud or coercion and impairs the State's interests; (2) there is malicious conspiracy causing damage to the interests of the State, of the collective or of a third party; (3) there is an attempt to conceal illegal goals under the disguise of legitimate forms; (4) harm is done to social and public interests; or (5) mandatory provisions of laws and administrative regulations are violated. The violation against the "mandatory provisions of laws and administrative regulations" as referred to in Article 52 of the *Contract Law* means the violation against the mandatory provisions on validity. It was found that the fact that the defendant signed the contract without having obtained relevant qualification or whether it matters that he obtained such qualification, the validity of the contract had no circumstance of violating mandatory validity provisions. The plaintiff also failed to produce any evidence that the Exclusive Agency Agreement signed between the parties was in any other circumstance for the invalidation of the contract. Therefore the claim of the plaintiff for the confirmation of the invalidity of the Exclusive Agency Agreement between the parties shall have no factual or legal basis and would not be supported. Because of the valid existence of the Exclusive Agency Agreement between the parties, the provision in the Agreement on the payment of RMB 2 million by the plaintiff to the defendant as contract deposit was an authentic declaration of the intentions of the parties. Therefore the parties should fulfill their obligations in accordance with the contents of the contract. The claim of the plaintiff for the refund of the RMB 2 million of deposit and payment of interest loss by the defendant shall have no factual or legal basis and would not be supported. The court ruled to reject the plaintiff's claims. The plaintiff refused to accept the ruling and made an appeal. The Intermediate People's Court of Suzhou City, Jiangsu Province ruled on 26 October 2015 to reject the appeal and upheld the original ruling.

[**Observations on the dispute**]

The focus of the dispute in the present case is: How to identify the validity of a contract beyond the business scope of the party? In other words, what is the validity of a general aviation service contract signed without the qualification for general aviation operations? According to the Provisions on the Administration of Business Licensing for General Aviation[27], "The Civil Aviation Administration of China (hereinafter referred to as the CAAC) conducts unified management on the business licensing for general aviation. The regional civil aviation administrative bureaus shall be responsible for the business licensing and market supervision of the general aviation within their respective jurisdictions. No entity or individual may prepare for establishing a general aviation enterprise or purchase or lease civil aircraft to undertake general aviation business activities without the approval of the regional civil aviation administrative bureau."[28] According to this provision, a general aviation business license must be obtained before conducting general aviation operations. If without approval, an entity or individual "prepares for establishing a general aviation enterprise or an aviation club or engages in general aviation business activities by purchasing or leasing civil aircraft, the CAAC or the regional administrative department of civil aviation shall order it/ him to suspend its/his illegal activities and impose a fine of not less than RMB 10,000 but not more than RMB 30,000 on it/ him if there are illegal gains or a fine of not more than RMB 10,000 if there are no illegal gains."[29] In the present case, the defendant indeed did not obtain a business license for general aviation. Then what will be the impact of reporting the absence of business qualification on the validity of the contract? Will it lead to the invalidation of the contract?

Under the existing law, the basis for judging the validity of the contract is the law and ad-

---

27 CAAC Decree No. 176, issued on 14 February 2007 and implemented on the date of issuance.

28 See Article 3 of the Provisions on the Administration of Business Licensing for General Aviation.

29 See Article 33 of the Provisions on the Administration of Business Licensing for General Aviation.

ministrative regulations. "After the implementation of the *Contract Law*, the people's court shall, when confirming the invalidity of a contract, base it on the laws enacted by the National People's Congress and its Standing Committee and the administrative regulations formulated by the State Council, rather than local regulations or administrative rules." [30]This provision explicitly excludes local regulations and administrative rules. From the perspective of the force of law, the Provisions on the Administration of Business Licensing for General Aviation is just an administrative rule, which naturally cannot be the basis for confirming the validity of the contract concerned in the present case. From a legal point of view, as cited above, the original court clearly pointed out in its judgment that the defendant's signing of the contract without the appropriate qualification is not a circumstance for the invalidation of a contract. Article 14 of the *Interpretation II of the Supreme People's Court of Several Issues concerning the Application of the Contract Law of the People's Republic of China* provides that "the 'mandatory provisions' in item (5), Article 52 of the *Contract Law* refers to the mandatory provisions on validity." Thus, only the contracts that violate the mandatory provisions on validity in laws and administrative regulations are invalid, and those that violate the mandatory provisions on administration in laws and administrative regulations are not necessarily invalid.

The question is, Article 10 of Interpretation I of the *Supreme People's Court of Several Issues concerning the Application of* the *Contract Law of the People's Republic of China* provides that "Where parties sign a contract beyond their scope of business, the court shall not invalidate the contract because of this, unless the contract violates the national provisions on restricted operations, franchise operations and the provisions of laws and administrative regulations on prohibition of operations." How to understand the "franchise operations" in this provision? The operations of general aviation require a business license for general aviation. Is this "franchise operations"? This question deserves further study.

IV. Hot Topics

UAV became the biggest highlight in the field of general aviation and flourished in 2015. UAV enterprises in China attracted huge amounts of funds from many investors and the UAV industry was booming. The "free" flight of UAVs triggered hot discussions on the security and regulation of UAV operations.

A. Widespread Commercial Use of UAVs

UAVs are widely applied in various fields as they can fly at a low altitude, provide a wide vision and are easily operable. They can be seen in many aspects of life and production such as surveying, leisure and tourism, search and rescue, agricultural production, traffic management and pipeline inspection.

In 2015, companies in China and the world started trying to use UAVs in courier services. For example, Taobao cooperated with YTO Express in the first attempt to deliver goods by

30 See Article 4 of the Interpretation I of the Supreme People's Court of Several Issues concerning the Application of the Contract Law of the People's Republic of China.

UAVs in Beijing, Shanghai and Guangzhou[31]; and Wal-Mart applied to the US Federal Aviation Administration for testing UAVs for commercial purpose and would experiment on goods delivery by UAVs.[32]

B. Security Problems Caused by the Commercial Use of UAVs

The extensive commercial operation of UAVs brings "barbaric" growth and "free" flight to the UAV industry, resulting in a number of security risks. The first is the threat to aviation safety. Because the legal system for the management of UAV flightsis deficient, and the relevant laws and regulations are not well-understood, UAV flights are very free, meaning the time, places and operators of the flights are completely decided by the parties themselves. This kind of lawless flights is likely to affect the safety of the normal civil aviation flights. For example, a company in Beijing operated a UAV to take aerial landscape photos without obtaining the qualification for aerial photography and mapping or applying for airspace, leading to the evasion and delay of several civil aircrafts.[33] The second is the threat to the life and property safety of third parties on the ground. For example, on 25 September 2012, an unmanned remote-controlled aircraft owned by a company in China made an emergency landing on the highway and collided with the car driven by Chen, resulting in the breaking of the tail and damage of the wings of the aircraft and the damage of the Chen's car[34].

C. Leakage of Personal Private Information due to UAVs

A UAV is a "flying camera". With the development and progress of technology, aerial photography by UAVs becomes hot. The market demand in this field is soaring, attracting more and more market players. Reports on the invasion of privacy by UAV aerial photography repeatedly hit the newspapers. UAVs may also fly to some sensitive areas such as military bases and government agencies, and this is likely to threaten the security or leak state secrets. For example, on 26 January 2015 the (local time), a senior official from the White House confirmed that the law enforcement agency found a small UAV landing on the ground of the White House on the same day[35]; and on 9 April 2015, a UAV landed on the roof of the Japanese Prime Minister's residence, which remained there until the staff accidentally found it on 22 A-

---

31 "Taobao and YTO Express Tried Delivery Service by UAVs, with No Plan of Rolling Out for the Time Being", published on 4 February 2015, see CNR network (http://finance.cnr.cn/gs/20150204/t20150204_517646247.shtml), accessed on 6 January 2016.

32 "Wal-Mart Can Not Longer Wait to Apply for Goods Delivery by UAVs", see Huanqiu.com (http://tech.huanqiu.com/news/2015-10/7850597.html), accessed on 6 January 2016.

33 "A UAV Controlled by Three Men Is Intercepted and Forced to Land by Two Military Aircraft When Illegally Taking Aerial Photos, published on 22 October 2014, see Xinhuanet.com (http://news.xinhuanet.com/mil/2014-10/22/c_127127945.htm), accessed on 6 January 2016.

34 See Civil Judgment (2014) Xia Min Zhong Zi No. 3864 of the Intermediate People's Court of Xiamen City, Fujian Province.

35 "An Intruding UAV in White House Causes Panic, A Naughty Government Employees Surrenders", 27 January 2015, see chinadaily.com.cn (http://world.chinadaily.com.cn/2015-01/27/content_19418254.htm), accessed on 12 January 2016.

pril 2015[36].

D. Strengthening Regulation on the Operations of UAVs in Many Countries

It is precisely because UAV operations brought many security and privacy issues, the safe operation and regulation of UAVs have become a common concern of the public and the government. To ensure security and strengthen regulation, China, the United States, Japan and other countries have introduced the regulatory laws and regulations on UAVs. The United States have FAA Modernization and Reform Act of 2012[37], the *Model Aircraft Operating Standards*[38], etc. China issued the *Measures for Civil UAV Air Traffic Administration* (MD-TM-2009-002), the *Interim Provisions on the Administration of Civil UAV Pilots* (AC-61-FS-2013-20) etc. Japan issued the *Amended Civil Aeronautics Act* on 10 December adding four prohibitions: UAVs are prohibited from flying in densely populated areas, near airports, above the facilities relating to security protection and the places with a large number of people gathering, or at night.[39]

In addition to law making, efforts are also intensified in law enforcement. On 6 October 2015, the US Federal Aviation Administration (FAA) announced a proposed USD 1.9 million record-hitting penalty against an aerial photography company for endangering the safety of airspace by illegal UAV operations. The FAA said in the announcement that SkyPan International, Inc. of Chicago conducted 65 unauthorized UAS flights in New York City and Chicago between March 2012 and December 2014. Of those, 43 flew in the highly restricted Class B airspace, the access to which one requires an air traffic control clearance. Additionally, the UAV of the company was not equipped with a two-way radio, transponder and altitude-reporting equipment, which are necessary for an aircraft with attended operation. FAA proposed the penalty against the company for operating the aircraft in a "careless or reckless manner endangering lives or property"[40]. In May 2015, an organization in Xinjiang used "Dabai II" UAV for aerial survey without applying for airspace and task approval or reporting the flight plan. Xinjiang Administrative Bureau of Civil Aviation imposed an administrative penalty of RMB 20,000 against the organization[41].

---

36 "Japanese Police Did Not Find the UAV Intruding into Prime Minister's Residence Until Two Weeks Later", published on 25 April 2015, see chinanews.com (http://www.chinanews.com/gj/2015/04-25/7233668.shtml), accessed on 12 January 2016.

37 See the official website of the US Federal Aviation Administration (https://www.faa.gov/uas/media/Sec_331_336_UAS.pdf), accessed on 12 January 2016.

38 See the official website of the US Federal Aviation Administration (http://www.faa.gov/documentLibrary/media/Advisory_Circular/AC_91-57A_Ch_1.pdf), accessed on 12 January 2016.

39 "Japan Amends Law to Restrict UAVs, with a Fine up to 500,000 yen Imposed on Violation", published on 12 January 2016, see CNR network (http://china.cnr.cn/qqhygbw/20160112/t20160112_521114197.shtml), accessed on 16 January 2016.

40 "Illegal UAV Flight in the US Receives a Penalty of USD 1.9 Million", published on 8 October 2015, see chinanews.com (http://www.chinanews.com/gj/2015/10-08/7557676.shtml), accessed on 16 January 2016.

41 "Xinjiang Imposes First Penalty Against UAVs: Unauthorized Flight Is Fined RMB 20,000", published on 9 October 2015, see Xinhuanet.com (http://news.xinhuanet.com/legal/2015-10/29/c_1116981873.htm), accessed on 16 January 2016.

V. Summary and Outlook

In 2015, the general aviation industry presented many highlights. General aviation was emphasized for the first time in the document of the country's highest authority, opening up broad prospects and injecting energy into the entire industry. The rolling off line of C919 aircraft and the commercial operation of ARJ21-700 aircraft were two major events in the aircraft manufacturing industry in China, illuminating the way forward for the rather weak general aviation manufacturing in the country. Their significance could not be overstated. The size of general aviation fleet and the number of enterprises in general aviation also grew significantly.

The rapid development of the UAV industry wrote a splendid page in the history of general aviation in 2015. Despite the problems in their operations, UAVs have brought great convenience to people's living and production. With the further development of the UAV market and the constant progress in the technology of UAV production, UAVs will have great development in the following years and are bound to bring more excitement to our production and life. At the same time, disputes on the sales and purchase and operations of UAVs have naturally arisen. The cases cited in this article are just a microcosm of the many cases involving UAV disputes.

In the traditional areas of the sales and leasing of general aviation aircraft, the failure to achieve the purpose of contract due to noncompliance of general aircraft with the laws and regulations on civil aviation is the main cause of disputes. Therefore, while paying attention to the *Contract Law* and other basic laws, one need to consider the requirements in the laws, regulations and rules on civil aviation. In addition, the sales, leasing, entrusted management and residual value disposal of general aircraft, especially business jets, have increasingly become the focus in the field of business jets, and the relevant legal issues are worth further study. In terms of the model of commercial operations of general aircraft, some mature approaches in foreign countries are being accepted by more enterprises and individuals in China. An example is the fractional ownership of business jets[42]. It also needs further study and research on how to fit foreign commercial practices into the domestic laws.

2016 is the first year of the 13th Five-year Plan period. Let us expect with the patience of accumulating short steps into a thousand-mile journey to see the concrete implementation of the relevant policies, the issuance of more laws and regulations on general aviation and the maturity of the general aviation market and its growth together with the general aviation industry.

---

42 Fractional ownership means that an air transport company buys a business jet and then sells the shares of the jet (1/16, 1/8, 1/4 or 1/2 of the ownership of the jet and the corresponding right to a certain number of flight hours) to the companies with the need. The buyer has a part of the ownership of the aircraft, which may be transferred. The fees paid include the one-time payment of the purchase price for the fractional ownership of the aircraft, the regular payment of the fixed costs distributed in proportion to the shares owned and the rent for each time one uses the aircraft.